Salzburg European Union Studies

herausgegeben von

Prof. Dr. Klaus Gretschmann
Prof. Dr. Stefan Griller
Prof. Dr. Sonja Puntscher Riekmann
Dr. Doris Wydra

Band 1

Sonja Puntscher Riekmann
Alexander Somek | Doris Wydra [eds.]

Is there a
European Common Good?

 **Nomos**

© Titel: Blick auf die Edmundsburg, Salzburg fotografiert von Magdalena Lepka

Die Deutsche Nationalbibliothek verzeichnet diese Publikation in der Deutschen Nationalbibliografie; detaillierte bibliografische Daten sind im Internet über http://dnb.d-nb.de abrufbar.

ISBN 978-3-8329-7976-8

1. Auflage 2013
© Nomos Verlagsgesellschaft, Baden-Baden 2013. Printed in Germany. Alle Rechte, auch die des Nachdrucks von Auszügen, der fotomechanischen Wiedergabe und der Übersetzung, vorbehalten. Gedruckt auf alterungsbeständigem Papier.

Inhaltsverzeichnis

The Common Good of European Institutions

Policy-Oriented Approaches to the European Common Good

Introduction: What is the Purpose of the Union?

Sonja Puntscher Riekmann, Alexander Somek, Doris Wydra

The president of the European Union, Herman Van Rompuy, has repeatedly defined the euro as the Union's 'common good'.[1] With the financial and fiscal crisis, debating the meaning of a European common good has lost its mere academic touch. Indeed, the demise of the common currency or the exclusion of one or more member states from the eurozone could entail detrimental implications for the whole integration project. However, it is far from clear whether a belief in the euro as a common good shared by all can be assumed without further ado. First, only 17 of 27 member states are also members of the eurozone. Thus, the common provision that the 'Union shall establish an economic and monetary union whose currency is the euro' enshrined in the Treaty of Lisbon (Article 3 para 4 TEU 3) is a work in progress. Moreover, the international agreements on credits and guarantees (ESFS/ESM) and on the Fiscal Compact were concluded outside EU law, although supranational organs are involved in the supervision of its implementation. Second, due to the massive financial packages set up to rescue states in distress, a rift between net payers and net receivers has opened out, whereas the traditional elite-citizens divide has deepened. Euroscepticism, be it a diffuse feeling or organised opposition, is gaining ground in most EU member states. Scharpf holds that the capitalist economy's performance has become a crucial argument for democratic legitimacy, which at the same time presupposes that democratically accountable governments have the capacity to shape their economies. But under the current rescue program reforms that are not self-chosen, 'cruelties' as Scharpf calls them, have to be proposed and defended by national governments. And as voters are 'not fair', governments may be punished for outcomes they were not able to control, leading at the same time to alienation and hostility against 'Frankfurt' and 'Brussels'.[2] Indeed, nationalist arguments have surfaced on both sides: in successful and in failing economies.

---

1   See e.g. the press conference after the Summit of the European Council, 8/9 December 2011 (http://www.european-council.europa.eu/home-page/highlights/european-council-concludes-discussion-on-the-new-fiscal-compact); Interview Van Rompuy with Businessweek 6 February 2012.
2   Fritz W. Scharpf (2011), Monetary Union, Fiscal Crisis and the Preemption of Democracy, MPIfG Disscussion Paper 11/11.

Is it then at all reasonable to postulate the euro being the European common good? What about peace being the very reason for which the Union was founded? Or prosperity for its peoples as mentioned in the preambles of all treaties? Or common values to be respected in particular by those who aspire to membership? Or security that has come to feature prominently among the Union's goals enshrined in the Treaty of Lisbon? And how is a common debate to be orchestrated in a club that is continuously growing and enlarging the circle of participants and perspectives? The Union's openness to new members, its teleological construction to potentially encompass the whole of Europe, enhances its proneness to re-open the common good debate at every turn of enlargement. In the European Union, the ideas of widening and deepening are a dialectical and often quarrelsome couple. Despite all successes in integration, it is an open question whether this Union is in fact more than the sum total of fragmentary compromises between and among the member states. Is there a European common good? Can the common good be defined as a state of affairs that is (or should be) desired by all people of a given community or is it something defined by those authorised by established (constitutional) rules (be them governments, parliaments or interest groups)? Or is the common good created by policies of redistribution introduced for the purpose of softening the gap between the poor and the better off? The nature and finality of the European transformation cannot be understood without taking these questions into account. One can hardly deny that the strictures of Economic and Monetary Union and their impact on security, health, social, and environmental policies require the Europeanisation of our understanding of a common good. However, a relevant discussion will be driven by current controversies over collective responsibilities and values.

As a matter of fact, the question 'What for are we together?' has elicited quite different answers in the course of time. The construction of a common narrative underpinning the togetherness has always been framed by the dynamics and the dilemmas of European integration. The future will tell whether the financial turmoil exposing the depth of internal and external economic interdependence will function as a new starting point for such narrative. Will a social contract emerge from the current dynamic that is either manifest in constitutional terms or can be made a subject of debate on the basis of established constitutional rules? These are questions at the specific critical juncture created by the financial crisis.

As the history of European integration shows, new initiatives establishing and consolidating common grounds and narratives have generally occurred at 'critical junctures'' driven by crucial political events and socio-economic developments. This holds true for the demises of the Bretton Woods system and of the Soviet empire, 9/11, and now the financial crisis. Herman Van Rompuy stressed this fact at a meeting on the European Semester for Economic Policy Coordination: 'The debt crisis, difficult and painful as it is, brings home the fact that the union is us ... We carry a common project... even if the choices are made nationally. Forgetting this in our actions undermines the common good.'[3] The construction of the Union is the result of a 'great transformation' of national orders through strategies of overcoming conflicting factors, and can thus not be anything other than a 'rocky, uncertain and unpredictable' process.[4]

It may be surprising that neither the negotiators of the Constitutional Treaty nor of the ensuing Treaty of Lisbon heeded to substantially overhauling economic coordination let alone creating true European economic governance capable of coping with the current problems. It took a crisis unleashed by events in the US subprime market to spur institutional developments that had previously appeared beyond reach. The ensuing debt crisis highlighted the 'adding up problem' as Ian Begg calls it, as the risks for any member states depend on policies that others adopt.[5] However, the response to the crisis by establishing rescue funds outside EU law and imposing fiscal reforms on terms of austerity may be at odds with the vision of a European common good. If, as some authors of this book hold, democracy, the rule of law, and the social model are to be part and parcel of a European common good, institutional solutions brought about since May 2010 may hardly appear as compatible. Democratic standards are thwarted by various factors: the EFSF/ESM is based on an international agreement that bypasses the European Parliament and leaves little to no room for manoeuvre to national parliaments pushed to give their consent by the argument that such arrangement is 'without alternative' (Merkel/Schäuble). Similarly, the international agreement establishing the so-called Fiscal Compact is presented to national parliaments and constituencies as the only way out of the crisis. Even when a referendum on the Fiscal Compact is staged, as in Ireland, political actors tend to engage in a rhetoric of pre-emption: 'I am confident that the Irish people will do what is necessary...' stated the Prime Minister Enda Kenny.[6]

In terms of rule of law, a number of European legal scholars and the European Parliament have voiced criticism in regard to inter-governmental agreements circumventing EU law and the peculiar effects on the consistency of European con-

---

3 Speech by President Herman Van Rompuy to the Interparliamentary Committee meeting on the European Semester for Economic Policy Coordination, Brussels, 27 February 2012. In this speech he even makes use of the musketeers' slogan, 'All for One; One for All!'

4 Neill Nugent (2010), The Government and Politics of the European Union, 7th edition. Houndsmill/ Basingstoke/ Hampshire: Palgrave Macmillan, p. 17.

5 Iain Begg (2012), The EU's response to the global financial crisis and sovereign debt crisis. Economic governance under stress? Asia Europe Journal, 9 (2-4), pp. 107-124.

6 Financial Times 29 February 2012, p.1; on 31 May 2012 60% of the Irish electorate voted in favour of the Fiscal Compact.

stitutionalism.[7] Last but not least, the vaunted term of solidarity is at stake, as well as the social market economy. Dominated by austerity discourse, the Fiscal Compact imposes heavy retrenchments of national social spending in order to reduce debts and deficits, thus potentially creating a vast number of losers among low- and medium-income strata. Moreover and quite insouciantly about social conflicts, the president of the European Central Bank, Mario Draghi, postulated in an interview with the Wall Street Journal that the European social model 'has gone'.[8]

However, these instances of change do not inexorably lead to the demise of the Union as some authors are speculating.[9] But they are omens of upcoming and most likely harsh conflicts between different interests and perspectives on the Union's future and its capability of finding a new consensus on what the European common good could possibly be. If Schumpeter was right in his verdict that there is no clearly defined common good to which people consent on the basis of rational arguments, for the simple reason that the common good means different things to different individuals and groups,[10] such a postulate is at best a historical and thus contingent compromise between diverging interests. The post-war European Social Model was such a temporary compromise in the context of the nation-state. While there was relative consensus about the principle, concomitant policies were the result of continuous negotiations between social partners, governments, and parliaments during the so-called *Trente Glorieuses*, those three decades of quantitative and qualitative expansion of social benefits for individuals participating in the workforce and those related to them. Outcomes differed considerably throughout the Union's members. That social contract had, however, already begun to erode before the financial crisis and to oppose reformers and supporters in the member states and at the Union level.[11] The crisis has only and

7   Paul Craig, The EU's Fiscal Compact, Lecture at the Faculty of Law, University of Vienna, 27 February 2012; Peter-Christian Müller-Graff (2011), Euroraum-Budgethilfenpolitik im rechtlichen Neuland, integration 34(4); Christian Calliess (2011), Das europäische Solidaritätsprinzip und die Krise des Euro – Von der Rechtsgemeinschaft zur Solidaritätsgemeinschaft, Forum Constitutionis Europae 01/11. Intriguingly, the Fiscal Compact stipulates in Article 2, para 1 that 'this Treaty shall be applied and interpreted by the Contracting Parties in conformity with the Treaties on which the European Union is founded....and with European law....'. Redundantly, the provision is repeated in para 2.
8   Mario Draghi literally said, 'You know there was a time when (economist) Rudi Dornbush used to say that the Europeans are so rich they can afford to pay everybody for not working. That's gone'. Wall Street Journal, 24 February 2012, p. 1.
9   See e.g. Walter Laqueur (2012), After the Fall: The End of the European Dream and the Decline of a Continent. New York: Thomas Dunne Books.
10   Joseph A. Schumpeter (1942), Capitalism, Socialism and Democracy. New York: Harper & Brothers, Ch. XXI.
11   Cf. Simon Hix (2008), What's Wrong with the European Union and How to Fix It. Cambridge: Polity, p. 1.

ultimately unveiled the shift of arenas of decision making in regard to one core element of national sovereignty: the prerogative of national parliaments to decide on the budget will be heavily curtailed. Actually, the shift had begun much earlier with the introduction of the Monetary Union and the Stability and Growth Pact. But it took the Fiscal Compact to make this transfer of sovereignty also visible to the citizens who are gradually discovering its implications for the welfare state. Contestation is looming large, with the protest movements and strikes in Greece, Spain, and Italy and the French presidential election of 2012 being important cases in point.[12]

Contestation, however, is the essence of democracy. It is about the chance of advocating different options in the pursuit of a common good that indeed is not a pre-ordained fact but the outcome of competition among interests and views. It does of course politicize the Union in an unheard-of way and it presupposes arenas and procedures that would allow actors to enter into such competition. Owing to the financial crisis and the considerable shift of budget powers from national parliaments to EU organs, the old academic controversy pro and contra 'politicisation' and further democratisation[13] will be rendered largely obsolete. If the Fiscal Compact is to enter into force after ratification by 12 of the 17 members of the eurozone, the decisions by the European Commission imposing sanctions on a member state infringing the fiscal rules can only be opposed by a reverse majority voting. These procedural changes are of paramount importance for European democracy: first, unanimity is no longer a requirement for this treaty to come into force; second, the reverse majority voting will be a much more powerful provision for constraining national preferences in fiscal policy. If it is still open to interpretation whether the European Social Model has gone, it is more certain that veto rights have gone in a policy field where member states had hitherto tried to preserve their sovereignty. Hence, politicisation will no longer be a choice but the very logic of European decision making, whereas the related question will be about the nature of politics: democratic or technocratic? And in regard to the common good: imposed from above or influenced from below?

---

12   Francois Hollande, the candidate of the Socialist Party, challenging the incumbent Nicolas Sarkozy, has indeed announced to renegotiate the Fiscal Pact in case of his election.

13   Such as the controversy between Simon Hix and Stefano Bartolini in a Policy Paper for Notre Europe (Stefano Bartolini and Simon Hix (2006), Politics: The Right or Wrong Sort of Medicine for the EU? Policy Paper No.19/2006, Notre Europe) or between Hix and Follesdal on the one hand and Majone and Moravcsik on the other (Simon Hix and Andreas Follesdal (2005), Why there is a Democratic Deficit in the European Union. A response to Majone and Moravcsik, EUROGOV No. 05/02; Andrew Moravcsik (2003), The EU ain't broke, Prospect, March 2003; Giandomenico Majone (1998), Europe's 'Democratic Deficit': The Question of Standards, European Law Journal 4 (1), pp. 5-28.

Politicisation and democratisation will complicate decision making as much as they will enhance the legitimacy of the outcome. Such a change of gears will raise difficulties for the integration process. Yet, integration has been difficult even at times when decision makers enjoyed the calm of the permissive consensus of citizens. In his memories of integration, Jean Monnet told the story of the Union's beginnings as a matter of functionalising challenges for advancing unification. By all means, the current situation holds the opportunity for building a true political Union, particularly if the agreements contracted at intergovernmental level will eventually become part of the European constitutional set-up.

With the onset of the financial crisis, the question about a European common good has attained a particular urgency. Unification can hardly be a common good in itself. Despite the number of appeals to the pursuit of a common good in the European treaties, the underlying normative positions and principles remain vague. The financial crisis has put the progress of integration to a test. The member states' willingness to provide the Union with resources needed for pursing the policies that citizens expect the Union to deliver is precarious, as demonstrated by the struggle for a financial 'bail-out' of Greece in 2010. This has also triggered intensive debates about European economic governance and better modes of coordination of economic policy, mutual surveillance, and sanctions. While the need for a closer political union remained hypothetical during the period of 'benign macroeconomic conditions' up to 2008, the crisis now highlights the tensions between domestic imperatives and the collective interest, thus also limiting the range of possible solutions.[14] In times of financial shortage, the conceptual pair of common good/common spirit develops into a code of appeals for a society's moral resources. While the problem of disproportionate allocation of burdens is crucial, it again emphasizes the importance of the question posed at the beginning: 'What for are we together?' The answer has to emerge from a democratic debate if it is to be acceptable to a considerable majority of European citizens. Yet, there is no tabula rasa with which to start such a debate. European citizens conceive their vision of a good life and concrete expectations based on traditions that are built on two centuries of struggles for democracy and welfare. If these achievements are simply to be discarded in the name of global competitiveness, it will become difficult to give reasons for European togetherness.

Before tackling some of these questions in greater detail, this book first endeavours to launch into an interdisciplinary debate on the theoretical foundations of the concept of common good and to relate them to institutions and specific poli-

---

14 Iain Begg (2012), The EU's response to the global financial crisis and sovereign debt crisis. Economic governance under stress? Asia Europe Journal 9(2-4), pp. 107-124.

cies pursued by the European Union. Any concept of a European common good is to be situated at an intermediate level between conceptions of a 'common good' of the individual member states on the one hand, and a universal understanding of a common good on the other. Problems and crises, like the financial crisis or climate change, demand reactions from the European Union and its member states. Reactions, however, are shaped by the tensions between different policy goals (such as upholding positions on global markets, guarantees for employment, social welfare, and a clean environment). All of this critically impinges upon the European social order and raises the question of how and under what conditions people live in the European Union, and whether as well as how the political, legal, and socio-economic systems contribute or don't contribute to a European Common Good.

The common good and how it can be pursued (indeed, *if* it can be pursued at all) is a contested question. It touches upon the core principles of a society, and it relates to the tensions between the individual and that society. It challenges political processes, institutional logics, and constitutional settings. In his chapter, *Gerhard Seel* takes up the challenge of searching for an entity that is effectively to the advantage of every citizen and is thus preferred by all – these are two criteria which he holds essential for his definition of a truly common good. In doing so, Seel focuses our attention on established European institutions that guarantee peace, democracy, and human rights, including those social rights whose operation is not tarnished by narrow concepts of sovereignty. He differentiates between different philosophical approaches towards the common good by clarifying some of the basic concepts connected to this abstract notion. In his analysis touching upon the question of what can be considered a common good, he asks the question of how externalities (which he defines as the relation between personal goods and evils, and common goods and evils), can induce market failures, thus allowing for 'free riders' to be counterbalanced by social institutions like legislation and democratic rules. This democratic constitution, and especially its juridical institutions, suggests that 'the freedom of one can coexist with everyone's freedom in accordance with a universal law of freedom' (Kant). He takes into account the common good of all Europeans, not because it is in everybody's preference, but because it is everybody's duty to realise them, and so the democratic state and its institutions, being fixed by positive law, result in deontic common goods for the consumption of all its citizens.

Thus, the European common good must not be taken for granted, but rather needs to be deliberated by free and open discussion to avoid losing its common meaning. This brings us back to the argument that contestation is the essence of democracy. Beginning with Aristotle's understanding of common goods as a result of cooperation (as opposed to the economic concept of the common good as a matter of distribution between shares and burdens), *Patrick Riordan* follows Charles Taylor's path on the search for the purely social good of Europe. The common good of a political community, through this emphasis on cooperation, is maintained by the shared meaning that enables all to participate in the communal activity. A common good thus is a good of collaboration, pursued together by cooperating parties. The social imaginaries that form the way people conceptualise their social existence, as well as their underlying normative concepts, form the market economy, civil society, and mode of government. This common understanding enables common practices and a widely shared sense of legitimacy, and according to Riordan, is what the European Union requires. On the other hand this also requires suitable rules and procedures that safeguard general rights, individual liberties, political entitlements, social positions and opportunities, and economic prospects. These procedures also allow for the acceptance of inequalities, as these inequalities appear to be justifiable for generally acceptable reasons.

Peter Koller introduces this concept of justice into the discussion on the common good. In regard to general rights, individual liberties, and entitlements to political participation, no acceptable reasons for inequality exist, and social and economic inequalities may be justifiable because these inequalities may benefit all members of society, including those who fare worse. In international economic cooperation, distributive justice applies to the benefits and burdens that are unequally distributed among nations, though in a system of prevailing state sovereignty the requirements of justice are hardly met. When studying the European Union, Koller draws the conclusion that the social deficit resulting from the struggles of the member states to maintain competitiveness reveals an unjust situation on the basis of the concept of economic distributive justice. Economic development and a flourishing economy, which are often regarded as central aims of European policy, are a common good only if this wealth is distributed fairly. He points towards the social deficit of the European Union, the insufficient cooperation in the spheres of social security, labour law, and tax policy. The injustice created can be overcome through cooperation in communities agreeing on common objectives. But, for the participation in a given community and the adherence to common objectives, a social imaginary is necessary (as Patrick Riordan stresses in his contribution) – a set of shared meanings constructed in deliberative processes.

Such a social imaginary builds upon the essential groundwork for the norms and rules necessary in order for a society to develop the common good for all its members. Constitutions have served the purpose of establishing a basic set of rules for political and legal communities, and so the constitutionalisation debate at the European level has gained notable prominence during the last decade. In his chapter *Alexander Somek* describes why the discourse on constitutionalisation incorporates constitutionalism with the mind-set of administrative problem solving, thus building on the culture and ethics of market societies instead of taming the 'administrative brute'. Constitutionalisation is a process that does not abide by procedural norms and is at first glance devoid of authorship, with courts acting as the main actors. During the course of this constitutionalisation project, the focus shifted from conduct to underlying structures underlining the process character aimed at transforming the structure of the constituted unit itself for the realisation of the common good, thus concentrating on problem solving. Therefore, constitutionalisation is not based on access to power but rather an appeal to a multiplicity of existing transactions. By critically evaluating questions of collective self-determination, deliberative democracy, and the rendering of externalities to public problems and collective individualism, Somek comes to the conclusion that constitutionalisation is not continuous with the tradition of constitutionalism, but an ironic reversal. The logic of political control is rendered to problem solving, and supranational authority becomes supra-political and supra-constitutional. To overcome this situation Europe needs a real constitution to move past provisional solutions. The European quest for a bona fide constitution must continue in order to counterbalance the self-reinforcing dominance of markets. This, Somek argues, allows for the broader social and cultural aspects of European society to develop.

Correspondingly, *Dragana Damjanovic* asks the question of whether we have already witnessed some kind of 'Social Constitution' within Europe as she describes an EU primary law order that provides for social integration within the Union. Damjanovic argues that economic integration has to find its limits where common European social values might be jeopardized. In her analysis she follows the process of the development of a 'European Social Constitution' derived from the 1957 Treaty of Rome. The foundational structures made for a 'Social Market Economy' that had to be realised at different levels (the safeguard of free market at the European level, and resource allocation at the national level), and an increasing emphasis on individual rights slowly and gradually brought about a social constitution of Europe by integration through the law. The Treaty of Lisbon now holds a social clause that mainstreams social policy into all policy fields, affirmations of the importance of social values, and a reference to the model of a 'Social Market Economy'. The fundamental social rights of the EU Charter have acquired binding legal force. For the regulative social policy fields, there now exists a solid EU primary law base; however, redistributive policy fields still remain within the competence of the member states. Yet, this is still only a limited version of a European social model.

Europe at the moment not only faces a debt crisis, but also Community law has entered into an existential crisis. *Augustín José Menéndez* draws our attention to this clear regression of European integration, if it is assessed by reference to the normative standards of a European social democratic *Rechtsstaat*. According to him three basic developments allow for such a conclusion: the structural democratic deficit resulting from constitutional asymmetries; the grave democratic shortcomings resulting from the Lisbon process; and the handling of the fiscal crisis of the eurozone. As we do not only have an ideal of Europe, but also an actual existing and well-developed European Union, there is a risk that during the course of integration options are wiped out and thus the process of democratic will formation is foreclosed. What had originally been constructed as genuine constitutional moment in Europe, the Laeken process, has become a hybrid process, and the more advanced the different crises in Europe have become (constitutional crises, financial crisis, crisis of democratic constitutionalism), the more the inconsistencies of the 'Collage' Union have become evident. Menéndez therefore calls for a European project that takes democratic constitutional law and democratic public law seriously as means of social integration.

But already Aristotle was rather pessimistic of people voluntarily refraining from pushing their advantages too far, as he was convinced that human socialisation requires the force of law. Accordingly, *Thomas Eilmansberger* and *Rainer Palmstorfer* argue that if social values are to be a common European good, they should be enforceable to guarantee for their implementation. It is often argued that common values are at the very heart of the integration project. While the original EC Treaty did not contain any reference to values at all (as it might have taken the existence of common values simply for granted), the Treaty of Amsterdam introduced the term 'value', and the Treaty of Lisbon now holds that the respect for human dignity, freedom, democracy, equality, the rule of law, and the respect for human rights are common to all member states in a pluralist, tolerant, and just society. But these values have to be enforced to have an impact, and infringements of values have to find effective legal remedies. By analysing the variety of legal instruments applicable in case of value infringement by the European Union and its member states by drawing on the existing case law of the European Court of Justice, Eilmansberger and Palmstorfer conclude that the European legal order provides for an adequate level of legal protection of such values, although the efficiency of enforcement is measured by the degree of precision with which the respective value is established in EU law.

A given set of norms and rules is not the only decisive factor for the development of a community, however. The procedures and institutional settings must also be analysed. The question then arises as to whether the common good can be negotiated, by whom, and according to what procedural norms. Whereas autocrats, monarchs, and tyrants upheld the fiction that the common good revealed its nature only to them, the Founding Fathers of the United States did not see any reason for debating the common good, as interest might have distorted it. But in democracy the common good must be negotiable because the interests and needs of people are ever-changing. While Jean-Jacques Rousseau argued that all citizens should participate in decision making for the sake of the general will, the second half of the twentieth century saw a shift from this individual participation to organisations and interest groups. The common good is thus no longer deliberated by a body specifically selected and authorised, but by an increasing number of interest groups. This leads to a blurring of accountability structures and forces citizens to organise, giving gatekeepers powerful positions. In his chapter, *Johannes Pollak* shows that stakeholder representation gained momentum in the European Union, where interest groups are no longer regarded as a completion of a parliamentary representative system but are treated as equal, with parliaments no longer negotiating the common good, but managing interest groups. The common good is thus ragged between particular interests, in a system not fulfilling the basic requirement of liberal democracies: accountability. Such a system may provide for a mutual 'blame-shifting' for outcomes, as accountability becomes increasingly blurred. Defining, negotiating, and finding ways to realise the common good builds the identity of a community and fosters unity.

This focus on outcomes also highlights that the European Union is expected to deliver benefits to all of its members, including a high standard of living, security, stability, and health. Several authors contributing to this publication have turned our attention to the different regulative instruments used to make good on these expectations. The rise of individualist concepts of society leads the common good to become increasingly connected to the well being of the individual members of the society, thus focusing on such questions as liberty, security, and property. Here, questions regarding the general framework of concepts of individual welfare and social justice (e.g. security of a material living foundation, promotion of economic growth, as well as public welfare) and about their realisation have to be raised. The financial and economic crisis has led to a search for solutions incorporating the European common good in the form of a common European economy and polity, as highlighted by the contribution of *Klaus Gretschmann*. But as member states have been affected by the crisis in different ways, a common approach becomes difficult because free-riding becomes an option. On the other hand, insufficient coordination could trigger a second wave of economic problems. The convergence of policy models is therefore crucial, though up to now the process of European integration has not been accompanied by strong coordination efforts in the macroeconomic realm. Consequently, governments can control domestic conditions only if they can influence the decisions taken in other countries, but issues of sovereignty, heterogeneity, the free-rider problem, and the weakest-link problem hamper cooperation for the common good. Especially in regard to global problems, it is essential that Europe creates a European public good and speaks with one voice, to ensure that its interests are duly defended at the global level. The crisis proved that deregulation, guided by the efficient market hypothesis, did not bring about a common good. Mastering the crisis therefore means 'reconstructing responsibilities'. The creation of an eco-efficient economy brings about a new green deal and may strike new balances and possibly change the economic and the financial system of the European Union.

Volkmar Lauber accordingly defines the common good as not just a matter of substantive goals, but also as a matter in which principles, rules, and instruments are considered appropriate for guiding government action. By analysing the instrument of emission trading as an instrument for slowing climate change, Lauber's article impressively highlights a threefold tension around the European common good: the tension between regulatory and deregulatory approaches, between the global and the European level, and between market and environment. By drawing analogies to the banking and finance sector, where also a policy change from regulation to more deregulation has taken place and was in the end not able to avoid the crisis, he analyses an approach in environmental policy, making emission trading market mechanisms the instrument of choice. Lauber demonstrates how this resulted in minimal effects for the improvement of the environmental situation and even hampered the development of new technologies for the use of renewable energies. Another important aspect of this chapter is that it highlights the interconnectedness on a global scale, analysing how pressure from the United States for trading schemes had an impact on the first reluctant European Commission during the Kyoto negotiations, which was followed by business support within Europe for emission trading, realising the potential for windfall profits. Regulatory approaches (like feed-in-tariffs) are developing only slowly and require a lot of regulatory imagination.

Sonja Puntscher Riekmann concludes that the European integration project has to define the common good in a field that encompasses tensions between fundamental freedoms and fundamental rights, between principles of openness and closure, and between the community and the individual citizen. European social discourses enjoy a century-long tradition, serving as the normative grounds for the modern welfare state. Drawing on Marhsall's seminal work on Social Citizenship she argues accordingly that civil and political rights remain incomplete without social rights. This argumentation was to inspire the political actors in post-war Europe in their engagement for welfare achievements that resulted in a European *differentia specifica*. However, the EU's commitment to the four freedoms and thus to a liberal market perspective is perceived as a power that dismantles those achievements. Whereas national social policy operates by

21

the logic of closure, European integration is based on the logic of openness. European political actors have repeatedly tried to overcome the dilemma of closure and openness by enshrining in primary and secondary law social concepts such as human dignity, freedom, equality, and solidarity, the latter becoming an important principle pervading the Treaty of Lisbon and the Charter of Fundamental Rights. This chapter first pursues the analysis of these concepts by asking to what extent these norms guide political action, or whether they may tend to function as rhetorical slogans assuaging European citizens. Secondly, it analyses the role of the Court of Justice in striking a precarious balance between social and market freedoms. This will finally advocate for social commitments as spelled out in primary law, substantiated by secondary law, and not left to the jurisdiction of the ECJ alone. Moreover, there is a need for public debate over European social citizenship. In this respect, Maurizio Ferrera's model of 'virtuous nesting' of three overlapping spaces in which the national welfare state is embedded in the EU economic and social spaces could become a valuable starting point.

The debt crisis has drastically highlighted the economic and social cleavages within the European Union and has thus put the whole integration project to a test. Governments and EU officials call for solidarity between member states, while discussions in national parliaments highlight the national interests that are at stake and public debates focus on questions of free-riding and unjust redistribution of scarce financial resources. The Slovak discussion on the Greek rescue plan in autumn 2011 has brought the question to the fore: can poorer countries be expected to subsidise rich ones? In many countries of the EU, the scepticism about the policies of the European Union has risen substantially, also fuelled by arguments brought forward by populist parties. This highlights that the question of whether there is a European common good is timely and that there also has to be an answer to the question of what we would miss if the European integration project fails. How can we answer the question, 'What for are we together?'

For Menéndez, European integration is a necessary condition for the realisation of democratic government in Europe. It is the political and juridical institutions that Europe has created, setting up norms and rules for regulating the increasing interaction and interference in each others' affairs, that make the European integration project unique (Gerhard Seel). It is the 'European way of life' as Somek calls it, with its shared meanings and values, also including its striving to realise a kind of 'social citizenship' across Europe (Eilmansberger and Palmstorfer; Damjanovic; Puntscher Riekmann). Still-recurring crises, most recently involving sovereign debt and pressure on the euro, reveal – as Riordan stresses – that we cannot afford to be complacent in thinking we already have a shared meaning. Until now there is no clear-cut conception of the common good of a European economy, because there is no consciousness of a European communality and no joint model of European economics. The crisis means that Europe has to move past provisional solutions (Somek). As Gretschmann stresses, mastering the crisis means 'reconstructing responsibility', transparency, control, and setting incentives correctly. And we have to be aware about the fragility of democratic processes and achievements. Pollak reminds us of the fact that the common good is no longer construed as an achievement but as an attribute of a complex negotiation process and we have to be careful that those few who claim to be in a better position to define the common good might become the norm-setters. The crisis puts into question both elements of the common good: social citizenship and democracy. In her article Puntscher Riekmann quotes Benjamin Franklin: 'We must, indeed, all hang together, or assuredly we shall hang separately'. In this vein the contributions of this volume are in search for an answer to the question in which areas 'hanging together' is necessary to safeguard the European common good from the hangmen of global financial markets.

Bibliography

Bartolini, S. and Hix, S. (2006), Politics: The Right or Wrong Sort of Medicine for the EU? Policy Paper No.19/2006, Notre Europe.

Begg, I. (2012), The EU's response to the global financial crisis and sovereign debt crisis. Economic governance under stress? *Asia Europe Journal*, 9 (2-4), pp. 107-124.

Calliess, C. (2011), Das europäische Solidaritätsprinzip und die Krise des Euro – Von der Rechtsgemeinschaft zur Solidaritätsgemeinschaft, Forum Constitutionis Europae 01/11.

Hix, S. (2008), *What's Wrong with the European Union and How to Fix It*. Cambridge: Polity.

Hix, S. and Follesdal, A. (2005), Why there is a Democratic Deficit in the European Union. A response to Majone and Moravcsik, EUROGOV No. 05/02.

Laqueur, W. (2012), *After the Fall: The End of the European Dream and the Decline of a Continent*. New York: Thomas Dunne Books.

Majone, G. (1998), Europe's 'Democratic Deficit': The Question of Standards, *European Law Journal* 4 (1), pp. 5-28.

Moravcsik, A. (2003), The EU ain't broke, *Prospect*, March 2003.

Müller-Graff, P.-C. (2011), Euroraum-Budgethilfenpolitik im rechtlichen Neuland, *integration* 34(4).289-307.

Nugent, N. (2010), *The Government and Politics of the European Union*, 7th edition. Houndsmill/ Basingstoke/ Hampshire: Palgrave Macmillan.

Scharpf, F. W. (2011), Monetary Union, Fiscal Crisis and the Preemption of Democracy, *MPIfG Disscussion Paper* 11/11.

Schumpeter, J. A. (1942), *Capitalism, Socialism and Democracy*. New York: Harper & Brothers.

Theorising the European Common Good

What is the common good and why should we pursue it? A philosophical foreword to a current European debate[1].

Gerhard Seel

I   Introduction

After having been almost forgotten for so many years, the concept of the 'common good' reappears today on the front pages of political agendas. It serves perfectly the ideological needs of those who – like Barack Obama or in Great Britain the Red Tories (Philip Blond) – want to fight the extremism of Chicago liberals and at the same time keep their distance to socialism and communism. It comes as no surprise that the current economic crisis fuels this movement. So, European politicians use to justify the current bail-out measures for Ireland, Portugal, and Greece, claiming that they are finally preserving and protecting the common good of all Europeans. We would be happy with this argument if we only knew what the European common good is exactly. However, before trying to define the European common good, we should know what we mean by the term 'common good' in general, and whether there is something to which it refers. If we couldn't answer this question, we should follow Schumpeter and completely renounce the use of this term.[2]

Questions of this kind are typically the business of philosophers.[3] They answer them either by turning to the history of concepts or by a systematic conceptual analysis. Though my main purpose is the latter, let me start with a short historical overview. As the history of our concept starts with Plato, we have to first look at his view. Plato uses the concept of common interest in order to distinguish the good government from the bad government, with the former pursuing the common interest, and the latter pursuing the proper interest of the ruler (Rep.

1   I am grateful to Iain Begg and Patrick Riordan for their helpful comments on the first version of this paper.
2   Joseph A. Schumpeter (1942), Kapitalismus, Sozialismus und Demokratie, Tübingen 1987, p. 399.
3   Philosophers rediscover this ancient concept as well. Especially Catholic thinkers see a welcome opportunity to remind the world of the traditional catholic defence of the common good (compare the foundational document, 'Rerum Novarum', a papal encyclical by Pope Leo XIII, issued in 1891). Catholic doctrine defines the common good as 'the sum of those conditions of social life which allow social groups and their individual members relatively thorough and ready access to their own fulfillment'.

412 d-e). According to Plato the city-state itself is an intrinsic good if it is built according to the principles of justice. This is a city where all the social classes live in perfect harmony with each other, with each citizen doing his proper job and thus contributing to the happiness of the whole. Though Plato himself doesn't explicitly say this, one could consider the just city-state as the 'common good'. Aristotle follows Plato on most points, but he differs from him on two very important topics. Firstly, he has a different conception of justice, and secondly, he does not attribute an intrinsic value to the city-state, i.e. a value that is independent of and prior to the good life of the citizens. According to Aristotle it is the 'common interest that brings men together according to which they partake in good life' (Pol.III, 6, 1278 b 21-23). Therefore, the 'political community' is only a means for the good life of every citizen. Only if the state observes the principles of commutative and distributive justice will every citizen have a happy life; this implies that some privileged people can abandon themselves to philosophy.[4] The difference between Plato and Aristotle sets the stage for the most important controversy in the history of political philosophy. On the one hand we have those who, like Aristotle, hold that the common good can be defined in terms of the goods of the individuals, and on the other hand we have those who like Plato believe that the common good is by no means reducible to the goods of the individuals. In the following, I call the first 'reductionists' and the last 'nonreductionists'.

Let me give some modern examples of both. Most modern reductionists hold that something has value because some individual desires it. This is the opposite of the traditional Aristotelian view who held, that people desire something because it has value. The reductionists differ concerning what the individuals desire. Thus, pleasure, satisfaction of informed preferences, fairness, opportunities, etc. are the key concepts that allow us to distinguish the different versions of reductionistic theories. The Utilitarians have identified the 'common good' with the utilitarian concept of 'the greatest happiness of the greatest number'. Today's 'welfare economics' hold that 'social welfare' is the common good, social welfare being defined as the sum total of the satisfaction of the informed preferences of all members of a given society. This position is called 'welfarism'.[5]

---

4   See Gerhard Seel (1990), Die Rechtfertigung von Herrschaft in der "Politik" des Aristoteles, in: G. Patzig (ed), Artistoteles' "Politik", Akten des XI. Symposium Aristotelicum Friedrichshafen/ Bodensee, 25.8. – 3.9. 1987, Göttingen, pp. 32-62; and Gerhard Seel (2011), The Citizen is a Ruler, in: E. Moutsopoulos and M. Protopapas-Marneli (eds.), The Notion of Citizenship in Greek Philosophy, proceedings of the 2nd International Conference of Philosophy, Alexandria, 4-6 March 2010, Athens, pp. 100-112.

5   Amartya Sen (1979), Utilitarianism and Welfarism, The Journal of Philosophy, 76(9), pp. 463-489.

Since Plato, the antireductionists hold that entities like the state are a kind of 'supra-person' and therefore have a value that cannot be defined in terms of the values of its members. Charles Taylor[6] for instance has argued that the common good has at least some elements, like culture, that are not reducible to personal goods.[7] Let me finally mention the contractualist theory of John Rawls, who appears to follow a third way between reductionism and antireductionism. On the one hand, he justifies his principles of justice independently of the conceptions of the personal good that everybody might have; on the other hand, he argues that the implementation of these principles in a system of institutions that guarantee a just distribution of primary goods and a just opportunity for everybody to acquire them will be to the advantage of everybody and thus be a 'good society'.[8]

To decide these controversies we would need to engage in complicated ethical and meta-ethical investigations. This I will not do in this chapter. I shall rather take an analytical approach and try to clarify some terms and make some key distinctions. However, I cannot avoid addressing one of the basic controversies in current philosophical value-theory – and value theory is very fashionable among philosophers today: on the one hand we have those who believe – like Aristotle – that we have duties because there are objective values that call for realisation; on the other hand we have those who hold – like Kant – that certain things have objective value only because we have binding obligations to realise them. This debate seems very academic and superfluous, but as we shall see, without answering it we can neither determine what the common good is nor justify the obligation to pursue it. However, there is a further question to be answered: 'Which kind of community should the European Union build according to easily justifiable standards of political philosophy?' Though I think that there are no easily justifiable standards, I will take up this challenge as well.

II   What entities are goods?

Let me start with some very simple basic distinctions and definitions. We should distinguish between values and the items that have value. Things that have value are called 'goods'. Confusing goods and values may have disastrous consequences. Values are normative propositions. Goods are entities that exist in the

---

6   Charles Taylor (1995), Philosophical Arguments. Cambridge, Mass.: Harvard University Press.
7   Patrick Riordan gives a good presentation of Charles Taylor's ideas in his chapter in this volume.
8   John Rawls (1972), A Theory of Justice. Oxford: Oxford University Press, p. 577.

real world in such a way that their description corresponds to the descriptive element of a normative proposition. That is what we mean when we say that something has value. Therefore goods can be produced and destroyed. Values can only be objects of thought. Furthermore, we distinguish between individual and socio-cultural values. The latter are often mistaken for objective values.

What kinds of entities can be said to have value? If we look to our current ontological distinctions we get the following categories: substances, persons, states of affairs and among them especially events, further abstract entities like scores and scientific theories, and finally rights, entitlements, obligations, and the like. However, if we ask what we mean when we say that an entity x has value, we see that strictly speaking not all of theses entities can be goods. According to the philosophical concept of value, 'x has value' means 'we prefer a situation where x is the case to a situation where x is not the case'; or, if you prefer a normative version: 'we should prefer a situation where x is the case to a situation where x is not the case'. It is useful to introduce the concept of negative value as well: x has negative value if and only if we prefer (should prefer) a situation where x is not the case to a situation where x is the case. Accordingly, we define evil as an entity that has negative value. As a consequence of these definitions, entities may be neutral concerning their value; they may be neither goods nor evils.

But the definition of 'good' given above is not the only one we find in the literature. Compare Harry Johnson's[9] definition of good 'as an object or service of which the consumer would choose to have more'. One sees immediately that, according to this definition, the entities we would normally classify as goods are substances or events whereas the entities that are goods according to the first definition are states of affairs and only states of affairs, for states of affairs are exactly those entities that either are the case or are not.[10] Though it is not the case that only philosophers use the term 'good' in the first sense and only economists use it in the second sense, for reasons of simplicity in the following I will call the first the 'philosophical definition' and the second the 'economical definition'.

So what I mean when I say 'this apple has value' is – according to the philosophical definition – 'I prefer a situation where it is the case that I have this apple at my disposal to an – in all other regards similar – situation where this is not the case'. According to the economic concept of good it means 'I would choose to have more apples'. In the following we should keep in mind the difference between the philosophical and the economic use of the term good.

9   Harry Johnson (1958), Demand theory further revisited or goods are goods, Economica, 25, p. 149.
10   One may reduce Johnson's definition to the first definition by arguing that what the consumer would prefer is the state of affairs that he has more of objects or services at his disposal.

III   Two criteria of common goods and evils

The next question is how to distinguish common goods and common evils from other goods and evils. In the history of philosophy and economics two quite different criteria have been introduced. The first was proposed by Eudoxos, a member of Plato's Academy. To be sure, he proposed it as a criterion for the highest good, but it serves perfectly well as a criterion for the common good. Eudoxos held that the highest good is the entity that is pursued by everybody.[11] I should emphasise that – in modern terms – what one pursues is the realisation of a state of affairs. Accordingly one can define the common good as the state of affairs that is pursued by every member of a given community, or more precisely: 'x is the common good of community y if and only if every member of y prefers the realisation of x to its non- realisation'. We can define the common evil accordingly inverting the places of "realization" and "non-realisation".

I call this criterion the 'preference-criterion'. I should emphasise that there is also a comparative version of this criterion. It says that the more people prefer the realization of an entity to its non-realisation the more this entity counts as a common good.[12]

According to their concept of goods, economists use a quite different criterion for the common good. They ask whether the consumption of a good by one person precludes its consumption by another person. If this is the case the good is a personal good; if not it is a common good.[13] I call this the 'use-criterion'. The first to give an analytic definition of personal and common goods – he used the terms private and public goods – was Paul Samuelson.[14] While for personal goods the total quantity of consumed goods is equal to the sum of the quantities consumed by all individuals taken together, in the case of common goods the to-

11   See Aristotle, Nicomachean Ethics, X, 2, 1172 b 9-15.
12   As preference is the basis of the ranking of goods – I may prefer one good to another – we can introduce a measurement standard that ranks good according to the product of the number of people who prefer an entity and the relative ranking it occupies on the value scale of each individual. Though this is a very powerful tool when we want to establish a value ranking of common goods in a given society, I will not use it here, because it is outside my present subject.
13   In the economic literature we find also the concept of a third kind of good, the so-called 'club-goods'. These are neither personal nor common goods, but goods of a more or less small group of persons. See James A. Buchanan (1965), An Economic Theory of Clubs, Economics 32, pp. 1- 14; Charles Tiebout (1956), A pure theory of local expenditures, Journal of Political Economy 64, pp. 416-424.
14   Paul A. Samuelson (1954), The pure theory of public expenditure, Review of Economics and Statistics, 36, pp. 387-389; Paul A. Samuelson (1955), Diagrammatic exposition of a theory of public expenditure, Review of Economics and Statistics 37, pp. 350-356.

tal quantity of consumed goods is equal to the quantity of goods consumed by just one individual.

Though I agree with Samuelson's definitions I would like to introduce a further difference that was almost neglected by Samuelson. A consumer can be precluded from the use of a good either by the very nature of the good or by legal dispositions. Consequently, I distinguish personal and common goods when the exclusion is natural and I use the terms 'private' and 'public' when the exclusion is a consequence of the law. In both regards, the excludability can be more or less great. Consequently consumer goods are to be placed on a scale between absolutely personal and absolutely common. The greater the number of people is who can use them without excluding one another from using them, the more the goods are common. In this regard, economists speak of 'pure' and 'impure' public goods.

On the same basis we can introduce the concept of common evil as well. Something is a common evil if the damage it causes to one person has as a consequence a damage to all or most other persons. I should emphasise that there is an asymmetry between the concept of common good and the concept of common evil.

IV   Using the criteria

Now I will try to find entities (or an entity) that are – according to the two criteria – useful for everybody and/or desired by everybody. However, as this conference is about the European common good I will always – as a secondary question – ask whether such an entity is to be found on the European level.[15] A first answer can be given immediately: neither the 'greatest happiness of the greatest number' nor its modern equivalent 'social welfare' can count as the common good, as they are just the sum total of personal goods. But let us proceed in due order taking one ontological category after the other.

1   Goods as substances

Let me first see whether there is a substance that could be considered as the common good. If we apply the preference-criterion we will find that no substance is possibly a common good. You certainly know Kant's ironical quotation

---

15   Klaus Gretschmann (in this volume) lists 'clean environment, health, knowledge, property rights, economic and monetary policy' as examples of global or regional public goods. As we shall see these belong to completely different ontological categories.

of the pledge of King Francis I (*Anheischigmachung*): 'What my brother Charles wants (Milan), that I want as well' (Critique of Practical Reason, AA, V, 28). The apparent accordance of the two desires disappears when we replace the object (Milan) by states of affairs. Of course what Francis I wants is that Francis I rules over Milan, and what Charles V wants is that Charles V rules over Milan; one excludes the other. Quite generally substances are not the proper objects of desires or preferences. Objects of desires and preferences are states of affairs. However, conflicts of interests like the one that opposed Francis I and Charles V arise only concerning personal goods. Therefore, personal goods and only personal goods need a just regulation of their use, while common goods yield the appreciable advantage that they give no rise to problems of justice of this kind.

If we now apply the use-criterion to substances, we see that some are personal goods and others impure common goods. When I use this apple, that is when I eat it, I thereby exclude everybody else from using it, and I even exclude myself from using it a second time.

Apples are 'personal goods' by their very nature. The situation is quite different in the case of pens, bicycles or airplanes. The fact that I use this pen now doesn't preclude that someone else uses it later. These entities don't lose their usefulness by being used or at least they don't lose it at short notice. Therefore they are called 'durable goods'. Durable goods are impure common goods. The fact that they are impure common goods has the consequence that their use must be regulated, as we shall see later. It is difficult to find substances that are common goods on the European level. The best example I can see is a system of highways linking Lisbon to Tallinn and Dublin to Athens.

2   Persons as personal and common goods

What I said about substances holds for persons as well. In this regard we should not trust our language too much. When I say 'I desire Maria', what I desire is not Maria but the state of affairs that Maria provides me a certain service. This doesn't exclude that certain states of affairs - with a reference to persons – are in fact desired by a large amount of people, for instance many desired that Obama was elected president of the United States. But, the example shows that it is rather unlikely that all desire the realisation of the same state of affairs referring to the same person. Not even the fact that , say Jack Nicholson gets an Oscar is an exception.

Aristotle was the first to recognise that persons can be useful to other persons and in this sense be goods. However, for ontological reasons the utility of persons is quite different from the utility of substances. As you know, the ontology of persons is very complicated and controversial. In a way persons are bodies.

This makes them look like substances. But inside these bodies occur strange psychic events, such as emotions, thoughts, and decisions. That's why normally a person is useful for another person if and only if she decided to provide the service the other wants. Services are to a certain degree non-exclusive. However, if we disregard political functions for the moment, services rarely reach a national or European level. No doctor cures the whole population of a country. However, the freedom of decision makes it possible that persons can harm other persons as well. That is why we want to have control over other people and to secure their services for ourselves.

According to the different kinds of service we can get from other people, Aristotle (NE, VIII, 1156 a 6 - b 32) distinguished three types of friendship: I may love another person because she provides me pleasure, because she is of some utility for me, or for her own sake. The first is friendship of pleasure, the second is friendship of utility, and the third is true or perfect friendship. Let me just make some remarks on the third type, i.e. perfect or true friendship, for it is important for our purpose. In the case of true friendship I don't love my friend for the sake of the services he provides but for his own sake. That means that I prefer whatever he does. Let me give an example. Mary uses my car at a moment when I need it myself. Now, if I truly love her, I sincerely will prefer that she uses the car though I wanted to use it myself. True friendship and envy have contrary effects: while envy makes me unhappy when the other is happy, true friendship yields that I am happy when my friend is happy.[16] So if I am an utilitarian I should promote true friendship in the society. The fact that friendship reverses the negative effects of rivalry and envy makes it the magical cement of societies. If everybody followed the Christian command to love one's enemy, we would not need justice anymore.

However, as Aristotle has already argued, one can have a relation of true friendship only with a few people, in the ideal case with only one. The reason is that it is impossible to have a deep insight into the character of the other and to create strong emotional bonds with the other if the number of these relations becomes too great. Therefore, a friend in the strong sense of the word is not a common but a personal good. That is why already Aristotle was sceptical about the possibility to base the unity of the city-state on friendship among the citizens.[17] The European Union doesn't hold together because each European is the

16 See Gerhard Seel (1990), Die Rechtfertigung von Herrschaft in der "Politik" des Aristotels, in: G. Patzig (ed), Artistoteles' "Politik", Akten des XI. Symposium Aristotelicum Friedrichshafen/ Bodensee, 25.8. – 3.9. 1987, Göttingen, pp. 45-47.

17 However, as Patrick Riordan rightly remarked, in Politics, III, 9, 1280 a 31-32, Aristotle emphasises that 'a state exists for the sake of a good life' and that as a consequence 'excellence must be the care of a state which is truly so called' (b 6-8). So clearly the basis

friend of every other European. The totality of the Europeans is not the common good for each European. Nevertheless, the coherence of the European Union will be certainly improved by the fact that ever more people of different member states provide services of all kinds to other people across the continent.

3   Goods as abstract entities

Abstract entities like music scores, scientific theories, literature, rules, and so forth are the backbone of a culture. The more Europeans have these entities in common, the more may we speak of a common European culture. But that is not yet the whole story. If we apply the use-criterion, we see that abstract entities are common goods "par excellence". They are in fact the purest common goods we can imagine. For, by using these goods I exclude nobody from using them as well, even at the same time. We should not confuse, though, the abstract entities with their material support. Abstract entities are at our disposal through a material support to which they are fixed. The material support of a theory limits its range of users. While I read this book you cannot read it. However, this doesn't diminish at all the non-exclusive character of abstract entities themselves. By their very nature they can be used by an unlimited number of users and an unlimited number of times. However, as abstract entities presuppose a language or a code to be laid down and made accessible to users, they can only be used by those who command the language or the code. To be sure, any language or code can be learned by a rational being and normally an abstract entity laid down in a given language can be translated into another language. Nevertheless, the dependence on a language or a code implies that even abstract entities are at a given time exclusive to a certain degree.

Given that abstract entities are non-exclusive, one may think that many people prefer to use them. This is in fact the case. However, as we shall see in the next paragraph, the users of abstract entities like theories or music scores form esoteric communities that normally exclude all the rest. A second distinction is important here. The use of a common good by many people is not the same as a common use. We speak of a common use of a score if an orchestra performs the piece of music in a common effort, not when a thousand musicians perform the same piece privately in their homes. So if we ask again whether we find a European common good among abstract entities, the answer is rather negative according to both criteria. Here the fact that culture becomes more and more esoteric

of the coherence among the citizens of a state cannot be friendship of utility or of pleasure only.

plays a decisive role. There is no abstract entity that could be used by all Europeans. In this sense it is wrong to speak of a common European culture.

4   Goods as events

Substances and abstract entities are used to make certain types of events happen or to bring about those events. I use my tennis racquet to play tennis and I use the score of a musical work to perform it. We normally say that substances and abstract entities are means for realising certain events, which we pursue as our ends. Here we encounter again our old fellow Aristotle who in fact believed that the only goods we pursue for themselves – the so called intrinsic goods – are types of events like searching for truth or ruling over city-states and that all the other goods are pursued for the sake of these. I doubt, however, that there are types of events the realisation of which everybody prefers.

There are of course many types of events like concerts, parties, festivities, and wars that presuppose the cooperation of many persons. And in most cases the participants desire that the event takes place because they enjoy taking part in it. As much as the activity of a certain person is a necessary element of the event, this person cannot be excluded from the event. So we see that these types of events fulfil both criteria of the common good. However, if we look to the European level we find that there is practically no social event that has a truly European dimension, not even the European Football Championship. Like the abstract entities that make them possible, types of cultural events are esoteric. They exclude all those who lack the knowledge or the skills to enjoy taking part in them. The only exception I know of is victory in a war. But should we wage wars to enjoy this common good?

5   Goods as entitlements

The last ontological category we have to consider are legal regulations like rights, obligations, entitlements, and so forth. Entitlements regulate the use of the goods we have considered so far. Therefore, we call the former 'first order goods' and the latter 'second order goods'. Entitlements, rights, and obligations are comparable to abstract entities in many aspects. They differ from the abstract entities we considered so far in two points:

1. They consist of modal propositions with a special deontic operator. In other words, they say that it is allowed or obligatory that somebody does something, for instance that I use this laptop.

2. Their existence presupposes a juridical system that enacts legal dispositions (laws) on which the validity of rights, obligations, and entitlements depend.

•

We have seen that first order goods are more or less exclusive by their nature. Second order goods make first order goods exclusive or non-exclusive by law, i.e. they transform them into 'private' or 'public goods'. This glass of water is a private good because I have the right to drink it and you have the obligation to refrain from drinking it.

The juridical character of entitlements and obligations has very surprising implications. One might surmise that the law always confirms and backs the natural exclusiveness or non-exclusiveness of first order goods. But this is a mistake. Entitlements and obligations can transform what is naturally a personal good into a public good, and what is naturally a common good into a private good. Let me give two examples:

1. We have seen that abstract entities are by their very nature common goods, but by copyrights and patents we transform them into private goods. The reason that is given for these legal measures is that there would be no motivation to produce these goods if the producer had no private ownership in them. This argument is questionable. During my career I have produced a lot of abstract entities fixed in books and articles. The more people use them, the happier I am.
2. There is also the transformation of personal goods into public goods by law. A herring on the table is a personal good by its nature. But as long as it swims freely in the sea it is a public good, for fishing rights entitle everybody to fish it. Commodities too are public goods, not in the sense of Samuelson's definition, but in the sense that everybody has the right to try to buy them.

The normal procedure, however, is to let naturally common goods become public goods. The examples mostly mentioned in the literature are national defence, communication systems, railways, roads, bridges, etc.[18] However, we should keep in mind that the definition of the concept of public good doesn't imply that every or some public goods are produced and owned by the state.

---

18   Klaus Gretschmann lists 'health' as public good. However, health as a state of an individual is a personal good; healthcare – as we have seen – is a personal good as well. The only thing that may be considered as a public good in this context is the institution of health insurance and legal provisions of health protection. So this is what Gretschmann must mean.

V   Externalities

The intervention of the lawgiver is especially requested because of a phenomenon that economists call 'externalities'. An externality is a specific relation between personal goods and evils on the one hand, and common goods and evils on the other, according to which a personal good or a personal evil implies a common good or a common evil. We have to distinguish four types of externalities:

1. A personal good implies a common good;
2. A personal good implies a common evil;
3. A personal evil implies a common good;
4. A personal evil implies a common evil.

Let me give some simple examples:

1. If somebody builds a bridge to reach his land on the other side of the river, he thereby creates a common good, for everybody can use the bridge.
2. If somebody builds a factory that pollutes the air in the whole country, his personal good implies a common evil.
3. If somebody sacrifices his life to save his country, his personal evil implies a common good.
4. If somebody catches a contagious disease and inadvertently infects the whole community, his personal evil implies a common evil.

In the economic literature – due to a lack of systematicity – the two latter types are completely neglected. Only the first two get due attention. In a market economy one effect of externalities will be that market prices don't reflect marginal social costs of production. This is called 'market failure', for in this case the market doesn't attain a state of efficiency. According to Pigou (1920) this kind of market failure calls for an intervention by the state. Let us consider the four types from a philosophical point of view:

First: if someone produces a common good in order to promote his personal benefit and people who didn't contribute to its production use it, we have the strong feeling that this is unjust. Here we are facing the so-called 'free-rider' problem. However, there is an economic argument in favour of allowing free riding. If the common good is already produced and financed, it is Pareto-suboptimal to exclude people from using it as long as this doesn't preclude others from using it. We must acknowledge, though, that in the case of impure common goods the latter may happen. Most of us know how it feels to be stuck in a traffic jam. This is the unpleasant consequence of the unrestricted entitlement to using public roads.

Or think of the crowded lecture halls in our universities. All of these are strong reasons to regulate the production and the use of common goods by law. But how should we regulate this?

The simplest solution would be to let the state produce and own all the common goods, which by this measure would become public goods. However, this involves another problem of justice. If the costs of the production of these public goods have to be paid by the taxpayers, regardless of whether they use them and to which degree they use them, we again get unwelcome externalities. To avoid these we need an institution that obliges the users to pay for the use of the common good to the degree that they take advantage of it. In other words, we need to introduce use- and profit-dependent fees, fares, and taxes.

Now, how should we fix these fees, fares, and taxes? In the case of public goods produced by the state, this amounts to the question of just taxation. I cannot go into the enormous amount of literature dealing with this question. Personally, I am very much in favour of Lindahl's and Johansen's proposal.[19] The simplified upshot of this is the following: each consumer of a public good pays a fee in terms of private goods she has to renounce. The amount of the private goods she renounces is determined by her marginal willingness to pay for the common good. This in turn depends on: a) the sum of private goods she is entitled to; b) the marginal benefit she gets from the consumption of these private goods; and b) the marginal benefit she derives from the public good. She should be willing to invest in the public good until the marginal utility of her consumption of the public good is equal to the marginal utility of the private good she has to renounce. One of the positive consequences of such a formula would be that poor people, who have to invest all of their income in private goods and thus cannot co-finance the public good, should nevertheless be entitled to use it in order to avoid a Pareto-suboptimal situation. However, the well-known problem with this proposal is that it is difficult to implement, because people have a tendency to misrepresent their preferences and thus pay less than they should.

Second: in the case of negative externalities, we see similar problems of justice. The simplest solution would be to avoid the externalities by forbidding the production of the personal good that causes the common evil, for instance by closing the polluting factory. However, this would lead to a Pareto-suboptimal situation. A better solution would be to oblige the polluter to pay damages to the members of the community. But how can we calculate these damages in a realistic way? In principle, the solution I favour for the first kind of externalities applies here as well. Each member of the community should receive damages from

19   Erik Lindahl (1919), Die Gerechtigkeit der Besteuerung. Lund: Gleerupa Universitets-Bokhandeln; Leif Johansen (1963), Some notes on the Lindahl theory of determination of public expenditure, International Economic Review 4 (3), pp. 346-358.

the polluter to the extent that his personal well-being is negatively influenced by the pollution. However, as in the former case, it is difficult to evaluate this in an objective manner, for the damage depends on the personal preferences of each person and everybody has an interest to misrepresent them. To resolve this difficult problem we would need to analyse the relevant economic literature, a task I cannot take on here.

In the third case we have the inverse situation. Here an individual has a disadvantage because of the production of a common good. This injustice has to be repaired by paying damages to the person in question. But in some extreme cases this is impossible. You cannot pay damages to a fallen hero who by his death saved his country.[20] The only way to guarantee justice in these cases is by following a fair procedure granting equal chances to everybody, when it comes to determining who has to sacrifice his life.

The fourth case seems to entail no problem of justice and therefore doesn't get much attention. However, this is a mistake. If somebody knowingly or even inadvertently causes damage to the community, he is responsible for this even if he suffers the same loss. He should be held responsible and be punished accordingly.

My last question is whether public goods fulfil the preference-criterion. Does every potential user desire the existence of a given public good? What a user prefers in the first place is his entitlement to use the public good. As he cannot have this without the equal entitlement of other users, he accepts this. In this sense, public goods fulfil the preference-criterion. However, I don't see a public good, the existence of which all Europeans would prefer.

VI   European juridical institutions as the European common good

Concerning the European common good, the result of our investigation has been negative so far. We found only some entities that can be considered as a European common good, but we didn't encounter anything that is without any doubt the European common good. However, this result is not only very unsatisfactory, it is also rather unlikely. Should there really be no European common good? Therefore I propose to reconsider our question and to analyse the topic more closely and more carefully. A look at the history of Europe shows that there were two main motives to create a community of European states. The first was the intention to make wars among European nations impossible, and the second was

---

20   Iain Begg suggested that one could pay damages to his family or his friends as in fact Buchanan's theory of clubs would argue. See James M. Buchanan (1965), An Economic Theory of Clubs, Economica 32, pp. 1-14.

the intention to foster and simplify economic relations between the European states and their citizens. This is no surprise, for wars are the most harmful interactions among states and just economic relations are the most advantageous ones. Should we not take peace and welfare as the true European common good?

However, before rushing to that conclusion, we should analyse this proposal in the light of our two criteria. If we apply the preference-criterion we come to a negative conclusion. It is simply not the case that all Europeans love peace and it is not the case that everybody loves the welfare of the others. But, one may think that the preference criterion is too strong anyway. So let us apply the use-criterion.

Are peace and social welfare non-exclusive goods? I have my doubts. As the ancients already knew, peace is a private good for the weak and a private evil for the powerful. This has certainly changed in the age of nuclear wars when even the aggressor himself can hardly escape the damage of nuclear destruction. However, below the level of nuclear warfare the ancient analysis is still valid. As I said before, welfare of a community is nothing but the sum of the private goods of its members or the statistically calculated average of them. As we have here a null-sum situation, welfare of the one clearly excludes the welfare of the other.

However, if we conceive of peace and welfare not as sociological states of affairs, but as legally warranted entitlements, we have to conclude that they are really common goods, for the right to live in peace is clearly non-exclusive, as is the right to equal economic opportunity. However, these rights can only be enacted and guaranteed by the juridical institutions of a state. This brings me to the main thesis of this chapter, that is that the European political and juridical institutions themselves are the true European common good.

In order to justify this claim let me first examine whether these institutions fulfil our two criteria of a common good. There is no doubt that they fulfil the use-criterion, because democratic institutions by definition cannot exclude any member from using them and the fact that one member uses a juridical institution doesn't exclude others from using it. Furthermore, as the activity of the political institutions is an event, the participations of all members in it – at least through voting – is necessary. But is this common good also desired by everybody, meaning, are the European institutions a common good according to the preference-criterion as well? Here the answer is negative, for it is obvious that not every European desires the existence of the institutions of the European Union. The existence of the Eurosceptics is sufficient to show this.

Do we have to renounce our claim that the European institutions are the real European common good? Not yet. For there is still another meaning of the term 'good' according to which these institutions are in fact a common good. To show this I will first introduce a deontic version of the preference-criterion. It says that an entity is a common good for a given society if all members of the society have the moral obligation to prefer it. You remember what I said at the outset: values may be the foundations of duties, but duties may be the foundation of values as well. Now, if we can show that all Europeans have in fact the duty to create European political and juridical institutions, these institutions have to be considered as the European common good.

Let me briefly justify these claims.[21] My starting point is a moral principle similar to Kant's categorical imperative and Fichte's basic moral principle. It obliges everybody to live in such a way that everybody else can accept his actions and live in agreement with him. Normally we agree with the actions of others if they are to our advantage and we disagree with them if they harm us or threaten to harm us. How is it possible that somebody agrees with the action of another that harms him? This would be reasonable for him to do if and only if the other acts according to a rule that the harmed person herself accepted and enacted. This is roughly speaking the justification of the establishment of positive law and this in turn can only be achieved through the creation of a state. A rule of action qualifies for positive legislation if and only if nobody has good reason to reject it. A good reason to reject a law would be the fact that it restricts one's freedom more than is necessary to protect the equal freedom of everybody, or more than it restricts the freedom of others.

Now, normally the probability that someone harms someone else by his actions is greater the more the interactions of people are frequent and important. The same is true of the probability of benefiting each other. Therefore, the need for a common legislation concerns, first of all, those people who actually interfere in each other's actions. Normally, close neighbours interfere more frequently with one another than do people who live at a greater distance. On the other hand it is much easier to reach a common agreement on laws of action among people who share cultural values and beliefs. This again is most likely the case with close neighbours. Therefore, it is quite natural that states have historically first been established on limited territories by culturally coherent communities and particular states get their legitimacy on the basis of the same considerations.

It was one of Kant's greatest insights that states that interfere with each other's actions directly or through the actions of their citizens are to be treated by the philosophy of right in the same way as individuals are. They have the obliga-

---

21 A more elaborated argument is to be found in: Gerhard Seel (2001), How to Justify the Rights of Political Minorities, in B.M. Leiser, T.D. Campbell (eds.), Human Rights in Philosophy and Practice, Ashgate: Burlington, pp. 215-233 and Gerhard Seel (2006), Wie lassen sich Rechte politischer Minderheiten rechtfertigen?, in: Gerhard Seel (ed.), Minderheiten, Migranten und die Staatengemeinschaft. Wer hat welche Rechte? Bern/ Wien: Lang, pp 19-57.

tion to regulate these interactions by commonly agreed positive law and, in order to put such laws in force, to form a state of states. So what practical reason really demands us to realise is not just a state, but also a federal state.[22] This means that, in the age of globalisation, where economic, cultural, and scientific interactions reach the remotest parts of the world, states and federal states have even the obligation to establish a federal world state. The principal of federalism is just this: regulate interactions among people according to their intensity and density on the geographically-defined levels where they occur. On each of these levels the political and juridical institutions are the deontologically-founded common good for those who take part in these institutions and fall under their regulations.

I take European integration to be the attempt to realise step by step[23] this kind of common good for the 'old' continent in the form of a federal European state.[24] I know that in the current political context politicians have good reasons to insist that the EU is not yet a federal state, and that its member states are still sovereign. But the concept of sovereignty is an invention of nationalistic thinkers of early modernity, and it should be put out of order together with nationalism.[25] So, the European political and juridical institutions are the truly European common good, not because everybody in fact prefers them, but because it is everybody's duty to realise them. Saying that the European Union as a political body and a political process is the only common good for all Europeans, I should emphasise that this implies that the European institutions guarantee human and civil rights for all Europeans, and these include in my view the so-called social human rights, like equal opportunity,[26] social security, health insurance, and a safe environment[27] That is why in the current economic crisis conjuring up a European common good defined in terms of welfare doesn't really solve the problem. The only way out is the improvement and development of the European institutions towards more economic and financial federalism.

22 So I use what Alexander Somek calls the 'federalist imagery'.
23 The different steps are convincingly marked by Dragana Damjanovic in her paper in this volume.
24 This is partly done by a process of 'constitutionalization' as Alexander Somek describes it in his chapter, but the most important steps toward it are the different treatises and conventions among the member states as described in Dragana Damjanovic's paper.
25 I agree with Alexander Somek who claims that the concept of sovereignty is 'atavistic, primitive and dangerous'.
26 I should emphasise that the aim of political institutions is not – as Johannes Pollak puts it in his chapter – the happiness of the citizens, but rather – as the American Declaration of Independence has it – the 'pursuit of happiness', which means equal opportunity to pursue one's own happiness.
27 See the passage from the Preamble of the Charter of Fundamental Rights of the European Union quoted in front of Sonja Puntscher Riekmann's contribution to this volume.

Some years ago a German critic of the European Constitution argued that a state, i.e. a constitution every citizen adheres to, presupposes a common sacrifice of blood and that the Europeans haven't made such a sacrifice.[28] He means that the Europeans should have waged war against a common enemy to acknowledge the need of unity. He didn't see that the Europeans already made an enormous sacrifice of blood, though of a different kind. I mean the bloodshed in the wars they waged against each other. If you still ask for a justification of the European federal state, here it is.

Bibliography

Aristotle, *Nicomachean Ethics,* X, 2, 1172 b, pp. 9-15.

Buchanan, J.A. (1965), An Economic Theory of Clubs, *Economics* 32, pp. 1- 14.

Johansen, L. (1963), Some notes on the Lindahl theory of determination of public expenditure, *International Economic Review* 4 (3), pp. 346-358.

Johnson, H. (1958), Demand theory further revisited or goods are goods, *Economica*, 25.

Lindahl, E. (1919), *Die Gerechtigkeit der Besteuerung.* Lund: Gleerupa Universitets-Bokhandeln.

Rawls, J. (1972), *A Theory of Justice.* Oxford: Oxford University Press.

Samuelson, P. A. (1954), The pure theory of public expenditure, *Review of Economics and Statistics* 36, pp. 387-389.

Samuelson, P.A. (1955), Diagrammatic exposition of a theory of public expenditure, *Review of Economics and Statistics* 37, pp. 350-356.

Schumpeter. J.A. (1942), *Kapitalismus, Sozialismus und Demokratie.* Tübingen.

Seel, G. (1990), Die Rechtfertigung von Herrschaft in der "Politik" des Aristoteles, in: G. Patzig (ed), *Artistoteles' "Politik", Akten des XI. Symposium Aristotelicum Friedrichshafen/ Bodensee,* 25.8. – 3.9. 1987, Göttingen, pp. 32-62.

Seel, G. (2001), How to Justify the Rights of Political Minorities, in: B.M. Leiser, T.D. Campbell (eds.), *Human Rights in Philosophy and Practice.* Ashgate: Burlington, pp. 215-233.

Seel , G. (2006), Wie lassen sich Rechte politischer Minderheiten rechtfertigen?, in: Gerhard Seel (ed.), *Minderheiten, Migranten und die Staatengemeinschaft. Wer hat welche Rechte?* Bern/ Wien: Lang, pp 19-57.

Seel. G. (2011), The Citizen is a Ruler, in: E. Moutsopoulos and M. Protopapas-Marneli (eds.), *The Notion of Citizenship in Greek Philosophy,* Proceedings of the 2nd International Conference of Philosophy, Alexandria, 4-6 March 2010, Athens, pp. 100-112.

Sen, A. (1979), Utilitarianism and Welfarism, *The Journal of Philosophy,* 76(9), pp. 463-489.

Taylor, Ch. (1995), *Philosophical Arguments.* Cambridge, Mass.: Harvard University Press.

---

28   The Europeans of course made some sacrifices for the creation of the EU. The most important is the partial renunciation of sovereignty. However, to formulate it in a Rousseauian model, they renounced a dangerous and arbitrary sovereignty and gained an autonomy guaranteed by law and the force of the community.

Tiebout, Ch. (1956), A pure theory of local expenditures, *Journal of Political Economy* 64, pp. 416-424.

Europe's Common Good: Ideas and Ideals

Patrick Riordan SJ

I   Introduction

Klaus Gretschmann makes nice play on words in contrasting *deals* and *ideals* at the heart of European cooperation.[1] Deals are bargains that the member states make with each other in pursuit of their national interest. Ideals by contrast are aspirations to values such as equality and participation, which motivate the construction and renewal of European institutions. Both are at play in the development of the European Union, and Gretschmann suggests that deals are more to the fore in times of economic pressure while a certain sense of economic well-being seems to be a prerequisite for pursuing ideals. This is a useful contrast facilitating a helpful analysis. However, it is also potentially misleading, if the *deal-ideal* pair is applied too widely. There is a danger that other significant concept pairs could be mapped on to it and receive novel but distorting interpretations. For instance, in the context of discussing Europe's common goods, it is necessary to distinguish between public goods and common goods. It would lead to a distortion of the concept of the common good if the *deal-ideal* pair was paralleled with the *public-common* pair, such that public goods are seen as the outcome of deals, and common goods seen as the content of ideals. In this investigation of the notion of Europe's common good I suggest that attention to ideas and ideals can help us recover the distinctive meaning of the common good and show its relevance to the on-going processes of operation and development of the European Union, whether in pursuit of deals or of ideals. This chapter argues that the intellectual capital of both ideas and ideals are central to Europe's common goods.

---

1   Klaus Gretschmann in his chapter on 'Joint Action or Free Ride: EU Economic Strategies as a Common Good' in this volume.

II   Public goods and common goods

The relevant definitions and distinction of public and common goods are well-presented in other chapters, especially in Gerhard Seel's contribution.[2] However, it is worth recalling the different contexts and therefore different interests generating the two concepts. For the sake of clarity I suggest that we have to look to Aristotle and the Aristotelian tradition for the background to the political philosophical concept of common goods, while the concept of public goods was clarified in the development of economics. When viewed this way, the radical difference between the Aristotelian approach to common goods and the economist's approach to public goods emerges.

Aristotle understands goods as ends of action: all action is for the sake of some good.[3] Similarly, common action, cooperation, is for the sake of some good in common. He makes the jump from the local forms of cooperation (households, athletic clubs, religious societies) to the highest form of cooperation (the *polis*), and thinks that the good of the highest form of common action will be the highest good. He concentrates on the fact that people cooperate for the sake of some good, but he does not immediately consider questions of distribution. How the good is distributed among the cooperating parties, how the burdens and costs of cooperation are allocated among them, how the good is enjoyed and in what proportions: these might all be relevant questions with regard to some instances of cooperation for the good. Aristotle does not raise them straight away when reflecting on common goods. I presume he would want to say that the answers to various questions will vary, depending on the nature of the good in question, and hence the nature of the cooperation. For instance, one case of cooperation might be a student with a tutor preparing for examination for a degree. The good of their cooperation might be labelled as 'knowledge' in some field of study, or 'truth', or 'skill'. In this case, the beneficiary of the cooperation is primarily the student who is to grow in knowledge, skill, or mastery. Their cooperation is for a common good, but the enjoyment of that good is predominantly on one side of the partnership. Aristotle relegates the questions of distribution to his discussion of justice.[4] Distribution as such does not enter into his clarification of common goods, beyond noting that different goods are pursued in different instances of cooperation or community. So, for instance, for

---

2   Gerhard Seel in his chapter on 'What is the Common Good and why should we pursue it?' in this volume.
3   Aristotle, The Politics. Translated by T.A. Sinclair. Harmondsworth: Penguin Press, 1972, Bk I, chap. 1.
4   Aristotle, The Ethics of Aristotle, The Nicomachaen Ethics. Translated by J.A.K. Thomson. Harmondsworth: Penguin Press, revised edition, 1981, Bk V.

Aristotle the various questions that might be asked of people who cooperate in a joint project are distinguishable. For the sake of clarity these can be numbered as follows:

- Q1. 'What is the point of your collaboration, what good are you pursuing?'
- Q2. 'Who will benefit in the enjoyment of that good and in what proportions?'
- Q3. 'Who bears the cost and makes the effort and in what proportions?'

Aristotle does not ignore the second and third questions, as is evident from his discussion of oligarchy, for instance, where he points to issues of distribution of outputs in proportion to inputs.[5] And his discussion of *eudaimonia* in the *Ethics* underlines the distinction between the good pursued and the satisfaction enjoyed by the agent in successful achievement.[6] So the question about the good that is the purpose of cooperation is distinguishable from the questions of distribution of costs and benefits.

This is very different to the economist's concepts of different types of goods – private, public, collective, or club – whereby the distribution of costs of production and of enjoyment or benefit is central in each case. This is completely meaningful in terms of the orientation of the economist to efficiency: maximum benefit at minimum cost. It also fits well with the recognition that there is competition for many goods. Paul A. Samuelson introduced the concept of collective consumption goods in a 1954 paper entitled 'The pure theory of public expenditure': these are goods 'which all enjoy in common in the sense that each individual's consumption of such a good leads to no subtractions from any other individual's consumption of that good'.[7] This characterisation focused on the feature of non-rivalry associated with public goods; the other feature of non-excludability is that no one can be excluded from the enjoyment of the good once it is available. The latter feature in particular has implications for the provision of such goods: who is prepared to carry the burden of provision when many others will stand to benefit without having to share the cost. These concerns with distribution of burdens and benefits are central to the specification of public goods, in contrast to common goods. The common currency of the euro is a pub-

5   Aristotle, The Politics. Translated by T.A. Sinclair. Harmondsworth: Penguin Press, 1972, Bk III c.9.

6   Aristotle, The Ethics of Aristotle, The Nicomachaen Ethics. Translated by J.A.K. Thomson. Harmondsworth: Penguin Press, revised edition, 1981, Bk I, v.

7   Paul A. Samuelson (1954), The pure theory of public expenditure, Review of Economics and Statistics 36(4), pp. 387-89.

lic good in this sense, and the political difficulties arising from the questions of competence and responsibility focus on this difficult question: who is prepared to continue to bear the burdens of maintaining the public good when it appears that many are willing to be free riders, enjoying the benefits of what others produce?

One consequence of this clarification of the distinction between common and public goods is that it is possible in an Aristotelian sense to speak about private goods as common goods, while it could not be meaningful to do so in an economic sense. So for instance, collaborators in a housing association have as their common good, the point of their associating, the provision of a house (a private good) for each participant. And they could also have as one of their common goods the provision of street lighting (a public good) in the housing estate. Similarly, the participant states in the eurozone can have as a common good of their collaboration the maintenance and strengthening of the public good, which is their common currency. For that to happen, however, the net contributors must have reasons that allow them to see their effort as reasonable and worthwhile.

III   Taylor on irreducibly social goods

The economist's notion of a good influences many other disciplines and especially their models of rational choice. So prevalent is this that Charles Taylor has found it necessary to ask whether there is any purely social good.[8] He is one of several authors who have sought to recover the common good from reduction to economic categories. Taylor asks whether there are intrinsic social goods, or do common goods ultimately reduce to individual and private goods? The assumption that public goods do reduce to the goods of individuals, prevalent in the welfarism that he sees as guiding public policy, is labelled atomism. Taylor challenges the assumption that social welfare is an aggregate of the utilities enjoyed by individuals, and to counter this atomism he distinguishes different kinds of public goods. He wants to show that there are some public goods that are irreducible to private goods. He takes as an example of a public good a dam constructed to prevent flooding. The dam provides each homeowner whose dwelling is threatened by flooding with security. The public good of the dam is instrumental to the individual goods of the beneficiaries. At the same time, the beneficiaries enjoy such public goods severally. Each one's enjoyment is independent of the benefit derived by others. Are all public goods of this order?

Taylor identifies two kinds of irreducibly social goods. On the one hand there are the goods of a shared culture, which make possible the feelings, decisions,

---

8   Charles Taylor (1995), Irreducibly social goods, in: Charles Taylor (ed.), Philosophical Arguments. Cambridge, Mass.: Harvard University Press, pp. 127-145.

and actions of individuals. On the other hand, there are goods that essentially incorporate shared understandings of their value. As an example of the first he discusses language. He draws on the distinction introduced by de Saussure between *parole* and *langue*. *Parole* refers to the speech of anyone, who draws on the resources of her language, *langue*, considered as a system. For any speaker attempting to express herself the language is a shared resource that makes such expression possible for her. Taylor points out that it is impossible to give an atomist account of language as a good. Similarly, culture, understood as the background of practices, institutions, and understandings that makes social action possible, is irreducibly social.

For the second type of irreducibly social good, he points to the shared understanding and reciprocal acknowledgement involved in certain qualities of relationships such as friendships. In such relationships there is recognition of the goodness and rightness of the quality of the interaction, which at the same time is mutually acknowledged. Where people deal with one another on the basis of equality and respect there is a reciprocal acknowledgement that this is the case and that this is appropriate. Communities, including political societies, are constituted by such relationships, but these are not reducible to private goods enjoyed severally by individuals. They are not simply instrumental, but constitutive. Subscription by citizens to the rule of law, whereby they understand themselves as cooperating in making that law, is an example of this kind of good.

The examples for both kinds of irreducibly social goods are drawn from dimensions of meaning. A shared language, a shared culture, shared expectations, and reciprocal acknowledgement in the context of relationships all belong to the realm of the symbolic. This is not surprising, since the Aristotelian tradition has always considered intellectual goods as essentially common. Knowledge, for instance, can be shared without any diminishment in the quantity of knowledge enjoyed by individuals. On the contrary, the sharing of such goods builds and sustains a community among those whose knowledge and commitment is common. This is critical for Aristotle's understanding of political community, as grounded in a shared view of what is good or bad, right or wrong, just or unjust, lawful or unlawful.[9] In this context knowledge can be both a common good and a public good.

Our world sometimes chooses to treat knowledge as a private good, for reasons which include the fostering of innovation and discovery. But that intellectual goods might be considered as private goods in this manner would be shocking to medieval philosophers. For them intellectual goods are inherently public, not private. As Herbert McCabe has written, theologians like Aquinas saw the

---

9   Aristotle, The Politics. Translated by T.A. Sinclair. Harmondsworth: Penguin Press, 1972, Bk I, chap. 2.

spiritual and intellectual as inherently common and public; what individuates and privatises is the material and the particular. Ever since Descartes, we are more likely to think of this contrast in the reverse direction, considering the spiritual in the sense of self-awareness as especially private, and the bodily, being visible and tangible to others, as especially public.[10]

IV   Types of common goods

Taylor's examples select dimensions of meaning as examples of intrinsically social goods, but this should not be read as confining all common goods to spiritual or symbolic domains. In this chapter I want to focus on common goods within horizons of meaning. But in order to situate these within a broader spectrum I recall briefly how, according to Aristotle's account, any kind of good can be a common good.[11] The primary sense of the term, following Aristotle, is to indicate the good for the sake of which people cooperate; and since people cooperate for many different purposes, there are many different goods in common corresponding to the different instances and various forms of cooperation. A 'good' for Aristotle is what *can be* the object or end of action, not necessarily what *must be* pursued on any particular occasion. One can recognise the worthiness of many goals and objects, without being obliged to pursue any of them. To identify a good, or a possible good in common, is not to issue a precept or imperative that since it is good, it *must be* pursued. Accordingly, the concept of 'common good' is used analogously. Without claiming to be exhaustive, the following is a list of possible meanings for the common good of cooperation.

a. People can cooperate to achieve *an identifiable concrete good*, realising some value, pursued as the objective of cooperation. Examples are a school place for a child, a game of tennis, a meal, a house, and a piece of legislation.

b. Sometimes the good in common is a *means to some desired goal*. On occasion, deliberate action must be undertaken to put means and conditions in place for the pursuit of concrete goods. So we build a school, a tennis court, cultivate a garden, or master the skills of legal drafting. Or within Europe we adopt a common currency, the euro, as a means to the many ends of action.

---

10   Herbert McCabe, OP (2005), The Good Life: Ethics and the Pursuit of Happiness, edited by Brian Davies. London: Continuum, pp. 36-7.
11   I summarise here what I have published elsewhere on the notion of the common good: Patrick Riordan (2008), A Grammar of the Common Good. London: Continuum.

c. Sets of such conditions appear as systems, and so we require cooperation to put in place and maintain in good working order the education system, the health care system, and the security and justice systems. And in relation to the euro, there is a system including such institutions as the European Central Bank, and national Central Banks. These have a role in maintaining the value and reliability of the currency, their goods in common, but the system in its own right can be a common good of action to create and sustain it.

d. People who cooperate in constructing and operating any such complex system, a justice system, for instance, face difficult questions on which they have to take a position. What is the purpose of the law? How do we determine the dividing line between issues of criminal law and issues of civil law? What is the point of punishment? How much discretion should be left to judges? Is indeterminate sentencing ever warranted? What rights are those punished assumed to forfeit? Any complex system will exhibit such series of questions, and it is part of the common good of those cooperating in maintaining the systems that there be a memory and *mastery of the decisions* arrived at, *skilled professionals* to deal with further questions, *educators and researchers* to initiate recruits into the relevant competencies and to develop the body of skills available. A brief overview of the table of contents of any textbook in jurisprudence or philosophy of law quickly confirms the range of knowledge and competence that belongs among the common good of co-operators in a legal system. It is part of the common good of a law governed society to have a body of competent professionals, and accordingly, to have the means of training them, resourcing them, and facilitating their functioning. To be noted here is that the common good can include persons, the network of their relationships, and their competencies.

e. Skilled professionals usually have to function in conflicted contexts. There are disagreements and disputes about the various courses of action open to them. Pedagogies, therapies, remuneration schemes, family support policies, childcare, bank rescue measures, and penal policies are all disputed territories. It is also part of the common good of the relevant community *that there be such dispute, and even conflict*, so that questions are raised and clarified, and experience can be gathered to determine the good, better or best options. It is not entailed by the notion of common good that the parties in cooperation already know in advance what their common good consists of in every detail. They only know that the outcome of the dispute, were it to be fully satisfactory, would be their common good. Commentators frequently presume from reference to common goods of co-operators that it must be something known by them already.

f. Some kinds of goods listed above for the sake of which we cooperate are relatively specific and identifiable. Sometimes, to make sense of our cooperation, we have to rely on a vaguer and more aspirational language. What is the purpose of our educational system? What is the goal of the health-care system, law-courts, and penal system? To answer these questions we rely on shorthand formulations of our values, such as love, truth, life, justice, harmony, peace, and friendship. And because these might be distinguishable but not separable, since together they make up what Aristotle labelled the good life, we use terms like happiness, well-being, and public welfare to bundle them together and evoke a *coherent vision of the kind of existence we aspire to*. When the common good is used to name this objective of our cooperation, then it is evidently a heuristic term. It labels something to which we aspire, but which we have not yet achieved. It remains to be discovered, even as it is being constructed. This is all the more relevant when there is conflict about policies to be implemented. We speak of a common good in terms such as justice, or welfare, or freedom for all, as naming an objective of our search, even as we dispute the appropriate policy for bringing it about. For instance, we know we want a stable currency with low inflation and the confidence of creditors, without being yet in agreement about how to achieve those ambitions. With reference to the common good we might wish to apply one or other of its linked criteria with which we can filter out policies or proposals unlikely to serve the common good.[12]

g. Participation in political community is a very particular case of cooperation, and it has its appropriate common good. Aristotle thought that this would be the highest possible good, which he understood as the good life, the life of excellence in the performance of distinctively human actions, noble actions, because he was of the view that political community was the highest possible form of cooperation. Most today would agree that Aristotle was too optimistic, or idealistic, about the nature of political community. This scepticism about the possibilities for political community emerged very soon as Aristotle's ideas were received in a Christian worldview. Especially under the influence of Augustine, the idea that the political community was the highest form of cooperation pursuing the highest good was clarified as follows:[13] The *polis* is not the highest form of cooperation to which corresponds the highest good. Instead, *the highest form of cooperation is the City of God in which the highest good is the enjoyment of God* (the beatific vi-

---

12 See my article: Patrick Riordan (2009), Europe's Common Good: The Contribution of the Catholic Church, in: Šimon Marinčák (ed.), Religion: Problem or Promise? The Role of Religion in the Integration of Europe. Orientalia et Occidentalia Vol.4. Košice, Slovakia: Centrum spirituality, pp. 279-294.

13 Augustine, The City of God, edited by David Knowles (1972), translated by Henry Bettensen. Harmondsworth: Penguin Press; Robert A. Markus (1970), Saeculum: History and Society in the Theology of St Augustine. Cambridge: Cambridge University Press.

sion). The instruments of political domination available to humankind are unable to make people good or excellent, as Aristotle had expected the *polis* to do for its citizens; consequently, the goods in common available to political community in history are not the highest goods. There is the religious perspective, which can acknowledge that God is the highest common good and that community with Christ in the Resurrection is the ultimate good to which all are invited. But even for those who share the religious perspective, there is no expectation that the political community in pursuit of its own common good would have to acknowledge the religiously-known common good as higher or more ultimate. In this respect it is important to note how the Catholic Church's Second Vatican Council in its treatment of the common good was content to emphasise the *conditions* facilitating human fulfilment, both individual and social, without insisting on its vision of human fulfilment. In other words, the notion of the common good corresponds to the senses (b), (c), and (d) summarized above.[14]

h. As a result of this clarification, it is no longer assumed that to consider the common good of a political community, whether that of a national state or that of a union of states such as the European Union, is to seek the highest good. Accordingly, in asking about a European common good, I distinguish this from the question of whether there is a universal common good as a good for all humanity. The European Union is a particular instance of cooperation among a growing number of states. It is a *complex instance of a system of systems*, and, as in the cases considered above, its common good is disputed. That is, the good in common for the sake of which the member states cooperate, might be spoken of in the kind of abstract terms that conceal real disagreements and real conflicts. Freedom, well-being, welfare support, participation, peace, and security are the sort of terms that everyone endorses and supports, but at the same time there can be real conflict of interests in how each expects freedom to be maintained or affluence achieved. The common good of the EU is not given or prescribed, or known in advance. It is in the process of being worked out, through conflict, as well as in debate and discussion. This is not simply about ideals. It is a way of understanding deal making, the search for ways of conciliating conflicting interests in such a way that everyone gets something of what they look for and all together support the arrangements which enable them to make deals.

---

14 Vatican Council II (1965), Gaudium et spes: The Pastoral Constitution on the Church in the Modern World, in: Austin Flannery (ed) (1996), Vatican II: Constitutions, Decrees, Declarations. Dublin: Dominican Publications, pp. 163-282, para. 26.

Summarising the reflection to this point, we can note the distinction of different meanings for the common good, the good pursued in collaborative activity:

a. A concrete good
b. Means or condition for (a)
c. A system in the manner of (a) and (b)
d. A system of systems
e. A heuristic as outcome of disputes and conflict in (d)
f. Vision of the good in inspirational language
g. A religious version of (f) specifying the highest common good
h. The European common good: a case of (f) + (e) + (d) + (b) + (a)

This listing is not yet complete, since more needs to be said about the dimensions of meaning in social goods. The discussion of a particular example may help elucidate this.

V   Shared meaning as a common good

The question, 'What is a parliament?', might be asked by a tourist in any of our capital cities to whom the London Houses of Parliament, Berlin's *Bundestag*, or the Buildings of the European Parliament in Brussels or Strasbourg are pointed out. Understanding the answer given will require a grasp of many concepts and their integration in a unified idea. So for instance, if the tour guide relied on the definition offered by the Oxford *Concise Dictionary of Politics*, the questioner would need to comprehend many different ideas. That dictionary explains a parliament as 'an elected assembly, responsible for passing legislation and granting government the right to levy taxation. Typically it combines this role of legislature with providing the personnel of government, thus fusing legislature and executive in a system of parliamentary government.'[15] The many ideas combined here include the notions of election, legislation, government, taxation, right, responsibility, legislature, and executive. It is difficult to see how, without prior familiarity with the practices and institutions of parliamentary government, the answer could be understood by the tourist. This is not just a matter of mastering the language; there is an intellectual achievement involved in interpreting the concepts and definition, which can be easily overlooked by those who take such distinctions for granted. Of course there are levels of comprehension, and political scientists and lawyers will bring more to bear in their understanding. But the

---

15   Iain McLean and Alistair McMillan (eds.) (2003), The Concise Oxford Dictionary of Politics. Oxford: Oxford University Press, pp. 393-394.

citizen faced with a choice of candidates for election to parliament must have a basic understanding of what is going on in the election, and what a parliament is for, and why it is a good thing that such a thing exists, and why they should cast their vote. All the elements of understanding and evaluation involved here illustrate what is meant by the assertion that our social and political world is mediated by meaning. To recognise a building as a house of parliament is a complex act of interpretation: it is to operate within a horizon of shared meaning, beyond what can be simply observed.

To determine what kind of good a parliament is requires attention to that horizon of shared meaning. It is evident that a parliament building is valued by those who cooperate to create and maintain it for what it accommodates: namely, the assembly, and its deliberations and decisions. Street lighting, a standard example of a public good, being both non-exclusionary and non-rivalrous, is also valued for what it makes possible: ease and safety of movement at night. That safety is valued in turn for what it makes possible: all the individual and communal projects or undertakings that people pursue in the realisation of their good, from social to educational, sporting to cultural. Ultimately it is human liberty and the liberty of association that is facilitated by the available public good of street lighting. A parliament building serves an analogous function, in facilitating individual and communal projects. But unlike the example of street lighting, a parliament building makes something possible only because of other factors shaping the shared meaning that the building has for its users.

Much more than a building is needed for an assembly to be and to function as a parliament. Constructing a parliament and caring for it goes beyond the construction of the building. It can also mean the organisation of occasions on which citizens or their elected representatives assemble, debate, and deliberate. Maintaining the parliament means engaging in the corresponding practices. A political community's pursuit of its common goods will include the maintenance of shared meaning, which enables all to participate in the same communal activity. A strengthening of the horizon of meaning occurs automatically in a self-reinforcing process when public life flourishes, but it becomes an object of attention and requires deliberate action in two kinds of situation. The first is the context of construction, when new practices and institutions are being introduced and operated for the first time. The creation and introduction of the euro as a common currency provides an example of deliberate construction. The second kind of situation is the context of crisis when there is a risk of losing what has been already achieved, or disintegration or distortion of what had been taken for granted. The sovereign debt crisis in Europe putting pressure on the euro and raising questions of its viability without a common fiscal policy that would presuppose greater political integration is an example of the second kind of situation. In both cases, construction and rescue, deliberate attention to the dimension of shared meaning is necessary, and this horizon of meaning is the common good of the cooperators.

Civic republicans draw attention to another dimension of the common good of public spaces, which is the civic virtue of participants in public life. Without citizens capable of reasoned deliberation and appropriate self-restraint there will be no public life in the relevant sense.[16] Their capacities for participation in public life on the basis of respect and reciprocity are not extrinsic to the flourishing of citizens, but when in operation constitute the quality of their participation. No one does well in these matters without others also doing well, and others doing well is not an extrinsic means to but a constitutive part of any citizen's flourishing. One cannot engage in parliamentary debate or committee work without others equally skilled and motivated, even if opposed on issues or principles. Accordingly, since civic virtue is constitutive of doing well, the virtue of the other is part of the flourishing of the whole, and so part of the common good. It is part of what a political community that relies on parliamentary process for handling its conflict would wish to sustain. Civic virtue is renewed automatically when the processes of public life are well functioning, but it requires specific attention when public life is in jeopardy, when corruption in the sense of the predominance of particular interests over the common good prevails.

While an individual participant in deliberation might take the horizon of meaning and the civic virtues of fellow participants for granted, is it defensible for a political community to do so? Unless some crisis makes it necessary to focus attention deliberately on one or other aspect of these common goods, they can remain unremarked. For instance, the density of shared meaning is particularly significant for public life, but would its absence from the list of a society's public goods be noticed? Once it is recognised and valued then it will be included, but its neglect would not necessarily lead to an immediate experience of loss, as might, for instance, the failure of the street lighting system. The political community might continue to enjoy the social capital inherited from the past without being aware that it is being exhausted, consumed without being renewed. Ernst-Wolfgang Böckenförde, former judge of Germany's Constitutional Court, warns that this poses a particular dilemma for a liberal state. He has formulated a paradox that subsequently bears his name:

> The liberal secular state lives on premises that it cannot itself guarantee. On the one hand, it can subsist only if the freedom it consents to its citizens is regulated from within, inside the moral substance of individuals and of a homogeneous society. On the other hand, it is

---

16   Iseult Honohan (2002), Civic Republicanism. London: Routledge, p. 161.

not able to guarantee these forces of inner regulation by itself without renouncing its liberalism.[17]

In other words, a liberal state cannot survive unless it is sustained by a political culture in which some elements are constantly at work strengthening and renewing the civic virtues of citizens and fostering their shared meanings and values.

The political common good is worked out by citizens as they shape their common life. In one sense it is constructed through the process of deliberation. Some aspects of what is constructed, as for instance the social capital of shared understandings and expectations, as well as the virtuous habits of citizens, are built up by the activity and the process without necessarily being the deliberately pursued goal of the process.

The discussion so far enables us to specify the different senses in which one can speak of the common good of a parliament. In this complexity, the common good can have several referents. A common good is a good of collaboration, a good pursued together by cooperating parties. People can work together to construct and maintain the parliament building; they can attempt to establish, operate, and improve the practices of deliberation and decision making; they can seek a reasonable solution to some issue. In each of these three cases there is a common good of the collaborators, a building, or practices, or a resolution. The building is a means for accommodating the assembly, which, however, is only a legislative assembly to the extent that it is structured by practices oriented to achieving a reasonable management of conflict. Those practices as common good of the parties involved are instrumental to the generation of reasonable and just resolution of concrete issues.

There is another sense in which common goods are common apart from being the deliberate goal of collaboration. Just as health is taken for granted while it obtains and only illness or injury obliges one to pay attention to health, so there are many dimensions of common goods which are taken for granted and relied upon in communal and collaborative life. In this way parliamentary government relies upon a horizon of meaning, without always having to make it an explicit object of attention. Similarly, the practices of parliamentary procedure and debate are relied upon in the day-to-day working of the assembly. And that a reasonable resolution of some issue would be one which met the requirements of the common good is assumed in the pursuit in detail of a viable resolution.

The common good in the sense of what pertains to and constitutes the good functioning of a community and its members is always partially realised – otherwise there could be no social or political life. And it is real, even if not ac-

---

17 Ernst-Wolfgang Böckenförde (1976), Staat, Gesellschaft, Freiheit. Frankfurt (english translation: State, Society, and Liberty: Studies in Political Theory and Constitutional Law). New York: Berg, 1991, p. 60.

knowledged as such. The common goods of a parliament include not only the shared goals towards which it strives in its deliberations and resolutions, but also the shared meanings and values, and the shared skills and practices, the social capital that sustains it.

VI   Europe's common good: use it or lose it

1   Challenging and preserving the common good

The European Parliament is just one of many institutions which are central to the life of the Union. It can serve as an example for the notion of common good, as we ask about Europe's common good. But the same questions can be asked about each of the institutions and about all together: what kind of good are they? In what senses are they common goods?

We are still in the process of constructing an expanding European Union. Europe's common good is not already achieved so that it can be taken for granted. This was the mistake of the mainstream political parties in Ireland during the first referendum in 2008 to ratify the Lisbon Treaty: they took it for granted that their electorate was sufficiently convinced of the value and point of the European Union and its expansion, and so they failed to make the investment of time, effort, and money to conduct a vibrant campaign. As a result, they lost out to all the peripheral opposition parties who were adept at provoking anxieties and capitalising on specific issues. They had not heeded Mill's warning about the importance of keeping alive the awareness of fundamental reasons even for established convictions.

John Stuart Mill in his essay *On Liberty* provides a set of arguments for why there should be toleration of opinions and no restriction or interference with the freedom to express opinions. The first two are often cited because they most conveniently fit with a liberal culture that favours open debate and criticism of establishments. Mill's first point is that silencing of discussion by the state or any public authority would be an unwarranted assumption of infallibility. And his second point stresses the value of open debate: the confrontation of opposed opinions is necessary to reach the truth. The third and fourth reasons reflect real elements in our experience that are relevant to my topic on the common good of Europe. This is a sophisticated version of the familiar saying: 'if you don't use it you lose it'. If we don't have controversy and vigorous debate about it, we will lose the vitality, urgency, and appreciation, e.g., of the value of parliamentary government.

> Thirdly, even if the received opinion be not only true, but the whole truth; unless it is suffered to be, and actually is, vigorously and earnestly contested, it will, by most of those

who receive it, be held in the manner of a prejudice, with little comprehension or feeling of its rational grounds. And not only this, but, fourthly, the meaning of the doctrine itself will be in danger of being lost, or enfeebled, and deprived of its vital effect on the character and conduct: the dogma becoming a mere formal profession, inefficacious for good, but cumbering the ground, and preventing the growth of any real and heartfelt conviction, from reason or personal experience.[18]

Here Mill is not writing about the dynamics of discovery, as in the first two points, but about the dynamics of preservation of what has already been discovered. What has been learned and is now taken for granted can be lost if not vigorously debated. In other words, using the example of a parliament, people might be able to repeat the dictionary definition of a parliament and hold it 'in the manner of a prejudice, with little comprehension or feeling of its rational grounds'. Similarly, the concepts may become even more abstract, unrelated to personal experience or personal understanding, and so the meaning of the definition could evaporate.

The argument to this point might be in danger of appearing to endorse uncritically anything that is proposed as belonging to the common good of the Union. The language of the common good can appear to be purely conservative at best, or reactionary at worst. The reference to Mill's concern with keeping alive established or accepted truths might confirm this impression. However, the preservative concern is neither primary nor exhaustive. Testing and refinement can be rigorous, insisting on change and development to meet new circumstances. Change can be guided both by the exigencies of critical reason drawing attention to new situations and new questions, and by the operative criteria of the common good. Those criteria are, first, that no person or group be arbitrarily excluded from participation in the enjoyment of the goods for the sake of which people cooperate. And second, that no dimension or aspect of the human good be arbitrarily excluded from the range of goods for the sake of which they cooperate.[19] In the application of these criteria, concern for the common goods of the European Union can be a source of critical challenges to economic, social, external relations, and security policies, as much as it can be a source of consolidation of the good which has been achieved.

18   John Stuart Mill (1859), On Liberty, edited by Harry B. Acton (ed.) (1972). London: Dent, pp. 120-21.
19   See Patrick Riordan (2009), Europe's Common Good: The Contribution of the Catholic Church, in: Šimon Marinčák (ed.), Religion: Problem or Promise? The Role of Religion in the Integration of Europe. Orientalia et Occidentalia Vol. 4. Košice, Slovakia: Centrum spirituality, pp. 279-294.

2 Intrinsically social goods: social imaginaries

I began with reference to a question posed by Charles Taylor. I return to that in conclusion, but also to a related topic that he discusses. Taylor wanted to show that there are some social goods that are irreducible to private goods. He identified two kinds, the goods of a shared culture, which make possible the feelings, decisions, and actions of individuals, such as a language. And second, the goods that essentially incorporate shared understandings of their value, such as friendship, or civil citizenship, which are relationships with certain qualities. If these things are intrinsically social goods, then so is the culture that sustains them, since it is intrinsic to the particular goods and not external to them in a merely instrumental way.

Taylor has coined the expression 'social imaginary' to designate 'the way people imagine their social existence, how they fit together with others, how things go on between them and their fellows, the expectations that are normally met, and the deeper normative notions and images that underlie these expectations'.[20] The moral order invoked by this set of images and assumptions embraces the market economy, civil society, and forms of government answerable to the governed. This is a convenient expression for the shared meaning which sustains a population's common life. So we can reformulate the question of Europe's common good in terms of its social imaginary.

Is the social imaginary available to the peoples of Europe today satisfactory to carry and sustain the developing European Union? The sense of belonging, for instance, or solidarity, has been shaped via a number of institutional forms, such as Church membership or religious allegiance, ethnic identity or membership of a nation-state, or solidarity with fellow workers across national boundaries. What resources are available in the second decade of the twenty-first century to sustain solidarity and a sense of belonging within Europe? The urgency of this question is underlined by the sovereign debt and euro crises of 2011. Are the bonds of solidarity between the members of the Union sufficiently strong to sustain a real sharing of economic burdens? Will political leaders who make the effort to develop Europe-wide solutions find their domestic electoral support withdrawn and transferred to candidates who advocate nationalist or local concerns? 'Look after us, let them look out for themselves' is a perennially possible stance, fostering a divisive 'us-them' polarity, in contrast to a sense that 'we are all in this together'. So the question is urgent: what resources of shared meaning, what images, what vision can sustain a sense of solidarity in the common project?

20   Charles Taylor (2004), Modern Social Imaginaries. Durham, NC: Duke University Press, p. 23.

In the face of contemporary crises, with the lack of a strong shared sense of communality among present populations, it would be a mistake to think that the answers to the questions and the sources of solidarity are available, in storage as it were, simple waiting to be invoked and brought to the table. That one group, or party, or even nationality is in a position to provide an answer to its own satisfaction does not mean that this answer will serve the purpose throughout the Union. In the debates around the proposed constitution we saw the attempt to revert to an earlier vision, that of Christendom, but for various reasons, including also theological reasons, that was not viable. What has proved useful in the past, such as the heritage of social democracy, as well as themes from Catholic Social Teaching such as solidarity and subsidiarity, may no longer evoke the same senses of allegiance and provide the resources for solving current problems. Similarly, the inherited commitment within the European Union to the values of the free movement of capital, goods, and people may not find the same endorsement among European electorates recovering from crises partly caused by the lack of regulation of financial markets, not just in Europe but globally. The resonance among the peoples of Europe needs to be more than intellectual acknowledgement of the validity of ideas. The required imaginary must be such that it can arouse emotional commitment. For instance, the debate about the incorporation of Turkey has focused on the ideas and values that sustain the European cooperation. These are important and fundamental: civil liberties, the freedom of movement of people, capital and goods, and democratic accountability. The question is whether these are sufficiently emotionally laden to actually provide the necessary social imaginary?

The European Union requires what Taylor writes about as a social imaginary, a 'common understanding that makes possible common practices and a widely shared sense of legitimacy.'[21] This would be among its common goods. Because it is still in process of being constructed, it must be sought and pursued in open debate. And because it is also in crisis, since that which is already achieved is controverted and challenged by many, it needs to be vigorously debated, as Mill recommends. Answers that served well in the past, no matter how exalted their heritage in Christianity or democratic tradition, will not be plausible for present purposes unless they prove resilient to the challenges of open debate. And similarly, they will not be of any help in current crises unless they are demonstrated to be fertile in generating ideas and solutions to deal with entirely new problems, such as those of sovereign debt within the eurozone and the consequent threat to the survival of the euro.

---

21 Charles Taylor (2004), Modern Social Imaginaries. Durham, NC: Duke University Press, p. 23.

3   The social imaginary in times of crisis

Crises bring to light both the need for shared meaning, a social imaginary, to sustain collaboration through the crisis, and at the same time the fragility and weakness of inherited meanings that are not robust enough to provide the necessary solidarity. In the midst of a crisis, particularly an economic one, the pressure on the political leaders is to reach a deal which is a source of a stable solution, not at all easy in the context of fluctuating markets. The sovereign debt crisis reveals how the pressure to find a deal comes not only from the need to protect national interests, but also from the need to safeguard common institutions such as the shared currency. Commitment to safeguarding the euro presupposes a loyalty beyond the national or local. What is the source of that loyalty, if it cannot be seen simply in terms of national interest? Can deals to secure common assets or institutions make sense without a dimension of the ideal? The vision and images at the heart of a social imaginary are needed to sustain deal-making which protects common as distinct from particular goods.

Social imaginaries are linked to conflict in two different ways. On the one hand, we rely on our social imaginary to make sense of the prevalence of conflict within our social experience and orient us in our handling of it. On the other hand, social imaginaries are themselves contested, in that there are competing ideas available to us from our heritage to make sense of our current experience. An obvious relevant example is the tension between latent and persistent nationalism, and universalism or globalism. Linked to this polarity are tendencies towards protectionism versus integration. Among our goods in common are these shared meanings which can sustain cooperation, but it follows that shared meanings will only provide resources in crises if they are constantly renewed and developed through robust debate. That debate itself is among our goods in common, much more fundamentally than any particular tradition of answer or proposed vision that might be brought to the table.

VII   Conclusion

The argument from this review of Europe's common goods can be summarized as follows. There are ideas and ideals that are shared by participants in any common effort. Concern with success of the common effort will require attention to the set of sustaining ideas and ideals so that they remain effective. This is all the more true in the case of political cooperation, which depends so heavily on the shared meaning of participants. The need for deliberate attention to shared meanings is all the greater for the project of the European Union for which a further level of interpretative understanding beyond that necessary for national politics is required of participating citizens. As Mill has argued, achieved meanings are in danger of being lost if they are not vigorously debated and constantly kept under review so that the commitment to the ideas and ideals is rooted in genuine personal conviction. Europe's common good is pre-eminently this social imaginary, or set of shared meanings sustaining its collaboration. There are many other goods in common in the European Union, so that this good in common at the level of shared meaning is not intended to be exhaustive. Other common goods include concrete goods, public goods, and the institutions and other instrumental goods required for the functioning of the Union. The shared meaning, the common dimension most taken for granted, is the one which is in greatest jeopardy, and so requires focused deliberate attention in public debate about purposes and values. Recurring crises, most recently involving sovereign debt and pressure on the euro, reveal that we cannot afford to be complacent in thinking we already have a shared meaning. Reflection and experience show that supposedly shared meanings are hotly contested and so further collaboration in this context will require deliberate examination of our resources of conviction and value. Without robust answers, net contributors in the eurozone are unlikely to find reasons to motivate their efforts to secure and protect the common currency. Deals won't work, ultimately, unless they are sustained by shared ideas and ideals.

Bibliography

Aristotle, *The Ethics of Aristotle, The Nicomachaen Ethics*. Translated by J.A.K. Thomson. Harmondsworth: Penguin Press, revised edition, 1981, Bk V.

Aristotle, *The Politics*. Translated by T.A. Sinclair. Harmondsworth: Penguin Press, 1972, Bk I, chap. 1.

Augustine, *The City of God*, edited by David Knowles (1972), translated by Henry Bettensen. Harmondsworth: Penguin Press.

Böckenförde, E.W. (1976/ 1991), *Staat, Gesellschaft, Freiheit*. Frankfurt: Suhrkamp (english translation: State, Society, and Liberty: Studies in Political Theory and Constitutional Law). New York: Berg.

Honohan, I. (2002), *Civic Republicanism*. London: Routledge.

Markus, R.A. (1970), *Saeculum: History and Society in the Theology of St Augustine*. Cambridge: Cambridge University Press.

McCabe, H., OP (2005), *The Good Life: Ethics and the Pursuit of Happiness*, edited by Brian Davies. London: Continuum.

McLean, I. and McMillan, A. (eds.) (2003), *The Concise Oxford Dictionary of Politics*. Oxford: Oxford University Press.

Mill, J.S. (1859), *On Liberty*, edited by Harry B. Acton (ed.) (1972), London: Dent.

Riordan, P. (2008), *A Grammar of the Common Good*. London: Continuum.

Riordan, P. (2009), Europe's Common Good: The Contribution of the Catholic Church, in: Šimon Marinčák (ed.), *Religion: Problem or Promise? The Role of Religion in the Integra-*

tion of Europe. Orientalia et Occidentalia Vol. 4. Košice, Slovakia: Centrum spirituality, pp. 279-294.

Samuelson, P.A. (1954), The pure theory of public expenditure, *Review of Economics and Statistics* 36 (4), pp. 387-89.

Taylor, Ch. (1995), Irreducibly social goods, in: Charles Taylor (ed.), *Philosophical Arguments*. Cambridge, Mass.: Harvard University Press, pp. 127-145.

Taylor, Ch. (2004), *Modern Social Imaginaries*. Durham, NC: Duke University Press.

Vatican Council II (1965), Gaudium et spes: The Pastoral Constitution on the Church in the Modern World, in: Austin Flannery (ed) (1996), *Vatican II: Constitutions, Decrees, Declarations*. Dublin: Dominican Publications, pp. 163-282.

Economic Distributive Justice

Peter Koller

I   The Relationship between the Common Good and Justice

It appears obvious that justice and the common good are closely interrelated. But how they are interrelated mainly depends on our understanding of the notion of the *common good* (cf. the articles by Riordan and Seel in this volume). As far as I see, there are two competing interpretations of this notion, a wide and a narrow interpretation. According to its *wide understanding*, the common good embodies the *totality of values* that appear to be generally acceptable among an aggregate of people, be it a particular social community, a national society, or even humankind as a whole. Understood in this way, the common good comprehends a variety of standards for evaluating social affairs, including the universal standards of morality and justice as well as the particular standards of the public interest and efficiency of individual social orders. This wide interpretation, however, raises the question of how to specify these various standards and their relationships. By contrast, according to its *narrow understanding*, the common good represents more *specific social values*, namely the values of particular social communities in regard to their long-term well-being and appropriate way of life. I would like to explain this interpretation a bit more.

Remember that Kant proposed to differentiate between three sorts of 'imperatives' or guidelines of individual human conduct, which together exhaust all standards of its evaluation: (1) *technical* guidelines focusing on a conduct's expediency in the light of the agent's accidental goals, (2) *pragmatic* guidelines concerning a conduct's prudence in view of the agent's long-term interests, and (3) *moral* guidelines regarding a conduct's defensibility towards other people from an impartial viewpoint.[1] It appears promising to apply this differentiation not only to the personal, but also to the *institutional level* of social action. Accordingly, the standards for evaluating social affairs may roughly be divided into three sorts: (1) standards of *efficiency*, which deal with the overall utility of social affairs in regard to the actual preferences of the individuals involved in the respective *status quo*; (2) standards of the *common good*, that concern the collec-

---

1   Immanuel Kant (1968), Grundlegung zur Metaphysik der Sitten (Orig. 1785), in: Wilhelm Weischedel (ed.), Kant-Werkausgabe in zwei Bändern, Vol. VII. Frankfurt/Main: Suhrkamp, pp. 44 et seq.

tive welfare of a social community in the light of an impersonal consideration of the well-considered interests of its members; and (3) standards of *morality and justice*, representing generally binding requirements that a social order must meet in order to be acceptable to its members and defensible towards its social surroundings. Of course, these sorts of normative standards cannot be kept separate, but must be combined in order to achieve a *comprehensive evaluation* of social affairs. This raises the question of how they are interrelated and how they may be combined, a question that is particularly important if the various aspects are in conflict rather than in harmony. As a rule, we assume a ranking order according to which the precepts of morality and justice have priority over the common good, whose demands again take precedence over efficiency. This assumption has to do with the fact that requirements of morality and justice usually have weaker motivational force than the demands of the common good, which themselves are actually often dominated by the striving for efficiency. This makes it necessary to reverse their normative order, since otherwise morality and justice would remain completely ineffective, and even the common good would have not much weight.[2]

Although the second, narrow understanding of the notion of the common good appears preferable to me, it does not make much difference in the present context, whether this notion is understood in the wide or the narrow sense. In the first case, the common good includes justice, whereas, in the second case, it is distinct from, but dominated by justice. And even if the wide interpretation is taken for granted, it will be necessary to differentiate within the domain of the common good between various sets of more specific standards on the analogy of the proposed classification, where the universal demands of morality and justice would also take precedence over the particular needs of collective welfare and social efficiency.

At any rate, there is reason to pay attention to problems of justice in the context of considerations about the common good in the European Union. In the following, I will deal with a special issue of justice that is not only of central importance, but also highly disputed in political discourse: economic distributive justice. And it is also clear that this issue becomes increasingly important for the European Union in the course of its on-going widening and deepening.

---

2   Peter Koller (2002), Das Konzept des Gemeinwohls, in: Winfried Brugger, Stephen Kirste, Michael Anderheiden (eds.), Gemeinwohl in Deutschland, Europa und der Welt. Baden-Baden: Nomos, pp. 41-70.

II   The Concept of Economic Distributive Justice

Economic distributive justice is a highly complicated and contested matter. While some authors are of the opinion that the very idea of economic distributive justice makes no sense at all, others simply take it for granted that all basic economic resources are subject to distributive demands, which they often interpret in a more or less egalitarian way. But things are not so easy, I think. In my view, the idea of economic distributive justice must be based on a sound general conception of justice on the one hand, and on an appropriate understanding of its object, the economy, on the other. So I begin with some remarks on justice in general in order to determine the place of distributive justice within its domain, and then turn to the proper object of economic distributive justice.

In order to identify some substantial, though rather abstract principles of justice, it is requisite to distinguish between four elementary kinds of justice, each of which applies to a particular basic type of social relationships: (1) distributive justice – communal relationships, (2) transactional justice – exchange relationships, (3) political justice – power relationships, and (4) corrective justice – wrongness relationships.[3] Among these kinds of justice and their respective social relationships, the first two are of particular importance for economic orders. So let me sketch them briefly.

Distributive justice applies to *communal relationships*. These are social constellations in which a number of people have a common claim to certain benefits or a common responsibility in regard to certain burdens. Justice demands that such benefits or burdens are to be distributed in a way that is reasonably acceptable to all people involved. Despite the fact that the demands of distributive justice are not only highly disputed, but also varying with their respective contexts, there is one widely shared fundamental principle of distributive justice that works for all communal relationships and their distributive problems, even though the specific criteria that apply to them depend on their special features. This is the *principle of equal treatment* which may be put as follows: the benefits and burdens of a communal relationship are to be distributed *equally* among the parties involved, unless inequalities appear to be justifiable for generally acceptable reasons.[4]

By contrast, *transactional justice* refers to *exchange relationships*, i.e. voluntary agreements on a mutual transfer of certain goods among independent parties

---

3   Peter Koller (2001), Zur Semantik der Gerechtigkeit, in: Peter Koller (ed.), Gerechtigkeit im politischen Diskurs der Gegenwart. Wien: Passagen, pp. 27 et seq.

4   David Miller (1976), Social Justice. Oxford: Oxford University Press, pp. 24 ff; Peter Koller (2001), Zur Semantik der Gerechtigkeit, in: Peter Koller (ed.), Gerechtigkeit im politischen Diskurs der Gegenwart. Wien: Passagen, pp. 29 et seq.

who are entitled to dispose of these goods respectively. The paradigm case is contractual transactions. Justice demands that such transactions occur in a way which makes sure that they are to the benefit of all parties involved, so that none of them has reason to complain about the outcome. In general, exchange transactions qualify as just, if the parties involved voluntarily agree on them under *fair conditions* that justify the assumption that the transactions are to the benefit of every party involved. In particular, these conditions require that all parties have equal legal competence, knowledge of the relevant facts, and sufficient capacities of rationality in order to make choices guided by their well-considered interests. Furthermore, the contractual agreements must be performed in absence of power so that no party is able to dictate the terms of trade.[5]

In social reality, the elementary kinds of justice and their respective demands are not independent, but interconnected in multiple ways, since human interaction usually occurs within complex social networks, such as families, working units, and political communities, that combine different elementary types of social interaction. Furthermore, there are some conceptual relations among the different kinds of justice and their respective demands. Most significant is the fact that distributive justice has priority over all other kinds of justice, because transactional as well as political and corrective justice presuppose an acceptable initial distribution of the parties' rights and duties in exchange, power, and wrongness relationships. Consequently, *distributive justice*, insofar as it applies, is a central issue within complex social practices, since it is a precondition of the proper application of all other demands of justice. So I should elaborate on its features a bit further.

First of all, there is the question of how communal relationships come about. A simple way to bring a communal relationship into existence is a respective compact among its members. In this case, the communal relationship results from a contract on the basis of an acceptable previous allocation of individual assets, which itself, however, must have its origin in some basic arrangement of individual rights and duties that is to be judged in the light of general morality and distributive justice. As to communal relationships that are not based on contractual agreements, we usually assume that people form such a relationship under the following conditions: when they jointly encounter a source of benefits or burdens to which all of them are equally entitled or obliged (such as a joint gift or a joint task), when they are involved in a cooperative enterprise that requires their united collaboration (such as a joint venture or a social order), and when

---

5   Peter Koller (2010), Market Effiency and Contractual Justice, in: Tadeusz Czarnecki, Katazyna Kijania-Placek, Olga Poller, Jan Wolenski (eds.), The Analytical Way. Proceedings of the 6th European Congress of Analytic Philosophy. London: College Publications, pp. 167-186.

they are confronted with a situation of joint needs that makes it necessary to divide certain goods or burdens in order to secure the existence of the individuals involved (such as coping with an emergency or a misfortune).

Second, it should be emphasised that distributive justice does not simply demand an equal distribution, but allows a wide range of inequalities, if they appear justifiable for generally acceptable reasons from an impartial viewpoint. The basic principle of distributive justice, the principle of equal treatment, merely provides a starting point for the resolution of distributive problems that may be overruled by appropriate reasons for a more or less unequal distribution of communal benefits or burdens. Even though these reasons are variable and context-dependent, they must make plausible that the inequalities under consideration are acceptable to all members, including the worse off, upon impartial and informed reflection. In general, such reasons have to do with three sorts of properties of the people involved: first, their *contributions, achievements, and qualifications*, second, their *legitimate expectations and well-established rights*, and, third, their *basic needs*.[6]

Finally, I want to counter the view that distributive justice would necessarily require a supreme authority endowed with the power to assign benefits and burdens among people at discretion. This view is confused. As such, distributive justice requires nothing more than suitable rules and procedures that regulate the distribution of communal benefits or burdens. As to whether and to what extent the implementation of those rules and procedures need social institutions endowed with powers is a contingent matter depending on the size and structure of the respective communal relationships under consideration. While small communities usually are able to resolve their distributive conflicts informally without any supreme authority, it is clear that large communities, such as modern societies, cannot do without formal procedures and authorised powers. Yet, even in this case, what distributive justice requires is not a distributive authority, but a legal order that regulates the distribution of societal benefits and burdens effectively.

This concludes my remarks on distributive justice in general and leads me to the more specific notion of *economic* distributive justice. What does 'economic' mean in this context? I'll take first a glance at the general notion of economic justice before I turn to economic distributive justice in particular.

Economic justice obviously applies to the sphere of social life that we usually call 'economy'. This sphere, which has to do with the *production, allocation, exchange, and use of scarce means of human subsistence and well-being*, includes

---

6   David Miller (1976), Social Justice. Oxford: Oxford University Press, pp. 24 ff; Peter Koller (2001), Zur Semantik der Gerechtigkeit, in: Peter Koller (ed.), Gerechtigkeit im politischen Diskurs der Gegenwart. Wien: Passagen, pp. 24 et seq.

a large variety of different sorts of individual and collective action that raise problems of justice. There are two levels of such action: on the one hand, the *individual level* that contains individual economic activities, such as the use of natural resources, the production and the interpersonal transfer of goods, etc., all of which require appropriate rules of just conduct, and, on the other hand, the *institutional level*, which concerns the economic order, whose rules and institutions are required to be not only efficient, but also just, as, for example, the arrangement of property rights, the rules of trade and business, the regulation of entrepreneurial activities and labour relations, and so on.[7]

Now, it is possible to define economic justice in general, and, within its domain, the scope of economic distributive justice as follows: *Economic justice* requires, on the *individual* level, that people comply with the respective demands of justice that apply to their economic activities, and, on the *institutional* level, that the economic order regulates these activities in a way that they satisfy the respective demands of justice, so that market transactions are performed under fair conditions and that the benefits and burdens of communal ventures are distributed among the participants in accord with the principle of equal treatment. Accordingly, *economic distributive justice* comes into play when individual economic activities or entire economic orders involve communal relationships and, therefore, are subject to distributive justice, whose requirements, insofar as they apply, take precedence over other demands of justice, leave alone efficiency.

This definition, which admittedly is highly abstract, raises the question as to what extent the demand for distributive justice actually applies not only to individual economic activities, but also to an entire economic order. This question, however, cannot be decided in the abstract without paying attention to the special features and functions of the respective economic order in the context of the comprehensive social system to which it belongs. In the present context, the economic order of the European Union is of particular interest. However, in order to identify the requirements of economic distributive justice that apply to it, it is helpful to regard two other types of economic order first: the economic order in modern national societies on the one hand, and the international or even global economic order on the other. Since there is reason to suppose that these economic orders differ in regard to their problems of distributive justice, I am going to inquire them separately in the following sections.

---

7   Kenneth Kipnis, Diana T. Meyers (eds.) (1985), Economic Justice: Private Rights and Public Responsibilities. Totowa, NJ: Rowman & Allenheld; Stephen Nathanson (1998), Economic Justice. Upper Saddle River, NJ: Prentice Hall.

III   Economic Distributive Justice in National Societies

Even though it is generally agreed on that every society, or rather its institutional order, is subject to justice, there is significant disagreement about the particular requirements that apply. In modern times, it has become usual to speak of *social justice* in order to designate the demands of justice that extend to the institutional order of a society. Consequently, social justice contains economic justice, including distributive justice, insofar as the latter applies to the economic order of a modern society, its 'national economy'. In view of this fact, I am going to delineate the very idea of social justice first and then proceed to the demands of economic distributive justice that may apply to a national economy.

For a first approximation, social justice may be defined as the *totality of demands of justice that concern the institutional order of a modern national society*, understood as a relatively independent and comprehensive organisation of social life with a centralised state power and a differentiated socio-economic structure.[8] Understood in this way, social justice includes a plurality of demands. A society's institutional order is subject to distributive justice insofar as it comprehends communal affairs among its members; to transactional justice to the extent in which it coordinates individual activities through contractual transactions; to political justice insofar as its order makes use of authorised power; and to corrective justice in cases of wrongdoings that call for correction. The resulting demands of justice are interconnected in multiple ways, one of which is of particular importance: the pivotal role of *distributive* justice, as far as it applies.

Thus, an entire society appears to be subject to distributive justice insofar as it is to be considered as a communal arrangement whose members share common benefits or burdens. However, as to whether and to what extent this is the case is a highly contested issue. The positions reach from extremely individualist to radically collectivist views.[9] An extremely *individualist* position conceives of a society nothing more than an aggregate of independent individuals who unite only in order to take benefit from peaceful coexistence and trade, with the result that the members owe to each other not much more than refraining from violent aggression and keeping contractual agreements, so that the demand for distributive justice is completely displaced.[10] By contrast, a radically *collectivist* view re-

---

8   Peter Koller (2003), Soziale Gerechtigkeit – Begriff und Begründung, Erwägen Wissen Ethik 14 (2), pp. 237-250.

9   Peter Koller (1994), Gesellschaftsauffassung und soziale Gerechtigkeit, in: Günter Frankenberg (ed.), Auf der Suche nach der gerechten Gesellschaft. Frankfurt/ Main: S. Fischer, pp. 129-150.

10   Friedrich A. Hayek (1976), Law, Legislation and Liberty, Vol. 2: The Mirage of Social Justice. London: Routledge; Robert Nozick (1976), Anarchy, State, and Utopia. New York: Basic Books.

gards a society as a total community that completely shapes the opportunities and prospects of its members, so that all benefits and burdens are common to all members and, therefore, must be distributed fairly.[11] I think both views highly implausible. A society is neither a market place where independent individuals spontaneously meet, nor a commune in which everything belongs to everybody. So an acceptable view of society will lie somewhere between those extremes. Every society involves a number of communal matters whose extent is contingent upon its development. In order to specify these affairs, it is helpful to differentiate between three types of communities: ownership, cooperation, and solidarity communities.[12]

An *ownership community* is a communal relationship among people who commonly own certain goods, because, for example, they have inherited them jointly or produced them through their cooperative work. I think it plausible to interpret a society as such community in regard to two sorts of goods to which all members have a common claim: these are the society's natural resources on the one hand, and the achievements of its cultural heritage on the other. This fact implies the demand for distributive justice to the effect that all members of a society must get a fair share of the natural and cultural goods in the sense that they have access to the benefits of their use.[13] A *cooperation community* is a communal constellation in which people cooperate in order to produce certain goods that, however, will come into existence only if most members are prepared to bear the burdens of cooperation too. It seems also clear that every society represents a cooperation community. This is particularly true of a modern society with its dense network of social cooperation in which everybody is affected by and dependent on the activities of others. Therefore, every member has to have access to social cooperation and get a fair share of its outcomes.[14] Finally, people form a *solidarity community* to the extent in which they are mutually responsible to take care for each other, as, for instance, the members of a family. Modern societies have become communities of this sort, since smaller social units, such as

11 Karl Marx, Friedrich Engels (1968), Manifest der Kommunistischen Partei (Orig. 1948), in: Karl Marx, Friedrich Engels, Ausgewählte Schriften in zwei Bänden, Vol. I, 16th edition, Berlin (East), pp. 17-57; Michael Walzer (1983), Spheres of Justice. Oxford: Blackwell.

12 Peter Koller (1993), Gemeinschaft und Gerechtigkeit im Disput zwischen Liberalismus und Kommunitarismus, in: Andras Balogh, Johann A. Schülein (eds.), Soziologie und Gesellschaftskritik. Wien: VWGÖ-Verlag, pp. 75-109.

13 Hillel Steiner (1994), An Essay on Rights. Oxford/ Cambridge, Mass.: Blackwell, pp. 231 et seq.

14 John Rawls (1971), A Theory of Justice. Cambridge, Mass.: Havard University Press, pp. 520 et seq.

kinship and small-scale local communities, which in previous times were responsible for the sick, the handicapped, and the elderly, have collapsed.[15]

As a result, a modern society combines a number of communal features to a significant extent, which has even grown in the course of its development, so that its social order is required to bring about a just distribution of the benefits and burdens that flow from these features. This raises the question as to the particular objects of social distributive justice. In general, one may say that these objects consist in those social resources that are of fundamental importance for the individuals' prospects and can be effectively distributed by a society's institutional order. Let us call them *fundamental social resources*. Although the particular things that qualify as such resources partly depend on contingent social conditions, it appears pretty clear that, in a modern society, they include the following prerequisites of individual well-being: (1) general rights, (2) individual liberties, (3) political entitlements, (4) social positions and opportunities, and (5) economic prospects.

So I assume that, in a modern society, the mentioned resources are subject to distributive justice and, therefore, ought to be arranged through the societal order according to the principle of equal treatment, which may be translated into the following *principle of social distributive justice*: all members of society ought to have an equal share of fundamental social resources unless an unequal distribution appears to be justifiable for generally acceptable reasons. In order to derive from this principle more specific requirements, we have to deal with the further question as to what reasons may be suitable to justify social inequalities to what extent. Even though this is also a highly controversial matter, we can identify a number of argument patterns that are usually used to justify social inequalities. Most important are the arguments from achievement, from liberty, and from need.[16]

The *argument from achievement* justifies inequalities that reflect the respective contributions or achievements of the participants in a cooperative venture which, in general, is to the benefit of all parties concerned. According to the *argument from liberty*, inequalities are also defensible, if they emerge spontaneously from individual activities that comply with generally beneficial rules of individual conduct. In addition, the *argument from need* admits or requires unequal claims to goods or services, if the respective differences are necessary to satisfy

15   Peter Koller (2007), Solidarität und soziale Gerechtigkeit, in: Hermann J. Große Kracht, Tobias Karcher, Christian Spieß (eds.), Das System des Solidarismus. Berlin: LIT, pp. 179-205.

16   William K. Frankena (1962), The Concept of Social Justice, in: Richard B. Brandt (ed.), Social Justice. Englewood Cliffs, NJ: Prentice-Hall, pp. 1-29; David Miller (1999), Principles of Social Justice. Cambridge, Mass.: Harvard University Press, pp. 93 et seq.

unequal needs of people. The common ground of these arguments is the principle that social inequalities are justifiable, if they are to the long-term benefit of all people concerned, including the worse-off.[17]

Admittedly, this principle is not only very vague, but needs also a lot of empirical information in order to be applicable to social reality. But it sets a rough frame for the justification of social inequalities. If we apply it to the fundamental social resources previously mentioned, we are led to a twofold result. In regard to the first three resources, i.e. general rights, individual liberties, and entitlements to political participation, there are *no* acceptable reasons justifying inequalities, since it appears implausible that an unequal arrangement of general legal rights, individual liberties, and political rights could be to the advantage of all members, including those with lesser rights. By contrast, the situation is different when we look at the last two sorts of resources, the social positions and opportunities, and the economic prospects. Here, it seems plausible that some social inequalities may be justifiable, since there is reason to assume that such inequalities may be to the benefit of all members, including those who fare worse.

These considerations result in five *fundamental requirements of social distributive justice*, which, in principle, find widespread acceptance in most advanced societies, even though there are significant disagreements about their precise understanding: (1) legal equality, (2) civil liberty, (3) democratic participation, (4) equal opportunity, and (5) economic equity. Apart from legal equality, which overarches all other requirements, these may be split in two groups: one that mainly concerns the society's legal-political order (2 and 3), and another one that primarily applies to its socio-economic system (4 and 5). Accordingly, the requirements of the latter group – equal opportunity and economic equity – represent the major principles of economic distributive justice within national societies. So let us take a closer glance at them.

Equality of opportunity demands that social positions – understood as social functions, professions, and roles that are connected with greater or lesser income, reputation, influence, and power – are equally open to all members of society so that everybody with equal qualifications has equal prospect of achieving any position. This demand admits that inequalities in social position may be justifiable for certain reasons, such as the provision of incentives, but it subjects such inequalities to the condition that the various positions are filled in a fair way according to people's merits, achievements, or qualifications irrespective of their accidental social background. This condition implies three requirements: first, that no member of society is legally excluded from any social position; secondly, that social positions are assigned through fair procedures in which the best appli-

---

17   John Rawls (1971), A Theory of Justice. Cambridge, Mass.: Harvard University Press, p. 62.

cants or competitors succeed; and, thirdly, that all individuals of a society's younger generation are provided with an appropriate basic stock of human skills and material assets that enable them to active participation in economic cooperation and social life according to their talents and ambitions.[18]

Although these requirements are still vague and open to various interpretations, they clearly exclude certain positional inequalities as inadmissible. As to the second requirement, it seems plausible that, if social positions are assigned through the market process, this process, in order to operate in a fair way, must not be distorted by gross inequalities of social power that enable stronger parties to take advantage of the weak through urging them to contractual agreements that would not occur under fair conditions. And it appears also quite clear that the third requirement implies the right of all young members of society to a solid education and professional training that provides them with sufficient capabilities for participating in economic cooperation and social life. However this requirement may be specified in more detail, when we look at the present course of affairs, it becomes quickly obvious that most societies, including our own, are developing in a direction which brings them into increasing conflict with the demand for equal opportunity.[19]

Undoubtedly, the most contested issue of social distributive justice is the demand of *economic equity*. Anyway, I would like to phrase this demand in a very general and weak way that is compatible with a great variety of political views. Accordingly, economic inequalities, i.e. inequalities in income, property, and opportunities of living, are acceptable to the extent in which they are a necessary feature of an efficient economic order that, in the long run, is to the benefit of all members of society, including the worse-off. This appears to be the case, if these inequalities are requisite to provide sufficient incentives for stimulating generally desirable contributions and achievements, if they unavoidably emerge from a market economy based on private property that fosters a generally beneficial allocation of resources and economic competition, or if they result from a generally beneficial practice of supporting people in need.[20]

This formulation, which should be acceptable both to moderate leftists and reasonable right-wing libertarians, is not completely devoid of substance. At any

18   John Rawls (1971), A Theory of Justice. Cambridge, Mass.: Harvard University Press, pp. 83 et seq.; John E. Roemer (1998), Equality of Opportunity. Cambridge, Mass.: Harvard University Press; Brian Barry (2005), Why Social Justice Matters. Cambridge: Polity Press, pp. 37 et seq.
19   Brian Barry (2005), Why Social Justice Matters. Cambridge: Polity Press, pp. 169 et seq.
20   Alistair Macleod (1985), Economic Inequality: Justice and Incentives, in: Kenneth Kipnis, Diana T. Meyers (eds.), Economic Justice: Private Rights and Public Responsibilities. Totowa, NJ: Rowman & Allenheld, pp. 176-189; David Miller (1999), Principles of Social Justice. Cambridge, Mass.: Harvard University Press.

rate, it makes clear that economic inequalities are subject to certain constraints that reflect the common interest of all members of society. Perhaps the following consideration may help to specify these constraints a bit further: if we assume that economic inequalities must be justifiable with reference to their general acceptability against the background of an equal or less unequal distribution of economic assets, then they appear to be justifiable only to the extent in which they go hand in hand with an increase of societal welfare which is not only to the benefit of the upper, well-off classes, but also improves the situation of the worse-off members. Consequently, a social constellation in which the still-growing societal wealth is only benefiting a small number of well-off members of society, while most people of the worse-off classes suffer considerable losses, is clearly unjust. And just this presently occurs in most advanced societies.

IV   Economic Distributive Justice in the Global Order

In recent decades, we have experienced a growing debate on international and global justice, which obviously reflects the far-reaching changes of our world that are usually addressed through the talk about *globalisation*.[21] Yet, since the idea of global justice is still in the course of development, which has not yet led to a widely-shared concept with a stable profile, it is not easy to grasp. A particularly controversial issue is the question as to whether and to what extent the demand for global justice also includes requirements of distributive justice, especially economic distributive justice. In view of this situation, I will start with a fairly general and formal definition of global justice, which, taken alone, leaves the question open, but provides a basis for identifying some requirements of economic distributive justice that apply to international relations and the global order.

For a first approximation to the notion of global justice, I want to pursue a similar strategy as in the discussion of social justice. Accordingly, global justice may be defined as the *totality of demands of justice that can be reasonably extended to international relationships among individual countries or the entire global order*.[22] This raises the question as to what demands may apply. I want to

---

21   Georg Kohler, Urs Marti (2003), Konturen der neuen Welt(un)ordnung. Beiträge zu einer Theorie der normativen Prinzipien internationaler Politik. Berlin/ New York: Walter de Gruyter; Frank J. Lechner, John Boli (eds.) (2004), The Globalization Reader, 2nd edition. Oxford: Blackwell; Peter Koller (2006), Die globale Frage. Empirische Befunde und ethische Herausforderungen. Wien: Passagen.

22   Peter Koller (2009), International Law and Global Justice, in: Lukas H. Meyer (ed.), Legitimacy, Justice and Public International Law. Cambridge: Cambridge University Press, pp. 186-206.

argue that again all kinds of justice come into play, namely distributive, transactional, political, and corrective justice. Since this may appear not so clear in regard to distributive justice than in the other cases, I take a glance at transactional justice first and then deal with distributive justice, leaving political and corrective justice aside.

The global order is subject to *transactional justice* when different nations as a whole or their individual members maintain trade and exchange relationships. Accordingly, international trade relations and global market processes are required to take place under *fair rules and framing conditions* which make sure that all participating peoples and nations can derive benefit from them. To this end, these rules and framing conditions must make sure that no nation is able to dictate unilaterally the terms of trade to its own advantage, and that international trade is not distorted by asymmetrical market restrictions. International trade differs from domestic trade in the respect that the government of each country defines the conditions under which its citizens may enter in international trade relationships. A prudent government will tend to regulate these relationships in a way that they are to the benefit of its own country. One feasible option is *protectionism*, consisting in measures that obstruct the import of foreign goods or foster the export of domestic products. In order to avoid a destructive escalation of such measures, countries conclude international trade agreements that determine the conditions of their mutual transactions. In last decades, a great many countries have entered in a series of agreements that have led to a successive liberalisation of global trade.[23]

A system of free trade, however, is not necessarily a fair system. Yet, a well-known theory of international trade, the theory of comparative advantage, maintains that free international trade relationships are to the benefit of all countries involved, even if these countries may start from very different initial stages of economic development, provided that their markets are equally open.[24] Although this theory seems to be correct in general, it fails to pay attention to some significant features of present global trade, particularly the role of transnational companies and the effects of the international credit system and finance markets. Consequently, one may say that transactional justice implies the following requirements on a system of international trade: first of all, equal openness of markets, unless exceptions are justified by other requirements of justice; secondly, sufficient control of transnational companies, in order to prevent them from

23   Michael J. Trebilcock, Robert Howse (2005), The Regulation of International Trade, 3rd edition. London: Routledge.
24   Paul Krugman (1996), Pop Internationalism. Cambridge, Mass., London: MIT Press.

causing market distortions by their activities; and thirdly, an unbiased international credit and finance system which operates to the benefit of all countries.[25]

Now, I want to turn to the most contested issue of global justice, the question as to whether and to what extent international and global affairs are subject to *distributive justice*. While some authors think that its demands do not have any significance in the context of global justice[26], others advocate the view that they apply to the global order in the same way as to national social orders[27]. Contrary to these positions, I want to advocate a concept of global justice that integrates distributive justice in a differential way. Accordingly, the global order is subject to distributive justice to the extent in which it has distributive effects in regard to the communal affairs of different nations or humankind as a whole. On the basis of this interpretation, the impact of distributive justice on international affairs depends on contingent facts, especially the degree of international and global interdependencies. The more individual nations become mutually interdependent by the external effects of their domestic political orders, their activities across borders and their cooperation based on division of labour, the greater is the domain of their communal affairs that create problems of distributive justice. When we consider the present constellation of the world, we encounter at least three issues that concern communal affairs among nations and, therefore, give raise to the demand for distributive justice: (1) the extent of the individual nations' political autonomy, (2) the nations' uses of global natural resources and the negative effects of societal activities across borders, and (3) international economic cooperation.

The first issue, the *extent of national political autonomy*, is already present in a world in which the countries' national economies are relatively separated and independent, but its importance increases with the process of globalisation. I assume that a just international order ought to grant to each nation the right to equal political self-determination to the greatest extent in which it is compatible with basic internal and external conditions of a peaceful and generally beneficial international order. I propose to specify these conditions in a rather weak way as follows: internally, a domestic political order ought to respect and protect the

25   Oxfam (2002), Rigged Rules and Double Standards. Trade, Globalisation and the Fight against Poverty. Oxford: Oxfam International; Joseph E. Stiglitz, Andrew Charlton (2005), Fair Trade for All. How Trade Can Promote Development. Oxford: Oxford University Press; Ethan Kapstein (2006), Economic Justice in an Unfair World. Princeton, NJ, Oxford: Princeton University Press, pp. 45 et seq.
26   John Rawls (1999), The Law of Peoples. Cambridge, Mass.: Harvard University Press; Thomas Nagel (2005), The Problem of Global Justice, Philosophy and Public Affairs 33(2), pp. 113-147.
27   Charles R. Beitz (1979), Political Theory and International Relations. Princeton, NJ: Princeton University Press.

most important human rights, including social and economic rights; and, externally, it must not be detrimental to the peaceful coexistence among nations. I think these conditions exclude a principle of extensive state sovereignty that concedes to each state government unconstrained powers to dispose of its country's natural resources at will and to raise credits in behalf of its country, as the present international system does.[28]

The second issue, the *nations' uses of natural resources and the negative effects of their ways of life across borders*, concerns the social and economic activities of individual societies that have negative effects on other countries and even the whole world. At present, a great deal of natural resources that belong to the common heritage of humankind are endangered by industry, traffic, and leisure activities; many other natural goods are progressively exploited and decimated; and there is also an increasing proliferation of technical facilities, such as energy plants and military systems, that cause significant dangers across borders or even threaten humankind as a whole. All these facts raise distributive problems among nations that imply the demand for a just distribution of the benefits and costs of border-crossing social and economic activities. In my view, this demand requires that, insofar as useful activities unavoidably cause negative effects across borders, the individual nations' costs of these effects must be in proportion to the benefits that they take from those activities. If such a distribution cannot be achieved by market regulations, the nations who fare better ought to pay appropriate compensation to those who are worse off.[29]

Third, there is the issue of *international economic cooperation*, which results from the fact that individual nations, though not all to an equal extent, increasingly grow together to more comprehensive units of social and economic cooperation based on division of labour in which all contribute to the production of earthly wealth, but also become increasingly dependent on each other. Even though international economic cooperation is mainly coordinated through markets, it creates a need for distributive justice, because markets alone can never secure a just distribution of their results. This is because, on the one hand, fair markets already presuppose an acceptable initial distribution of economic resources among the parties; and, on the other, even if they start from a fair initial distribution, they may lead to unacceptable outcomes, since their inherent dy-

28 Thomas Pogge (2002), World Poverty and Human Rights. Cambridge, Oxford: Polity Press, pp. 168 et seq.; Urs Marti (2003), Globale distributive Gerechtigkeit, in: Georg Kohler, Urs Marti (eds.), Konturen der neuen Welt(un)ordnung. Beiträge zu einer Theorie der normativen Prinzipien internationaler Politik. Berlin/ New York: Walter de Gruyter, pp. 345-361.

29 Brian Barry (1989), Humanity and Justice in Global Perspective, Barry Brian (ed.), Democracy, Power and Justice. Essays in Political Theory. Oxford: Clarendon Press, pp. 434 – 462.

namics may generate economic, social or political inequalities that distort the subsequent market processes. Therefore, distributive justice also applies to the benefits and burdens of international cooperation based on division of labour. This demand may be put as follows: The global order has to make sure that international economic cooperation is to the benefit of all peoples, in particular the less-developed and poor nations. And this does certainly not admit that some nations take the benefits, while others are left with empty hands.[30]

As a result, the idea of global justice includes at least three significant demands of distributive justice. While the first (the demand for an appropriate extent of the nations' political autonomy) primarily concerns the political structure of the global order, the two latter (the demands for a fair distribution of the benefits and costs that result from the nations' use of natural resources and from their international economic cooperation) immediately affect the global economic order, so that they may be understood as demands of economic distributive justice. At a closer glance, however, it turns out that the first demand is also of major importance for the global economy, because it requires appropriate restrictions of national sovereignty that prevent corrupt regimes from selling their countries' natural resources and raising credits in behalf of their countries.[31]

Even though all demands of global distributive justice mentioned are rather vague, it appears pretty obvious that the present international system greatly fails to meet them. The demand that the scope of national political autonomy must fit with a peaceful and generally beneficial global order is undermined by the prevailing principle of state sovereignty, which concedes to national governments extensive powers that foster corrupt and predatory regimes. Furthermore, the present international system grossly violates the demand for a proportional distribution of the benefits and costs of the nations' exploitation of natural resources and of their societal activities across borders, because the wealthy nations derive the lion's share of the benefits at the cost of the poor peoples and future generations. Finally, this system is also far from meeting the demand for a fair distribution of the benefits and burdens of international economic cooperation, since the prevailing global economy operates in a way that is to the main benefit of wealthy nations, while most less-developed countries are left behind.

---

30 Charles R. Beitz (1979), Political Theory and International Relations. Princeton, NJ: Princeton University Press; Peter Singer (2002), One World. The Ethics of Globalization. New Haven, London: Yale University Press, pp. 51 et seq.

31 Thomas W. Pogge (2002), World Poverty and Human Rights. Cambridge, Oxford: Polity Press, pp. 112 et seq.

V   Economic Distributive Justice in the European Union

My considerations on economic distributive justice in national societies on the one hand, and in the global order on the other support the conclusion that its demands have more impact on the former than on the latter. This conclusion, which appears to be in full accord with the widely shared opinion, mirrors the fact that the order of modern national society involves a much greater extent of communal affairs among its members than the international order among different peoples. On the basis of this result, I would like to address the significance of economic distributive justice within the European Union.

It is common knowledge that the EU is neither a national society with a centralised state power, nor a mere international confederation whose member states remain fully sovereign. Rather, it is a pretty new type of a plurinational community whose main institutions are endowed with considerable supranational powers over its member states.[32] So the EU is a social entity that lies somewhere between a national state and the international system. This fact suggests the thesis that economic distributive justice applies to the EU in an intermediate way between its pivotal standing within domestic social justice and its less extensive, even though by no means negligible role in the context of global justice. In fact, this thesis also finds support by the actual policy of the EU. For, on the one hand, the EU does not even pretend to be a comprehensive political community that ought to guarantee all its citizens equal opportunity and a fair share of economic assets; on the other hand, the EU not only provides its citizens with equal rights and freedoms in a wide range of matters, such as movement, residence, work, and trade, but it also aims at a harmonious social and economic development of its member countries through a variety of means, from minimum standards in labour relations, social security, and health protection up to considerable financial transfers to less-developed regions.[33] As the Amsterdam Treaty put it, the EU intends to become 'an area of freedom, security and justice'.

Admittedly, these features are much too indeterminate to allow a precise answer to the question as to what extent the EU should be understood as a community whose economic benefits and costs call for distributive justice. In general, however, it appears reasonable to assume that a plurinational community, such as the EU, is subject to demands of distributive justice to the extent in which its in-

---

32   David Phinnemore (2007), Towards European Union, in: Michelle Cini (ed.), European Union Politics, 2nd edition. Oxford: Oxford University Press, pp. 30-45; John Pinder, Simon Usherwood (2007), The European Union. A Very Short Introduction. Oxford: Oxford University Press.

33   Gerda Falkner (2007), The EU's Social Dimension, in: Michelle Cini (ed.), European Union Politics, 2nd edition. Oxford: Oxford University Press, pp. 271-286.

stitutional framework exerts distributive effects on its member states and their populations. Accordingly, a weak general principle of distributive justice applying to such a community may be put as follows: the institutional framework of a plurinational community is to be arranged in a way that (a) enables its member states to establish or preserve a just societal order meeting the demands of social justice previously mentioned, and (b) takes care that the overall advantages flowing from political or economic integration are both to the benefit of each member country as a whole and to the benefit of all citizens of each member country as well. Thus, socio-economic inequalities that may emerge from the process of economic integration through establishing a single market are justifiable only to the extent to which the economic surplus of this process is of benefit to all citizens, including the worse-off groups in each member country.

Against the background of this principle, the EU has brought great achievements, but also created significant social injustices. Its main achievement is that it has contributed to stabilising or promoting liberal democracy in its member states, but also succeeded in diminishing the differences of their overall welfare levels to a significant extent through its devices of financial subsidies for poorer regions. On the other hand, however, the EU also suffers from severe injustices. Beside some disputed distributional issues that are still unresolved, such as sharing the burdens of increasing immigration streams of asylum-seekers, its most important failure, I think, is its *social deficit* that results from the discrepancy between the highly advanced stage of the common market on the one hand, and the insufficient cooperation in the spheres of social security, labour law, and tax policy on the other. Whereas the member states have always succeeded in agreeing on the steps leading to a single market, such as the opening of their national economies, the liberalisation of economic competition, the privatisation of public companies, the standardisation of their finance policies, and the establishment of a common currency, they have been greatly ineffective in issuing binding *standards concerning the protection of workers, social security, and taxation.*[34]

Consequently, the member states have been exposed to an intensifying struggle to maintain the competitiveness of their national economies, which has not only weakened the position of employees and minor business people, but also undermined the financial basis of national social security systems. As a result, the large companies have achieved rapidly growing profits that have led to an enormous increase of income for well-off groups, particularly investors and managers, while the lower classes, such as workers, employees, and many other people, have experienced significant losses through the decrease of real incomes,

---

34 Stefano Giubbione (2006), Social Rights and Market Freedom in the European Constitution. A Labour Law Perspective. Cambridge: Cambridge University Press; see also Dragana Damjanovic in this volume.

the weakening of workers' rights, the diminishing bargaining-power of trade unions, the reduction of social transfer payments and public services, and the social exclusion of low-qualified people.[35]

It appears doubtful whether the EU will be able to cope with the detrimental social effects of this development on the basis of its presently highly limited powers in matters of social and fiscal policy (see the contributions by Puntscher Riekmann, and Somek in this volume). And, under present conditions, it is also doubtful whether the individual member states will be able to make use of their powers in these matters to counteract the growing social injustices, for they would face competitive disadvantages by doing so without acting in accord.

The current crisis of the European monetary union even tends to aggravate the EU's social deficit, for it not only forces all member states to pursue a rigid cost cutting policy in order to diminish their national debts, but also requires the richer countries to render further financial support to poorer countries in order to save the common currency. This constellation, however, may foster the project of 'a new European economic governance' through a considerable strengthening of the EU's powers to set common standards for the economic and fiscal policies of the member states.[36] If this project succeeds, there is also some hope that the EU could take appropriate steps to a common social policy that should decrease its present social deficit and promote more economic distributive justice in Europe.

Bibliography

Barry, B. (1989), Humanity and Justice in Global Perspective, in: Barry Brian (ed.), *Democracy, Power and Justice. Essays in Political Theory*. Oxford: Clarendon Press, pp. 434 – 462.

Barry, B. (2005*), Why Social Justice Matters*. Cambridge: Polity Press.

Beitz, Ch. R. (1979), *Political Theory and International Relations*. Princeton, NJ: Princeton University Press.

Falkner, G. (2007), The EU's Social Dimension, in: Michelle Cini (ed.), *European Union Politics*, 2nd edition. Oxford: Oxford University Press, pp. 271-286.

Frankena, W.K. (1962), The Concept of Social Justice, in: Richard B. Brandt (ed.), *Social Justice*. Englewood Cliffs, NJ: Prentice Hall.

Giubbione, S. (2006), *Social Rights and Market Freedom in the European Constitution. A Labour Law Perspective*. Cambridge: Cambridge University Press.

35 Max Haller (2008), European Integration as an Elite Process. The Failure of a Dream? London: Routledge.
36 European Commission (2010), A New EU Economic Governance – A Comprehensive Commission package of Proposals. http://ec.europa.eu/economy_finance/articles/-eu_economic_situation/2010-09; see also Klaus Gretschmann in this volume.

Haller, M. (2008), *European Integration as an Elite Process. The Failure of a Dream?* London: Routledge.

Hayek, F.A. (1976), *Law, Legislation and Liberty*, Vol. 2: The Mirage of Social Justice. London: Routledge.

Kant, I. (1968), Grundlegung zur Metaphysik der Sitten (Orig. 1785), in: Wilhelm Weischedel (ed.), *Kant-Werkausgabe in zwei Bändern*, Vol. VII. Frankfurt/Main: Suhrkamp.

Kapstein, E. (2006), *Economic Justice in an Unfair World*. Princeton, NJ/ Oxford: Princeton University Press.

Kipnis, K. and Meyers, D.T. (eds.) (1985), *Economic Justice: Private Rights and Public Responsibilities*. Totowa, NJ: Rowman & Allenheld.

Kohler G. and Marti, U. (2003), *Konturen der neuen Welt(un)ordnung. Beiträge zu einer Theorie der normativen Prinzipien internationaler Politik*. Berlin/ New York: Walter de Gruyter.

Koller, P. (1993), Gemeinschaft und Gerechtigkeit im Disput zwischen Liberalismus und Kommunitarismus, in: Andras Balogh, Johann A. Schülein (eds.), *Soziologie und Gesellschaftskritik*. Wien: VWGÖ-Verlag, pp. 75-109.

Koller, P. (1994), Gesellschaftsauffassung und soziale Gerechtigkeit, in: Günter Frankenberg (ed.), *Auf der Suche nach der gerechten Gesellschaft*. Frankfurt/ Main: S. Fischer, pp. 129-150.

Koller, P. (2001), Zur Semantik der Gerechtigkeit, in: Peter Koller (ed.), *Gerechtigkeit im politischen Diskurs der Gegenwart*. Wien: Passagen, pp. 41-70

Koller, P. (2002), Das Konzept des Gemeinwohls, in: Winfried Brugger, Stephen Kirste, Michael Anderheiden (eds.), *Gemeinwohl in Deutschland, Europa und der Welt*. Baden-Baden: Nomos, pp. 41-70.

Koller, P. (2003), Soziale Gerechtigkeit – Begriff und Begründung, *Erwägen Wissen Ethik* 14 (2), pp. 237-250.

Koller, P. (2006), *Die globale Frage. Empirische Befunde und ethische Herausforderungen*. Wien: Passagen.

Koller, P. (2007), Solidarität und soziale Gerechtigkeit, in: Hermann J. Große Kracht, Tobias Karcher, Christian Spieß (eds.), *Das System des Solidarismus*. Berlin: LIT, pp. 179-205.

Koller, P. (2009), International Law and Global Justice, in: Lukas H. Meyer (ed.), *Legitimacy, Justice and Public International Law*. Cambridge: Cambridge University Press, pp. 186-206.

Koller, P. (2010), Market Effiency and Contractual Justice, in: Tadeusz Czarnecki, Katazyna Kijania-Placek, Olga Poller, Jan Wolenski (eds.), *The Analytical Way. Proceedings of the 6th European Congress of Analytic Philosophy*. London: College Publications, 167-186.

Krugman, P. (1996), *Pop Internationalism*. Cambridge, Mass./ London: MIT Press.

Lechner, F.J. and Boli, J.(eds.) (2004), *The Globalization Reader*, 2nd edition. Oxford: Blackwell.

Macleod, A. (1985), Economic Inequality: Justice and Incentives, in: Kenneth Kipnis, Diana T. Meyers (eds.), *Economic Justice: Private Rights and Public Responsibilities*. Totawa, NJ: Rowman & Allenheld, pp 176-189.

Marti, U. (2003), Globale distributive Gerechtigkeit, in: Georg Kohler, Urs Marti (eds.), *Konturen der neuen Welt(un)ordnung. Beiträge zu einer Theorie der normativen Prinzipien internationaler Politik*. Berlin/ New York: Walter de Gruyter, pp. 345-361.

Marx, K.; Engels, F. (1968), Manifest der Kommunistischen Partei (Orig. 1948), in: Karl Marx, Friedrich Engels, *Ausgewählte Schriften in zwei Bänden*, Vol. I, 16th edition, Berlin (East), pp. 17-57.

Miller,D. (1976), *Social Justice*. Oxford: Oxford University Press.

Nagel, T. (2005), The Problem of Global Justice, *Philosophy and Public Affairs* 33(2), pp. 113-147.

Nathanson, S. (1998), *Economic Justice*. Upper Saddle River, NJ: Prentice Hall.

Nozick, R. (1976), *Anarchy, State, and Utopia*. New York: Basic Books.

Oxfam (2002), *Rigged Rules and Double Standards. Trade, Globalisation and the Fight against Poverty*. Oxford: Oxfam International.

Phinnemore, D. (2007), Towards European Union, in: Michelle Cini (ed.), *European Union Politics*, 2nd edition. Oxford: Oxford University Press, pp. 30-45.

Pinder, J.; Usherwood, S. (2007), *The European Union. A Very Short Introduction*. Oxford: Oxford University Press.

Pogge, T.W. (2002), *World Poverty and Human Rights*. Cambridge/ Oxford: Polity Press.

Rawls, J. (1971), *A Theory of Justice*. Cambridge, Mass.: Havard University Press.

Rawls, J. (1999), *The Law of Peoples*. Cambridge, Mass.: Harvard University Press.

Roemer, J.E. (1998), *Equality of Opportunity*. Cambridge, Mass.: Harvard University Press.

Singer, P. (2002), *One World. The Ethics of Globalization*. New Haven/ London: Yale University Press.

Steiner, H. (1994), *An Essay on Rights*. Oxford/ Cambridge, Mass.: Blackwell.

Stiglitz, J.E.;Charlton, A. (2005), *Fair Trade for All. How Trade Can Promote Development*. Oxford: Oxford University Press.

Trebilcock, M.J.; Howse R. (2005), *The Regulation of International Trade*, 3rd edition. London: Routledge.

Walzer, M. (1983), *Spheres of Justice*. Oxford: Blackwell.

The Common Good of European Institutions

Constitutionalization: Constitution-Making for Individualists

Alexander Somek

I   Significance

It is time to take stock of the intellectual consequences of Europeanisation. The integration process has given rise not merely to momentous transformations in the economic sphere, but also to remarkable alterations in the field of ideas. Among these alterations figures, most prominently, the new perception of international relations as a realm of opportunity where states can reap their share of the positive sum brought about by cooperation.[1] With regard to the democratic process, the emphasis has moved considerably towards deliberation and away from political choice by majorities.[2] Matters of distributive justice have been basically toned down to questions of equality of opportunity, in particular to matters of protection from discrimination.[3]

Quite remarkably, these shifts have not only pushed certain elements of an idea to the front while others receded into the back, but they also confront us with the built-in claim of improvement. The new understandings implicitly claim to provide a normatively better understanding of old practices and ideals. International cooperation with a net benefit is presented as an approach to international relations that is substantively superior to the power-thirsty world envisaged by realism. Deliberation is believed to be a more sober and morally more agreeable foundation of democratic legitimacy than dark appeals to the opaque will of the people. And it is taken for granted that at the end of the day one can make sense of questions of justice only by casting them in the form of equality of opportunity.

Of course, these developments are associated with movements of thought that are prevalent well outside the Union. It is striking, however, that they have been

---

1   For a beautifully polemical identification of the European perception of international relations, see Robert Kagan (2003), Of Paradise and Power: America and Europe in the New World Order. New York: Alfred Knopf.

2   Markus Höreth (2009), Überangepasst und realitätsentrückt: Zur Paradoxie der Theorie der deliberativen Demokratie, Zeitschrift für Politikwissenschaft 19, pp. 307-330.

3   On the respective shift in the conception of solidarity, see Wolfgang Streeck, Competitive Solidarity – Rethinking the "European Social Model", http://www.mpi-fg-koeln.mpg.de/pu/workpap/wp99-8/wp99-8.html.

particularly successful in Europe. Apparently, they fall on fertile soil. In contrast to nations whose populations yield to the lure of one or the other moral absolutism, Europeans have been predisposed to obtain guidance from historical transformations as though history were a court for adjudicating ideals. *Historia locuta, cause finita.* Communism and socialism are imagined to be lost causes, very much in a manner in which monarchy and religion-based political communities are deemed to be a matter of the past.

But not all Europeans buy into such a facile philosophy of history. Some – the author included – sense that what purports to be the ruling of history cannot be trusted without critical inquiry into its broader social significance. Shifts as those referred to above may reveal as well as conceal. Hence, they merit critical attention with the appropriate 'hermeneutics of suspicion'.[4] It needs to be asked, therefore, whether the assumption of continuity in the relation between old and new – or worse and better, respectively – does not indeed conceal a *break* with past. If that were the case we would witness not the growing perfection of international relations, democracy, and justice, but rather their *replacement* with international administration,[5] deliberation,[6] and the creation of equality of access to opportunities, for the generation of which political communities are no longer supposed to play an active role.[7]

In what follows, I would like to explore the meaning of a concept that undoubtedly partakes of this ideological process of Europeanisation. What I have in mind is the notion of 'constitutionalization'. It fits the transmutational pattern sketched out above. Until recently, constitutions were deemed to be constructs that are brought about by a constituent power. This idea has fallen into disrepute. Not only does the existence of such power all of a sudden seem mystical, it is also associated with the allegedly atavistic, primitive and dangerous concept of sovereignty.[8] The concept of constitutionalization, by contrast, promises to have overcome the attendant moral and intellectual limitations and to capture accurately developments beyond the nation-state.

The questions remains, however, whether constitutionalization represents indeed, as it implicitly claims, a more rational form of constitution making. Even

4   Paul Ricoeur (1970), Freud and Philosophy: An Essay on Interpretation (trans. Denis Savage). New Haven: Yale University Press.
5   See Perry Anderson (2009), The New Old World. London: Verso, p. 62.
6   Alexander Somek (2008), Demokratie als Verwaltung: Wider die deliberativ halbierte Demokratie, Soziale Welt, pp. 323-348.
7   John Roemer (2000), Equality of Opportunity: Cambridge, Mass.: Harvard University Press.
8   Mattias Kumm (2010), The Best of Times and the Worst of Times: Between Constitutional Triumphalism and Nostalgia, in: Martin Loughlin & Petra Dobner (eds.), The Twilight of Constitutional Law: Demise or Transmutation? Oxford: Oxford University Press, pp. 201-219 at 205, 207.

more importantly, is it still continuous with the broader tradition of constitutionalism?

I would like to argue that constitutionalization falls short in both respects. Putting it bluntly, the discourse on constitutionalization assimilates constitutionalism to the mind-set of both the common law and administrative problem solving.

Throughout this chapter I will refer frequently to the European Union for the simple reason that it is generally believed to represent the *avant-garde* of constitutionalization.

II   Constitutionalism and constitutionalization

It is a commonplace that the European Union has been mightily transformed in the course of its constitutionalization.[9] In the final result, the Union's legal operative system has been altered from international to constitutional law. No constitutional text was needed for that. Even the failed 'Constitution for Europe', arguably motivated by many factors,[10] was merely supposed to bring to a conclusion what had been under way for quite some time. Constitutionalization is a process, not an act.

In what follows, I would like to explore the concept of constitutionalization and what it means for the larger tradition to which it supposedly belongs. The underlying question is simple. What is the significance of constitutionalization for constitutionalism?

Evidently, answering this question presupposes some background conception of the latter.[11]

Broadly understood, constitutionalism is the project of submitting public power to the discipline of legal norms.[12] Historically, it marked a decisive break with a way of approaching politics that regarded constitutions as basically fragile equilibriums between and among contending forces.[13] Constitutionalism involves a specific justification for the exercise of (state) power. It is based on the premise

---

9   See, in particular, Joseph H.H. Weiler (1999), The Constitution of Europe. Cambridge: Cambridge University Press, pp. 19-25.

10   Jean-Claude Piris (2006), The Constitution for Europe: A Legal Analysis. Cambridge: Cambridge University Press, pp. 38-41.

11   Dieter Grimm (2005), The Constitution in the Process of Denationalization, Constellations 12, pp. 447-463.

12   Thus understood, constitutionalism is a view of political morality that favours limited government. See Martin Loughlin (2010), What is Constitutionalization? In: Martin Loughlin, Petra Dobner (eds.), The Twilight of Constitutional Law: Demise or Transmutation? Oxford: Oxford University Press, pp. 47-69 and 55.

13   Glenn Burgess (1992), The Politics of the Ancient Constitution: An Introduction to English Political Thought, 1603-1642. London: Macmillan, p. 6.

that the authors and the addresses of authoritative directives are free and equal.[14] It is not by accident that *law* is essential to the justification of power among those who conceive of one another in these terms. The form of law – legality – is supposed to lend adequate expression to the type of relationship that obtains, by default, between people who are equally free. Having law govern their dealings is right for them. It may not be right, by contrast, for those who share, for example, the experience of libidinous identification with their leader. Consequently, ruling by means of constitutional legality is different from seeing the sustainability of legitimate and good government depend on the reproduction of civic virtue, obedience towards a priestly elite, the terror-aided implementation of the world-historical roadmap, or the participation in common problem solving. Choosing constitutional law over these alternatives is not merely relevant at some hypothetical point zero of public life; it is at stake at every stage of constitutional project.

Constitutional legality, even though lending expression to a certain relationship, has never been an end in itself. As I will point out below,[15] submitting public power to legal discipline has been supposed to serve three objectives, namely, the protection of rights, the facilitation of intelligent problem solving, and, finally, the pursuit of collective self-determination.

It is not altogether trivial that we may owe the term 'constitutionalization' in fact to accounts of European integration. I cannot make out who had been the first to use it in this context – perhaps Eric Stein[16] – but I think one does not go wrong in assuming that it first emerged as a referent for fundamental legal transformations concerning what had been then still the European Economic Community. Indirectly, the concept is Europe's most recent contribution to the Olympus of legal ideas.

Remarkably, the concept has quickly migrated to other areas of transnational law, notably, to general international law. The debate over the constitutionaliza-

---

14   See, quite accurately, Mattias Kumm (2009), The Cosmopolitan Turn in Constitutionalism: On the Relationship between Constitutionalism in and beyond the State, in: Jeffrey Dunoff, Joel Trachtman (eds.), Ruling the World? Constitutionalism, International Law, and Global Governance. Cambridge: Cambridge University Press, pp. 258-324 at 322.

15   See below p. 10.

16   Of course, when Stein wrote about the transnational constitution of the European Union—without, however, using the term 'constitutionalization' itself—he was taking his cue also from the language of the European Court of Justice. See, for example, Eric Stein (1981), Lawyers, Judges, and the Making of a Transnational Constitution, American Journal of Public International Law 75, pp. 1-27. It may well be the case that it was indeed Weiler who coined the term, even though first using it in quotation marks. See Weiler note 9.

tion of international law is already under way.[17] Likewise, functionally special-ised regimes, for example the international trade system, are at least considered to be candidates of constitutionalization or already perceived to be 'in' the requi-site process.[18]

Even more remarkably, no area of transnational law seems to be *a priori* im-mune to constitutionalization. One already expects to read soon about the consti-tutionalization of international commercial arbitration or international freight law. The impression of universal susceptibility is further nourished by the fact that constitutionalization is widely believed to be a mark of distinction. Ostensi-bly, it invests fields of law with a higher dignity. Constitutionalization is like an upgrade to the first class. The more constitutionalised, the merrier. Understanda-bly, no field of law wishes to stay behind.

III   Inferential constitution making

'In the process of' is the key idiom of constitutionalization. In contrast to the old-fashioned adoption of a constitution, which was supposed to be an act, constitu-tionalization involves the passing of time. Indeed, this is key to understanding what makes it special.

Constitutionalization is a process. But it does not abide by procedural norms. That is, in contrast to referenda or the use of convention parliaments, constitu-tionalization, as a legal process, happens *somehow*. It is jurisdictionally unspeci-fied and substantively indeterminate.

Since constitutionalization is also not an act of will, but a development, it is based neither on choice nor on a decision. It has no source.[19] Constitutionaliza-tion merely draws out something that is purportedly already there. It merely ren-ders inferentially explicit what is deemed to be implicit. It states what may not yet have been obvious. Constitutionalization is a matter of reason and not of will. Hence, constitutionalization appears, at first glance, to be devoid of authorship

---

17   For an overview, see Bardo Fassbender (2007), The meaning of international constitu-tional law, Nicholas Tsagourias (ed.), Transnational Constitutionalism. Cambridge: Cam-bridge University Press, pp. 307-328.

18   See, notably, Deborah Z. Cass (2005), The Constitutionalization of the World Trade Or-ganization: Legitimacy, Democracy and Community in the International Trade System. Oxford: Oxford University Press.

19   Martin Loughlin (2010), What is Constitutionalization? In: Martin Loughlin, Petra Dobn-er (eds.), The Twilight of Constitutional Law: Demise or Transmutation? Oxford: Oxford University Press, pp. 47-69.

by a *pouvoir constituant*.[20] Neither monarchs nor peoples enter the picture. Amazingly, not unlike a perfect constitution, constitution *making* may be even imagined to be a machine that goes of itself.[21]

Constitutionalization is a result of a reasoning process that is conducted in an institutional setting where reason matters and gives rise to real effects. More precisely, constitutionalization is widely believed to be the work of adjudicating bodies. At any rate, initially, it is the work of courts on which subsequent legislative reform might build. With courts envisaged to be the main agents, the protection of rights is likely to provide the major avenue of constitutionalization. Not by accident, the concept is intrinsically tied to a liberal, rather than a republican, rendering of the constitutional project.[22] The constitution is seen as an instrument that limits political action. It is not supposed to create the channels for collective energy to gush into transformative action.

The groundwork done by adjudicating bodies is manifest in the inferential development of norms that trump others ('higher law')[23] and of individual rights that are directly effective vis-à-vis ordinary laws. Most often, both come in tandem. What are believed to be *ius cogens* norms in a constitutionalised international system are, of course, also the most fundamental of all fundamental rights.

Finally, constitutionalizations *grow out* of a certain field of law. They stem from processes that involve legal reasoning. But it is not the case that as a result of these processes the emerging constitutional elements become somehow severed from the rest of this field. It is not the case, in other words, that certain fields of law are pregnant with constitutional ideas until after gestation and through judicial delivery these ideas take on a life of their own. Rather, in a very profound manner the constitutional ideas are *intrinsic* to the field of law from which they originate. This explains why that which is being constitutionalised is often a most fundamental element of a certain compartment of law.

---

20   I may note, without paying undue regard for my own work, that I believe that even transnational legal entities avail of a constituent power. Alexander Somek (2008), Individualism: An Essay on the Authority of the European Union. Oxford: Oxford University Press.

21   See Michael Kammen (1986), A Machine That Would Go of Itself: The Constitution in American Culture. New York, Alfred Knopf.

22   As has been perceptively observed by Martin Loughlin (2010), What is Constitutionalization? In: Martin Loughlin, Petra Dobner (eds.), The Twilight of Constitutional Law: Demise or Transmutation? Oxford: Oxford University Press, pp. 47-69.

23   See Erika de Wet (2006), The Emergence of International and Regional Value Systems as Manifestation of the Emerging International Constitutional Order, Leiden Journal of International Law 19, pp. 611-632.

IV Fundamental Law

It is not difficult to imagine how this works. Imagine private law constitutionalised. One is immediately drawn to choose freedom of contract and private property to be part of its core constitutional principles. These principles are fundamental, for they lay the foundation for much of the rest. It explains why they are deemed relevant for the interpretation of other parts of private law. The principles *overdetermine* its meaning. They radiate into the rest. Their fundamental nature may even constrain you to interpret narrowly certain rules that you believe to be irregular and abnormal, for example, the obligation to enter into a contractual agreement even against your will when the provision of public goods appears to require this. Consequently, you may scoff at the legislature for tinkering with the integrity of the field's composition when it concedes, for example, to all customers the right to revoke agreements that originate from doorstep selling.

At any rate, this is what you are likely to do when you work within the *civil law* tradition. You censure the legislature, and you interpret narrowly, but you do not declare a statutory provision void for reasons of inconsistency with fundamental principles.

If your task is to administer a *common law* system you are equally drawn to identifying fundamental principles.[24] Good doctrine requires precisely this type of work regardless of whether you do common or civil law. However, in contrast to *ius civile,* the common law permits you to 'overrule' certain precedents that do not fit a set of principles that you perceive to emerge from other cases. This is what it takes to work with fundamental law.[25] Certain principles arrive on the horizon and attain a central and organising importance. In order to provide consistency, clarity, predictability, and rationality, you may have to overrule. The fundamental principles trump the holding of cases that reflect old or inconsistent doctrines.

I suspect that constitutionalization is a more stylized form of fundamentalisation; in fact, it is a stylized form that tacitly re-conceives all legal systems from the perspective of the common law.[26] Arguably, for an internal market funda-

---

24 On the following, see Melvin Eisenberg (1988), The Nature of the Common Law. Cambridge, Mass.: Harvard University Press, pp. 43-49 and pp. 104-145.

25 This notion has been long recognised by the Common Law tradition. See Glenn Burgess (1996), Absolute Monarchy and The Stuart Constitution. New Haven: Yale University Press, p. 134.

26 This should not come as a surprising development. In seventeenth-century England the common law, owing to its customary nature, has been deemed to be the 'ancient constitution'. See J.G.A. Pocock (1987), The Ancient Constitution and the Feudal Law, 2nd edition. Cambridge: Cambridge University Press, 1987, pp. 16-19; Glenn Burgess (1992), The Politics of the Ancient Constitution: An Introduction to English Political Thought, 1603-1642. London: Macmillan, p. 6.

mental freedoms are of foundational importance. Using them as trumps constitutionalises. The laws of the member states are treated as though they were 'bad law' that no longer fits an emerging pattern of new ideas. The substance of the new ideas is articulated by the judiciary. The findings of judges account for what is deemed to be expressive of common understandings. The elite consensus of lawyers is expressive of the morality of the relevant community.[27] This is how the common law looks at the world.

By working in this manner, constitutionalization is clearly different from constitution making, which originates from an act. Thomas Paine would have dismissed as utter mockery the idea that a constitution might be constructed by lawyers who assume that certain fundamental principles exist.[28]

V   Distant goals: Innovation

I would like to add one further observation. Constitutionalization may also come invested with a teleological orientation. This has been the case, undoubtedly, in the European Union where the treaties have been construed with an eye to the objective of Europe-building as market-building.

When a set of norms is seen against the background of larger goals, the substance of norms becomes subject to a teleological reservation. Their meaning is supposed to mean what it means only in as much as it contributes to attaining the objective. Hence, the application of norms becomes fine-tuned with regard to their instrumentality. The meaning of the fundamental principles governing the common market, for example, becomes recalibrated such as to best serve their aim. The interpretation of norms is thereby covertly transformed into a means-ends test in which norms are submitted to instrumental scrutiny and consequently adjusted and readjusted in light of their purpose.

But what if the ends are not entirely clear? It seems as though they have to be determined in some process of discovery. When objectives are open-ended and the causal pathways leading to their realisation difficult to make out, it becomes essential that the interpretative process abounds in new ideas. The teleological reservation opens the door to experimenting with creative solutions to interpreta-

---

27   Melvin Eisenberg (1988), The Nature of the Common Law. Cambridge, Mass.: Harvard University Press.
28   See Thomas Paine (1984), Rights of Man, Eric Foner (ed.). London: Penguin Press, p. 185.

tive problems. The process of adjudicative constitutionalization is then disposed to draw on *innovation* as its major legitimating factor.[29]

Ordinary common-law-style reasoning is different from such a feast of teleology. The set of cases comprising a doctrine are expected to fit a set of principles. But the principles are not understood to be social aims that are to be realised at some point in the future. Rather, principles are taken to be woven already into the fabric of society. They are to be respected or given adequate articulation. Nevertheless, a common-law-style administration of fundamental laws can be taken tacitly over by the spirit of innovation.

This is of consequence not merely for the interpretation of rights but also for questions of jurisdiction. It is one thing to adapt the interpretation of rights to the pursuit of social objectives; but effective goal-attainment needs to go beyond mere substance and also allocate jurisdiction in the body engaged in substantive fine-tuning. In other words, the body in charge of attaining an objective needs to ascribe to itself, in light of weighty objectives, the respective power to issue the rulings necessary to attain them. Instrumentalism is a mode of self-empowerment.[30]

The power to issue rulings in which sweeping constitutionalization claims are made is part of these self-(in-)(re)ferential attributions of competence. Of course, it should not be forgotten that the more open-ended the goals, the more open-ended the requisite powers to attain them.

VI   Constitutionalism's core asymmetry

Constitutions establish barriers and bulwarks on the one hand, and introduce trajectories on the other. They foreclose as much as they constitute opportunities. Barriers and bulwarks are erected against what might be termed a polity's *prime suspects*. It is not the case that these suspects are by their very nature somehow alien elements that constitution-makers have been forced to accept (for example, a king or a bishop). Rather, they are an integral, but risky, part of government. The prime suspect is believed to be more powerful and more effective than other constituted agents. The most notorious prime suspect is the executive branch.

Constitutions do not merely introduce agents whose powers and capacities give rise to agency costs. They also contain grants of opportunities for what is considered to be a *prima facie benign force*. This explains why constitutions

---

29   See my interpretation in 'Legalität heute: Variationen über ein Thema von Max Weber' (2008), Der Staat 47, pp. 428-465.

30   See the discussion in Neil MacCormick (1999), Questioning Sovereignty: Law, State and Nation in the European Commonwealth. Oxford: Oxford University Press, pp. 101-121.

have been experienced by those sharing the aspirations of that force as an act of *emancipation*. For example, for quite some time parliaments elected on the basis of general suffrage offered a real promise of empowerment to a social democratic proletariat.[31]

Traditionally, constitutions have been built around various asymmetries in the relation of prime suspects and *prima facie* benign forces. The tension was clearly defined, originally, in the relation between monarch and parliament (or any other people's representation). What Carl Schmitt later came to describe and to debunk as the 'legislative state' (*Gesetzgebungsstaat*)[32] with its astoundingly idealised conception of the legislature reflects what it means to perceive the constitution from the vantage point of the *prima facie* benign force *alone*.

In federalist systems, the positions occupied in the asymmetrical structure depend on the allocation of distrust. At the founding of the American republic, the federal government was clearly cast as the prime suspect. The provisions of the Bill of Rights were originally supposed to protect the majoritarianism of the states.[33] This changed with reconstruction. Then the bigots sitting in state legislatures became prime suspects, and the federal court system the representative of the benign force.[34]

I do not want to claim that every constitution is based on only one of these tensions. They may comprise several overlapping tensions. What I would like to claim, nonetheless, is that constitutionalism is a distinctive and appealing political ideal only if constitutions create new opportunities for groups and, even more intriguingly, thereby redefine what legitimate political action comes to. In a sense, they also presuppose a certain mode of being political.

Originally, constitutionalism is a bourgeois project.[35] The Third Estate laid claim to being the nation.[36] That is, participating in the benefits of the constitutional project required accepting the terms and conditions of participation laid down by this group. Previous access conditions and modes of exercising influence were disparaged as 'privileges'. Groups or movements give life to the universal ideas and aspirations of modern constitutional law, in particular as regards fair and effective participation in politics. The thresholds introduced by the

---

31 See Colin Crouch (2004), Post-Democracy. London: Polity Press, pp. 6-11.
32 See Carl Schmitt (2004), Legality and Legitimacy (trans. Jeffrey Seitzer). Durham: Duke University Press, pp. 17-38.
33 Akhil Reed Amar (1998), The Bill of Rights: Creation and Reconstruction. New Haven: Yale University Press, pp. 7, 26, 285.
34 Ibid, p. 244.
35 Dieter Grimm (1991), Die Zukunft der Verfassung. Frankfurt am Main: Suhrkamp, pp. 39-43.
36 Abbé Sieyès, Political Writings, edited by Michael Sonenscher (2003). Indianapolis: Hackett, p. 140.

bourgeoisie were later overcome by parliaments elected on the basis of general suffrage. Political parties with comprehensive visions of social life became the type of group that would benefit from occupying the position of the *prima facie* benign force. But also a strong presidential leader may in one person represent the energy and resolve of a self-determining body. Throughout the New Deal and even long thereafter, the American presidency enjoyed the constitutional support that goes along with occupying the place of the *prima facie* benign force.[37] In the transition from parliamentary inclusion to presidential rule, the mode of being political changed from subscribing to, and working towards the realisation of, grander social visions to identification with leaders who emerge victorious from contests to find the support of a largely passive electorate.

The point of constitutional arrangement is, to repeat, not to let the *prima facie* benign force prevail in a long-term battle against the prime suspect. Rather, the art of modern constitutionalism consists in sustaining a legally asymmetrical relation under conditions of reverse capacities. Parliaments need to be legally superior to executives for the reason that executives are by virtue of what they do better equipped to excel in short-term problem solving. Therein, however, lurks the danger associated with expedient action. It is likely to lack rationality and morality. Contrariwise, a national chief executive may have to be conceded some leeway in order to be able to overcome resistance exercised by inert parochial forces. But this does not mean that countervailing suspect forces are supposed to be wiped out.

VII   The European Union: From sustaining asymmetry to structural transformation

Something closely resembling the basic asymmetry of modern constitutional law was manifest also in the European Community, at any rate, until the mid 1970s. The member states and cooperating businesses were clearly cast in the position of prime suspects, while the Commission and Parliament were wearing the shoes of the benign force.[38] This is reflected in the long-standing distinction between supranationalism and intergovernmentalism. The intergovernmentalist *modus operandi* of the member states was always seen as posing a threat to the Community's supranational constitution.

---

37   Bruce Ackerman (1991), We the People, vol. 1: Foundations. Cambridge, Mass.: Harvard University Press, pp. 106.
38   David J. Gerber (1998), Law and Competition in Twentieth Century Europe: Protecting Prometheus. Oxford: Oxford University Press, pp. 257-265.

Moreover, the asymmetry was also manifest in what was believed to be the economic constitution.[39] Competition law was targeted at big businesses and at governments colluding with local clientele. The fundamental freedoms were understood to be bans on protectionist conduct. They were taken to be anti-discrimination norms.

As long as the emerging European constitution had this focus it could have been said to be targeted at the behaviour of prime suspects. Their *conduct* was to be controlled by it. It is not inaccurate to say that the first round of constitutionalization merely pushed the control of conduct to a higher level. It was addressed to agents and what they potentially do.

The constitution is law. It regulates conduct. It grants powers and it immunises existing permissions from legal erasure. This is what constitutions do.[40]

The constitutionalization process, however, took a surprising turn. It changed the direction of control from agents to structures. It is the structure of a system of nation states and the structure of certain market situations that became the prime suspect.

Usually, constitutions do not address *directly* the structural questions. They do so, if at all, in institutional guarantees and they may appeal to transformation in aspirational provisions in which governments are admonished to take proactive steps into a certain direction. Tackling structural problems, however, is the task of the political process and not of the constitution itself. The political process may decide to institute an administrative scheme in order to address such problems, for example, an Equality Body. But this is a matter of administrative problem solving.

The European constitution, when the EU had been still merely a Community, began tackling structural problems. That is, it not merely introduced powers for actors to become active if they desired to do so; rather, it became a proactive force itself. The existing *structure* of regulated markets and the *system* of nation-states became a matter of constitutional concern.[41]

I am not sure if this is a unique development. Most likely it is not. The German Federal Constitutional Court went into a similar direction when exploring, for example, the structure of broadcasting[42] or the organisation of scientific re-

---

39   Christian Joerges, What is Left of the European Economic Constitution? A Melancholic Eulogy, http://www.arena.uio.no/cidel/WorkshopStockholm/Joerges.pdf.

40   For this highly elementary concept of the constitution, see Neil MacCormick (1999), Questioning Sovereignty: Law, State and Nation in the European Commonwealth. Oxford: Oxford University Press, p. 103.

41   The case in point is, of course, Cassis de Dijon. See Case 120/78, Rewe-Zentrale AG v. Bundesmonopolverwaltung für Brandwein, ECR 649 (European Court of Justice 1979).

42   See BVerfGE 12, p. 205.

search.[43] What the Federal Constitutional Court did, in certain instances, was to determine the substantive reach of rights with an eye to the public good that is to be created by their collective exercise. This is clearly a structural problem. Rights are then considered protected in as much as and to the extent that they contribute to processes, such as independent scientific research or public opinion formation. Undoubtedly, a very strong teleological element is thereby introduced into the interpretation of the constitution. The effective scope of fundamental rights becomes calibrated with an eye to the reproduction of structural states.

Arguably, the structural strain of the Federal Constitutional Court's jurisprudence is generally more backward-looking and therefore concerned with preserving existing structures. In the case of the ECJ, by contrast, the story is more remarkable. The public good is such that its realization requires transforming the structure of the constituted unit itself.

I cannot say much about how this development is manifest in competition law. It may well be reflected in the protection against 'structural abuse', that is, a situation in which an undertaking has become so dominant in the market that no matter what it may do in order to secure long-term success through dominance, its conduct will be considered abusive.[44] It is, however, most clearly manifest, as I argued elsewhere,[45] in the manner in which the ECJ interpreted fundamental freedoms with an eye to protecting economic activities against disadvantages that do not arise from conduct, but rather as systemic consequences of the co-existence of nation-states. The protection against so-called obstacles is accompanied by a horizontalisation of proportionality. The application of this principle is triggered by a difference between and among national regulatory regimes.

These steps have been of great significance, not only for the member states whose regulatory powers and, most recently, systems of social protection have come to be more narrowly circumscribed, but for constitutionalism in general. Obviously, the constitution is turned into an instrument to pursue some kind of project that is different from facilitating political action and limiting government. It is no longer about constraining, without disabling, a prime suspect and enabling, without unleashing, the *prima facie* benign force. It is supposed to be a blueprint for 'structural transformation'.[46]

---

43 See BVerfGE 35, p. 79.
44 See Case C-27/76 United Brands Company and United Brands Continentaal BV v. Commission [1978] ECR 207 at para. 198.
45 See my article (2010), The argument from transnational effects I: Representing outsiders through freedom of movement, European Law Journal 16, pp. 315-344.
46 Much could be said, at this point, about the fate of the German basic law, which was ironically, qua constitution submitted to constitutionalization. The constitutionalization of the German Constitution was the work of a court that read it as instituting a 'value order'. On the most basic characteristics of reading the constitution qua 'value order', see Thilo

All forces constituted by the constitution thereby become basically part of the same mission. They participate in a joint enterprise. Welcome on board. The constitution is the meta-program of all programs. More to the point, the constitution itself is taking the place of the benign force. Hence, all agents are also in the position of primary suspects. Are they adequate to the task? Or do they fall short?

Once a constitution has attained the rank of the benign force, those in charge of purveying its meaning partake of its authority. This explains why, even though the context has changed, constitutionalization retains the *form* of the common law. A judicial tribunal is in charge of precipitating most fundamental principles and ascribing to them the status of higher law. *Substantively*, however, this process is no longer based upon the received jurisprudential techniques of generalisation and specification. Rather, as I tried to point out above, if the ends are unclear it will be driven by charisma of innovation, which feeds into the voyage of legal transformation. Transnational governance without government, in particular management processes such as the OMC, are not the antithesis, but rather the *essence* of what is brought about in the course of constitutionalizations.

VIII   Administered individualism

The European Union is only one paradigmatic case. In what follows, I would like to develop a more general ideal type. This idea is to contrast constitutionalizations, wherever they might occur, with what we have hitherto understood to be constitutions.

Let me begin by summarizing some general points.

First, constitutionalization is a process whose success depends on the exercise of judicial imagination. Second, it results in the use of fundamental law *as* higher law, in particular, vis-à-vis prime suspects or whole structures. Third, its major avenue is the protection of rights.

But for whom is constitutionalization the right exercise of the constituent power? What kind of being would one have to be in order find it desirable?

Rensmann (2006), Wertordnung und Verfassung: Das Grundgesetz im Kontext grenzüberschreitender Konstitutionalisierung. Tübingen: Mohr Siebeck, p. 412; on the genesis, see also Dieter Grimm (2010), The Basic Law at 60 – Identity and Change, German Law Journal, 11, pp. 34-46 and 42-43 http://www.germanlawjournal.com/pdfs-/Vol11-No1/PDF_Vol_11_No_01_33-46_GG60_Grimm.pdf at

The answer to this question depends, in my view, on the link between administrative action and modern individualism. The normative vision underpinning constitutionalization is individualistic. It is manifest in the view that what matters in life is personal advancement and the happiness of those to whom one feels personally attached, be they members of the family, fellow believers, or pets. The claims made by society at large are met with scepticism, possibly because individualists are generally even sceptical as regards the existence of a body capable of representing society as a whole.

Belief in political transformation has abated. If there were such belief nobody would have time to act on it. All are busy pursuing their personal ends. Nevertheless, in societies where individualism is strong, social cooperation is complex and risky. Governments are imagined to be bodies that rely on knowledge in order to sustain a structure of complex webs of interaction and to contain various risks. The fabric of society is not entirely self-stabilising. It requires constant monitoring and intervention.

Individualists have no time for public affairs. They are interested in amassing wealth, in how their persona is perceived by their superiors, or in planning their children's weddings. Individualists are, therefore, in a fix. They know that complex societies require permanent intervention. But they cannot and do not want themselves to invest any time or effort in these matters. Rather they long for good reasons in order to rationalise their indifference.

To that end one merely needs to realise that one lives in a knowledge society. In a society of this type all knowledge exists dispersed in specialised expertise. Against this backdrop, one is in a position to explain to oneself and others that deference to expertise, which feeds into centralised regulation, is in one's long-term interest. This explanation undergirds the belief that it is in the rational self-interest to have a centralised administration exercise the power of the social to organise itself. The belief, in turn, is manifest in a daily plebiscite of political indifference. The votes in favour of passivity are cast in the form of rationalisations. For don't these administrative bodies develop and implement standards for food and drink? Don't they adopt traffic regulations in order to make us safe? Don't they screen immigrants in order to prevent terrorism? And how should ordinary people be able to make well-informed choices? Everyone has reason to trust expertise.

The administrative system concomitant to individualism is different from the administrative state envisaged by Max Weber.[47] To begin with, it is no longer backed up by sovereignty. This increases the pressure to derive legitimacy from

47 Max Weber (1966), Staatssoziologie, 2nd edition, edited by Johannes Winckelmann. Berlin: Duncker & Humblot, p. 46.

rationality. Second, it is no longer based on what Weber called faith in legality,[48] but rather on the faith in one's own rationality and the rationality of others. Transnational societies shift from *Legalitätsglaube* to *Rationalitätsglaube* as a major legitimating factor.

Individualistic societies are burgeoning cages of rational obedience. Confidence in social power – the power of transnational networks of expertise – gives rise to a form of collective self-determination where the prevalence of private pursuits and faith in the rational expertise of others results in submission to the demands of an administered life.

IX   Substance matters

If it is this substance of constitutionalized arrangements that distinguishes them from old-fashioned constitutions then it is obvious why approaching them from a federalist perspective does not reveal much. In the case of the EU, transnational constitutional arrangements are often described as though they have given rise to a somewhat incomplete or deficient federalist system. They are taken to involve a plurality of potentially colliding regimes, with no legal order mediating between and among them.[49] The essence of a transnational constitution is presented as though it instituted federal authority without supremacy or any clear-cut allocation of powers. It is like federalism, just a bit messier.[50]

Albeit not without merit, this perspective tends to obscure the substance of transnational arrangements. Transnational constitutionalizations, if they occur, do not crystallise around the problem of generating the wherewithal of political power. Rather, they concern modes of dealing with regulatory responses to market failure and perceived risks. The latter may arise spontaneously across state administrations. This, at any rate, has been Anne-Marie Slaughter's observation regarding the new world order.[51] At a global level, policymaking is increasingly the work of transnational networks in which the sharing of expertise translates

48   See ibid, p. 28.
49   See, for example, Daniel Halberstam (2009), Constitutional Heterarchy: The Centrality of Conflict in the European Union and the United States, in: J. Dunoff & J. Trachtman (eds.), Ruling the World? Constitutionalism, International Law, and Global Governance. Cambridge: Cambridge University Press, pp. 326-355.
50   According to long established doctrine, federalism is always messy. See Georg Waitz (1862), Grundzüge der Politik nebst einzelnen Ausführungen. Kiel: Homann, p. 213; Carl Schmitt (2008), Constitutional Theory (trans. J. Seitzer). Durham: Duke University Press, p. 388; Carl Schmitt (1989), Verfassungslehre, 7th edition. Berlin: Duncker & Humblot, p. 371.
51   See Anne-Marie Slaughter (2004), A New World Order. Princeton: Princeton University Press.

into control. Such networks are sometimes referred to as sources of global law, or global 'soft law', beyond the state.

Administrative processes create public goods, for example, banking rules addressing liquidity and lending rules. They help to create and to sustain trust. Substantively, they are examples of good governing. They represent administration without sovereignty. Since they are not tied to a single constituency, the only manner of controlling them is through monitoring by civil society and review by courts on civil rights grounds. In the course of such reviews, courts may well begin to constitutionalize.

It bears emphasis how different, even from the ideal perspective of public justification, the world of constitutionalizations is from the world of constitution making. Constitutions, traditionally understood, constitute access to political power, which can then be used to bring about social change by peaceful means. The constitution is a compact among citizens. It is on their reasonable agreement that all authority rests. Self-government is based thereon. Ideally, constitutions originate from a hypothetical situation prior to society.

Constitutionalizations, by contrast, would typically emerge from adjudicative responses to various sites of regulatory or managing authority. The basic idea is that the exercise of market-correcting and risk-managing expertise needs to be controlled on the basis of legal expertise regarding transparency, accountability, and fundamental rights protection. Constitutionalized legal structures are not a compact based on the reasonableness of citizens; rather, they incorporate principles of rational trust in expert networks and controlling legal expertise. Questions of redistribution do not arise. Only civil liberties are at stake.[52] *Problem-solving plus civil rights protection is the default common good pursued by sector-specific constitutionalizations.*

X   The loss of national political self-determination

I have claimed that constitutionalization is most adequate to the mind-set of administered individualism. It fits the needs of people who want to have their private pursuits rationally channelled and protected by some spontaneously established expert body. Now I would like to examine in which respect the rise of constitutionalization involves a decisive break with the constitutionalist tradition.

---

52   Using old-fashioned constitutional language I understand by 'civil rights' those fundamental rights that do not guarantee the rights of active citizenship. They are non-political rights. Akhil Reed Amar (1998), The Bill of Rights: Creation and Reconstruction. New Haven: Yale University Press, pp. 48-49.

Taking up an idea first articulated by Ackerman,[53] it makes sense to assume that constitution-makers select a specific allocation and separation of powers in order to attain three formal objectives. These are the objectives that we expect constitutions *generally* to attain. First, we oblige public decision making to respect or even to enliven our rights. Second, we want public power to be in a position where it can engage in intelligent and efficient problem solving. Finally, we expect constitutions to facilitate self-determination. Of the three core expectations regarding constitutional performance – rights, problem solving, and self-determination – the third is notoriously the most difficult to apprehend. What does it mean for *individuals* to be *collectively* self-determining?

Part of constitutionalization's appeal may be owing to the fact that it avoids addressing this third question. Constitutionalization can accommodate problem solving and fundamental rights protection. Indeed, under a liberal administrative regime, be it national or transnational, this is all that it takes for there to be constituted power. Constitutionalization is about entrenching rights-respecting, liberal bureaucracies. Through the common withdrawal from the public sphere political liberty is given a genuinely *private* articulation.

From the perspective of the constitutionalist tradition this entails a loss. Constitutionalizations do not constitute the conditions of active liberty. They are oblivious to the objective of political self-determination, publicly defined.

Any self-determination involves both activity and passivity. The paradigmatic instance of its active dimension, at any rate in a democratic polity, is that of a political movement successfully garnering the support of the majority of the electorate. Remarkably, in an age in which public action exhausts itself in either strategic or concerted adjustments to shifting circumstances, the conception of a political movement appears to be out of place. Undeniably, nonetheless, modern constitutions accommodate and channel mobilisation. They do not do so, however, without establishing obstacles, too. These obstacles point to the passive side of political self-determination, that is, to that someone who is, at first glance, determined without ostensibly actively determining him- or herself. That someone merely lets it happen.

Usually, constitutional analysis is interested in the active side of political liberty. However important it is, for example, to ponder how many electoral victories are required in order to translate political energy into normative entrenchment,[54] the passive side of political self-determination is ultimately more essential. It presupposes that individuals are willing to accept as their choices the

---

53   Bruce Ackerman (2000), The New Separation of Powers, Harvard Law Review 113, pp. 633-729.

54   See Bruce Ackerman (2000), The New Separation of Powers, Harvard Law Review 113, pp. 633-729.

choices made by others. This is not to say that embracing these choices implies making them one's own. Ideally, choices are respected as choices made by strangers. This is what respecting the law – rather than respecting a moral precept – is all about. Respecting another's will as if it were one's own is the very essence of legality.

Activity and passivity, however, must not fall on two different sides. Otherwise, we would be confronted with a case of heteronomy. Self-determination is possible only if passivity is also expressive of an element of active endorsement. Viewed from the passive angle, people are collectively self-determining when respecting choices by others is necessary in order to sustain their life *as members of a community*. The will to sustain the bond is the active element underlying passive acceptance that reconciles being determined by others with being oneself (or, rather, *Beisichsein*). This will is thereby expressive of a general will in the sense that it is over and above[55] the political choices made either by oneself or others.

It may be suspected that what I have in mind here is tantamount to Carl Schmitt's way of conceptualising the self-determination of a homogeneous democratic society. Accordingly, citizens remain self-determining even in the event that their initiatives become defeated, for the occasional loss in a vote does not exclude them from the sweet harmony of agreement that obtains on the ground of indivisible national commonality.[56] The latter would be what constitutes and constrains from a position above and beyond all choices.

It is well known that this is a dangerous fiction. But there is a kernel of truth to it. Citizens are self-determining even when they grudgingly accept the determinations made by others as long as these others are part of their world. The *views* of others may appear strange. But their *presence* is taken for granted. The unfamiliar is familiar not because one could imagine being like them (who could ever imagine being a liberal democrat?), but rather because they are part of a form of life that is experienced as one's own. What makes the unfamiliar look familiar is what we call a nation.

My explanatory task is gravely exacerbated, I sense, even by merely suggesting a possible proximity to Schmitt. But the proximity is only apparent. The conception of collective self-determination proposed here is exceedingly more plausible when we abandon the fiction that the range of what appears familiar among various strange encounters is based upon a natural fact. Nations familiarise the unfamiliar. This materialises in acts which make it possible that we recognise

---

55   See, again, M. Korsgaard (2009), Self-Constitution: Agency, Identity, and Integrity. Oxford: Oxford University Press, pp. 72, 75, 126, 134.

56   See Carl Schmitt (2004), Legality and Legitimacy (trans. Jeffrey Seitzer). Durham: Duke University Press, p. 24.

people from a different social setting as our own. This is what it means that nations are imagined communities.[57] The imagination is real. It bridges the gap that would otherwise exist among us, taken as individuals.

Contrary to the Schmittian imagery, therefore, homogeneity is neither a given nor the dominant experience. Every act of political self-determination is an empirical test of its conditions of possibility. At any rate, as long as the constitution as law is adhered to, self-determination is in place. Societies may be relatively pluralistic. In fact, the more pluralistic they are, the more enlightened societies have become about their internal constitution, for they realise *in practice* that their sustainability depends on familiarising the unfamiliar. It is through pluralism that nation-states realise for themselves what they are in themselves (*an sich*).

Just like passivity needs to encompass an active element, activity needs to be the activity *of* some passively existing unit. Its existence is signalled through tenacity. In fact, much can be learned about the homogeneity of a society by attending to constitutional entrenchment. Societies that give room to quick transformations are either relatively impervious to change or willing to accept it. In both cases, they are homogeneous.

XI   Unpalatable alternatives: Deliberative democracy

Functionally understood, a nation is that which makes collective self-determination possible. The question that arises of course, in a transnational age, is whether it is a necessary ('quasi-transcendental') condition or rather merely one empirical condition among others. Are there no alternatives to political self-determination?

In a transnational context, the question is usually posed more narrowly. Transnational regimes are confronted with the expectation to be democratic. This expectation is then either characterised in terms of 'output' or 'input' legitimacy.[58] Democratic output legitimacy is believed to be realised when the folks on the ground are satisfied with what effective leadership delivers. Thus understood, Singapore is democratic, assuming, for the sake of the argument, that Singapore's population is happy. Input legitimacy, by contrast, affects the voice that is had by those likely affected in the process leading up to decision making. As is well known, the more refined forms of democratic input are deemed to be those

---

57   See Benedict Anderson (1991), Imagined Communities: Reflections on the Origin and Spread of Nationalism (2nd edition). London: Verso, p. 6.

58   I guess we owe the distinction to Fritz W. Scharpf. See his Governing in Europe: Effective and Democratic? (1999). Oxford: Oxford University Press, pp. 10-23.

that rely on the use of arguments that claim to be universally acceptable. In other words, instead of raw (and vulgar) acts of voting, the public-spirited exchange of argument is deemed to provide the relevant input for democracy. Self-government thus comes to be redefined in terms of 'deliberative democracy'. Since this type of democracy can in principle dispense with representative assemblies and general elections as long as provision is made that affected groups are given a 'voice' it is perfectly compatible with a style of governance that perceives a central administrative unit involved in deliberations with transnational and local stakeholders. Since the participation of stakeholders varies with the issues affected, it is sensible to vest final decision-making authority in the bureaucratic body. As I tried to explain elsewhere,[59] it so happens that under conditions of transnational government and concomitant constitutionalization self-government is prey to *administrative assimilation*.

XII   Unpalatable alternatives: sectoral transnational constitutionalizations

One may still want to object that it is more then merely unimaginative, namely bland, to assume that a nation is the only locale for collective self-determination. Why is it impossible to see the same relation realised in fragmentary form in a variety of circumstances? Why, in other words, couldn't there be self-determining bodies across nations that deal with sectoral issues, constituted by partial instruments for the governance of, say, health or safety?

Above all, the idea of sectoral constitutions is inconsistent. In order to realise their own aspiration, sectoral constitutions would have to abide by their own jurisdictional constraints. Conceptually, they would presuppose, *pace* pluralists, a comprehensive constitution allowing them to put themselves into their proper place. The existence of an overarching constitutional framework is not merely a matter of logic. It is also a matter of empowerment. Political choices cut across a variety of sectors. Reductions of spending on public universities, for example, have an impact on various spheres of social life, ranging from childrearing to the job market. Constitutions that feature national governments and legislatures permit *addressing* these impacts systematically and comprehensively. Not only would sectoral constitutions have to rely on good faith coordination, by their very nature they would permit confronting other 'branches' with a *fait accompli*. When the educational sector decides to introduce a three-year undergraduate program among participating states, other sectors need to adapt. When the financial sector modifies liquidity standards for banks, this is it.

59   Alexander Somek (2008), Demokratie als Verwaltung: Wider die deliberativ halbierte Demokratie, Soziale Welt, pp. 323-348.

It is not the case, of course, that externalities exist as though their existence were a matter of fact. The musical predilections of the vast majority of people are a nemesis to the vanguard production of sonorities. It would be odd, however, to call this an externality. We consider folks entitled to their musical taste. Identifying an externality presupposes a normative baseline. It exists only in as much as its emergence is perceived to be engaging someone's responsibility.

There can be no collective self-determination among persons who are perfectly happy to adapt. Whatever happens to them, they take it as a given. Their experience does not register 'externalities', for they are vis-à-vis others in no position to appeal to the responsibility to respect their moral independence.

In many respects, this matches the situation of international society as described by so-called realists. The big shots are calling the shots. The little states have no other choice but to adapt. Even the big shots merely adapt. Expanding the sphere of influence is key to survival as a grand power.

As an alternative to mere adaptation, public liberty begins in the private sphere. It begins with people complaining about how the conduct of their neighbours interferes with their whim. This is the first step towards turning 'externalities' into public problems.[60] The belief that what happens affects an interconnected sphere – and not merely oneself personally – allows for such transubstantiation. Addressing public problems presupposes a common sphere of influence. Constitutions, traditionally conceived, are substantively and jurisdictionally comprehensive. They establish public liberty by rendering collective self-determination inevitable. Owing to representative institutions and political rights, decision makers are forced to deal with 'externalities' as public problems.

XIII   Unpalatable alternatives: collective individualism

Nations need boundaries. There is a weaker and a stronger version of explaining this necessity. The weaker version claims that, if it were not for boundaries, the totality of the social world would lose contours and dissipate into indeterminacy. The concern for a common future or a common way of life would be devoid of substance if it had to accommodate everything. One world would be nobody's world. The stronger version holds that a world with nationality realises more liberty than any post-national cosmopolitan alternative. This claim is best explained as a reply to an objection. For it may be reasonably objected that within the constraints set by principles of justice all societies actually ought to attempt to ac-

60   See John Dewey (1954), The Public and its Problems. Chicago: Swallow Press, p. 64.

commodate *any* permissible version of the good. Any liberal society is as good as any other. National differences matter only for reasons of historical path dependence. Liberal societies need to settle for something neutral in order to facilitate the realisation of various conceptions of the good. Apparently, a market economy is a neutral medium, for it allows interconnecting one's choice of a type of life with the choices of others through a matrix of opportunity costs.[61] One cannot expect others to pay for one's life choices unless one avails oneself of the necessary resources by tending to the needs and interest of others. The impression of neutrality, however, is a consequence of a perceived lack of alternatives, which, in turn, gives rise to the experience of necessity. Necessary is that which cannot *not* be. It is beyond the purview of choice. Hence, it is also neutral.

But it is the common mistake of political liberalism to assume that a market economy is a neutral medium for the realisation of a way of life. Rather, being successful in a market economy presupposes surrendering to the cultural ways of capitalism. For example, one can thrive only when adopting a long-term perspective and acquiring the ability to work for distant rewards. The predominance of certain socially rewarded personal attributes requires people to adapt their social visions to the conditions under which they can be maintained on the basis of trade and barter. As a consequence, many cultural practices that may survive on the basis of national solidarity (e.g., rural mountain dwellers, national opera houses) would likely disappear under conditions of cosmopolitan market liberalism, which would even bar them from struggling for survival outside the market, for this would be deemed to be unjust.[62]

An alternative to the bounded existence of national constitutional democracies would have to lock out any encounters with otherness from the sphere of collective self-determination. It has its dialectical vanishing point in the political phantasma of individualism.

The political phantasma of individualism has been first identified by Hegel.[63] It affects, indeed, the question of how individuals can be believed to be self-determining under circumstances that are not of their own choosing. Whoever needs to lead a life under circumstances one would not have chosen had one been given a choice is not fully free. Assuming that the person is not subject to coercion the person still can be said to be autonomous, albeit autonomous under conditions of heteronomy. She is foreign to her own social world. How can indi-

61 Ronald Dworkin (2001), Sovereign Virtue: The Theory and Practice of Equality. Cambridge, Mass.: Harvard University Press.
62 Will Kymlicka (1988), Liberalism, Community and Culture. Oxford: Oxford University Press, pp. 190-192.
63 See Gottfried W.F. Hegel (1977), Phenomenology of Spirit (trans. A. V. Miller). Oxford: Oxford University Press, p. 359.

viduals be believed to be fully self-determining under circumstances that they have not reflexively endorsed as their own?

The answer given by the phantasma of individualism is that full autonomy can only be established by recreating the social world in the person's image. Under the ordinary conditions of collective self-determination – that is, where it is necessary to recognise a foreign will as one's own – this is impossible. The need for compromise and accommodation would prevent closing the gap yawning between autonomous choice and heteronomous circumstance. The only way out that remains is identification with an omnipotent leader taking charge of social transformation. His is the active side of political self-determination while individuals identify with his choices. This is their road to freedom. They adapt. It is by means of political passivity – obedience, in other words – that they are 'collectively' autonomous. In the event that self-determination by means of surrender should cause psychological pain, shrinks and pills will take care of the problem.

Of course, the most prominent applications of the political phantasma of individualism are instances of authoritarian rule. It is possible, however, to reconcile the phantasma with a world that permits the pursuit of private ambition guarded by benevolent administrative social engineering. The engineers say 'avoid X'. Consequently, the subjects avoid X and enjoy their collective autonomy as private individuals. The phantasma endorses an apolitical version of self-determination that is fully compatible with the belief in, and identification with, bureaucratic rationality.

XIV Conclusion

In this chapter, I tried to sketch how and why the discourse on constitutionalization assimilates constitutionalism to the mind-set of both the common law and administrative problem solving. Constitutionalization is supposed to be a process by which governance arrangements identify fundamental, higher-ranking principles underlying certain transformative projects. The articulation of these principles is the province of adjudicative bodies. This may include the formulation of rights.

Advocates of constitutionalization assume that the relevant processes are continuous with the tradition of constitutionalism. But they are wrong, for these processes result, in fact, in an ironic reversal. Rather than taming the administrative brute (*i.e.*, the state sans glamorous adornments of sovereignty),[64] they surrender political control to the logic of problem solving.

Since the term 'supranational' suggests that authority is vested in a sphere over and above the nation-state, it is accurate to amend this attribute in the case of constitutionalizations. Supranational authority, when constitutionalised, is also supra-political and, ironically, supra-constitutional. It is compatible with collective self-determination only if the latter is understood to be as public autonomy taken over by private autonomy. The result is public liberty poorly achieved, very much in the sense in which, by analogy, oligarchy is a deficient mode of aristocracy or populist democracy a shabby version of republican government. If we expect constitutions to facilitate self-determination, the existence of boundaries is essential. Otherwise, what is deemed to be transnational self-determination is likely to reflect the highly homogeneous conception of individuality that is build into the culture and ethics of market societies.

For the European Union this means that the quest for a European constitution has to continue. However, it needs to continue in a different key. Instead of retrieving popular approbation for convoluted outputs of warily negotiated reforms, Europe needs (and deserves) a real constitution.

Europe needs to move past provisional solutions. The Union needs to realise that what is at stake in Europe is a form of life. It is, I submit, a decidedly Western European form of life,[65] which counterbalances the self-reinforcing dominance of market dealings with arrangements that are supposed to elevate human pursuits from the dictates of necessity. They range from lifting the burden of choosing one's health insurance over six week vacations to sustaining a high culture that is decidedly unpopular.

Half a century of quest for defining a transnational polity or identifying acceptable forms of governance beyond the nation-state may have taught us a lesson that is different from what we might have expected. Instead of introducing a New Jerusalem, the journey to an unknown destination might have merely enabled us to rid ourselves of illusory foundations of the nation-state that were imagined to lie in an ethnically well-defined people, a clear-cut culture, common destiny, or legally unconstrained state power. Why should not the European Union present an opportunity to create a nation-state on the basis of a clearer conception of what such an entity truly is?

---

64 See my article (2009), Administration without Sovereignty, in: Martin Loughlin, Petra Dobner (eds.), The Twilight of Constitutional Law: Demise or Transmutation? Oxford: Oxford University Press, pp. 267-286.

65 See, more generally, Tony Judt (1996), A Grand Illusion? An Essay on Europe. New York: Hall & Wang, pp. 110-112.

Bibliography

Abbé Sieyès, *Political Writings*, edited by Michael Sonenscher (2003). Indianapolis: Hackett.

Ackerman, B. (1991), *We the People*, vol. 1: Foundations. Cambridge, Mass.: Harvard University Press.

Ackerman, B. (2000), The New Separation of Powers, *Harvard Law Review* 113, pp. 633-729.

Anderson, B. (1991), *Imagined Communities: Reflections on the Origin and Spread of Nationalism* (2nd edition). London: Verso.

Anderson, P. (2009), *The New Old World*. London: Verso.

Burgess, G. (1992), *The Politics of the Ancient Constitution: An Introduction to English Political Thought, 1603-1642*. London: Macmillan.

Burgess, G. (1996), *Absolute Monarchy and The Stuart Constitution*. New Haven: Yale University Press.

Cass, D.Z. (2005), *The Constitutionalization of the World Trade Organization: Legitimacy, Democracy and Community in the International Trade System*. Oxford: Oxford University Press.

Crouch, C. (2004), *Post-Democracy*. London: Polity Press.

De Wet, E. (2006), The Emergence of International and Regional Value Systems as Manifestation of the Emerging International Constitutional Order, *Leiden Journal of International Law* 19, pp. 611-632.

Dewey, J. (1954), *The Public and its Problems*. Chicago: Swallow Press.

Dworkin, R. (2001), *Sovereign Virtue: The Theory and Practice of Equality*. Cambridge, Mass.: Harvard University Press.

Eisenberg, M. (1988), *The Nature of the Common Law*. Cambridge, Mass.: Harvard University Press.

Fassbender, B. (2007), The meaning of international constitutional law, in: Nicholas Tsagourias (ed.), *Transnational Constitutionalism*. Cambridge: Cambridge University Press, pp. 307-328.

Gerber, D.J. (1998), *Law and Competition in Twentieth Century Europe: Protecting Prometheus*. Oxford: Oxford University Press.

Grimm, D. (1991), *Die Zukunft der Verfassung*. Frankfurt am Main: Suhrkamp.

Grimm, D. (2005), The Constitution in the Process of Denationalization, *Constellations* 12, pp. 447-463.

Grimm, D. (2010), The Basic Law at 60 – Identity and Change, *German Law Journal* 11, pp. 34-46.

Halberstam, D. (2009), Constitutional Heterarchy: The Centrality of Conflict in the European Union and the United States, in: J. Dunoff & J. Trachtman (eds.), *Ruling the World? Constitutionalism, International Law, and Global Governance*. Cambridge: Cambridge University Press, pp. 326-355.

Hegel, G.W.F. (1977), *Phenomenology of Spirit* (trans. A. V. Miller). Oxford: Oxford University Press.

Höreth, M. (2009), Überangepasst und realitätsentrückt: Zur Paradoxie der Theorie der deliberativen Demokratie, *Zeitschrift für Politikwissenschaft* 19, pp. 307-330.

Judt T. (1996), *A Grand Illusion? An Essay on Europe*. New York: Hall & Wang.

Kagan, R. (2003), *Of Paradise and Power: America and Europe in the New World Order*. New York: Alfred Knopf.

Kammen, M. (1986), *A Machine That Would Go of Itself: The Constitution in American Culture*. New York: Alfred Knopf.

Korsgaard, M. (2009), *Self-Constitution: Agency, Identity, and Integrity*. Oxford: Oxford University Press.

Kumm, M. (2009), The Cosmopolitan Turn in Constitutionalism: On the Relationship between Constitutionalism in and beyond the State, in: Jeffrey Dunoff, Joel Trachtman (eds.), *Ruling the World? Constitutionalism, International Law, and Global Governance*. Cambridge: Cambridge University Press, pp. 258-324.

Kumm, M. (2010), The Best of Times and the Worst of Times: Between Constitutional Triumphalism and Nostalgia, in: Martin Loughlin & Petra Dobner (eds.), *The Twilight of Constitutional Law: Demise or Transmutation?* Oxford: Oxford University Press, pp. 201-219.

Kymlicka, W. (1988), *Liberalism, Community and Culture*. Oxford: Oxford University Press.

Loughlin, M. (2010), What is Constitutionalization? In: Martin Loughlin, Petra Dobner (eds.), *The Twilight of Constitutional Law: Demise or Transmutation?* Oxford: Oxford University Press, pp. 47-69.

MacCormick, N. (1999), *Questioning Sovereignty: Law, State and Nation in the European Commonwealth*. Oxford: Oxford University Press.

Paine, T. (1984), *Rights of Man*, Eric Foner (ed.). London: Penguin Press.

Piris, J.-C. (2006), *The Constitution for Europe: A Legal Analysis*. Cambridge: Cambridge University Press.

Pocock, J.G.A. (1987), *The Ancient Constitution and the Feudal Law*, 2nd edition. Cambridge: Cambridge University Press.

Reed Amar, A. (1998), *The Bill of Rights: Creation and Reconstruction*. New Haven: Yale University Press.

Rensmann, T. (2006), *Wertordnung und Verfassung: Das Grundgesetz im Kontext grenzüberschreitender Konstitutionalisierung*. Tübingen: Mohr Siebeck.

Ricoeur, P. (1970), *Freud and Philosophy: An Essay on Interpretation* (trans. Denis Savage). New Haven: Yale University Press.

Roemer, J. (2000), *Equality of Opportunity*. Cambridge, Mass.: Harvard University Press.

Scharpf, F.W. (1999), *Governing in Europe: Effective and Democratic?* Oxford: Oxford University Press.

Schmitt, C. (1989), *Verfassungslehre*, 7th edition. Berlin: Duncker & Humblot.

Schmitt, C. (2004), *Legality and Legitimacy* (trans. Jeffrey Seitzer). Durham: Duke University Press, pp. 17-38.

Schmitt, C. (2008), *Constitutional Theory* (trans. J. Seitzer). Durham: Duke University Press.

Slaughter, A.-M. (2004), *A New World Order*. Princeton: Princeton University Press.

Somek, A. (2008), Demokratie als Verwaltung: Wider die deliberativ halbierte Demokratie, *Soziale Welt*, pp. 323-348.

Somek, A. (2008), *Individualism: An Essay on the Authority of the European Union*. Oxford: Oxford University Press.

Somek, A. (2008), Legalität heute: Variationen über ein Thema von Max Weber, *Der Staat* 47, pp. 428-465.

Somek, A. (2009), Administration without Sovereignty, in: Martin Loughlin, Petra Dobner (eds.), *The Twilight of Constitutional Law: Demise or Transmutation?* Oxford: Oxford University Press, pp. 267-286.

Somek, A. (2010), The argument from transnational effects I: Representing outsiders through freedom of movement, *European Law Journal* 16, pp. 315-344.

Stein, E. (1981), Lawyers, Judges, and the Making of a Transnational Constitution, *American Journal of Public International Law* 75, pp. 1-27.

Waitz, G. (1862), *Grundzüge der Politik nebst einzelnen Ausführungen.* Kiel: Homann.

Weber, M. (1966), *Staatssoziologie*, 2nd edition, edited by Johannes Winckelmann. Berlin: Duncker & Humblot.

Weiler, J.H.H. (1999), *The Constitution of Europe.* Cambridge: Cambridge University Press.

The constitutional dérapage of European integration: the dark side of the last two decades of European integration

Agustín José Menèndez

Si é cosi profondi, ormai, che non si ve de più niente. A forza di andare in profondità, si è sprofondati. Soltanto l'intelligenza, l'intelligenza che è anche 'leggerezza', che sa essere 'leggera', può sperare di risalire alla superficialità, alla banalità

Sciascia, Nero su Nero, 717

Bien entendu, on peut sauter sur sa chaise comme un cabri en disant l'Europe!, l'Europe!, l'Europe! ... mais cela n'aboutit à rien et cela ne signifie rien

Charles De Gaulle, 14 December 1965

I   Introduction

There are many good reasons to celebrate the political, economic, and constitutional dimensions of the process of European integration. Any historical comparison between Europe's *Stunde Null* in 1945 and its present configuration would prompt us to consider why a continent devastated by the second war in two generations could transform itself into a union of social and democratic states that have attained unparalleled levels of social justice. A key part of the answer (even if, quite obviously, not the whole of the answer) would be the process of integration unleashed by the Coal and Steel Community, the Economic Community, and the Euratom. As lawyers, we would probably like to stress the key role that community law has played in the process of integration, something which is by itself revealing of the peculiar nature and the very success of the Union. It is telling that the integration process has had law as the social means of integration *of choice*. Community law has become the supranational law of all European lands (even of states which are not full members of the Union). Community law has become the constitutional law through which constitutional states could integrate, and in the process, transform their very identity, from autarchic sovereign states into member states of a federal polity in the making.

This *normative horizon* (*European integration triumphant*) is the one in which most of community lawyers have tended to place themselves, and by that proving the allegedly *engaged* role that legal scholars have played in the process of integration. This chapter will be rather heterodoxical in striking a rather different note. Without putting into question the historical pertinence of most of the narrative and of the *drive* of European legal scholarship, it seems to me that the very *normative engagement* which traditionally underlay legal dogmatics of community law requires us to concentrate on the emerging *dark side*, not only of European politics, but also of European law.

Indeed, the central thesis of this article is that community law entered into an existential crisis already in the late 1970s, and that after a long and uncompleted constitutional season, such crisis has resulted in a *clear regression* of European integration, if we assess it by reference to the normative standards of the European (one should always say Hellerian) social and democratic *Rechtsstaat*. In particular, I will refer to three basic developments in that regard: Firstly, the emergence of a *structural democratic deficit* as a result of the coupling of judge-crafted economic freedoms with horizontal constitutional force and a consequently fragmented political decision-making process after the Single European Act. Secondly, the grave democratic shortcomings of the Lisbon process leading to the Lisbon Treaty, which did not only reverse the democratic *achievements* of the Laeken process (very especially the affirmation of the power of citizens to decide on constitutional reforms, as proven by the consequences of the negative vote in France and in the Netherlands) and substituted them by naked executive dominance, but also has led to a major questioning of the very core substance of community law (in particular, through negotiation around the Charter of Fundamental Rights). Thirdly, the virtual foreclosure of democratic decision-making (and for that matter, genuinely political decision-making) on what concerns socio-economic policy, resulting from both the asymmetric design of Economic and Monetary Union and from the peculiar way in which the manifold crisis of the last five years has been governed at the supranational and national levels.

I am no Eurosceptic. On the contrary, my claim is that European integration has reached the point in which Altiero Spinelli's thesis that the only relevant political cleavage was that separating those in favour of integration and those against integration has to be nuanced. Because we do not only have the ideal of Europe, but a really existing and much developed European Union, the proper realisation of the socio-economic objectives of the democratic *Rechtsstaat* cannot be trusted to the growth of competences, to further integration ('More Europe' cry those who claim themselves to be 'pro-federal', a ragbag including odd bedfellows such as Schäuble and Fischer). Not only the automaticity is no longer there, but also the politics of different integration options is far from homogeneous. The task of public law is not of course to predetermine which of these options is to be followed, but should ideally be to make us aware of the risk of options being simply wiped out, and thus the process of democratic will formation being foreclosed. And that is unfortunately the trend into which the process of European integration has been moving in the last decades.

115

II   The Three Nemeses of Democracy in Europe

1   Structural and substantive review of European constitutionality and the division of competences

At first sight, the bold proportionality review of national laws seems to result from the transposition to the supranational level of the practice of national constitutional courts when protecting fundamental rights. Given the key role that such courts played (in some Member States) in the consolidation of national democracies in the critical early decades of postwar period, the European "copying and pasting" of the national constitutional syntax would seem to be entirely comendable. However, two caveats must be added. The first one is that the critical reconstruction of the case law of the European Court of Justice reveals that the standard three-stepped reconstruction of proportionality (adequacy, necessity, and proportionality) pays insufficient attention to two previous and occasionally decisive steps, namely, the elucidation of the constitutional principles underlying the colliding norms, and the assignment of the argumentative benefit and burden. In these two steps, courts contribute to the concretisation (conceptualisation) of the conflicting principles and determine how the conflict is to be understood: from which principle, so to say, are we going to start the argument? The second is that proportionality is a formal principle; this necessarily entails that resort to proportionality guarantees the formal correctness of the decision, but cannot ensure the substantive correctness of the decision. That cannot but depend on the substantive justifiability of the substantive choices with which the formal argumentative syntax of proportionality is 'filled in'. Indeed, far from being a *legitimising* principle, proportionality must be understood as a critical analytical tool, equipped with which we can reveal the substantive choices made by a court, and assess whether they are properly grounded on previous legal authoritative decisions, on good substantive reasons put forward by a court, or on the contrary, are largely unjustified.

In a second sight, so to say, the ECJ practice reveals itself as far from self-justified. Indeed, if we take seriously the structure of proportionality and what it entails, we are forced to engage into a critical analysis of what the ECJ has been doing. This leads me to four key problems in the fleshing out of European constitutional law in the jurisprudence. Firstly, I find that the while the affirmation that economic freedoms constitute a key part of the canon of European constitutionality is well-grounded, the European Court of Justice has shifted its characterisation of economic freedoms from operationalisations of the principle of non-discrimination on the basis of nationality and building blocks of a common market, to concretisations of a self-standing and transcendental economic freedom and vanguard of the single market. Such a shift may seem to have been endorsed (even if, *ex post casu*) by the Treaty amendments introduced by the Single European Market and the Treaty of Maastricht. However, I claim that it remains hard to reconcile with the constitutional identity of the European Union and impossible to square with the constitutional identity of the member states as social and democratic *Rechtsstaaten*. Indeed, it seems to me much more plausible to conclude that the jurisprudence of the European Courts took a *wrong turn* when it shifted from one conception of economic freedoms to the other, or what is the same, that *Cassis de Dijon* and the later jurisprudence expanding the 'obstacles' conception of breaches to economic freedoms are properly characterised as part of a 'constitutional dérapage' in the development of Community law. Secondly, I find extremely problematic the tendency of the European Court of Justice to invariably assign the argumentative benefit to the economic freedoms and the argumentative burden to the principle underlying the colliding norm. That is difficult to reconcile with the fact that fundamental rights have long been acknowledged to be part of the yardstick of European constitutionality, and become formally and undeniably so after the formal incorporation of the Charter of Fundamental Rights to the primary law of the Union. The opinions of Advocate General Geelhoed in *American Tobacco* and of Advocate General Cruz Villalón in *Santos Coelho* could be so constructed as to become precedents of a more flexible and balanced approach. Thirdly, I have serious objections to the standards that the European Court of Justice employs to determine the probability of events when assessing the adequacy and necessity of the norms colliding with an economic freedom. While the ECJ assumes without paying much attention to any evidence that all breaches of economic freedoms would result in a *grave infringement*, it eventually sets a too high threshold to prove the adequacy and necessity of infringing norms. This can be illustrated by reference to the fully unrealistic assumptions the ECJ makes on the alternative means on the hands of member states to ensure the effectiveness of fiscal supervision (flatly contradicted by the several legislative initiatives of the Commission, only partially successful, to increase the degree of tax assistance, especially in the form of automatic exchange of tax data). Fourthly, the European Court of Justice tends to fail to approach on its own terms the principles underpinning the norms colliding with economic freedoms. The breadth and scope of these principles is not only defined in the most restrictive manner, but the inner normative logic of these principles tends to be neglected. This may well be exemplified by considering the peculiar characterisation of the overriding national interest in the coherence of the national tax system. These four major flows combine into the two major structural problems of the case law, already mentioned: (1) the maximalistic understanding of the constitutional force of economic freedoms, turned de facto and de jure into the yardstick of validity of all national norms; (2) the ideologically biased understanding of what faculties the economic freedoms comprise, what they entitle the holders of such economic freedoms to do. Viking and Laval, shocking as they were, are but mere scribblings in the margins of a case law which was launched by Cassis de Dijon, and which has rendered dysfunctional progressive tax systems and social expenditure programmes since. The rub of the matter, as also already mentioned, is that these biases are hard to rectify through politics. Starting with the Single European Act, and under the rationale of empowering the European Parliament, and thus improving the democratic legitimacy of the European Union, European decision-making processes have been split. In some areas (essentially those relating to market-making) there has been a shift towards co-decision and consequently majoritarian processes, while on the matters that concern the core of the Social and Democratic Rechtsstaat, the old unanimitarian Community method has resisted. After enlargement, rectifying the ECJ so as to defend and guard socio-economic protections requires unanimity within the Council, a unanimity which is so elusive that the Commission does rarely bother to launch legislative initiatives beyond the occasional strategic and symbolic one (like the one on the European "Tobin" tax, born dead from the presses).

2   Executive Constitutionalism: Laeken and Lisbon

In general terms, the mounting tensions cumulating within the process of European constitutional synthesis resulted in Laeken and Lisbon as representing two attempts at transcending the synthetic constitutional path through which the Union has trod in its first fifty years of history; they can be characterized as attempts at transcending constitutional synthesis.[1] It is to be noticed that Laeken and Lisbon seemed at first glance to have been intended to redraw the constitutional path of the Union in opposite directions: towards a full-blown constitutional track through a constitutional moment (Laeken), and towards an *octroyé* constitutionalism through an executively controlled change in the substantive content of the primary law of the Union, justified by the rhetorics of 'constitutional crisis'.

---

[1]   On the meaning and implications of the theory of constitutional synthesis, see John Erik Fossum and Agustín José Menéndez (2011), The Constitution's Gift, Lanham: Rowman and Littlefield.

(a)   Laeken

Laeken was partially propelled by the vision of a constitutional moment, in which *We the People* writes or rewrites the constitution. The signalling act of the process, the Laeken Declaration, was the first occasion at which the reform of the primary law of the Union was framed in explicit constitutional terms (indeed, quite cunningly, the European Parliament avoided the constitutional idiom in 1984). The Laeken Declaration (2001) was thus by many seen as an appropriate response to Joschka Fischer's clarion call in 2000 for a European federation founded on a democratic constitution. The Laeken Declaration also included a new reform vehicle that further seemed to amplify or give credence to its constitutional vocation, namely the Convention on the Future of Europe.[2]

However, it should be stressed that on both these counts, the actual situation was more ambiguous. While clearly more inspired by the federalist vocation of the Belgian Presidency, and clearly more so than previous treaty reform platforms, the final text of the Laeken Declaration was the product of consensus making in the European Council, which rendered the constitutional foundation of the reform more of an afterthought than of an explicit constitutional reform mandate. The upshot was that the constitutional nature of the eventual Reform Treaty was merely hinted at. The literal tenor of the Declaration, steeped as it was in the spirit and language of 'simplifying reforms', or 'simplification',[3] noted that this might require the drafting of a text of constitutional import (a phrase that revealed its political overtones in its substantively illogical nature).[4] Further, the Laeken Declaration's ambiguous constitutional vocation also shown up in the formal role assigned to the Convention: The Laeken Declaration merely set the Convention up with the limited remit to produce one or several *reform proposals* for the subsequent IGC. This formally assigned role is indicative of the clever underlying political strategy of simultaneously seeking to placate what were diametrically different positions and underlying conceptions of the charac-

---

2   This was clearly inspired by the success of the Convention that forged the Charter of Fundamental Rights of the European Union and was also recognition of the dismal failure of the Nice IGC to produce a viable treaty reform.

3   Paul Magnette has argued that 'In the context of this Convention, the notion of "simplification" soon became the label of minimum compromise the members could reach, and the conceptual tool used to forge it.' See Paul Magnette (2005), In the Name of Simplification: Coping with Constitutional Conflicts in the Convention on the Future of Europe, European Law Journal 11, pp. 432-451.

4   'The question ultimately arises as to whether this simplification and reorganisation might not lead in the long run to the adoption of a constitutional text in the Union. What might the basic features of such a constitution be? The values which the Union cherishes, the fundamental rights and obligations of its citizens, the relationship between Member States in the Union?'

ter of the EU within the European Council. Labelling a Convention immediately brought up the association to the Philadelphia Convention, a body of high symbolic constitutional salience (even if the ambiguity of Philadelphia in democratic terms escaped the attention of most observers, perhaps uninterested in substantive American constitutional history); but then at the same time confining it to a formal role of preparative body was akin to effectively ascribing it (or circumscribing it) to a body more similar to the Reflection Group that had preceded the Amsterdam Treaty than to a constitutional assembly proper.

There was however considerable support for a European constitutional arrangement outside, but notably also within, the Convention. Valery Giscard d'Estaing, the Convention President, was well aware of the fact that a vast majority of the Convention was willing to reach an ambiguous agreement, or at the very least ambiguous enough as to reinforce their own profile in European history. He thus affirmed during the first session that the Convention should try to achieve 'broad consensus on a single proposal (…) (that) would thus open the way towards a Constitution for Europe.' In so doing it is fair to argue that the Convention sought to exceed beyond its initial formal mandate and instead set itself up and act *as if* it were a constitution-making body. Thus the Convention not only appropriated an explicit constitutional mandate, it also set itself the concrete task of writing a constitutional proposal.

In its first weeks, this also seemed to be its main game, and with it came efforts to heighten the democratic legitimacy of a body with rather convoluted and mixed democratic credentials. The Convention also seemed intent on addressing itself to the European public, as attempts were made to gain visibility in national public debates, and even to connect to civil society organisations (although the latter seem to be more inspired by the aim of managing public relations than by a sincere constitutional intention). The latter, however, came to be highly critical of what they saw as a top-down Convention-run orchestration rather than inclusion of civil society actors,[5] and civil society organisations complained that the Convention offered limited access and paid even less heed to the concerns of civil society organisations.

As time progressed it became increasingly clear that the Convention would not and could not foster a constitutional moment for Europe (a constitutional moment that would realise the democratic potential of the rewriting of the primary law of the Union and thus ensure the democratic legitimacy of the Union in a direct and unmediated way). The main reason for this resided in the fact that, whereas the Convention declared itself as a constitution-making body, the European Council would still be the body with treaty-based authority to amend the

5   This was for instance expressly stated in connection with the Youth Convention. Interview with civil society activist.

EU's material constitution. This was a major structural constraint that the Convention leadership was not only wholly aware of, but also as the process proceeded proved well ready to accept and to ensure through political manipulation.[6] The Convention leadership, through contacts and various other means, structured the Convention's work in such a manner as to ensure that it could anticipate in an on-going manner what the European Council would accept from its work.[7] The upshot was for the Convention to have to pay a rather high price for raising the constitutional card. In thus aligning itself with the European Council it effectively eluded the political constitutional terrain, and instead framed its constitutional role in the language of consolidation and simplification of Community law. The unavoidable political battle in any constitution-making process, the battle for the constitutional soul of the polity, was thus basically avoided. This meant that the Convention largely shirked away from clarifying the political stakes and the larger polity and constitutional implications of the many specific reform proposals that were addressed. For instance, when the time came to decide on the primacy of the constitutional law of the European Union, the political implications of the issue were hidden behind legal expertise on the present state of Community law. The normatively loaded choice of the term 'law' as a substitute for 'regulations' and 'directives' was presented as a mere exercise in clarification. The incorporation of the Charter of Fundamental Rights was justified on its being a mere consolidation of existing law; and still, instead of opening the constitutional text, it was confined to an intermediary section between the constitution proper and the set of norms of constitutional import proper. This formal abandonment of the constitutional ground paved the way for the progressive involution of Laeken from a moment of constitutional promise to at most an exercise in managed constitution making.

Key to this re-orientation was clearly the European Council, and the imprint it had on the Convention's work. This was apparent in the ambiguous role attributed to the Convention and the strong steer the European Council exerted (mainly if not exclusively through the appointment of the Convention leadership). This effectively led to a major re-orientation to the Convention's main constituency. The Convention was of course barred from making a constitutional proposal directly to the people. Instead, precisely because it had been inters-

6   The presidency and the presidium played a central role in this regard according to George Tsebelis and Sven-Oliver Proksch (2007), The Art of Political Manipulation in the European Convention, Journal of Common Market Studies 45, pp. 157-86.

7   Each national government had its own government representative in the Convention. The European Council went so far in its steer as to decide the identity of the three leading members of the Convention, its president and its two vice-presidents Valéry Giscard d'Estaing was nominated President, and Giuliano Amato and Jean Luc Dehane Vice-Presidents.

persed into the IGC treaty amendment framework rather than replacing it, the Convention had to concentrate much of its effort – if it wanted a material result that would last – on ensuring safe passage of its draft through the next, European Council stage. This effectively altered its main constituency from: *We the European Peoples*, to *We the European Council*. Such a re-orientation was symbolised through several leading member states directly participating in the Convention through their foreign ministers, which in itself gave a strong governmental steer to the Convention process. This was later translated into the generalisation of the argument of 'second-guessing', namely rendering part of the process of constitutional debate an assessment of whether a given drafting will be *acceptable* to the IGC, thus losing sight of the fact that constitutional acceptability cannot but be dependent on what the final holder of the constituent power thinks (*We the People*). With the benefit of hindsight, the change of audience was the first step towards the ratification disaster of the spring of 2005.

Second was the act of appropriation of constitution-making power by the European Council itself. The European Council was after all the body in charge of treaty amendment and it exercised this role also through the Convention. This was readily apparent through the way it set the Convention up and also on the constraints it imposed on the Convention's operations. This appropriation of constitution-making power by the European Council took place within the confines of the Convention. Government representatives – notably *foreign ministers* serving as government representatives – were part of the Convention's deliberations but they would also *re-enter the process as direct participants* at the deciding, European Council, stage. Each government was equipped with veto at the European Council meeting; hence, the government representatives in the Convention – and notably the foreign ministers – could exercise credible quasi-veto threats in the Convention. This also made one author refer to the Convention as 'deliberating in the shadow of the veto'.[8] Another element of this appropriation is seen in the fact that the European Council had directed the Convention to work within a fixed time frame: the Convention was given a year to deliver its proposal(s).[9] Despite requests for more time, the time limit was only very modestly increased, and this worked as a major constraint on the Convention. This became particularly evident when the European Council denied the Convention time to debate Part Three, a decision that upset many Convention members (and proved

8   See Paul Magnette (2004), Deliberation or Bargaining? Coping with Constitutional Conflicts in the Convention on the Future of Europe, in: Erik Oddvar Eriksen, John Erik Fossum, Agustin José Menéndez (eds.), Developing a Constitution for Europe. London: Routledge, pp. 207-225.

9   'Proceedings will be completed after a year, that is to say in time for the Chairman of the Convention to present its outcome to the European Council'. See the Laeken Declaration on the Future of the European Union.

deadly in national ratification debates, very especially in France). This effectively substituted the Convention with a set of national legal experts, contradicting the very purpose of simplifying the primary law of the Union and notably the very idea that the exercise was an exercise in constitution making. Inserting the entire body of specific provisions that makes up Part Three into the document labelled the Constitutional Treaty cannot but be understood as devaluing the constitutional currency of the draft.

The European Council's appropriation of constitution-making power was further confirmed by the decision to convene an IGC which considered the Convention Draft as a mere point of departure (proving the naiveté of the calls for the IGC to rubber-stamp the Convention's draft, and the self-defeating character of the Convention second-guessing the IGC). This subjected the draft to diplomatic hardball (and the rather peculiar Berlusconi's seduction tactics, which did not necessarily impress his colleagues, even if they sold newspapers) in the Brussels European Council of December 2003, when the parties failed to come to agreement. The fate of the draft was thereafter the subject of the diplomatic manoeuvrings of the Irish presidency during the winter of 2004, when the Irish presidency through secretive bilateral meetings sought to build up enough support to restart the IGC.

Thirdly and finally, the ratification debates were designed as endorsement processes, in which the rather empty constitutional shell of the draft approved by the IGC was to be mobilised so as to ensure a pacific consensual debate. This would take place in the standard IGC ratification context. The Constitutional Treaty would enter into force if and only if all member states of the European Union were to ratify it (former Article 48 of the Treaty of European Union, confirmed by Article 448 of the Constitutional Treaty).[10] These ratification provisions were based on unanimity and national idiosyncrasy (in terms of procedure and timing). They sat better with the notion of international law as a legal order *equal but separate* from national legal orders,[11] than they do with any possible

---

10 The Constitutional Treaty did contemplate modest changes in the amendment rules applicable once it entered into force. Besides making the convening of a Convention part of the standard amendment procedure (but not a mandatory requirement), some streamlined procedures were contemplated for some of the provisions contained in Part III of the Constitutional Treaty (policies). Paradoxically enough, such changes were introduced by the Intergovernmental Conference, and were not to be found in the draft elaborated by the Convention.

11 Under such a conception, international law determines in a fully autonomous way the legal force of its own norms *within its scope of application* (basically, in relations between states), each national legal order is equally autonomous to determine the *legal force of international norms* within the scope of application of national law; national courts and administration are in most cases bound by their own national constitution to follow the latter characterisation when in conflict with the one stemming from international law.

notion of a European constitutional order. These ratification rules also stand in clear tension to the common constitutional standards as a regulatory ideal. It is this norm set that can serve as *autonomous norms*, as the norms that render credible the quintessential democratic notion, namely that citizens have given themselves the norms, rather than have had the norms heteronomously imposed upon themselves. Such a normative condition cannot be satisfied by a ratification procedure that only counts *aggregate national wills*, and does not consider the *individual will* of each citizen.

It is important to note that the simultaneous persistence of the *unanimity rule* and the *national idiosyncratic rule* resulted in different national ratification procedures *explicitly* or *implicitly* characterising the Constitutional Treaty in *different legal-constitutional* terms. Thus, the 25 national decisions were only apparently *decisions on the same thing*; substantially, they are better understood as a *collection of different types of decision*, not only due to the eventual endorsement or rejection of the text, but due to the fact that they would be rejections or endorsements of different things, of different legal qualifications of the text. Indeed, the national ratification procedures in place actually reflect the three main conceptions of what the legal norms to be ratified are: a) a standard international treaty,[12] b) a hybrid between international treaty and constitutional norms, which can be labelled as a European integration treaty[13] (which can also be defined as an international treaty with wide constitutional implications), and c) a constitution.[14] That further proves the progressive abandonment of the idea of Laeken as a democratic constitutional moment. At any rate, both *positive* and *negative* outcomes of the ratification process became necessarily problematic. While the persistence of the unanimity and the national idiosyncratic rules are premised on the respect for national constitutional autonomy, which is said to require allowing for different characterisations of the text to be ratified, the *pragmatic* implication of the persistence of these rules results in different *democratic weights* of different national decisions. In abstract terms, the closer the national ratification procedure comes to characterise the Constitutional Treaty as a Constitution, the more weight it will have in shaping the final result of the ratification process.[15]

12 Article 121 of the Estonian Constitution, as there is no specific procedure for European treaties, but only for treaties 'by which the Republic of Estonia joins international organisations or unions' and 'the implementation of which requires the passage, amendment or repeal of Estonian laws'.
13 Article 23 of the German Constitution contains the European clause.
14 As is implicit in the choice of a referendum, and on the scrutinising of the Constitutional Treaty in accordance with the national constitution.
15 Thus, *the pursuit of the formal equality of all Member States and the respect of their national institutional autonomy* actually results in creating wide differences in weight and importance between states and ratification procedures.

On such a basis, the choice of a given procedure to ratify the Constitutional Treaty (and very significantly, whether citizens should be given the voice directly, through the holding of a referendum or through the election of a special body of representatives to take such a decision, or through general elections focused on the issue) should not only be regarded as a discretionary *national* issue, but also as a choice that determines the relative weight to be assigned to each national decision, to each positive or negative constitutional verdict, given the different degrees of fit between national procedures and the claim to constitutionality of the Constitutional Treaty.

The paradoxical outcome of Laeken was that the initial democratic constitutional promise was slowly but steadily rendered hollow, but in the very last moment was re-appropriated by French and Dutch citizens, only to say resoundingly 'no' to the concrete text with which they were being presented. By taking seriously the pretence of the process to be a constitutional moment, they engaged in a constitutional debate, and exercised the constitutional power of saying 'no' to the proposed text. Whether their act is properly to be characterised as an instance of *Fiat democratia, perit Europa* is another question

(b)   Lisbon

The very fact that the *non* of the French and the *nee* of the Dutch people put an end to the Laeken process constituted a confirmation *rigor mortis* of its constitutional nature *all through*. But quite ironically, the constitutional promise of the 'no' could not be transformed into a positive constitutional force precisely because Laeken floundered. The very institutions and structures rejected by *We the European Peoples* would have been more amenable to a positivisation of the democratic force underpinning the 'no'. A rather unsurprising dynamic was then unleashed, consisting in the progressive affirmation of an alternative way of transcending constitutional synthesis, namely the Lisbon strategy of appropriation of constitution-making power by national executives interacting in a rather managerial way.[16] The long and apparently sterile period of reflection following Laeken, during which national governments pretended to be fostering a debate

16   'The rejection of the *Treaty Establishing a Constitution for Europe* in referendums in France and the Netherlands has brought about a crisis in the EU.' See House of Commons, The Future of the European Constitution, Research Paper 05/45, available at http://www.parliament.uk/commons/lib/research/rp2005/rp05-045.pdf. Academic assessments of this crisis abound. See for instance Thomas König, Stephanie Daimer and Daniel Finke (2008), The Treaty Reform of the EU: Constitutional Agenda-Setting, Intergovernmental Bargains and the Presidency's Crisis Management of Ratification Failure, Journal of Common Market Studies 46, pp. 337-363.

on how to revive Laeken, was in reality the incubation period of a model of 'crisis constitution making'. It characterised Laeken as the foremost example of the embrace of the radical mirage of democratic constitution making in the European Union (which it was not, for the reasons which have just been laid out) and slowly but steadily presented to the public the idea that the reckless decision to open ratification to excessive and chaotic public participation (through the vehicle of referenda) had resulted in a crisis, which could only be solved by national governments mobilising their political judgment and technical expertise.

The reading was that Laeken failed because democratic constitution making was impossible at the European level. Some of the elites George Ross interviewed 'criticized Giscard d'Estaing and his Presidium for «pretentious and provocative" insistence on turning the Convention into an assembly with Philadelphia-like constitutional claims.'[17] Besides the strange persistence of the association of Philadelphia with democratic constitution making, this revealed the implicit belief that the kind of reforms the Union needed could be implemented if constitutional politics were avoided, and provided the cover under which it could be proposed that the traditional IGC model was disentangled from the democratising add-ons that had emerged through the Union's constitutional history (and indeed, we would claim, reversely engineered in a more executive fashion than ever). In other words, the solution was to formally revert back to the IGC understood as a classical secretive – diplomatic – inter-governmental conference mode of treaty amendment, and, in doing so, change the constitutional path, from that of constitutional synthesis to one of *octroyé constitutionalism*, in which the elites *do take the constitutional decisions* in the name of the people *without* the people.

The second concurrent rationale of the move was the just referred constitutional crisis that the misguided attempt at engaging in democratic constitution making at the European level had precipitated could be overcome if the heads of national governments would engage in pragmatic negotiations, and would make use of all their political leverage to get the text ratified by national parliaments without opening the constitutional Pandora's box of national referenda. From a democratic perspective, such referenda would prove unnecessary because the reforms to be undertaken were *managerial*, not *political*. The crisis facing the Union was economic: 'since the early 1990s ...the core European national economies [had failed] to grow and modernize.'[18] The Union's legitimacy credit needed to be replenished through *efficiency*, not democracy. Part of the problem

17   George Ross (2008), What do "Europeans" Think? Analyses of the European Union's Current Crisis by European Elites, Journal of Common Market Studies 46, pp. 389-412, at 402.
18   Ibid, p. 398.

facing the EU was a significant 'communications failure'; people lacked proper information on the many good things that the EU did for them.

In line with this reading, all the TEC's references to 'constitution' and other 'state-like' symbols, such as the characterisation of Community legal acts as laws and framework laws, flag, and national anthem were removed from the Lisbon Treaty. By removing the term constitution and state-type language and symbols, the European Council sought to reassure Europe's peoples that the EU was not a state; neither did it have the vocation to become one. Further, by removing all direct symbolic associations to constitution, they sought to declare that the Lisbon Treaty was not of constitutional salience, and hence did not require to be put to the people in popular referenda.

Similarly, the characterisation of Laeken as a failed constitutional project appeased qualms about the utter secrecy in which the Lisbon Treaty was drafted. The UK House of Commons European Scrutiny Committee concluded that it was 'an essentially secret drafting process conducted by the Presidency, with texts produced at the last moment before pressing for agreement. The compressed timetable now proposed, having regard to the sitting terms of national parliaments, could not have been better designed to marginalise their role.' [19] In this sense it could be argued that the Lisbon Treaty came about through a particular version of the IGC, that is, it was forged by a more secretive and self-referential type of IGC than the EU had used since the SEA. This approach has again shown its limits by now. The alleged efficiency of executive bargaining is contradicted by the baroque nature of the reforms endorsed by the Lisbon Treaty. The rhetoric of urgent crisis is contradicted by the long time that will pass before law-making takes place according to simplified rules;[20] while the very constitutional substance of European integration is clearly put into question by the strange opt-out clause concerning the Charter of Fundamental Rights of the European Union, 'a veritable dog's dinner, and not only due to its abominable drafting'.[21] The removal of the provision on the primacy of EU law from the body of the text in the TEC (eliminates Article I-6) increases uncertainty about the status of EU law. And the very possibility of orderly managed ratification was contradicted by the strange victory of the 'no' in the Irish referendum.

The Treaty will not add to, but may subtract from, the legitimacy basis of the European Union. Consider the remarkable constitutional double-talk: when we

19 UK House of Commons European Scrutiny Committee, 35th Report, Session 2006-07. p. 24, available at http://www.parliament.the-stationery-office.com/pa/cm200607/cmselect/-cmeuleg/1014/101402.htm.
20 Thus, the Lisbon voting rules easing qualified majority voting may take up to ten years to enter into force.
21 Michael Dougan (2008), The Treaty of Lisbon 2007: Winning Minds, not Hearts, Common Market Law Review 45, pp. 617-703.

consider how the leaders presented the Lisbon Treaty, we find quite contradictory renditions. There was a clear 'tendency of each Member State to sell the TL [Treaty of Lisbon] to its own domestic audience: countries which had previously ratified the CT promised their constituents that the TL was identical in every meaningful respect; those which had rejected the CT or wished to avoid putting it to a popular vote vowed that the TL was fundamentally different from its predecessor.'[22] Media across Europe has picked up on this mixed message, which will not increase citizens' trust in the process or in the leaders in charge of it.

Within this confusing setting, European constitutional norms are likely to be increasingly experienced as foreign, as radically heteronomous, and as such lacking the democratic dignity which in a *Rechtsstaat* is a precondition for citizens' voluntary compliance with them.

3   The Fiscal Crisis of European Integration

The Maastricht Treaty in 1991 and the Stability and Growth Pact in 1997 created a very asymmetric Economic and Monetary Union. On the face of it, monetary policy was federalised and depoliticised (not only the "federal" ECB, but also its "federal" components, national central banks, were to be configured as autonomous institutions, "freed" from political pressures and political cycles), while fiscal policies remained national and very political. The coherence of this unique and unprecedented split policy mix was trusted to "governance" arrangements (broad economic policy guidelines, open coordination within the Eurogroup) and to the disciplinary force of financial markets. For ten years, it seemed to work gingerly. EMU seemed to be homogeneising income and wealth within the Eurozone. In reality, as we know, EMU masked growing divergence, papering income and wealth differences with the flows of credit. From a political standpoint, it is important to notice that the formal national political autonomy was highly conditioned by the different structural position of the different States, which created powerful incentives to follow peculiar strategies of adaptation: exporting competitiveness in the Euro-core, real estate and consumption bubbles in the South, and specialisation on tax avoidance in the Benelux.

But if the design of EMU was unhappy, the way in which the consequences of such unhappy design have been dealt with since the explosion of the various European crises has been even more deleterious for European democracy. The "government" of the crisis seems to be in the verge of transforming the monstruous EMU into a full-size constitutional Frankenstein, which is increasingly

---

22   Michael Dougan (2008), The Treaty of Lisbon 2007: Winning Minds, not Hearts, Common Market Law Review 45, pp. 617-703

escaping any kind of political control. A full and systematic analysis is beyond my mandate and space here. Perhaps two constitutional "vignettes" would be sufficient to illustrate the extent to which European leaders have engaged into the search for empty constitutional spaces, confirming their aspiration- already visible in the Lisbon process- to become the puovoir constituent in the EU, and escape not only the democratic mandates shaped into constitutional constrains, but even public law in toto.

First: Among the tumble and fury of the eurozone crisis, a rather revealing story has been largely missed by the European public, and, to my knowledge, by European legal scholars. It is well known that in the rather stuffy nights of five days of May 2010 (critically, it seems on the European Council of 7-8 May), the decision to create a European Financial Stability Mechanism was adopted. This was said at the time to constitute a gigantic step to avoid the contagion of the fiscal implosion of Greece to other member states of the eurozone. This said Mechanism was rendered operative by a so-called European Financial Stability Facility. Relying on the guarantees provided by the member states of the eurozone (and decisively, of the AAA rated debts of Germany, France, and the Netherlands), the fund will raise money in the financial markets and will successively render that money available to the troika, so that it could lend it to countries suffering a liquidity crisis. What is less known but very telling is that the European Financial Stability Facility is legally speaking a *société anonyme* incorporated in Luxembourg, which apparently had the Luxembourgeois government as its sole shareholder, and of which the other eurozone member states became shareholders in a second step in early June 2010. These choices have been justified in the name of the speed necessary to actually make the arrangements work and avoid that uncertainty frustrated the goal of avoiding contagion. But the symbolism of the decision is hard to avoid. And its legal implications are far from banal. Firstly, this *legal* form is the one characteristic of hedge funds. So instead of public law, constitutional law, and administrative law shaping fundamental financial commitments of member states on which the future of our socio-economic order depends, we find the framework of the private law long used to serve as the vehicle of transnational capital. Secondly, the site of the Fund is Luxembourg (land of the hedge funds, and, according to the recent extremely well-documented book of Nicholas Saxshon[23], a tax haven at the core of Europe, as the French Parliament had already hinted at years ago). Thirdly, the appointed director of the European Financial Stability Facility, Klaus Regling, has a mixed background as a eurocrat and 'hedgie', in the very terms that *The Economist* used to comment upon his nomination.[24] This is not a vignette from which we

---

23   Nicholas Saxshon (2011), Treasure Islands, London: Bodley Head.
24   Chief bail-out officer, The new head of the euro-zone SPV, The Economist, 1 July 2010.

can conclude that public law and administrative law is *triumphant*. On the contrary, this is a story that tells us quite a lot about how public power has managed to escape the discipline of public law. And perhaps it speaks volumes about the actual implications of the repeated commitments to fight tax evasion on the side of the European Council, or of the convoluted compromise to harmonise the corporate income tax base included literally in a dark corner of the Euro Plus Pact. Not to talk of what it seems to bode for some of the interesting initiatives that the Commission has managed to launch from time to time (from the incomplete but fundamental savings income taxation directive of 2003, which put forward the idea of automatic exchange of information, to the recent administrative cooperation new directive, which would enlarge the categories of income for which there would be such an automatic exchange of information).

Second: the very establishment of the European Financial Stability Mechanism and Facility had been surrounded by a very polarised debate on the proper interpretation of certain articles of the Treaty on the Functioning of the European Union (provisions which, perhaps should be added, had remained unchanged since they were made part of the primary law of the European Union), and by extension, on the national and European constitutionality of providing financial assistance to a member state in financial dire straits.

Act I: as soon as the newly elected Greek prime minister informed his peers in the European Council on 10 December 2009 that the Greek deficit was on steroids, contrary to the estimates of the previous incumbent government led by Karamanlis Jr. (and, not without relevance, Papandreou, also Jr., further confessing to his peers the utterly corrupt state of the Greek political system and state, if we are to believe, and we have good reasons to do that, Tony Barber of the *Financial Times*),[25] it became rather obvious that it was a matter of time that the Hellenic State will run short of money. The federalisation of monetary policy deprived Greece (and all other member states) of the power to monetise the deficit by simply printing money. At the same time, Article 124 of the TFEU bars member states from using their sovereign powers to force financial institutions to extend credit on privileged, even less compulsory terms (a subject matter which caught the eye of a young scholar in the 1970s named Anibal Cavaco Silva[26]: history is very frequently rather ironic).[27] It was just a matter of time that the Greek state had to suspend payments for lack of financial resources. In the early

---

25   Tony Barber, 'Saving the euro: Tall ambition, flawed foundations', Financial Times, 11 October 2010.
26   "Forced Loans" in: D. Greenway and G.K. Shaw (eds.), Public choice, public finance, and public policy: essays in honour of Alan Peacock, Oxford: Blackwell, 1995.
27   For another Euro-irony, see Gordon Brown (ed.) (1975), Red paper on Scotland, Edinburgh: Edinburgh University Press.

weeks of 2010, however, the media informed us that the German Chancellor came equipped to all European meetings with copies of the Lisbon judgment of the German Constitutional Court (which might have been a matter of either inaccurate press-reporting, as the decisive judgment is that rendered on the Maastricht Treaty, so perhaps Merkel had copies of the two judgments; or perhaps the media was right, and other European political leaders took for granted that a Chancellor has immanent constitutional knowledge) and argued once and again that the no bail-out clause, the prohibition of acquisition of public debt by the European Central Bank or national central banks, together with the German Constitutional Court characterisation of the 'German' constitutionality of the monetary union as dependent on the monetary union guaranteeing financial stability, rendered any collective European solution to the Greek problem rather impossible *on account* of its being *doubly* unconstitutional: against the treaties as the constitutional charter of the Union and against the German Constitution. To this view, it was opposed that such an interpretation of the treaties did not take proper account of Article 122(2) TFEU, which let the door open to a modicum of financial assistance to one member state in case that state was affected by an unforeseeable event beyond its control. That Article would be of application because the trigger of the financial crisis of the Hellenic State was the financial crisis, on the wings since at the end of 2006 the American real estate market came to a halt, and fully unleashed by the momentous decision of ex-Goldman Sachs banker Henry Paulson letting Lehman Brothers fall. The moral of this first act seems to be that the German government flirted with the idea of *Fiat germanica constitutio, perit Europae*, or perhaps with the convenience of obtaining now what could not be obtained in 1999, that is, the definition of Euroland as an already optimum currency area. Counterclaimants endorsed a position that necessarily entailed that what had befallen Greece was a disaster of which the Greek state/government/citizenship was not responsible, or at the very least, was not fully responsible. So what was required was some form of financial solidarity, which quite obviously could not aptly be administered along IMF policy lines.

Act II: a compromise emerged at some point in March. Eventual stability concerns on the side of the German Constitutional Court could be assuaged by providing financial assistance to Greece *outside* of the Community framework (by means of bilateral loans somehow coordinated; something vaguely reminded us of the Austrian sanctions of 2000), and by subjecting such assistance to rather strict conditions. Not only will assistance be in the form of *loans* and not of *grants*, but the rates of such loans would be far from being concessional (so that, cunningly and rather puzzlingly, it was claimed that creditor states will reap a handsome profit, as they could borrow at much lower rates in the markets and lend it to Greece at a rather higher rate of interest), and, more to the point, the assisted member state would have its financial sovereignty in suspension for as long as the assistance persisted, as it would be required to follow *drastic* adjustment plans aimed at regaining competitiveness through internal deflation (which under the parameters of the monetary union, meant a reduction in real wage levels). In the public imagination, strict conditionality was confirmed by the rather odd decision to get the IMF involved in the process (something which carried with it a paraphernalia of peculiar legal sources, which perhaps should be the task of global administrative lawyers to systematise, such as the Memoranda of Understanding). But not only is such involvement justified in technical terms provided one accepts that assistance has to follow a conditionality pattern (as the IMF has been very long on the business, which is not the case of the Commission or the European Central Bank), but also participants' accounts reveal that the IMF personnel has tended to be less narrow-minded than the European ones (as the well-known Portuguese legal sociologist Boaventura dos Santos has recently commented as part of the negotiating term of his country).[28] The moral of this second act is that the search for a solution compatible with a certain interpretation of German constitutional law (the Chancellor's Office's) has resulted in the alleged finding of a constitutional 'empty space', where neither German constitutional law nor European constitutional law are applicable: hardly a victory for constitutional law and for the *Rechtsstaat*, and for the idea of integration through democratic constitutional law. In that regard, it is hard to escape the conclusion that the legal wrapping of the Greek rescue package was directly aimed at *dressing up* the true nature of what was been done, something which was especially necessary after the reckless use of *constitutional arguments* as a bargaining chip to block the rescue of Greece. It suffices to consider that the central role played by the Commission and the European Central Bank in the negotiation of the Memorandum of Understanding means that the 'bilateral' character of the loans is a mere gimmick to assuage the eventual constitutional doubts of the German Constitutional Court. And that the fact that such loans are fully 'junior' loans means that, in the event of Greece defaulting for good, the lending member states will suffer considerable losses.[29] The rescue package would become a transfer package, and thus its real nature, I am afraid, will be revealed (indeed, Martin Wolf has rightly argued again and again that the transfer was al-

---

28   Peter Wise, Portugal on holiday amid bail-out talks, Financial Times, 22 April 2011, http://www.ft.com/intl/cms/s/0/070c6c5c-6cfd-11e0-83fe-00144feab49a.html#axzz263-MNimEK.

29   The gimmicks oft he "PSI" (private sector involvement) spared the "official lenders" for the time being, although they had to pick the bill resulting from the extremely generous offer made by Greek creditors. On the generosity of the offer, see Nouriel Roubini, Greece's private creditors are the lucky ones, Financial Times, 7 March 2012, http://blogs.ft.com/the-a-list/2012/03/07/greece%E2%80%99s-private-creditors-are-the-lucky-ones/#axzz263OHBnzZ.

ready in the cards once the creditor states tolerated that banks in their national financial systems (and the deposits on which they guaranteed) engaged into massive loans to what are now the rescued PIGS).

Act III: as in characteristic in dramas, action rapidly accelerated after the end of the second act. The Community rescue package for Greece, duly camouflaged as congeries of bilateral loans, was approved on 2 May. On 7 May Trichet played the *prete ricordante* to the European Council and informed that contagion was knocking on the doors. On the night of 7-8 May, apparently inspired by a mystical vision that Trichet had managed to represent with the help of the Bank of International Settlements' graphic accounting for the entanglement of German, French, and Dutch institutions on PIGS public debt and on debt towards financial institutions of the PIGS states, the German Chancellor came to accept that something else had to be done, *no matter what her previous constitutional position*. Pierre Lellouche, the French Minister for European Affairs, claimed in a rare outspoken comment that what had been decided amounted to a mutation of the treaties.[30] Whether one agrees with such a claim or not, Merkel would have to agree on the basis of her previous position. Gone was the pretence of extending the loans outside of the framework of European constitutional law. The Mechanism and the Fund were created and came to be part of the European institutional setup (although, as we saw, the Fund was technically speaking a Luxembourgeois *société anonyme*). The temporal basis of the Fund seemed to have been thought of as reducing the constitutional sharp corners of the decision. But it seems rather difficult to fathom why a temporary fund will be less unconstitutional than a permanent one, especially when the fiscal liabilities and thus the ensuing transfers resulting from the temporal fund can be far from negligent for the public treasury (given that the credits are also junior credits). Furthermore, Germany came to accept that Article 122(2) TEC enabled the creation of this financial assistance mechanism. But this was a very odd argument. Indeed, if a member state should be assisted because it had been hit by an unforeseeable event of which the member state/government could not be held fully responsible, why should it be that the way out of such a state of affairs was a drastic structural reform *only* of that member state? Why should it be the case that only its citizens should bear the burden of the adjustment? How is it possible that Article 122(2) TEC could be used to justify a non-concessional and rather punitive loan guaranteed by the simple renunciation of fiscal sovereignty? The moral of the third act is that the European Council was ready to go beyond European constitutional law and *de facto* change its contents when it found itself on the cliff. The Constitution should not be a suicide pact, but then one should be especially attentive

---

30   Financial Times, 27 May 2010, http://www.ft.com/intl(cms/s/0/d6299cae-69b5-11df-8432-00144feab49a.html.

about what one writes into the constitution. Paraphrasing Romano Prodi, not only the original fiscal constitution of EMU was silly, but it seems that we have not had enough of that silliness, so we will 'constitutionalise' the Growth and Stability Pact, and either in the constitution or in a properly rigid norm, constitutionalise the prohibition of running budget deficits. The *gouvernement économique* has shrunk to the same size of the late French president Sarkozy and has become the *gouvernance economique*.[31]

Act IV: the Irish crisis provided a kind of intermezzo inside the drama. One of the rare occasions in which the coordination of economic policies framework put in place by the Maastricht Treaty and the Stability Pact actually worked well was in regard to the 2001 Irish budget. The Commission was rather concerned by a reckless pro-cyclical budget. Ireland was quickly sliding into a real estate bubble that will inflate its GDP until 2008 and leave a complete mess after 2008. But the Irish government was defiant and the Commission's warning was simply ignored. As a result, the Irish financial sector grew exponentially riding on real estate speculation. Caught unguarded by the fall of Lehman Brothers, the Irish financial sector runs the risk of making good the claim that the difference between Iceland and Ireland was a letter and three months and quite obviously, the very different politics of the subsequent economic and financial policies implemented in each country. Breaking ranks from an inchoate but emerging common and coordinated European response, the Irish government decided in a matter of hours to guarantee all bank deposits. This decision in itself reveals the extent to which integration through democratic constitutional law is in regression in Europe. A decision that implied compromising around 100 per cent of the national GPD was taken by night by the prime minister and five bankers, and then sped up through parliament in one day. This was presented (as all later similar national decisions) as a good affair for the government, which only incurred in contingent liabilities, and on the side saved the national financial system. The fact of the matter is that Ireland, a country with one of the lowest debts in the EU in 2008 at under 30 per cent, had become essentially illiquid by the fall of 2010. After severe pressures coming from the Eurogroup and the European Central Bank, the Irish government asked for the rescue, and the mechanisms approved in May and June were first applied.

Third: what is the point of all this? Given the high levels of indebtedness of the Greek and the Irish exchequer (Greece at 165 per cent GPD in 2012, with negative growth, and Ireland at 125 per cent GDP in 2012, with very moderate growth), the 'rescue packages' are not about providing these two countries with a temporarily missing liquidity, but with gaining time, time that is said and com-

---

31   "Un Chemin pour un pilotage économique européen", available at http://www.ladocu-mentationfrancais.fr/rapports-publics/114000011/index.shtml.

mented to be necessary to prepare the financial system for the eventual bankruptcy of the creditors, i.e. the banks. It is clear and obvious that were Greece and Ireland to suspend payments tomorrow, the financial system would get a serious hit (remember Merkel's vision prompted by the Bank of International Settlements chart). The state, and by that one can only mean the European Union, not the nation-states in isolation, will have to intervene and underpin the financial system to avoid economic chaos. I am far from denying that. But notice that up to now, the music that has been played in public is very different, and therefore, discussions about our public law have fostered the wrong debates. Because the question is not only whether we have to intervene, but according to which terms. In brief, the specific form and manner of organising the rescue is of substance. Who gets what and how from the rescue, or what is the same, whose rescue and who pays for it, are fundamental political questions that are avoided.

I know my Pigou and thus I know that one can only bend financial markets by surprise actions. But what we have here is no surprise (financial markets assume that debt will suffer severe haircuts before 2014, and some actors may try to force default before 2013). It is hard to escape the conclusion that what is at stake here is a rather problematic (and risky) use of fundamental instruments of our constitutional law to gain time, which furthermore advances the interests of some to the detriment of the interests of others.

III   Conclusion: the crisis of democratic constitutionalism itself

The European constitution has mutated. While the form remains, the substance has drastically changed. What we have, as argued in this chapter, is übereconomic freedoms set loose from any kind of political rectification, coupled with an asymmetric economic and monetary union which European leaders have tried to stabilise by means of escaping to empty constitutional spaces. Both Lisbon and the European crisis government have revealed the extent to which European leaders have tried to appropiate the *puovoir constituent* for themselves.

This "new" European constitution cannot but heighten the (already latent) tension between the deep constitution of the European Union, the constitutional law common to the member states, which is set on the constitutional identity of member states as social and democratic *Rechtsstaaten*, and the construction of the treaties as the constitution of a single market geared towards neoliberal principles, fostered by the jurisprudence of the ECJ on economic freedoms and competition law, and favoured by the Single European Act and the Maastricht Treaty. As one austerity plan after the other has been passed, the identity of the PIGS as social and democratic *Rechtsstaats* has been increasingly challenged. Acquired rights (such as those of public servants to tenure) have been set aside in some states, and are under challenge in others. The basic institutional structures on which the realisation of socio-economic rights depends have become so underfunded as to threaten the core of such rights (such as is the case of the right to health or the right to education). Indeed, the core principles of the social and democratic *Rechtsstaat* rule out a resolution of the crisis through the assignment of burdens in a fully regressive manner.

But the tension has come to affect the very concept of democratic constitutionalism, as through the Stability, Coordination and Governance Treaty (itself a most peculiar legal instrument) Member States seem bound to introduce into their constitutions the principle of balanced budgets. What is critical in that regard is that there is a clear political will to do so according to the template of executive emergency constitutionalism - that is, minimising public debate and avoiding the usual filters of the democratic constitutional state. The 'express constitutionalism' that characterises the snap constitutional reform in Spain is paradigmatic.

The Union has always been a rather complex and ambiguous political community. It does not seem to me that the Union is a *sui generis* and fully idiosyncratic polity, as is usually claimed, but the Union represents a rather novel experiment, namely, the integration of already constituted democratic and social *Rechtsstaaten* in a wider polity (which aims at being itself a democratic and constitutional polity aimed at realising the same principles and values of its constituent parts). While it is highly dubious that the Union transcends the state form, it clearly aims at transcending the *nation*-state form. This is the major *gift* of European integration. The *cunning* of the project lies in its opening a new constitutional path to establish a democratic constitution, a path in which the collective of national constitutions become the deep-rock fundamental law, partially explicated in the founding treaties. This leaves rather undetermined the final shape of the European Union.

This constitutional ambiguity has probably served the Union very well for decades. But it has clear drawbacks. In the absence of a clear constitutional template, it was unavoidable that a long-winded and protracted process of integration followed, and that different decisions at different times reflected different conceptions of what the Union is and what it should be. The economic constitution of the European Union is a clear example. The principle of national control and responsibility of fiscal policy clearly corresponds to an inter-governmental understanding of the Union. The assignment of monetary policy to the European System of Central Banks, with the European Central Bank at its head, clearly fits into the federal conception of the Union, while the governance arrangements through which monetary and fiscal policy are coupled respond to the 'post-national' vision of European integration.

The more the process of integration goes forward, the more a need for disambiguation has been felt. This accounts for the long series of processes of treaty reform, which in reality make up a long and unfinished constitutional season of the European Union. When the financial and economic crisis hit European shores, the Union was in a very delicate moment. What originally held the promise of becoming a genuine constitutional moment in European integration, the Laeken process, had become a hybrid process itself, and petered out as French and Dutch citizens rejected the draft Constitutional Treaty. The more the different crises have advanced, the more the inconsistencies of the 'Collage' Union, especially on fiscal matters, have become evident.

It is rather obvious that the crisis of European integration is not a theoretical crisis. It would simply be silly to pretend that, if we get the constitutional theory of the European Union right, all other aspects of the European crisis will be sorted out. What is however true is that, without a proper clarification of the visions of integration, and, consequently, of the constitutional theory of the Union that we advance, the crisis of European integration is unlikely to be sorted out. We will be condemned to be unable to calibrate the implications of different decisions. Indeed, what looks like the same decision (for example, the Euro Plus Pact) would actually translate into very different things, depending on the way in which we conceptualise and understand European integration. Furthermore, the actual implications of concrete policy measures get lost in such an ambiguous discourse. The net result is a unidimensional reduction of the debate to whether Europeans should opt for renationalising policies (which would entail, in the long run, a break up of the euro) or *more* integration (which means either transforming governance arrangements by means of adding to them hard law sanctions while keeping the *flu* form of the common action norms, or communitarising the public debt *apparently* without discussing the serious distributive implications of the specific way in which this is done). But this fails to take into account the other fundamental dimensions of the problem, such as the basic political question of who gets what, when, and how, affecting both the distributive implications of decisions, the timing of decisions, and the means of social integration through which they are implemented. Consider Eurobonds. While we could define Eurobonds in a rather technically neutral manner, what Eurobonds are depends on how they are issued and, above all, on how we pay for them, on how we, at the end of the day, want to tax Europeans. It is a strange form of federalism that which calls for debt without the means of paying for that debt.

To repeat it once more at the end: if I bother you with my qualms it is not because I share the Eurosceptic relish on what is wrong and defective with European integration. On the contrary, it is because European integration is in my view a necessary condition for the realisation of democratic government in Europe. I only find a trifle exaggerated the claim of a cherished colleague of mine that Europe is indeed the last hope of humankind (a world where the shift of paradigm following the war on terror is far from being finished). But the European political project of the 1980s and the 1990s may well have died on 9 May. There remains an institutional structure and a series of major achievements that can be mobilised for good. But we need an alternative project, a project that again takes seriously the centrality of democratic constitutional law, and of democratic public law as the means of social integration of choice.

Bibliography

Brown, G. (ed.) (1975), *Red paper on Scotland.* Edinburgh: Edinburgh University Press.

Dougan, M. (2008), The Treaty of Lisbon 2007: Winning Minds, not Hearts, *Common Market Law Review* 45, pp. 617-703.

Fossum, J.E. and Menéndez, A.J. (2011), *The Constitution's Gift.* Lanham: Rowman and Littlefield.

Greenway, D. and Shaw, G.K. (eds.)(1995), *Public choice, public finance, and public policy: essays in honour of Alan Peacock.* Oxford: Blackwell.

König, T., Daimer S. and Finke, D. (2008), The Treaty Reform of the EU: Constitutional Agenda-Setting, Intergovernmental Bargains and the Presidency's Crisis Management of Ratification Failure, *Journal of Common Market Studies* 46, pp. 337-363.

Magnette, P. (2004), Deliberation or Bargaining? Coping with Constitutional Conflicts in the Convention on the Future of Europe, in: Erik Oddvar Eriksen, John Erik Fossum, Agustin José Menéndez (eds.), *Developing a Constitution for Europe.* London: Routledge, pp. 207-225.

Magnette, P. (2005), In the Name of Simplification: Coping with Constitutional Conflicts in the Convention on the Future of Europe, *European Law Journal* 11, pp. 432-451.

Ross G. (2008), What do "Europeans" Think? Analyses of the European Union's Current Crisis by European Elites, *Journal of Common Market Studies* 46, pp. 389-412.

Saxshon, N. (2011), *Treasure Islands*, London: Bodley Head.

Tsebelis, G. and Proksch, S.-O. (2007), The Art of Political Manipulation in the European Convention, *Journal of Common Market Studies* 45, pp. 157-186.

Legal enforcement of Union values

Thomas Eilmansberger/ Rainer Palmstorfer

I Introduction

1 The Treaty of Rome: common values taken for granted

The EU is often referred to as a community of values, and it is often argued that common values (i.e. values that are shared by all the member states) are at the very heart of the integration project. That claim certainly has some merit at least. Although the Treaty of Rome, i.e. the treaty establishing the European Economic Community (EEC), did not contain any references to Community values, it seems clear that after the catastrophic experiences in the first half of the last century, only the existence of certain shared values (not least that of a peaceful co-existence of nations) not only among the political elites, but also among the societies concerned permitted integration efforts to succeed.[1]

Common values not only have this historical significance, but they are also still crucial for the functioning of the post-Lisbon EU: they are important for all modern pluralist societies because they provide the common platform on which differences can be accepted and balances and compromises be struck. For the EU, given its considerable ethnic, cultural, and political diversity, but also in view of its still somewhat problematic legitimacy, this is a particularly relevant aspect. Such values can be seen as the foundations on which the EU has been and is being built.

Against this background it is interesting, maybe surprising, that the original EC Treaty did not contain any references to values at all. An explanation might be that the existence of common values was simply taken for granted.[2] A state joining the EEC without safeguarding an adequate level of human rights protection was considered unthinkable.[3]

---

1   Benedikt Speer (2001), Die Europäische Union als Wertegemeinschaft: Wert- und rechtskonformes Verhalten als konditionierendes Element der Mitgliedschaft, Die öffentliche Verwaltung 54, pp. 981et seq.

2   Ibid. p. 981.

3   Walter Hallstein (1973), Die Europäische Gemeinschaft. Düsseldorf: Econ, p. 49.

2 From Amsterdam to Lisbon: the reference to values in the treaties

It was the Treaty of Amsterdam (1997) that introduced the term 'value' for the first time in Article 16 of the EC Treaty (ECT), which refers to the provision of services in the general interest as a common value. More importantly perhaps, the Treaty of Amsterdam laid down a number of legal principles in Article 6 TEU (providing that the Union is founded on the principles of liberty, democracy, respect for human rights and fundamental freedoms, and the rule of law), which must, of course, also be seen as expressions of central Union values.[4] With regard to contents, these legal principles undoubtedly formulate values. Similarly, the Charter of Fundamental Rights (2000), which has become legally binding after the coming into force of the Lisbon Treaty, declares that 'the peoples of Europe, in creating an ever closer union among them, are resolved to share a peaceful future based on common values' (Charter: Preamble).[5] Owing to the fact that 'the peoples of Europe' have different historical experiences, it is also clear, however, that these common values need to be formulated at a fairly abstract level.[6]

Unlike its predecessors, the Lisbon Treaty frequently – 13 times – uses the term 'values'. For example, according to the Preamble, the parties of the treaty draw 'inspiration from the cultural, religious and humanist inheritance of Europe, from which have developed the universal values of the inviolable and inalienable rights of the human person, freedom, democracy, equality and the rule of law.' Article 2 TEU holds that the 'Union is founded on the values of respect for human dignity, freedom, democracy, equality, the rule of law and respect for human rights, including the rights of persons belonging to minorities. These values are common to the Member States (MS) in a society in which pluralism, non-discrimination, tolerance, justice, solidarity and equality between women and men prevail.'

3 Enforcing EU values: general remarks

However, it is evidently not the number of references to values in a constitution or other basic legal texts which reveals the commitment of a political entity to

4   Christian Calliess (2004), Europa als Wertegemeinschaft – Integration und Identität durch europäisches verfassungsrecht? Juristenzeitung 59, pp. 1033et seq.
5   Charter of Fundamental Rights of the European Union OJ [2000] C364/1.
6   Benedikt Speer (2001), Die Europäische Union als Wertegemeinschaft: Wert- und rechtskonformes Verhalten als konditionierendes Element der Mitgliedschaft, Die öffentliche Verwaltung 54, p. 982.

these principles. Values are vulnerable concepts and they are, legally speaking, not self-executing; in this respect they differ from the four freedoms under EU law (i.e. the free movement of goods, the free movement of persons, the free movement of services, and the free movement of capital), which are designed as (enforceable) individual rights, that is to say, as rules. Dating back to the original treaties, these freedoms are also much older than the said EU values. Apart from that there is another striking difference: whereas the EU values can be found also at the national level (i.e. in national constitutions), the four freedoms are peculiar to the EU. In other words, EU values (e.g. the rule of law and democracy) have been originally developed in a national setting, but have been also transferred to the EU level.

By contrast, the four freedoms – all of them ultimately aiming at the making possible of economic activities in other member states – have been developed at the EU level and are tailored to the needs of the creation of an internal market. To put it differently, the concepts of the rule of law and human rights have – on principle – been already developed before 1957. The EU brought new ground insofar as it offers a means to safeguard these values in its member states and candidate countries. Thus the human rights in a given member state are enshrined in its constitution and not in EU law; EU law, however, offers instruments to make sure that this member state respects such rights. In addition, the treaties also reflect these values for the EU level. That is to say, the fact that democracy is referred to as a value does not only mean that member states and candidate countries are obliged under EU law to be democracies; it also means that the EU itself is committed to be democratic and based on the rule of law.

Values, however, are only as effective as the instruments provided for their protection and enforcement. As far as these instruments are concerned, one may distinguish between an external and an internal dimension.

The external dimension is represented by the possibilities and practical results of imposing the respect of these values on third countries (i.e. the exportation of these values), which the EU seeks to achieve in treaty negotiations with accession applicants or other third countries and, more importantly, by its foreign policy.[7] The internal dimension of the protection of EU values finds expression in their legal enforceability under EU law, i.e. the possibility to compel observance of or obedience to these EU values before a competent – EU or national – court, the possible infringers being the EU, EU citizens, or Member States. As this contribution focuses on the legal enforcement under EU law, the external dimension, being governed by international law,[8] will be only dealt with as regards the im-

7   Urfan Kaliq (2008), Ethical Dimensions on the Foreign Policy of the European Union. A Legal Appraisal. Cambridge: Cambridge University Press, pp. 7 et seq.
8   Ibid, pp. 19 et seq.

posing of EU values on accession applicants. But, as regards internal enforcement in the sense just defined, the picture shall be as comprehensive as possible. This picture is necessarily a complex one. Prior to looking at it, however, we will have a look at the role of EU values in the application process of prospective member states of the EU.

II   The external dimension: imposing the respect of Union values on accession applicants

According to Article 49 TEU, a provision introduced by the Treaty of Amsterdam, 'any European State which respects the values referred to in Article 2 [TEU] and is committed to promoting them may apply to become a member of the Union.' Article 49 TEU mirrors the accession requirements laid down by the European Council in Copenhagen in 1993:

> 'Membership requires that the candidate country has achieved stability of institutions guaranteeing democracy, the rule of law, human rights and respect for and protection of minorities, the existence of a functioning market economy as well as the capacity to cope with competitive pressure and market forces within the Union.'

As far as the nature of Article 49 TEU is concerned, there is no doubt that this provision is of legal nature. In other words, the accession requirements are not just programmatic guidelines.[9]

Despite its legal nature, Article 49 TEU is legally enforceable only to a limited extent. Firstly, fulfilling the accession requirements does not confer an enforceable claim on an applicant state. In addition, also the Member States are free to object to the accession. Secondly, an accession treaty cannot be the subject of a nullity action under Article 263 TFEU. Also as regards the possibility of a preliminary reference procedure under Article 267 TFEU, it seems questionable whether the ECJ is willing to elaborate on the preconditions for the accession of a given state.[10] For example, in a case concerning the forthcoming accessions of Spain and Portugal, the ECJ held that the legal conditions for an accession remain to be defined in the context of the accession procedure 'without its being possible to determine the content judicially in advance'.[11] Therefore, the ECJ refused to give a ruling on the form or subject matter of the conditions that might be adopted under the accession procedure. The EU institutions have a large mar-

---

9   Martin Nettesheim (2003), EU-Beitritt und Unrechtsaufarbeitung, Europarecht 38, pp. 44 et seq.
10   Martin Nettesheim (2003), EU-Beitritt und Unrechtsaufarbeitung, Europarecht 38, pp. 44; pp. 62 et seq.
11   Case 93/78 Lothar Mattheus [1978] ECR 2203, para 8.

gin of appreciation when assessing an application. This wide margin of appreciation is not only due to the vagueness and broad wording of the requirements of accession; it is also due to a lack of case law in this field. Nevertheless Article 49 TEU is endowed with a strong sanction: applicant states considered not to meet the Article 2 TEU criteria will not become member states. What is more, applicant states are subjected to a much more serious regime of human rights scrutiny and intervention than that applied to member states.[12] With the accession being dependent on the respect for the values under Article 2 TEU, the EU may strongly influence accession countries (provided that the latter are eager to join the EU). In other words, the EU as an international organisation provides for the necessary incentives to guarantee values at the national level.

III   The internal dimension

Because of the particular governance structure of the EU, there are three potential victims of relevant encroachments or interferences, namely the EU itself and EU citizens, but also the member states, which could see Union values threatened by the EU; and there are two potential infringers, namely the member states and the EU. As a result, there is wide variety of legal instruments applicable in these various constellations. In this respect we will not only look at the values mentioned in Article 2 TEU but also at other non-economic values, in particular values defining the social dimension of the EU.

1   Member states as infringers – value enforcement against member states

(a)   *The EU as potential victim and enforcer: fundamental EU values concerning the organisation of member states*

Article 2 TEU lists the principles common to the member states, i.e. liberty, democracy, respect for human rights and fundamental freedoms, and the rule of law. It seems remarkable that the Treaty – at a theoretical level – also provides for two safeguard mechanisms: firstly, as mentioned above, Article 49 TEU stipulates that the respect for these common values is one of the conditions for any state wishing to join the European Union; secondly, with regard to member states, Article 7 TEU (introduced by the Amsterdam Treaty and subsequently amended at Nice and Lisbon) and 354 TFEU seek to equip the Union institutions

---

12   Andrew Williams (2000), Enlargement of the Union and human rights conditionality: a policy of distinction? European Law Review 25, pp. 605-617.

with the means to secure compliance with these fundamental principles. Unlike the Amsterdam Treaty, which allowed only remedial action after a serious and persistent breach had already occurred, the Nice Treaty (Article 7 TEU) gave the Union the capacity to act preventively in the event of a clear threat of a serious breach of the common values. This procedure is still valid, provided for under the Lisbon Treaty.

As a result of this innovation, two independent mechanisms now coexist: (i) a procedure to determine that there is a threat of a serious breach (Article 7 para 1 TEU) and (ii) a procedure to determine that there is a serious and persistent breach of the common values (Article 7 para 2 TEU). Whereas the Council is competent to declare that there is a clear risk of a serious breach by a member state of the values referred to in Article 2 TEU, it is – with the coming into force of the Lisbon Treaty – now for the European Council to determine the existence of a serious and persistent breach, making the latter institution a watchdog on the proper application of the European values by member states.[13] Once the European Council has established the seriousness and persistence of a breach, the Council may apply penalties, but is not obliged to do so. The (European) Council's power is subject to democratic control by the European Parliament, in the form of the assent that it must give before the (European) Council can act. As far as legal remedies are concerned, the ECJ decides on the legality of an act adopted pursuant to Article 7 TEU in respect solely of procedural stipulations (cf. Article 269 TFEU).

This sanction mechanism is politically and legally very interesting and there is lively discussion not only in legal circles whether the procedure under Article 7 TEU constitutes a useful and efficient instrument for remedying perceived infractions, a discussion that gained momentum notably against the background of the bilateral member states sanctions against Austria in the wake of the entrance of the Freedom Party (FPÖ) into the Austrian government in 2000, not least because the said sanctions were not based on Article 7 TEU.[14] We will probably and hopefully never know whether and how this mechanism of sanctions would work in practice since it seems extremely unlikely that it will ever be activated and applied. After all, the threshold for finding an infringement is rather high since the provision is obviously not designed to remedy individual breaches. The risk or breach identified must go beyond specific situations and concern a more

---

13   José Mariá Beneyto (2008), From Nice to the Constitutional Treaty: Eight Theses on the (Future) Constitutionalisation of Europe, in: Stefan Griller, Jacques Ziller (eds.), The Lisbon treaty: EU Constitutionalism without a Constitutional Treaty? Wien: Springer, p. 5.

14   Tim Schönborn (2005), Die Causa Austria: Zur Zulässigkeit bilateraler Sanktionen zwischen den Mitgliedstaaten der Europäischen Union. Frankfurt am Main: Peter Lang, pp. 104 et seq.

systematic problem. In other words, whereas 'simple' breaches of the treaties may be persecuted under the 'ordinary' infringement procedure under Article 258 TFEU, persistent and serious breaches, i.e. breaches that may also qualify as or border on systematic infringements of human rights and/or crimes under international law, fall under the scope of Article 7 TEU.[15]

This sanction mechanism enables the EU to put peer pressure on a deviant member state. Such a pressure – exerted not only by a single state but by a group of states – may have considerable effects on this member state. As with accession candidates, the EU as collective may impose considerably more pressure than a single state. It may be submitted that the political cost in the respective member state would be considerable. In this respect, the existence of the EU does make a difference.

(b)   Individuals as potential victims and enforcers: enforcement of other non-economic Union values

While it may be unlikely that those fundamental values will be violated often, it is almost inevitable that Union values which found expression in sufficiently precise, albeit sometimes indirectly granted, individual rights will at least be occasionally disregarded. This applies also and in particular to those non-economic values that are of interest here: these are classic fundamental rights on the one hand, and the many – directly or indirectly – granted rights (e.g. in the social sphere) on the other. Fundamental rights protection in the EU context is primarily aimed at EU institutions; but the debtors or guarantors of those other non-economic rights (established by EU law) are typically the member states and their emanations (e.g. social security systems), and they are therefore the ones against whom those social rights will have to be enforced.

EU law now contains a considerable number of such rights and it's probably fair to assume that in no other field does EU law grant so many rights. These rights are (i) social rights typically in form of workers' rights regulations (cf. Regulation 1408/71[16] on the application of social security schemes to employed persons and their families moving within the Community) or directives to be transposed into national law by member states (e.g. the working-time directive);

---

15   Frank Schorkopf (2000), Homogenität in der Europäischen Union: Ausgestaltung und Gewährleistung durch Art. 6 Abs 1 und Art. 7 EUV. Berlin: Duncker & Humblot, pp. 149et seq.
16   Regulation (EEC) No 1408/71 of the Council of 14 June 1971 on the application of social security schemes to employed persons and their families moving within the Community OJ [1971] L 149/2.

(ii) social rights stemming from the demand of equal treatment (nationality) in the context of the free-movement-of-persons treaty provisions (i.e. the free movement of workers pursuant to Article 45 et seq TFEU and EU citizenship under Art 20 TFEU). As regards this context, member states are frequently direct debtors of these rights; (iii) rights to equal treatment or non-discrimination because of sex, which are protected both by the TFEU itself (cf. Article 157 TFEU) as well as by secondary legislation (e.g. Directive 2006/54/EC on the implementation of the principle of equal opportunities and equal treatment of men and women in matters of employment and occupation), making member states both debtors and guarantors[17], (iv) social rights provided in the Euroepan Social Charter.

With exception of the latter-mentioned Charter rights, all of these social rights are strong, i.e. enforceable, rights, and this is also, maybe mainly, due to the ECJ which strengthened these rights both as regards their substance and their enforcement. For example, as regards substance, the ECJ applies a very extensive interpretation of the above-mentioned sex-discrimination directive and its forerunner, by holding that it also covers discrimination on grounds of pregnancy resulting in high degree of protection especially against termination and discrimination in job applications (e.g. Case *Dekker*)[18] or discrimination of transsexuals (Case *P v S and Cornwall County Council*)[19]. Such extensive interpretation also occurred with regard to age discrimination, a field of law that produced a series of controversial judgements. For example, the ECJ held that there is a general principle of equal treatment, in particular in respect of age, which cannot as such be conditional upon the expiry of the period for the transposition of a directive (i.e. Council Directive 2000/78/EC of 27 November 2000 establishing a general framework for equal treatment in employment and occupation) intended to lay down a general framework for combating discrimination on the grounds of age (Case *Mangold*, para 75 et seq)[20]. Likewise, the ECJ decided on the application of the transfer of undertakings directive in the context of out-sourcing situations within the public sector (Case C-343/98, *Collino*)[21].

There is also a number of controversial rulings in the free movement area aiming at preserving unity of family by (probably over-) stretching relevant free-movement provisions, the high-water mark being Case *Metock*[22], in which the

---

17 Directive 2006/54/EC on the implementation of the principle of equal opportunities and equal treatment of men and women in matters of employment and occupation OJ [2006] L 204/23.
18 Case C-177/88 [1990] ECR I-3941.
19 Case C-13/94 P v S and Cornwall County Council [1996] ECR I-2143.
20 Case C-144/04 Mangold [2005] ECR I-9981.
21 Case C-343/98 Collino [2000] ECR I-6659.
22 Case C-127/08 Metock [2008] ECR I-6241.

ECJ held that the right of a national of a non-member country who is a family member of a Union citizen to accompany or join that citizen cannot be made conditional on prior lawful residence in another member state, and consequently found that a non-community spouse of a citizen of the Union can move and reside with that citizen in the Union without having previously been lawfully resident in a member state. There are many other remarkable judgements, remarkable also because these cannot really be explained by the internal market logic but only by the Court's ambition to protect family values and the right to family life. In Case *Carpenter*[23], for example, the ECJ found that the refusal to allow Mrs Carpenter, the non-community spouse of a British citizen, to enter the United Kingdom would result in a separation of the parties to the marriage and therefore would infringe Mr Carpenter's freedom to provide services pursuant to Article 56 TFEU. In that regard, also Cases *Baumbast* and *Chen*[24] should be mentioned. Though these judgements, in general, have a shaky legal basis, it has to be acknowledged that they make an important contribution to giving the EU a social face.

As regards enforcement, these social rights (which, as mentioned, need to be enforced against member states and their subjects), of course, greatly benefit from the legal principles governing the relationship between national law and EU law established by the Court early on, that is, the principles of (i) direct effect (they can be relied upon before a national court), (ii) supremacy (EU law overrides conflicting national law), and (iii) state liability (a state may be held liable for loss and damage caused to individuals by breaches of Community law for which the State can be held responsible). This is clearly demonstrated by Case *Francovich*[25], a landmark case on state liability that concerned Italy's failure to timely transpose Council Directive 80/987/EEC on the protection of employees in the event of the insolvency of their employer[26] into Italian law. Thus the legal enforcement of non-economic values (especially social values) is efficient to the extent that they manifest themselves and find expression in rights vis-à-vis member states (and their subjects).

This does, however, not necessarily reveal a particularly strong commitment to these rights, although that conclusion is not entirely wrong either, given the existence of the body of case law in which the ECJ appears to be genuinely interested in increasing the scope of social protection provided by EU law (i.e. where the ultimate motive clearly is not to further other goals, e.g. internal mar-

---

23   Case C-60/00 Carpenter [2002] ECR I-6279.
24   Case C-200/02 Chen [2004] ECR I-9925.
25   Case C-479/93 Francovich [1995] ECR I-3843.
26   Council Directive 80/987/EEC on the protection of employees in the event of the insolvency of their employer OJ [1980] L 283/23.

ket objectives). But as far as the enforcement technique is concerned, i.e. as regards the availability of legal remedies permitting the direct enforcement of these rights before national courts, the efficacy of value enforcement is simply owed to the concern of securing an efficient enforcement of EU law in general. Consequently, the main reasoning for the ruling in *Francovich* was that 'the full effectiveness of Community rules would be impaired and the protection of the rights which they grant would be weakened if individuals were unable to obtain reparation when their rights are infringed by a breach of Community law for which a Member State can be held responsible' (Case *Francovich*, para 33)[27]. In other words, the fact that the rights at hand in *Francovich* aimed at the social protection of workers was not emphasised and not decisive either.

2   The EU as infringer: defence and enforcement of Union values against the EU

(a)   *Individuals as potential victims and claimants: the example of human rights protection*

Human rights protection is certainly a central EU value. This can be seen from the fact that all member states are party to the European Convention on Human Rights (ECHR) and many have additional protection in their constitutions. In the EU context, however, national human rights protection is not sufficient, for national fundamental rights cannot protect against infringements by the EU and its institutions owing to the above-mentioned supremacy principle. Therefore, it is striking that the ECT originally did not provide for any kind of fundamental rights protection against such infringements by EC institutions. However, this omission is not necessarily due to a neglect of the importance of human rights protection in the EEC context, but may be put down to the fact that the drafters of the original ECT were of the opinion that human rights already enjoyed appropriate protection under national laws.[28] It should be remembered that the supremacy principle had not yet existed at that time (it was to be established by the ECJ in 1964)[29].

This neglect may however also be explained by the fact that, given the almost exclusive focus on economic integration, there may not have seemed to be much

27   Case C-479/93 Francovich [1995] ECR I-3843.
28   Benedikt Speer (2001), Die Europäische Union als Wertegemeinschaft: Wert- und rechtskonformes Verhalten als konditionierendes Element der Mitgliedschaft, Die öffentliche Verwaltung 54, p. 984.
29   Case 6/64 Costa v. ENEL [1964] 1253.

potential in breaching such rights. That may also help to explain why an express reference to human rights was made not until the Maastricht treaty amendment (1992) and why the Charter of Fundamental Rights was drafted only recently (2000).

It is therefore hardly surprising that also the ECJ in its first ruling demonstrated a marked disinterest in this issue (cf. Case *Stork*).[30] Quickly, however, at least the ECJ did recognise the importance of fundamental rights and single-handedly introduced these rights into the EC legal order, declaring that they were unwritten principles of law (Case *Stauder*, para 7).[31] This took place in the late 1960s and early 1970s. In Case *Internationale Handelsgesellschaft* (1970)[32], the ECJ held that 'respect for fundamental rights forms an integral part of the general principles of law protected by the Court of Justice' and that 'the protection of such rights, whilst inspired by the constitutional traditions common to the member states, must be ensured within the framework of the structure and objectives of the Community' (Case *Internationale Handelsgesellschaft*, para 4). Some years later, in *Nold* (1974)[33], the Court established another source of inspiration for EC human rights by holding that 'international treaties for the protection of human rights on which the member states have collaborated or of which they are signatories, can supply guidelines which should be followed within the framework of community law' (Case *Nold*, para 13). In particular, it was the ECHR that was to become the most important source of inspiration, as it was considered unacceptable not to have human rights protection in the EU that at least reached the level provided by the ECHR (Case *Hauer*, para 15).[34]

Interestingly enough, the ultimate motive behind this line of case law was originally probably not so much or not only the concern for human rights. Instead, it was also motivated by the ECJ's concern for the primacy of EC law. It should be recalled that the above-mentioned primacy principle met with resistance from certain national courts, especially the German Constitutional Court, fearing for the protection of their respective national human rights (see the so called *Solange* Decisions and Case *Bananenmarkt*).[35] Thus, not establishing an EU law concept of human rights might have resulted in national courts not accepting the supremacy principle, i.e. the fundamental principle governing the relationship between EU law and national law, and might have induced national courts to scrutinise EC law pursuant to national human rights. While the reasons

---

30 Case 1/58 Stork [1959] ECR 17.
31 Case 26/69 Stauder [1969] ECR 419.
32 Case 11/70 Internationale Handelsgesellschaft [1970] ECR 1125.
33 Case 4/73 Nold [1974] ECR 491.
34 Case 44/79 Hauer [1979] ECR 3727.
35 BVerfGE 37, 271, Solange I; BVerfGE 73, 339 Solange II; BverfG 2 BvL 1/97 Bananenmarkt.

for this ECJ jurisprudence might therefore seem to be pragmatic, the result, i.e. the implementation of ECHR standards in the EU legal order, is of course very positive.

While there is thus an acceptable level of protection now, there is still some room for improvement, both as regards substance and enforcement. Concerning substance, it is striking that it seldom happens that the ECJ actually finds an infringement, and occasionally there is also some divergence between Luxembourg and Strasbourg.[36] Nevertheless, there are also cases in which the ECJ considered an infringement of the freedoms of the internal market to be justified as the measure served the protection of human rights (Case *Schmidberger*).[37] Concerning enforcement, the ECJ is clearly much more restrictive when it comes to the possibility to challenge EU law compared with a challenge of national law, for, as a rule, the ECJ denies individual applicants standing against EU normative rules potentially in breach of fundamental rights. This is not unproblematic because there may not be an alternative way to achieve a review of the legality and human rights conformity of this act, as indirect challenges via national courts are often difficult.

However, the Lisbon Treaty brought about an improvement of legal protection in this context. As regards the substantive standard, there may be a slight improvement by the planned accession of the EU to the ECHR, as that would clearly establish the Strasbourg Court as ultimate authority, which could possibly result in a more generous interpretation of certain rights.[38] However, the negotiations between the European Union and the European Council regarding the required accession agreement are still in progress.[39] Concerning enforcement, Lisbon might bring about an improvement, as the deletion of the requirement of individual concern as to a regulatory act, which is of direct concern to the plaintiff and does not entail implementing measures (Art 263 para 4 TFEU), could open the way for direct challenges of EU legislation for breaches of fundamental rights by individuals. However, it remains to be seen whether regulations taking the form of legislative acts may also qualify as regulatory acts under Article 263

---

36   Guy Harpaz (2009), The European Court of Justice and its Relations with the European Court of Human Rights: the Quest for Enhanced Reliance, Coherence and Legitimacy, Common Market Law Review 46, pp. 105-141.

37   Case C-112/00 Schmidberger [2003] ECR I-5659.

38   Guy Harpaz (2009), The European Court of Justice and its Relations with the European Court of Human Rights: the Quest for Enhanced Reliance, Coherence and Legitimacy, Common Market Law Review 46, pp. 134f.

39   Council of Europe, Second negotiation meeting between the CDDH ad hoc negotiation group and the European Commission on the accession of the European Union to the European Convention on Human Rights, Relevant excerpts from the report of the 75th meeting of the CDDH, Strasbourg, 17-19 September 2012.

para 4 TFEU (in the negative the decision *Inuit*, the appeal against which is however still pending).[40]

As far as the human rights protection at the EU level is concerned, some critics argue that it is superfluous as human rights are already protected by national constitutions or by the ECHR. These critics, however, fail to see that, in the EU legal order, national law is not considered a yardstick by which to measure an EU measure, which, as shown above, called for the development of human rights at the EU level.

(b)   Member states and their societies as victims – issue of conflicting values – enforcement of Union values by member states against the EU

The provision of services of general economic interest (SGEI) was and still is the only Union value referred to as such in the TFEU; thus it is all the more interesting that it is at the same time a Union value which member states felt in need to be defended against the EU. That is very clearly the point of Article 16 and 106 para 2 TFEU.

One may wonder why an explicitly recognised Union value needs to be defended against the EU itself. The answer is that EU law potentially restricts the pursuit of that particular value (and, for that matter, of many other non-economic values such as certain social values of different kind, environmental protection, media plurality, etc.). The protection of those values, therefore, takes the form of exceptions to potentially restrictive EU provisions. These exceptions, however, need to be filled with life, and commitments to values can be measured by the ECJ's interpretation and the scope accorded to them in legal proceedings in which member states defend their laws against the charge of EU law incompatibility.

This is a very important, if not the decisive aspect and the determinant of the social dimension of the EU. The social face of the EU, and, more specifically, the internal market, is not only defined by social rights directly or indirectly granted by EU law, but also, and maybe more significantly, by the direct interference of these rules with the member states' organisation of the provision of these services. In other words, the discretion left to member states in providing those services is also an important indicator of the recognition of the social values by EU law, which is particularly relevant given the limited powers of EU to provide these services itself; it is in these cases that EU law needs to make tough choices, i.e. prioritise between potentially conflicting values (e.g. market values

---

40   Cases T-18/10 and C-583/11 Inuit [2011].

vs. social and other non-free-market values). In the following we will examine to which extent member states are able to defend legislation safeguarding fundamental societal values against the market logic of certain EU rules, in particular internal market freedoms and competition rules.

(i)   Internal market

With regard to internal market freedoms, all relevant provisions are accompanied by exceptions explicitly providing for the possibility of member states to restrict the freedom at issue. Some of these exceptions are clearly supposed to protect particular interests of member states (e.g. security interests); certain exceptions, however, clearly reflect the appreciation and recognition of EU values.

According to a literal reading of the relevant Treaty provisions, these exceptions are a limited, exhaustive list of grounds that permit member states to deviate from internal market logic and are clearly expressions of Union values. That may not have been a problem if the reach of the four freedoms, i.e. their restraining force, would have been defined narrowly by the ECJ. If, in particular, the Court had interpreted those provisions as prohibiting only discriminatory national rules, the discretion of member states to pursue and enforce certain non-economic values would not have greatly been restricted: it would not have been in violation of the internal market law, for example, if member states had restricted the sale of products because of their negative social or environmental impact, and it would not have been problematic to restrict certain activities because of their negative social effects (e.g. Sunday labour), or because of their effects on cultural institutions (ban of sale of videos within certain period to protect cinemas). That was however not the case: the four freedoms were interpreted extensively, which created the need for member states to justify restrictions of economic activities even though they were applied across the board. At the same time, however, the Court (Case *Cassis de Dijon*)[41] recognised and approved a series of additional grounds for justification.[42] This did not change the fact that the ECJ sometimes becomes the 'arbiter of delicate social choices, reconciling trade with competing social policies'.[43]

---

41   Case 120/78 Rewe-Zentral AG v Bundesmonopolverwaltung für Branntwein (Cassis de Dijon) [1979] ECR 649.
42   Stefano Giubboni (2006), Social Rights and Market Freedom in the Constitution of Europe: A Labour Law Perspective. Cambridge: Cambridge University Press, pp. 167 et seq.
43   Joseph H.H. Weiler (1999), The Constitution of the Common Market Place: The Free Movement of Goods, in: Paul Craig, Gráinne de Búrca (eds.), *The Evolution of EU Law*. Oxford: Oxford University Press, pp. 349-376.

In Case *Keck* (1993)[44], the ECJ, however, narrowed the scope of prohibition to national rules affecting in law and fact domestic products in the same way as imported products, herein significantly increasing the regulatory discretion of member states[45]. Moreover, the ECJ grants a higher margin of appreciation to national legislators when it comes to sensitive, fundamental values. For example, in the recent Case *Liga Portuguesa de Futebol Profissional and Baw International* (2009)[46], the ECJ held that a member state is entitled to take the view that the mere fact that a gambling operator lawfully offers services in that sector via the internet in another member state, in which it is established and where it is in principle already subject to statutory conditions and controls on the part of the competent authorities in that state, cannot be regarded as amounting to a sufficient assurance that national consumers will be protected against the risks of fraud and crime.

More importantly, the ECJ also accepted fundamental rights as justifications for the restriction of market freedoms. For example, in Case *Viking* (2007)[47], the ECJ held that a trade union's right to collective action is recognised under EU law and that restrictions of the freedom of establishment may, 'in principle, be justified by an overriding reason of public interest, such as the protection of workers provided that it is established that the restriction is suitable for ensuring the attainment of the legitimate objective pursued and does not go beyond what is necessary to achieve that objective' (*Viking*, para 90). Thus, the Court has struck defensible compromises between internal market demands and interests of member states in pursuing non-economic objectives, although, of course, there are judgements in the social field, such as *Rüffert* (2008)[48] or *Laval* (2009)[49], in which one might have preferred a different balancing of interests.

(ii)   Competition rules

The competition rules of the TFEU restrict private (cartel prohibition, abuse of dominance, merger control), but also public behaviour (state aid, public undertakings, public procurement). However, it is mainly public competition law that

---

44   Joined cases C-267/91 and C-268/91 Keck and Mithouard [1993] ECR I-6097.
45   Anthony Arnull (2006), The European Union and its Court of Justice. Oxford: Oxford University Press, pp. 427et seq.
46   Case C-42/07 Liga Portuguesa de Futbol Profissional and Baw International Ltd. [2009] ECR I-7633.
47   Case C-438/05 International Transport Workers' Federation and Finnish Seamen's Union v Viking Line ABP and OÜ Viking Line Eesti ("Viking") [2007] ECR-10779.
48   Case C-346/06 Rüffert [2008] I-1989.
49   Case C-341/05 Laval [2007] ECR I-11767.

potentially limits member states possibilities to pursue non-economic objectives, in particular to organise the provision of services in the general interest. For example, the discretion to finance public services is potentially restricted by state aid law, the possibility to pursue social and other non-economic goals in context of state purchasing is limited by public procurement rules, and the grant of special rights to permit the financing of a universal service is restricted by Article 106 TFEU. Without going into details, one can state that also in this respect the ECJ, in particular on the basis of Article 14 and 106 (2), seems to strike an acceptable balance between the objective of the protection of competition pursued by these rules and the concerns of member states to pursue certain social goals. As regards state purchasing, for example, the ECJ now recognises that this may be an instrument to pursue certain policy goals. In *Wienstrom* (2003)[50] the Court interpreted procurement laws in such a way that a contracting authority may – under certain circumstances – also take into consideration ecological criteria when identifying the most economically advantageous tender. As regards state aid law, the Court clarified in Case *Altmark* (2003)[51] that the subsidisation of the provision of social services is not necessarily state aid, making it, in principle, permissible to grant exclusive rights for the purpose of cross-subsidisation of universal services. Summing up, also in this context, the legal framework as interpreted and applied by the Courts can be considered to leave adequate discretion for member states to pursue social policies and put their social values into effect.

IV   Conclusion

As shown above, there are enforcement mechanisms for all possible victims of interferences with Union values, but as a general rule, the efficiency of enforcement correlates with, or turns on, the degree of precision with which the respective value is established in EU law. This is clearly true for the enforcement by individuals, for this is only possible with regard to values which have found expression in individual rights that the enforcement is particularly efficient vis-à-vis member states. As regards member states, the situation is different and more favourable, as values can be relied upon also if they only exist in the form of political principles governing legislative and other activities. Thus it is possible to conclude that, as is befitting for a political entity that likes to call itself a community based on law and on common values, the EU legal order provides for adequate level of legal protection for these values. If there is room for improve-

50   Case C-448/01 Wienstrom [2003] ECR I-14527.
51   Case C-280/00 Altmark [2003] ECR I-7747.

ment, it is with regard to protection against EU action, especially legislative action. All in all, the values to which the EU is committed are for the most part not new, as they already existed before the Treaty of Rome. However, the EU can undoubtedly be regarded as a new and powerful actor in order to safeguard these values.

Bibliography

Arnull, A. (2006), *The European Union and its Court of Justice*. Oxford: Oxford University Press.

Beneyto, J.M. (2008), From Nice to the Constitutional Treaty: Eight Theses on the (Future) Constitutionalisation of Europe, in: Stefan Griller, Jacques Ziller (eds.), *The Lisbon Treaty: EU Constitutionalism without a Constitutional Treaty?* Wien: Springer, pp. 1-19.

Calliess, Ch. (2004), Europa als Wertegemeinschaft – Integration und Identität durch europäisches Verfassungsrecht? *Juristenzeitung* 59 (21), pp. 1033-1045.

Giubboni, S. (2006), *Social Rights and Market Freedom in the Constitution of Europe: A Labour Law Perspective*. Cambridge: Cambridge University Press.

Hallstein, W. (1973), *Die Europäische Gemeinschaft*. Düsseldorf: Econ.

Harpaz, G. (2009), The European Court of Justice and its Relations with the European Court of Human Rights: the Quest for Enhanced Reliance, Coherence and Legitimacy, *Common Market Law Review* 46, pp. 105-141.

Kaliq, U. (2008), *Ethical Dimensions on the Foreign Policy of the European Union. A Legal Appraisal*. Cambridge: Cambridge University Press.

Nettesheim, M. (2003), EU-Beitritt und Unrechtsaufarbeitung, *Europarecht* 38, pp. 36-64.

Schönborn, T. (2005), *Die Causa Austria: Zur Zulässigkeit bilateraler Sanktionen zwischen den Mitgliedstaaten der Europäischen Union*. Frankfurt am Main: Peter Lang.

Schorkopf, F. (2000), *Homogenität in der Europäischen Union: Ausgestaltung und Gewährleistung durch Art. 6 Abs 1 und Art. 7 EUV*. Berlin: Duncker & Humblot.

Speer, B. (2001), Die Europäische Union als Wertegemeinschaft: Wert- und rechtskonformes Verhalten als konditionierendes Element der Mitgliedschaft, *Die öffentliche Verwaltung*, 54(23), pp. 980-988.

Weiler, J.H.H. (1999), The Constitution of the Common Market Place: The Free Movement of Goods, in: Paul Craig, Gráinne de Búrca (eds.), *The Evolution of EU Law*. Oxford: Oxford University Press, pp. 349-376.

Williams, A. (2000), Enlargement of the Union and human rights conditionality: a policy of distinction? *European Law Review* 25, pp. 605-617.

Political representation and the common good: a fragile relationship

Johannes Pollak

I   Introduction

Political representation is one of the cornerstones of liberal democratic systems. Together with accountability and transparency, representation is tasked to fulfill multiple functions vital for reaching collective as well as individual objectives. Theories of representation deal with the questions of who, what, and how is represented, and come up with different answers and justifications relying on widely diverging definitions of the core concept itself.[1] Obviously, those answers are historically contingent. Practical and theoretical debates about representation also involve ideological disputes of a kind that cannot be easily settled, and consequently one should position the different definitions to their historically and politically specific contexts. Yet this would be curiously defeatist and relativistic in implication. For what is the point of establishing contestability if we have no way of identifying winners and losers in the 'contest'? We need a set of elaborate criteria to assess what democratic representation is and what it is not, what is good and what is bad representation, how representation is institutionally endowed, and what kind of tensions are involved in theory as well as in democratic practice. One way to assess the quality of representation would then be to look at the general state of the common good in a polity, asking if the current representative regime allows for the achievement of collective and individual objectives. Tied to representation one has to ask how a polity sets out to define collective goods and what leeway individuals are granted in order to reach individual happiness. Thus, political representation is always about the reconcilement between public and private needs. A such, as Albert Weale points out, representative democracy is commonly justified not on the grounds that it allows a *whole* people to govern itself but on the grounds that it reconciles collective decision making with the continued autonomy of *each* individual.[2]

---

1   Johannes Pollak (2007*), Repräsentation ohne Demokratie. Kollidierende Modi der Repräsentation in der Europäischen Union.* Wien, New York: Springer.
2   Albert Weale (1999), Democracy. London: Macmillan.

This contribution deals with four broad questions. Section 2 asks if the common good is self-evident truth and charts some of the answers given in political philosophy. The following section assumes that the common good has to be negotiated and fine-tuned all the time – but who can do so in times of mass societies? Subsequently the contribution adopts the idea of representation as claims making and asks what can possibly go wrong in times of crises. Going beyond the confines of the well-ordered nation-state, Section 4 sheds some light on political representation in a supranational polity characterised by multiple interacting levels, the interplay of state and non-state actors, and non-coercive politics. A final section sums up the argument.

II   Can the common good be negotiated?

Throughout human history we can discern two major approaches to the question if the common good can be negotiated, or, to put it in other words, if the common good is flexible, i.e. adaptable to time and circumstances. As such, this is also a question about the changing or constant nature of human *eudaimonia*:

There were those who started from the assumption of a predestined common good, discernible only for the chosen ones.[3] Those few extraordinary men were able to grasp the common good due to their invested powers and/or overarching intellect. The former were the ones anointed by the Church and acted as God's representatives on earth[4] – sometimes with the help of a privy council. The later, among them also some of the Founding Fathers of the United States and all those who were scared to death by the idea of an extension of the franchise, thought a minimum of education to be the precondition for the deliberation of how to achieve the common good. James Madison made this explicit in The Federalist No. 10, where he argues for the refinement of the public views 'by passing them through the medium of a chosen body, whose wisdom may best discern the true interest of their country, and whose patriotism and love of justice, will be least

---

3   Maude V. Clarke (1936), Medieval Representation and Consent: A Consent of Early parliaments in England and Ireland. With Special reference to the Modus Tenendi Parliamentum. New York: Russel & Russel; Otto Hintze (1931), Weltgeschichtliche Bedingungen der Repräsentativverfassung, Historische Zeitschrift 143, pp. 1-47; Hasso Hofmann (1974), Repraesentation. Studien zur Wort- und Begriffsgeschichte von der Antike bis ins 19. Jahrhundert. Berlin: Duncker & Humblot; Walter Ulmann (1975), Medieval Political Thought. Harmondsworth: Penguin Press.

4   Hence the catching name 'descendence theory'. See Adalbert Podlech (1984), Repäsentation, in: Otto Brunner, Werner Conze, Reinhart Koselleck (eds.), Geschichtliche Grundbegriffe: Historisches Lexikon zur politisch-sozialen Sprache in Deutschland, Bd. 5. Stuttgart: Klett, 1974-1997, pp. 509-547.

likely to sacrifice it to temporary and partial considerations'.[5] Or compare Boissy d'Anglas who wrote in the introduction to the French Constitution of 1795:

> 'We must be ruled by the best citizens. And the best are the most learned and the most concerned in the maintenance of law and order. Now, with very few exceptions, you will find such men only among those who own some property, and are thus attached to the land in which it lies, to the laws which protect it and to the public order which maintains it…You must, therefore, guarantee the political rights of the well-to-do…and [deny] unreserved political rights to men without property, for if such men ever find themselves seated among the legislators, then they will provoke agitations…without fearing their consequences…and in the end precipitate us into those violent convulsions from which we have scarcely yet emerged'[6].

Nota bene, not the common good is negotiated, but only the means and instruments to achieve the objective. The difference between those two positions lies in the number of people being able to recognise the common good and thus allowed to choose the way leading towards it. Moreover, whereas despots and monarchs, autocrats, and tyrants had (and have) at least to uphold the fiction that the common good is out there, revealing its nature to them and only them, Madison, Jay, Hamilton, and the other less well-known creators of the modern republic accounted for the interests distorting or fostering this common good. Thus, while the former established an eternally unchanging common good, the latter conceded that the secret in achieving this common good lies in the mediation between diverging interests. A discussion of the nature of the common good seemed superfluous to both as the Assyrian marble slabs in the British Museum and the rites of anointment[7], as well as the Federalist papers or the American Declaration of Independence show.

Secondly, there are those who, out of ethical, moral, and practical considerations, regard every human being as the best judge of his/her *eudaimonia*. Consider J.S. Mill (1861) who considered it a principle of universal truth

> 'that the rights and interests of every or any person are secure from being disregarded when the person is himself able, and habitually disposed, to stand up for them…Human beings are only secure from evil at the hands of others in proportion as they have the power of being, and are, self-protecting'.[8]

Neither property nor education is a necessary precondition for recognising the common good. Modern liberalism is founded on the belief that freedom and the

---

5   Thus Burke and Madison are much closer in their elitist conception of representation than it is usually presumed.
6   Christopher Hibbert (1980), The French Revolution. London: Penguin Books, p. 282.
7   Arthur Bloch (1990), Compounded Representation in EU-Multi Level Governance, in: Beate Kohler-Koch (ed.), Linking EU and National Governanne. Oxford: Oxford University Press, pp. 81-110.
8   John Stuart Mill (2008/1861), Considerations on Representative Government. Ithaca, NY: Cornell University Press; John Stuart Mill (1972/ 1861), Utilitarianism, On Liberty and Considerations on Representative Government. London: Dent.

right to achieve happiness attaches to men and women as such, from birth. The political system in which we are born (i.e. the way the common good is perceived) may in fact make an enormous difference to our life chances. But the polity is not meant to make a difference to our rights to follow our own personal happiness or natural inclinations.[9] Logically, only a way of direct governing guarantees that the common good can be shaped and approximated. And this common good, above all, must allow the individual to reach personal objectives.

And here, at the latest, all our troubles start, because in the first case the common good is not negotiable, it is revealed to the chosen one by whomsoever, or, in only a slightly less parochial way, the common good is taken to be self-evident. Take the example of a remarkable document, the American Declaration of Independence:

> 'We hold these truths to be self-evident, that all men are created equal, that they are endowed by their Creator with certain inalienable Rights, that among these are Life, Liberty, and the pursuit of happiness.'

In fact, it seemed so self-evident to the authors that no further specifications were made.[10] Again, the common good is not negotiable, but at least we can discuss about the ways how best to foster it. But there are some, like Edmund Burke, who know better how to foster the self-evident (although with the help of divine guidance) than others:

> 'But his unbiased opinion, his mature judgement, his enlightened conscience, he ought not to sacrifice to you [the electorate of Bristol], to any man, or to any set of living men. These he does not derive from your pleasure, – nor from the law and the Constitution. They are a trust from Providence, for the abuse of which he is deeply answerable.'[11]

The second case, let us call it the democratic case, has an entirely different point of departure. The common good is and must be negotiable *per se* because interest and needs of people change and no one is in a better condition to tell others what this elusive common good is. It is a basic human right indeed, to set one's own objectives.[12] Cohorts of students have learned that a political community

---

9 It is not unknown for modern thinkers to criticise ancient thinkers for the belief that freedom and thus happiness could only be achieved within the polis. However, one also has to bear in mind that Plato as well as Aristotle did not believe that men in general were capable of political freedom. This is why they need the polis, since only the well-ordered and just polis offers them at least a chance to become virtuous.

10 We should disregard for the moment that then and long thereafter quite a considerable lot of people were deprived not only of political rights but also of many other 'inalienable rights' essential to life, liberty, and the pursuit of happiness.

11 Edmund Burke (1866), Speech at the Conlusion of the Poll. The Works of Edmund Burke, 12 Vols., Vol. 2, Boston.

12 Compare Dworkin's two liberal principles: the principle of the 'intrinsic value of human life' and the principle of 'personal responsibility' hammered out in his book (2008) Is

needs to provide for security, freedom, justice and order, and welfare. And scores of students have learned that there are endless variations in detail. What remains is the fact that the common good is not plainly out there, apart from its most simple and general form and that we are all equal in recognising it. At least, this insight holds true for the democrats among us. And within the general borders set by the most basic state functions we shall all find happiness. Small wonder, then, that the negotiations about the nature of the common good have shifted to the question of who can negotiate it. Henceforth, one rather talked about 'common interests' and no longer the common good.

III   Who can negotiate it and how is it negotiated?

The modern 'father of all direct forms of government', Jean-Jacques Rousseau, argued that, for the sake of the general will, all citizens should participate in decision making or in the search for the common good. From James Mill to Montesquieu and William Patterson, from Noah Webster to Thomas Paine[13], all of them easily realised that such a participation of all would have dire consequences. Thomas Hare formulated in the nineteenth century:

> 'Representation is a matter of daily occurrence and common necessity. It is the vicarious performance of duties which cannot be personally executed. It intervenes in commerce, in jurisprudence, in education, and in a thousand other forms. In a multitude of circumstances people are compelled to place themselves and their interests in the hand of others'[14].

Thus, the necessity of political representation arises. In addition, representation also becomes a necessity[15] beyond mere practical consideration because it allows a community to act and be perceived as an actor by others. Representation is indeed an existential precondition for building a collective identity. As simple as this sounds, the struggle to arrive at a legitimate selection of people representing a community took quite some while and is closely connected to our first point. In a democracy representatives are authorised via elections 'to act in the best inter-

Democracy Possible Here? Principles for a new political debate. Princeton: Princeton University Press.

13   See John A. Fairlie (1968), Das Wesen politischer Repräsentation, in: Heinz Rausch (ed.), Zur Theorie und Geschichte der Repräsentativverfassung, Darmstadt: Wissenschaftliche Buchgesellschaft, orig. 1940, pp. 28-73.

14   Quoted in Fairlie (1968), p. 47.

15   *Nota bene*: it is a practical necessity not a normative requirement or a moral right. This goes hand in hand with the fact that representation was not invented to make democracy possible in large polities, rather it was invented to bar the advance of democracy by granting participatory rights only to a tiny fraction of the population. See Frank R. Ankersmit (2002), Political representation, Stanford, Cal.: Stanford University Press. .

est of the representatives'.[16] On what grounds are they selected? Let us differentiate between common identity, common interests, and epistemic reasons.[17] In the first case, citizens select one of them; in the second case, they select not because of a perceived overlapping identity (be it local, regional, national, ethnic, gender, etc.) but because of shared interests. And in the last case, the expertise of the representative tips the scale. A question that is not solved by the authorisation method concerns the (in-) dependence of the representative from the represented (imperative or free mandate). While Burke can be said to lead the camp of the independence supporters, Madison (Federalist No. 52) acts as the spearhead of those who see in the dependence of the representatives the most important guarantee[18] against the development of a class of political mandarins. Frequent elections should ensure this dependence. Liberal representative democracies apply an uneasy balance between the need for consistency and the imperative mandate, i.e. frequent elections but long terms of office. Today, it increasingly seems the electorate mandates her representatives via mass media, opinion polls, and beauty contests.

The enterprise of comparative politics tells us about various ways to negotiate the common good, the focus of attention being parliaments 'mandating' the executive after they have deliberated the common good or managed the clash of interests. Recently, i.e. since the late 1960s, more encompassing ways have come into fashion: societal participation via interest groups. Greven distinguishes two big waves of societal participation in the second half of the twentieth century.[19] A first wave focused on the participation of citizens who had been historically restricted by structural barriers or lack of social resources. The second wave contained a shift from individual participation to organisations and collective actors or interest groups. It was no longer the education effect or justice arguments that were brought forward to justify participation but considerations on effectiveness, problem-solving capacity, and compliance with regulations:[20] the more participants, the more effective, and less costly in terms of supervision, coercion, and

---

16 Hanna F. Pitkin (1976), The Concept of Political Representation. Berkeley, Los Angeles, London: University of California Press.
17 John O'Neill (2001), Representing People, Representing Nature, Representing the World, Government and Policy 19, pp. 483-500.
18 In addition a big government, depicting all interests and a rigorous separation of power were thought to keep representatives in check.
19 Michael Greven (2007), Some Considerations on Participation in Participatory Governance, in: Beate Kohler Koch, Berthold Rittberger (eds.), Debating the Democratic Legitimacy of the European Union. Lanham: Rowman & Littlefield, pp. 233-248.
20 There is no shortage in theories trying to explain the pluralisation of political actors or the informalisation of politics: from a state-centred perspective we find pluralism and neo-corporatism; from a self-regulatory perspective we find associative and deliberative democracy.

resources. A 'normative de-individualization of political participation'[21] took place, which directs the discussion today. Consequently we find more and more groups demanding their say in the political process. All of them point to their representativeness as a justification for participation. Such a pluralist system has undeniable advantages under the conditions of a stable institutional/constitutional frame which defines roles in the policy-making process, a transparent decision-making system and clear accountability procedures for all participating actors: (1) The involvement of multiple representatives (or individuals/organisations claiming to be representative) allows for a wider range of societal concerns to be raised. Noticing these concerns and allowing them a place in the decision-making system could strengthen the legitimacy of a political system. (2) Interest groups have a short chain of delegation, i.e. they are closer to the citizens. (3) Interest groups are privileging specific policy issues rather than strategic party politics. Due to this focus on issues rather than on obtaining political power, they are potentially transnational in character. (4) A pluralist system allows the citizens to direct their support to alternative groups instead of venturing their frustration against the system *per se*. (5) Interest groups demand a higher degree of participation and political activism than formal structures of representation. They may thus be capable of increasing 'citizenship practice' (Wiener 1998).[22] (6) Pluralist representation can increase the inclusiveness/ representativeness of politics. Thus it potentially reduces transaction costs in implementation.[23] (8) Last but not least, a pluralist system, by allowing for consultation with specially affected groups, enables polities to take account of those variations in the *intensity* of preference that are widely agreed to be worthy of consideration instead of just counting heads of people who might be affected only marginally by a specific decision.

This strand of thinking was taken up by the 'claims-making' approach introduced by Michael Saward.[24] Political representation is understood as an on-

---

21 Michael Greven (2007), Some Considerations on Participation in Participatory Governance, in: Beate Kohler Koch, Berthold Rittberger (eds.), Debating the Democratic Legitimacy of the European Union. Lanham: Rowman & Littlefield, pp. 233-248 at 247.

22 A Neo-Aristotelian argument which is beautifully explicated in Hannah Arendt (1967), The Human Condition, Chicago: Chicago University Press. See also Frieder Naschold (1969), Organisation und Demokratie: Stuttgart: Kohlhammer; John Dewey (1927), The Public and its Problems, London: George Allen and Unwin.

23 Bob Jessop (2002) argues that participation, or participatory governance, is a means of coping with the omnipresence of governing failures (Bob Jessop (2002), Governance and Metagovernance: On Reflexivity, Requisite Variety, and Requisite Irony, in: H. Heinelt et.al (eds.), Participatory Governance in Multi-Level Context.Concepts and Experience, Opladen: Leske+Budrich, pp. 33-58.

24 See e.g. Michael Saward (2003), Representing Nature and the Nature of Representation, Paper presented at the 2nd European Consortium for Political Research Conference,

going, tripartite dialogue between representatives, their representative claims they put forward to an audience of potential represented, and the ones who are subject to the decisions by the representatives. It is a fluid and endogenously defined standard in which some actors – be they parliamentarians, NGOs, interest groups, civil society associations, etc. – make claims to represent others which are, in turn, accepted, amended, or rejected by various (sometimes overlapping) social groups or audiences. Such a claim presents an offer to the represented to be understood in a specific form. Potential representatives make claims about themselves (that they possess certain characteristics which enable them to represent a constituency) and their constituency (they describe or understand the constituency in a specific way). The representatives constantly present a claim comprising an idea of the political community they want to represent and a specific course of action that allows for the realisation of its principals' best interest (Saward 2006). Political representation is not confined to those that citizens vote into offices, which allows them to make binding decisions (i.e. formal representatives), but also social groups which are increasingly part and parcel of modern governance systems (i.e. informal representatives).

On a conceptual level representation as claims making comprises the following elements: (1) A representative; (2) The mandate that comprises the area for which a representative is expected to deliver justifications; (3) The form and language in which the dialogue takes place. The dialogue makes use of a certain 'prose', i.e. there are standard questions the audience wants to have answered in a standard way ranging from the economic and parsimonious employment of resources to formal rule adherence and to the ethical behaviour of representatives; (4) The context in which claims are offered; (5) Finally, we find the audience that is part of the context but also structurally different from it. Ideal democratic theory would want to see one unified audience assembled in the *agora* receiving the justifications of the representatives, entering into a rational discourse about their performance resulting in praise or ostracism. Democratic practice, however, is a bit more complicated, since representatives are faced with many different audiences showing divergent interests, demands, and capabilities and therefore asking for different forms of accountability. Given this complexity it is hardly surprising that we find several layers of indeterminacy, or in other words, turns where representation can go wrong.

The first layer of indeterminacy concerns the question of who is authorised or entitled to make claims. As stated, it is no longer just elected politicians but also grass-roots movements, NGOs, and interest groups who voice claims to

Marburg, September 2003; Michael Saward (2006), The Representative Claim, Contemporary Political Theory 5, pp. 297-318; Michael Saward (2010), The Representative Claim. Oxford: Oxford University Press. .

represent. But, crucially, such unelected representatives do not just lack the authority to speak on behalf of the whole citizenry.[25] They do not seek that authority, instead preferring to give voice and influence to specific membership groups. What remains is a cacophony of claims and a fog of accountability.

The second layer of indeterminacy concerns the question of language. Representative and audience have to speak the same language; they have to be able to formulate representation requirements such as the scope of representation, and they have to be able to decipher the justificatory prose. Given the undeniable fact that every social group and institution uses specific terminology in its justificatory claims, the giving of account may become unintelligible. Combine this with the rising complexity of politics, the vagueness of legal prescriptions ('soft law'), and the rising number of actors, the chance for misapprehension is considerable. Justifications may become intelligible for an expert community, which can only lead to the frustration of the wider public. Intricately linked to this indeterminacy is the problem of translation. This does not denote the simple translation from one language to another, but on the one hand the translation from technical reports into everyday language, and on the other hand the translation for different audiences. The first requirement is not necessarily rooted in a Schumpeter-like scepticism about the ability of an audience, but rather in the fact that politics is not the primary interest of the wider public, given that time resources are scarce and that there are differences in audience capability. The second one takes account of the fact that every political community disposes of multiple audiences. In a liberal representative democracy we would expect representatives to fulfill these translation requirements since they are installed by the principal to hold to account (and are themselves held to account). However, one has to consider the possibility of different, sometimes even contradictory, accounts and justifications delivered to different audiences by the same representative. Only the public exchange of claims and their discussion can provide for the identification of public goods. And even then striking examples of contradictory justifications by one and the same representatives conveyed to fragmented audiences are part and parcel of democracy. Assuming that a representative has delivered a comprehensive and coherent claim to a specific audience based on stable non-shifting criteria, this audience has to process the information, i.e. it has to be capable of establishing causal relations between activities and effects. This may be difficult to achieve in complex polities, but it is even more difficult if the public lacks the capability or the interest to do so.

To sum up, the common good is no longer deliberated by a body specifically selected and authorised for that purpose, but supplemented by an increasing

25   Alex Warleigh (2001), "Europeanizing" civil society: NGOs as agents of political socialisation, Journal of Common Market Studies 39 (4), pp. 619-639.

number of 'claims-makers'. It just sounds like the deliberative paradise. Hierarchical systems of policymaking are dissolved for the benefit of pluralist negotiation systems in which no actor is privileged. Yet dissolved is too strong a word, since even in pluralist systems some basic rules of the game have to be observed by the participants in order to keep at least the illusion of accountability. This inclusion of multiple actors (and also the agencification, i.e. the transfer of specific decisions to non-majoritarian bodies) is increasingly justified by pointing to the rising complexity of politics and the need for special expertise.

One result is that (1) The common good becomes an unplanned side-effect or an indirect result of negotiations between different interest groups only caring for particular objectives and definitely not with an eye for wider societal welfare;[26] (2) Such a system of 'organised chaos' tends to privilege 'rich' groups, thereby aggravating or at least continuing power asymmetries. This leads to a situation which leaves some interests well entrenched in the policymaking process while others are left to grapple with the difficulty of getting organised for action at all; (3) The complexity of such an 'organised chaos' can easily lead to duplication and thus to efficiency losses; (4) Accountability structures are blurred, and shirking and blame-shifting can become rampant; together with point three, this can contribute to a rising frustration of the citizens with their political system; (5) In absence of clear rules, central players have to act as gatekeepers/sluice gates, which gives them a considerably powerful position. (6) Last but not least, it forces citizens to organise themselves in order to get their share, thereby sacrificing a major advantage of representative liberal democracies, *viz.* to strive for individual happiness. Those who do not organise themselves are not 'represented', and subsequently have no voice in the negotiation processes.

Those unwelcome side-effects are kept at bay, at least to a certain extent, by party-based politics. In addition, every liberal democratic system shows a good deal of those negative symptoms. What has kept democracies from plunging into the abyss of 'might is right' is the existence of a balance of interests, party-based politics, and an independent judiciary acting on the basis of well-entrenched constitutions. This was exactly the argument of James Madison: let us understand the parliament as a 'congress of ambassadors' representing local, specialized interests and hope they balance each other out (see Federalist 10 and 52). But can we still trust that such a balance exists?

---

26 A Habermasian would find it most apt that the common good is negotiated by multiple interest groups in order to achieve rational consensus. My point is that the common good is never explicitly deliberated and negotiated in the 'light of the day' as J.S. Mill argued in 1861 in his book on Utilitarianism (John Stuart Mill (1972/1861), Utilitarianism, On Liberty and Considerations on Representative Government. London: Dent).

IV   How is it done in the European Union?

If we hold that the common good in liberal democratic systems is the by-product of intense and complex negotiations (and not of deliberate planning or grasping) in which no longer one specific group claims to be in a better position (be it because this group is specifically authorised by e.g. national elections), how does it look in systems which can be defined by 'policies without politics'?[27] According to black letter law it is quite clear who is the actor tasked with upholding the European common good: whereas the Council of the European Union represents the member states and the European Parliament (EP) represents the European Peoples, the European Commission shall act as a neutral arbiter, its eyes set on the European good impartially. How does this work?

In its 'White Paper on Governance' (2001), the Commission defined its own role as an arbiter between those democratic interests represented by the Council and those represented by the EP. Of course, the Commission's claim – that its representative role is based on the idea of a neutral bureaucracy safeguarding the general interest in the clash of national interests in the Council of Europe and the European Council – only begs questions of how a mixture of independence and technocratic understanding can ground claims to regulate relationships between different categories of elected representatives.[28] Does this mean the Commission represents a given common good while Council and EP are democratic addenda? Or is the common good the result of brute institutional and interest representation to which the Commission adds the common good? The best answer the White Paper could give was to show how the Commission can formulate its claims in a dialogue with the other institutions, interest groups, and the citizens at large, though that, of course, still left unanswered how it would arbitrate competing claims.[29] Having the monopoly of initiative in important policy fields, the steering capacity of the Commission and thus its influence on the conditions of achieving a common or individual good are considerable.[30] A clearer definition of the Commission's representative role in the cacophony of claims is needed.

---

27   Vivian Schmidt (2006), Democracy in Europe. The EU and National Politics. Oxford: Oxford University Press.

28   Andreas Føllesdal (2003), The Political Theory of the White Paper on Governance: Hidden and Fascinating, European Public Law 9 (1), pp. 73-86.

29   Christopher Lord, Johannes Pollak (2010), The EU's Many Representative Modes: Colluding? Cohering? Journal of European Public Policy 17(1), pp. 117-136.

30   The literature on the Commission shows quite some divergence when it comes to the influence of the Commission ranging from an assessment seeing 80 per cent of the Commission's initial draft in the final legislative act (Robert Hull (1993), Lobbying Brussels: A View from Within. In: Sonia Mazey, Jeremy J. Richardson (eds.), Lobbying in the European Community. Oxford: Oxford University Press, pp. 82-92), to a mere superficial resemblance between draft and legislative act (Michelle Cini (1996), The European

The European Commission's White Paper on European Governance awarded a prominent place to civil society organisations for the sake of efficient and democratic governance. This new-found love for inclusive policymaking found a sequel in the Constitutional Treaty (CT), where in a section about participatory governance the importance of the participation of representative associations is emphasised (Article I-47), and also in the Lisbon Treaty (Article 11 TEU). Although the hapless differentiation between representative and participatory democracy was dropped in the Lisbon Treaty, Article 11 obliges EU institutions 'to maintain an open, transparent and regular dialogue with representative associations and with civil society'.

Such a dialogue, also in the form of public consultations, is highly important in the policy formation phase and certainly increases the legitimacy of the supranational level. However, the European Council, the 'centre of the executive'[31], turns out to be the decisive institution in terms of final decision making. Certainly landmark decisions, from the Currency Union to enlargement, from the European Financial Stability Facility (EFSF) to treaty reforms, support this assumption. And the Treaty of Lisbon's provisions strengthen the role of the European Council even further. Consisting of the heads of state and government and supported by a secretariat and, since the Treaty of Lisbon, a permanent president (Article 15), the European Council claims to represent the member states, sharing this role with the Council, both being 'democratically accountable either to their national Parliaments, or to their citizens' (Article 10 TEU). During the financial crises starting in 2008 and culminating in the dramatic Greece-related events in 2011, the European Council acted in an entirely unbound way.[32] Although a number of commentators were not at ease with the way decisions were made and justified, the general mood was asking for decisive and swift action. Once again it was the German Federal Constitutional Court, who already at the occasion of the Lisbon Treaty assigned the German *Bundestag* a watchdog role[33],

Commission: Leadership, Organisation and Culture in the EU Administration. Manchester: Manchester University Press.

31   Peter Ludlow (2005), Die Führung der Union durch den Europäischen Rat: Übergang oder Krise? Integration 28(2), pp. 3-15.

32   E.g. Martin Seidel (2010), Aktuelle Probleme der europäischen Währungsunion, Integration 36(4), pp. 334-351.

33   Dimitrios Doukas (2009), The Verdict of the German Constitutional Court on the Lisbon Treaty: not guilty, but don't do it again, European Law Review 34 (6), pp. 866 - 888; Jo Eric Murkens (2010), Bundesverfassungsgericht (2Bve 2/08): "We want our identity back" – the revival of national sovereignty in the German Federal Constitutional Court's decision on the Lisbon Treaty, Public Law, pp. 530-550; Dieter Grimm (2010), Zum Lissabon – Urteil des Bundesverfassungsgerichts: das Grundgesetz als Riegel vor einer Verstaatlichung der Europäischen Union, Der Staat 48(4), pp. 476-495; Peter-Christian, Mül-

who upped the ante for the German government and thus, indirectly, for the Council. In the case of the ESFS a procedure was enacted guaranteeing the participation of the *Bundestag* resembling a parliamentary reserve. If the economic crisis requires an exceptionally rapid reaction, a new body consisting of nine members of the Parliamentary Budget Committee was created (Article 3 section 3 StabMechG[34]). Against this 'Committee of Nine' a successful appeal by oppositional members of the *Bundestag* was launched. The German Constitutional Court ruled that no committee can usurp the decision rights of the *Bundestag* (see BVerfG, 2 BvE 8/11, 27.10.2011). This ruling puts at least a certain limit to the discretionary power of the European Council in the current financial crises. In addition to the European Council, Article 10 TEU sees the member states also represented by their governments in the Council. The Council is the place for political bargaining between the member states, most decisions being taken at civil servant level, either in the COREPER or the multiple working groups. It is not descriptions or images of the represented which clash in the Council but state interests. The claim that the ministers are responsible to their national parliaments in practice meets largely uninformed and unwilling national parliaments.[35]

The Treaty of Lisbon also maintains that 'citizens are directly represented at Union level in the European Parliament' (Article 10(2) TEU). On top of that, the Treaty stipulates that 'political parties at the European level contribute to European political awareness'. At the level of the EP we are confronted with an unequal representation of the member states, itself not unknown also within some member states.[36] It is well known that, e.g. in Luxembourg, there is one MEP for every 40,000 electors whereas in Italy there is one MEP for every 696,000 electors, a difference of 17 to 1. The principle of degressive proportionality is enshrined in the Lisbon Treaty, with a provision that the smallest states should have at least 6 seats and a maximum of 96 reserved for the largest, a ratio of 16 to 1. However, the German electorate outnumbers the Luxembourg electorate by a ratio of more than 250 to 1. In the EU, a single German MEP represents 0.17 per cent of the total EU population. A single MEP from Malta represents 0.01 per cent of the EU population. The range of difference between these two ex-

ler-Graff (2009), Das Karlsruher Lissabon-Urteil: Bedingungen, Grenzen, Orakel, und integrative Optionen, Integration 32(4), pp. 331-360.

34   Stabilisierungsmechnismusgesetz, see http://www.gesetze-im-internet.de/stabmechg/3.-html

35   Johannes Pollak, Peter Slominski (2009), Zwischen De- und Reparlamentarisierung: der österreichische Nationalrat und seine Mitwirkungsrechte in EU-Angelegenheiten, Österreichische Zeitschrift für Politikwissenschaft 2, pp. 193-212.

36   Anne Peters (2001), Elemente einer Theorie der Verfassung Europas, Berlin: Duncker & Humblot; Lionel S. Penrose (1946), The Elementary Statistics of Majority Voting, Journal of the Royal Statistical Society 109 (81), pp. 53-57.

tremes is therefore 0.16 per cent. Figure 1 displays these difference ranges in percentage of population represented in the most and least populous constituency. It shows that the difference of population represented by a single MEP in the EU, 0.16 per cent, is more than in Austria, Belgium, Germany, and the USA, but less than e.g. in Australia, Canada, France, and Switzerland. In other words, although the initial ratio of citizens represented in the EU is very high due to the principle of degressive proportionality, the EU to a large extent balances out this distortion by having a relatively large number of total representatives (750 MEPs).[37]

Figure 1: Range of difference in percentage of population represented

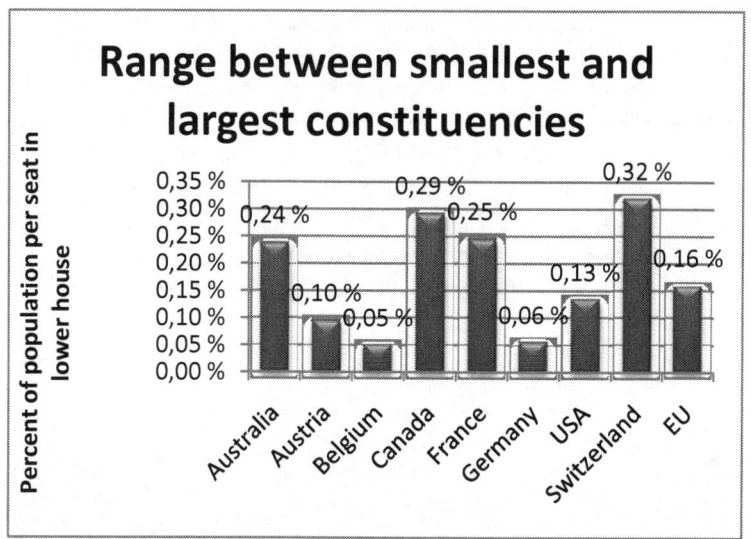

This reflects the problem of bringing the principle of international law of equal representation of states into line with the democratic principle of equal representation of citizens. However, the principle of digressive proportionality, which privileges smaller member states again, as in the case of European Council and Council, emphasises the territoriality of representation. It is the political organisation of the EP that effectively counters this territoriality, in the most cases

37   Johannes Pollak et. al. (2011), Citizen's weight of vote in selected federal systems, Directorate general for internal policies, Policy Department C: Citizens' Rights and Constitutional Affairs, PE 453.168.

ranging from party cohesion[38], to the basic rules allowing for the formation of EP factions.[39] As is the case with the Commission and the Council, dialogue between incumbents and citizens is a precondition for representation as claims making. According to an analysis of the year 2000[40], 56 per cent of the MEPs spend some time per week in their home states, and 34 per cent can only do so during the weekends. Contact to the voters is indirect via a permanently staffed office for 82.7 per cent of the MEPs. Regular contact with the respective constituency was only the case for 31.9 per cent of MEPs. It stands to reason that the claim to represent a constituency is mediated by citizens organised in interest groups, the media, or party offices. Such indirect contact to the voters is part and parcel of the modern mass society. What contributes to a certain kind of alienation between the representative and the represented at the European level is the high level of aggregation. The higher this level, i.e. the more citizens a single MEP has to represent, the more general will be the representative claim, and the more fuzzy will be the description of the constituency.

What we find at the European level is thus a form of highly complex compound representation, describing the co-existence of different channels and institutions claiming to represent Europe's citizens.[41] National parliaments, a directly elected European Parliament, the European Council, the Council, European parties, and civil society organisations all claim to represent the citizens in his or her multiple facets. In this compound system the danger of the above-said indeterminacies become a reality.

---

38   See e.g. Simon Hix (2002), Parliamentary Behavior with two Principals: Preferences, parties and Voting in the European Parliament, American Journal of Political Science 46(3), pp. 688-698; Simon Hix et. al. (2006), Democratic Politics in the European Parliament. Cambridge: Cambridge University Press; Simon Hix, Christopher Lord (1997), Political Parties in the European Union. London: Macmillan; Amie Kreppel (2002) European parliament and Supranational Party System – A Study in Institutional Development. Cambridge: Cambridge University Press.

39   See the Rules of Procedure of the 7th parliamentary term, September 2011: http://www.europarl.europa.eu/sides/getDoc.do?pubRef=-//EP//NONSGML+RULES-EP+20110926+0+DOC+PDF+V0//EN&language=EN

40   Data from the European parliamentary Research Group at the LSE. See http://www2.lse.ac.uk/government/resgroup/EPRG/MEPsurveyDasta.aspx.

41   Arthur Benz (2003), Compounded Representation in EU-Multi Level Governance, in: Beate Kohler-Koch (ed.), Linking EU and National Governance. Oxford: Oxford University Press, pp. 81-110; Joanne B. Brzinski et. al (1999), Compounded Representation in Western European Federations. London. Franc Cass; Christopher Lord, Johannes Pollak (2010), The EU's Many Representative Modes: Colluding? Cohering? Journal of European Public Policy, 17(1), pp. 117-136.

V   Conclusion

The supranational system seems to aggravate what we know from policymaking at the nation-state level: well-endowed and entrenched interest groups shape the policymaking process under the watchful eyes of a benevolent executive. The common good is no longer construed as an achievement, but as an attribute of a complex negotiation process, and politics not as a vehicle for expressing and realising our human nature as political animals, but as the price for pursuing our own private aims. The institution hitherto tasked with the deliberation of the common good, the legislative assembly, becomes one player among others, and not the most highly regarded one if we are to follow countless opinion polls about politicians. Instead, a myriad of interest groups, not necessarily hostile towards each other but certainly indifferent, following hardly any collective logic, determine particular interests. Viewed from above, the common good is a rag rug of particular interests. But what is wrong with it if this patchwork allows us to achieve private happiness? First, such a system does not fulfil a basic requirement of liberal democracies, *viz.* accountability. Who is responsible for what becomes increasingly blurred and deteriorates into a game of mutual blame shifting. Secondly, the equal representation of citizens in one body becomes an empty shell because parliaments tend to lose out in the integration process. Instead of deliberating the common good, parliaments are occupied with the management of particular interest groups. It is a short way from the well-founded need for advice by particular interest groups to the mere juggling of those groups. Thirdly, W. Hennis defined the discussion of objectives as a precondition for being worthy of recognition/acceptance (Annerkennungswürdigkeit)[42]. And this discussion should take place in the body foreseen for it: parliaments. If we renounce this common visualisation/discussion by legitimately authorised representatives, we renounce politics. Those few who claim to be in a better position to define the common good might then become the norm again.

Bibliography:

Ankersmit, F.A. (2002), *Political representation*. Stanford, Cal.: Stanford University Press.

Arendt, H. (1967), *The Human Condition*. Chicago: Chicago University Press.

Benz, A. (2003), Compounded Representation in EU-Multi Level Governance, in: Beate Kohler-Koch (ed.), *Linking EU and National Governance*. Oxford: Oxford University Press, pp. 81-110.

---

42   Wilhelm Hennis (1976), Legitimität. Zu einer Kategorie der bürgerlichen Gesellschaft, Politische Vierteljahresschrift, Sonderheft 7, pp. 9-38.

Brzinski, J.B. et. al (1999), *Compounded Representation in Western European Federations.* London: Franc Cass.

Burke, E. (1866), *Speech at the Conlusion of the Poll. The Works of Edmund Burke*, 12 Vols., Vol. 2, Boston.

Cini, M. (1996), *The European Commission: Leadership, Organisation and Culture in the EU Administration.* Manchester: Manchester University Press.

Clarke, M.V. (1936), *Medieval Representation and Consent: A Consent of Early parliaments in England and Ireland. With Special reference to the Modus Tenendi Parliamentum.* New York: Russel & Russel.

Dewey, J. (1927), *The Public and its Problems.* London: George Allen and Unwin.

Doukas, D. (2009), The Verdict of the German Constitutional Court on the Lisbon Treaty: not guilty, but don't do it again, *European Law Review* 34 (6), pp. 866 – 888.

Dworkin, R. (2008) *Is Democracy Possible Here? Principles for a new political debate.* Princeton: Princeton University Press.

Fairlie, J.A. (1968), Das Wesen politischer Repräsentation, in: Heinz Rausch (ed.), *Zur Theorie und Geschichte der Repräsentativverfassung.* Darmstadt: Wissenschaftliche Buchgesellschaft, orig. 1940, pp. 28-73.

Føllesdal, A.(2003), The Political Theory of the White Paper on Governance: Hidden and Fascinating, *European Public Law* 9 (1), pp. 73-86.

Greven, M. (2007), Some Considerations on Participation in Participatory Governance, in: Beate Kohler Koch, Berthold Rittberger (eds.), *Debating the Democratic Legitimacy of the European Union.* Lanham: Rowman & Littlefield, pp. 233-248.

Grimm, D. (2010), Zum Lissabon – Urteil des Bundesverfassungsgerichts: das Grundgesetz als Riegel vor einer Verstaatlichung der Europäischen Union, *Der Staat* 48(4), pp. 476-495.

Hennis, W. (1976), Legitimität. Zu einer Kategorie der bürgerlichen Gesellschaft, *Politische Vierteljahresschrift*, Sonderheft 7, pp. 9-38.

Hibbert, Ch. (1980), *The French Revolution.* London: Penguin Books .

Hintze, O. (1931), Weltgeschichtliche Bedingungen der Repräsentativverfassung, *Historische Zeitschrift* 143, pp. 1-47.

Hix, S. (2002), Parliamentary Behavior with two Principals: Preferences, parties and Voting in the European Parliament, *American Journal of Political Science* 46(3), pp. 688-698.

Hix, S. and Lord, Ch. (1997), *Political Parties in the European Union.* London: Macmillan.

Hix, S. et. al. (2006), *Democratic Politics in the European Parliament.* Cambridge: Cambridge University Press.

Hofmann, H. (1974), *Repraesentation. Studien zur Wort- und Begriffsgeschichte von der Antike bis ins 19. Jahrhundert.* Berlin: Duncker & Humblot.

Hull, R. (1993), Lobbying Brussels: A View from Within, in: Sonia Mazey, Jeremy J. Richardson (eds.), *Lobbying in the European Community.* Oxford: Oxford University Press, pp. 82-92).

Jessop, B. (2002), Governance and Metagovernance: On Reflexivity, Requisite Variety, and Requisite Irony, in: H. Heinelt et.al (eds.), *Participatory Governance in Multi-Level Context.Concepts and Experience.* Opladen: Leske+Budrich, pp. 33-58.

Kreppe, A.l (2002) *European Parliament and Supranational Party System – A Study in Institutional Development.* Cambridge: Cambridge University Press.

Lord, C. and Pollak J. (2010), The EU's Many Representative Modes: Colluding? Cohering? *Journal of European Public Policy* 17(1), pp. 117-136.

Ludlow, P. (2005), Die Führung der Union durch den Europäischen Rat: Übergang oder Krise? *Integration* 28(2), pp. 3-15.

Mill, J.S. (1972/1861), *Utilitarianism, On Liberty and Considerations on Representative Government*. London: Dent.

Mill, J.S. (2008/1861), *Considerations on Representative Government*. Ithaca, NY: Cornell University Press.

Müller-Graff, P.-Ch. (2009), Das Karlsruher Lissabon-Urteil: Bedingungen, Grenzen, Orakel, und integrative Optionen, *Integration* 32(4), pp. 331-360.

Murkens, J.E. (2010), Bundesverfassungsgericht (2Bve 2/08): "We want our identity back" – the revival of national sovereignty in the German Federal Constitutional Court's decision on the Lisbon Treaty, *Public Law*, pp. 530-550.

Naschold, F. (1969), *Organisation und Demokratie*. Stuttgart: Kohlhammer.

O'Neill, J. (2001), Representing People, Representing Nature, Representing the World, *Government and Policy* 19, pp. 483-500.

Penrose, L.S. (1946), The Elementary Statistics of Majority Voting, *Journal of the Royal Statistical Society* 109 (81), pp. 53-57.

Peters, A. (2001), *Elemente einer Theorie der Verfassung Europas*. Berlin: Duncker & Humblot.

Pitkin, H.F. (1976), *The Concept of Political Representation*. Berkeley, Los Angeles/ London: University of California Press.

Podlech, A. (1984), Repäsentation, in: Otto Brunner, Werner Conze, Reinhart Koselleck (eds.), *Geschichtliche Grundbegriffe: Historisches Lexikon zur politisch-sozialen Sprache in Deutschland*, Bd. 5. Stuttgart: Klett, 1974-1997, pp. 509-547.

Pollak, J. (2007), *Repräsentation ohne Demokratie. Kollidierende Modi der Repräsentation in der Europäischen Union*. Wien/ New York: Springer.

Pollak, J. and Slominski, P. (2009), Zwischen De- und Reparlamentarisierung: der österreichische Nationalrat und seine Mitwirkungsrechte in EU-Angelegenheiten, *Österreichische Zeitschrift für Politikwissenschaft* 2, pp. 193-212.

Pollak, J. et. al. (2011*), Citizen's weight of vote in selected federal systems*, Directorate general for internal policies, Policy Department C: Citizens' Rights and Constitutional Affairs, PE 453.168.

Saward, M.(2003), *Representing nature and the nature of Representation*, Paper presented at the 2nd European Consortium for Political Research Conference, Marburg, September 2003.

Saward, M. (2006), The Representative Claim, *Contemporary Political Theory* 5, pp. 297-318.

Saward, M. (2010), *The Representative Claim*. Oxford: Oxford University Press.

Schmidt, V. (2006), *Democracy in Europe. The EU and National Politics*. Oxford: Oxford University Press.

Seidel, M. (2010), Aktuelle Probleme der europäischen Währungsunion, *Integration* 36(4), pp. 334-351.

Ulmann, W. (1975), *Medieval Political Thought*. Harmondsworth: Penguin Press.

Warleigh, A. (2001), "Europeanizing" civil society: NGOs as agents of political socialisation, *Journal of Common Market Studies* 39 (4), pp. 619-639.

Weale, A. (1999), *Democracy*. London: Macmillan.

Integration through Law and the Social Constitution of Europe

Dragana Damjanovic

I   Introduction

The title of this chapter covers two very broad concepts of European Law: 'integration through law' and the 'Social Constitution of Europe'.

The first refers to a whole body of legal scholarship – the 'integration through law school'[1] – which deals with the various functions of law and its relationship to the politics within the EU integration process. Under the concept of 'integration through law', the law is analysed:

First, as an 'instrument of political actors', i.e. as a medium with which political decisions for an economic, social, and cultural integration at the EU level are implemented. From this angle, the EU integration process is primarily conceived as a political process and the law as the dependent variable of it.[2]

Secondly, as a factor that defines the political actors and the framework within which they have to operate. The role of the law is here denominated to be 'the agent of integration' and the politics the dependent variable of it.[3]

Third, as an 'integrative factor of its own', meaning that also the legal actors themselves by applying the law (mostly debated the ECJ) can act as a motor of integration.[4] This is also circumscribed as the process of 'legal integration',[5] in

---

1   For the key obligatory references on this body of legal scholarship, see the overview on the topic provided by Gráinne de Búrca (2005), Rethinking Law in Neofunctionalist Theory, Journal of European Public Policy 12(2), pp. 310-326.

2   Most of the political science presents law essentially as a passive and functional tool of integration. Gráinne de Búrca (2005), Rethinking Law in Neofunctionlist Theory, Journal of European Public Policy 12(2), pp. 310-326 at 314. On the perspective that integration is fundamentally a political process see i.p. Mauro Capelletti et al (1986), Integration through Law, Book 1, Vol. 1, Chap. 2. Berlin/ New York: Walter de Gruyter.

3   On this more complex conceptualisation of the role of law as an institution, see Kenneth A. Armstrong (1998), Legal Integration: Theorizing the Legal Dimension of European Integration, Journal of Common Market Studies 36 (2), pp. 155-174 at 156 et seq.

4   It is a rather formal and doctrinal approach to EU law to construct the ECJ as a 'legal' and not a 'political actor' whose task is simply to apply the law. But see also the many in particular Anglo-American studies in which the courts are analysed as political actors. For such an analysis on the ECJ, see the various essays in Karen Alter (ed.) (2009), The European Court's Political Power – Selected Essays. Oxford: Oxford University Press.

5   See Gráinne de Burca (2005) and the further references therein.

contrast to the process of political integration (where the law just takes the role of a passive functional tool of political actors).

The concept of the 'Social Constitution of Europe' again connotes the whole debate of whether the EU can be regarded as an entity capable of an own constitution[6] and whether the EU treaties can be qualified as constitutional law;[7] and if so, whether this Constitution of the EU is just of an economic nature (i.e. focusing primarily on the integration of economic aspects of the European society)[8] or of an already broader one; respectively, whether it should be of a broader nature, allowing for an integration at the EU level also with regard to the broader social and cultural aspects of the European society. The term 'Social Constitution of Europe' is in this context, then, very broadly used, describing very generally an EU primary law order which enables a societal integration within the EU, i.e. for an integration of the European society as such, covering not only the core 'social' areas (the welfare state), but all the other relevant policy fields beyond economic issues of a society, such as e.g. migration, external, environmental, or security policy, etc.[9] In relation to the title of this book, such a societal integration could be also circumscribed by the 'development of a European Common Good'.[10]

From a legal perspective it is difficult to deal in just one chapter with all the above-mentioned facets and policy fields the title of this contribution potentially involves. So I had to make a selection of the aspects on which I will go into closer detail in this paper. This looks as follows:

6   I.e. whether in the context of the EU it is helpful to use the language of Constitutionalism. On this debate, see e.g. Stefan Griller (2005), Die Europäische Union: Ein staatsrechtliches Monstrum? In: Ingolf Pernice, Ulrich Haltern, Gunnar Folke Schuppert (eds.), Europawissenschaft. Baden-Baden: Nomos; in particular on the significance of constitutionalisation for constitutionalism, see the contribution of Somek in this book (Constitutionalisation and the common good).

7   The ECJ has already beginning of the 1980s described the EC treaty as forming the '*basic constitutional charter*' of a '*Community based on the rule of law*', C- 294/83 [1986] ECR 1339.

8   On these aspects of the European Constitution, see Julio Baquero Cruz (2002), Between Competition and Free Movement. The Economic Constitutional Law of the European Union. Oxford: Hart Publishing, pp. 63 et seq.

9   In particular when the term 'European social integration' is used by sociologists, it signifies the integration of society and has no special focus on social policy. See e.g. Jan Delhey (2004), European Social Integration. From Convergence of Countries to Transnational Relations between Peoples, WZB Discussion Paper, Berlin, http://skylla.-wzb.eupdf/2004/i04-201.pdf.

10   For the various understandings of the notion common good, see the contributions of Koller, Riordan and in particular Seel in this volume.

First, I will start from the premise (and I will not question that issue anymore in this paper), that the EU treaties do qualify as constitutional law of the EU. So, when I refer to the EU Constitution I basically mean the EU primary law.

Second, I will choose a much narrower conceptualisation of the term 'Social Constitution of Europe', which by the way is also quite commonly used within the literature,[11] meaning by it not the EU primary law order which enables EU societal integration as such, but just the part of the EU primary rules which enables an integration of the 'social core' within the EU, i.e. for an integration of those policy fields which are dealt with at the national level within Europe, typically under the concept of 'social policy' or the 'welfare state'. In concrete these cover: labour and equality law, the social security systems, the provision of social assistance (both in cash or kind), as well as public health care and public education.[12]

With regard to the so conceptualised 'Social Constitution of Europe' I basically want to show how its legal structure looks like today, i.e. of which treaty norms it is exactly made up, how it has developed over time, and which of the actors of EU integration (ECJ, Commission, EU legislator) have taken which role within this developmental process. To put it in the 'integration through law' diction: how have politics and law – i.e. the political and the legal integration process at the EU level – so far interacted with each other in the creation of the current 'Social Constitution of Europe'.[13]

The overall aim is to identify – from a legal perspective – today's still open fundamental problematic issues within this process of an EU social integration and to give an estimation of which direction the future developments within these policy fields at the EU level might take.

---

11 I.p. the lawyers use the term 'social integration' of Europe and 'Social Constitution' in the narrower sense, focusing on core social policy issues, see e.g. in Jo Shaw, Jo Hund, Chloe Wallace (2007), Economic and Social Law and Policy of the European Union. London: Palgrave Macmillan, pp. 341et seq.

12 Following the broad definition of 'social policy' by Thomas H. Marshall (1975), Social policy in the twentieth century, 4th edition. Hutchinson University Library, p. 15: the use of 'political power to supersede, supplement or modify operations of economic systems in order to achieve results which the economic system would not achieve on its own...guided by values other than those determined by market forces.' See also the definition of the 'welfare state' by Nicholas Barr (2004), The Economics of the Welfare State. Oxford: Oxford University Press, pp. 6 et seq.

13 In the edited volume of Höpfner and Schäfer this issue is also analysed from the economic perspective. More concretely, it is examined how politics and economics have interacted with each other within the EU economic integration process and how this has changed the member states' social regimes so far. See Martin Höpfner, Armin Schäfer (2008), Die Politische Ökonomie der europäischen Integration. Frankfurt/ New York: Campus, p. 14.

II   Stages and Phases in the Developmental Process towards an European Social Constitution

1   Treaty of Rome 1957: A 'mixed economy' to at different levels

Starting at the bottom of this process, i.e. the Treaty of Rome as the primary law order from which today's EU Social Constitution originated, the following picture is displayed:

European integration was focused almost entirely for the well-known reasons[14] on economic integration, i.e. its primary goal was the development of an open and competitive common market within the EEC. This focus was, however, not meant to establish within the EC a neoliberal market economy, i.e. a system in which the allocation of resources for the society is almost entirely organised by a 'free market'. The political idea of the then founding member states of the EU was rather to preserve the system that was generally predominant back then in Western Europe of a 'mixed economy' (in various member states also labelled the 'Social Market Economy')[15] also within the EC context, and just to realise it within this context at different levels:[16] the establishment and safeguard of a free market – as just one component to organise the resource allocation within the European economic system – would become the primary task of the Community. The organisation of the resource allocation by public policy instruments (i.p. through special social policy, respectively welfare state measures and special public utilities regulation) – as the other central element of such an economic system – would remain the primary task of the member states.

This political concept of a 'mixed economy for Europe to be realised at different levels' was transposed in the legal realm through the following elements:

The EC market rules (free movement and competition including state aid)[17] were installed as the core legal basis with which to pursue economic integration, i.e. the establishment of a free market at the EC level. They would apply to services, goods, economically active persons, and capital in a cross-border context, respective to undertakings, but not – and this was at that time beyond any doubt

---

14   Basically, within the negotiations leading to the Treaties of Rome a political compromise on Social Europe could not be reached, see Fritz W. Scharpf (2002), The European Social Model: Coping with the Challenges of Diversity, Journal of Common Market Studies 40, pp. 645-670 at 646.

15   In general as to the system of a mixed or social market economy, see Paul A. Samuelson, William Nordhaus (2005), Economics, McGraw Hill, pp. 8 et seq.

16   In this sense the EU economic system is conceptualised as a multi-level system, just alike the EU legal system and the EU welfare system.

17   And the public procurement rules as a concretisation of the free movement rules at the secondary level.

– to any form of resource allocation by social policy and welfare state instruments. The services and goods provided by the welfare regimes were not regarded as services/goods that would fall under the free movement rules, and the entities providing the services or goods – at that time mostly public – not as undertakings under the competition, respective to state aid rules.

The title on social policy[18], which did not embrace the welfare state as such but in a rather narrow sense just workers' rights (thus labour law) and some equality law issues – we will refer to them in the following as the regulative social policy fields[19] – only made some concessions for an EC integration through policy instruments, not through law. The explicit wording was: '*the Commission shall encourage cooperation between the Member States.*' The title on Social Policy was originally conceived as a confirmation of the member states' responsibilities for the regulative social policy fields.[20] As to the redistributive social policy fields,[21] the member states' primary competences followed from the general rule of conferred powers[22] and the fact that these policy areas originally were not mentioned at all within the treaty.

Only with regard to the member states' social security systems and to some labour-related social benefits, the treaty also enabled for an 'integration through law', but only insofar as this constituted 'an indispensable precondition' to ensure the efficient effectuation of the free movement of workers within Europe.

18 Art 117-128 EECT
19 In contrast to the redistributive social policy fields the task of the State *just* consists in regulating the relationships between the individuals and to provide an institutional framework for collective bargaining. For this categorisation of the regulative social policies, see Simon Deakin, Jude Browne (2003), Social Rights and Market Order: Adapting the Capability Approach, in: Tamara K. Hervey, Jeff Kenner (eds.), Economic and Social Rights under the EU Charter. A Legal Perspective. Oxford: Hart Publishing, pp. 27-43 at 28.
20 Gerda Falkner (1998), EU Social Policy in the 1990s. Towards a Corporatist Policy Community. London: Routledge, p. 57.
21 Within the redistributive social policy fields the task of the state consists in generating resources and distributing them among the population, in short to provide certain services to the citizens (as eg. social assistance services, public health care or public education services). For this categorisation of social policy and its differentiation from the so-called regulative social policy fields, see Dragana Damjanovic, Bruno de Witte (2009), Welfare Integration through EU Law: The Overall Picture in the Light of the Lisbon Treaty, in: Ulla Neergard, Ruth Nielsen, Lynn Roseburry (eds.), Integrating Welfare Functions into EU-Law. From Rome to Lisbon. Copenhagen: DJØF, pp. 53-97.
22 The general rule of 'conferred powers' was back then literally perceived to allow the Community to exercise only as much power as explicitly conferred upon it. As to this rule (also denominated the principle of attributed powers) and its further development by the ECJ, see Armin von Bogdandy, Jürgen Bast (2002), The European Union's Vertical Order of Competences: The Current Law and Proposals for its Reform, Common Market Law Review 39(2), pp. 227-269 at 232 et seq.

The EU integration of the member states' social security systems was conceptualised as an element of economic integration rather than social integration, which is why its legal base was not inserted within the title on social policy, but among the EU market rules, more precisely the free movement of workers provisions.[23] As such it was very narrowly construed a merely 'market motivated social integration' provision[24] by the drafters. It was meant to be confined to the workers in the narrow sense and to labour-related social services. Furthermore, it explicitly only allowed for an 'integration through coordination' (in contrast to the 'integration through harmonisation') and required above unanimity voting.

Finally, the member states have included a provision in the treaty (Article 90 EECT) which at that time was perceived to leave also the outer ring of the member states welfare systems – the resource allocation by public utilities, comprising e.g. the provision with energy, postal services, public transportation, etc.[25]– in principal outside the EC economic integration process and thus within the primary responsibility of the member state. In contrast to the welfare state areas, this was legally however not implemented by not applying the market rules at all to these sectors or by not mentioning them at all within the treaty, but just by providing in Article 90 para 2 EECT for a special possibility of derogation from the market rules for these sectors (at the EU level denominated the SGEI), if so necessary to ensure a universal provision with these services within the member states. For a long time – as long as the ideology prevailed that public utilities are to be considered as natural monopolies (in Europe until the late 1980s) – that derogation clause was read to allow *per se* for monopoly rights within these sectors and so to leave these sectors *per se* outside the EU internal market and within the primary domain of the member state.[26]

---

23 Art 51 EECT.
24 Therewith a provision is meant which aims at EU social integration merely for market making reasons and not for genuine social policy reasons. For this differentiation of EU social integration, see Jo Shaw, Jo Hund, Chloe Wallace (2007), Economic and Social Law and Policy of the European Union. London: Palgrave Macmillan, pp. 344et seq.
25 As to this link between the MS' public utilities and the MS welfare systems, Dragana-Damjanovic, Bruno de Witte (2009), Welfare Integration through EU Law: The Overall Picture in the Light of the Lisbon Treaty, in: Ulla Neergard, Ruth Nielsen, Lynn Roseburry (eds.), Integrating Welfare Functions into EU-Law. From Rome to Lisbon. Copenhagen: DJØF, pp. 53-97 at 54.
26 David Edward, Mark Hoskins (2005), Article 90: Deregulation and EC Law. Reflections arising from the XVI Fide Conference, Common Market Law Review 32 (1), pp. 157-186.

2   Focus on economic integration and debate on 'market-making': EU social integration with regard to the regulative social policy fields

This approach of a 'mixed economy to be realised at different levels within the EC' remained at the beginning of the EU integration process pretty uncontroversial. Social policy and social integration were in general not a big issue in the initial phase of the EU integration process. Two regulations were just put in place to realise the market-motivated coordination of the member states' social security systems according to Article 51 EECT.[27] Apart from that, at that time the focus was rather on economic integration through the market rules, which the ECJ considerably pushed forward – as is well known – by interpreting the market rules as being primary over national law and directly effective. With that it considerably transformed the structure of the treaties; it 'constitutionalised' them is the term often used[28] to describe the process. This has again changed the dynamics of the EU integration process considerably. The construction of the market rules as subjective rights on which basis the individuals in the EU can now lodge complaints before the courts, has given them as well as the ECJ itself considerable power to co-design the EU integration process,[29] and this not only with regard to the economic aspects, but in the following also indirectly – as will be shown in detail later – with regard to the social aspects of EU integration.

Only with that intensified economic integration within the EU, the first controversies as to the EC's approach to social policy issues arose, but at first only with regard to the regulative social policy fields (and here again in particular the workers' rights).[30] As to these it was argued that a further economic integration would also make a further social integration necessary: on the one hand for 'market making reasons' – only minimal harmonisation of certain working conditions could prevent distortions of competition – and on the other hand also for

27   Regulation 3/58 [concerning social security for migrant workers, OJ 1958 L 30/561] was put in place almost immediately after the EECT came into force, but became of true practical relevance only in its adapted version of Regulation 1408/71 [on the application of social security schemes to employed persons, to self-employed persons and to members of their families moving within the Community, OJ 1971 L 149/2], which followed shortly after the adoption of Regulation 1612/68 [on freedom of movement for workers within the Community, OJ 1968 L 257/2] with which free movement of workers was firmly institutionalised in the EC.

28   See e.g. Kenneth A. Armstrong (1998), Theorizing the Legal Dimension of European Integration, Journal of Common Market Studies 36(2), pp. 155-174, at 161.

29   On this thought in more detail: Renaud Dehousse (2000), Integration through Law Revisited: Some thoughts on the Juridification of the European Political Process, in: Francis Snyder (2000), The Europeanisation of Law. The Legal Effects of European Integration. Oxford: Hart Publishing, pp. 15-30.

30   The redistributive social policy areas and the public utilities, on the other hand, have at that time not yet become an issue of European integration.

genuine 'social policy reasons' – i.e. to prevent the levelling down of workers' rights (social dumping), which could result from the competition of the member states' labour markets.[31] In the context of this debate the notion of the European Social Model (ESM), which became popular again 30 years later, arose for the first time.[32]

Following this argumentation, the member states already introduced in the Single European Act of 1986, which in principle was just meant to further economic integration, a slight extension of the EC competences as to the regulative social policy fields. In concrete they authorised the EC to issue – by qualified majority – directives establishing minimum requirements for the health and safety of workers.[33] Apart from that, they adopted the Community Charter of Fundamental Social Rights of Workers in 1989, but just in the form of a non-binding legal document.[34]

Approximately about the same time as the debate on the necessity of a further social integration came up, the ECJ also started with its line of case law in which it gradually extended the coordination of the member states' social security systems, originally very narrowly constructed by the EU legislator (both the primary and the secondary one), on the basis of Art 51 EECT. It continually broadened the term 'worker' to cover basically any economically active person, as well as the term 'social benefits' to cover virtually all welfare benefits (and not only those closely related to labour as originally intended). Basically, the Court argued this extension with the rationale that it was 'an indispensable precondition for effectuating the free movement of workers within the EC', and with a rather 'market-making' than 'genuine social policy' argument.[35] With the same rationale, but just on the basis of the general non-discrimination clause of the treaty, it also already opened the beginning of the 1980s cross-border access to higher education within the EU.[36]

---

31 Jo Shaw, Jo Hund, Chloe Wallace (2007), Economic and Social Law and Policy of the European Union. London: Palgrave Macmillan, pp. 344 et seq.
32 As to the emergence of this term in the EU political discussion by the late 80s, see Gerda Falkner (1998), EU Social Policy in the 1990s. Towards a Corporatist Policy Community. London: Routledge, p. 67.
33 Art 118 A EECT.
34 The Charter was then incorporated into EU law by simple reference in the Preamble to the 1997 Treaty of Amsterdam. Today, the rights of the 1989 Charter reappear in the EU Charter of Fundamental Rights.
35 For an overview of this case law of the ECJ see Eleanor Spaventa (2007), Free Movement of Persons in the European Union. Barriers to Movement in their Constitutional Context. Alphen aan der Rijn: Kluwer, pp. 1-33; Anne Pieter Van der Mei (2003), Free Movement of Persons within the European Community: Cross-border Access to Public Benefits. Oxford: Hart Publishing.
36 Fundamentally, see C-293/83, Gravier [1985] ECR 593 and Case C-24/86, Blaizot v University of Liège [1988] ECR 379.

3   The treaty of Maastricht (1992): The high-water mark of the EU pro-
      social integrationist tide[37]

These 'pro-social integrationist developments' within the initial phase of the EU
integration process finally led, with the Maastricht Treaty reformations in 1992,
to a considerable extension of the Community competences within the regulative
social policy fields.[38] In the following treaty revisions these have been gradually
evolved, so that the EU today possesses as to almost all labour law issues the
competence to provide for minimum harmonisation by majority voting[39] and as
to almost all equality law issues by unanimity voting.[40]

      Above all, with the Maastricht revisions, for the first time the member states
also included provisions relating to the redistributive social policy fields: a title
on health care and a title on education. As to these, the member states, however,
explicitly excluded any harmonisation at the EC level and provided (as in the
case originally of the regulative social policy fields) only for a political integration through policy instruments *to encourage cooperation between the Member
States.*[41]

      The provision on the coordination of the social security systems, already inhe-
rent in the original version of the EC treaty, was left unchanged in its wording,
but was clearly accepted in its by then already substantially broadened meaning
through the case law of the ECJ: allowing cross-border access to virtually all social benefits for any economically active person within the EU.

      Finally, Maastricht also introduced the Union citizenship chapter (Article 8 –
8e ECT), which at that time, however, was perceived to be just of a symbolic nature (i.e. not constituting any rights). The same was held for the number of social
values that the Maastricht Treaty also newly inserted in EU primary law.[42]

---

37   On this terminology see Mark Kleinmann (2002), A European Welfare State? European
     Union Social Policy in Context. Basingstoke: Palgrave Macmillan, p. 90.
38   As to the Community competences within the regulative social policy fields under the
     Maastricht Treaty, see Gerda Falkner (1998), EU Social Policy in the 1990s. Towards a
     Corporatist Policy Community. London: Routledge, p. 81.
39   Except for aspects of 'pay, the right of association, the right to strike or the right to im-
     pose lock-outs' (Art 153 TFEU).
40   On EU equality law – as a part of the EU regulative social policy – see the overview at Jo
     Shaw (2005), Mainstreaming Equality and Diversity in European Union Law and Policy,
     Current Legal Problems 58 (1), pp 255-312.
41   Art 126 and 129 ECT.
42   Art 2 and 3 ECT.

The extended EU competences for the regulative social policy fields, in the following, put in motion the adoption of a remarkable body of secondary legislation on issues such as free movement of workers, gender equality at work, health and safety of workers, working and employment conditions, and the fight against all forms of discrimination. Today, this legislation is in its entirety described to form a quite elaborated and solid EU framework on labour and equality law.[43]

Beyond these developments within the core welfare state fields, post-Maastricht also brought major changes to the so called 'outer-ring' of the welfare state: public utilities. In the 1990s the transformation of these sectors from state monopolies to competitive markets had reached its peak. It was a process primarily initialised by the private actors and the Commission who, due to the ECJ's interpretation of the market rules as subjective rights, could lodge complaints before the ECJ asking for an opening of public utilities to the markets. The Court then gave a main impetus to this process by deciding in its first telecom cases[44] that public utilities can no longer *per se* be regarded as justified exemptions from the market rules under Article 106 para 2 TFEU (back then: Article 90 para 2 EECT), and that the Commission is in principal empowered under Article 90 para 3 EECT to take legal actions also by the means of directives to abolish special or exclusive rights in the public utility sectors. Even if the Court, in the following cases dealing with the liberalisation of the postal, the energy, or the railway sector, remained rather neutral on the issue of the necessity of abolishing exclusive or special rights in the public utility sectors, with its first telecom cases it provided the Commission with enough power to put pressure on the member states to issue secondary EC law measures on the further liberalisation of public utilities.[45]

In reaction to these developments in the public utilities fields (the traditional SGEI), the Commission has started to issue Communications dealing with the de-regulation and re-regulation of these sectors. The first of these Communications was published in 1996[46] and even if this clearly just dealt with public utili-

---

43   See COM (2007) 726: Opportunities, access and solidarity: towards a new social vision for 21st century Europe, p. 10.
44   The telecom sector was the first sector of the public utilities to be liberalised by the EU. The major cases are: C-188/80 relating to the transparency directive and C-202/88 relating to the telecommunications equipment market.
45   As to this strategic power of the Commission see the analysis of Susanne K. Schmidt (2008), Europäische Integration zwischen judikativer und legislativer Politik, in Martin Höppner, Armin Schäfer (eds.), Die Politische Ökonomie der Europäischen Integration. Frankfurt/ New York: Campus Verlag, pp 101-127, at 112f.
46   COM (96) 443: Communication on services of general interest from 1996.

ties at that time (the SGEI as referred to in the treaty), its title already back then referred to a broader concept: the services of general interest (SGI), defined by the Commission to cover both economic (in any case public utilities) and non-economic services of general interest. Back then, the Commission identified such non-economic services as the redistributive social policy fields (such as welfare, public health, education and training, and culture) and core public authority services (such as security, justice, diplomacy, or the registry of births, deaths, and marriages). The Commission has therewith from the very beginning of the liberalisation process of public utilities established a connection between the public utilities and the welfare regimes of member states.

5   Amsterdam and Nice Treaties: A more cautious approach to EU social integration

The way in which the member states' public utilities were transformed to open markets by EC law and the linkage established by the Commission between public utilities and the redistributive social policy fields through the invention of the term SGI might explain why the member states within the treaty revisions of Amsterdam (1998) and Nice (2001) took an extra reluctant and negative approach with regard to a further social integration at the EU level, in particular with regard to their redistributive social policy fields.[47] This they expressed by repeating and underlining Europe's limited competences in the fields of health care, public education, and social protection (including social security and social assistance) and, by adding to the explicit prohibition of any harmonisation in these fields (which has been already stated by the Maastricht Treaty), there was an extra obligation for the EC *'to fully respect the responsibilities of the MS'* in these fields.[48] Above all, they introduced a new 'safeguarding clause' for the SGEI (Article 16 TEC), by which they tried to clarify what should have actually already followed from Article 86 para 2 TEC: that the EC has to take care, in particular when applying the EU market rules, that the SGEI operate on the basis of principles and conditions which enable them to fulfil their missions. With the same intention – to safeguard their welfare regimes – the member states included the fundamental social rights in the EU Charter of Fundamental Rights, which

47   In contrast, in relation to the regulative social policy fields the member states have constantly made some concessions to the EU. With the Amsterdam Treaty they have in particular added a 'general non-discrimination' legal base (Art 13 ECT), which enabled the adoption of measures combating discrimination also outside employment and on other grounds than nationality.

48   Art 152 ECT, Art 149 ECT and Art 137 ECT.

was adopted in Nice (2000), but remained legally non-binding until the entry into force of the Lisbon Treaty.

6   Post Amsterdam and Nice: An increase of cases before the ECJ within the redistributive social policy fields

In light of the above-described developments in the post-Maastricht phase, it's quite interesting to observe a significant increase of cases before the ECJ in relation to the redistributive social policy fields starting off at the beginning of this century, so just after the treaty revisions of Nice and Amsterdam and after the major part of the public utilities liberalisation had been accomplished at the EU level.

These cases are, on the one hand, based on the EU market rules (free movement, competition, and state aid). On this basis they in essence deal with the question of whether the public entities providing welfare services[49] are to be qualified as undertakings (respectively the welfare services as economic services) to which the EU market rules would apply.[50] The Commission puts this question typically in a more universal way, namely, whether and to what extent are the redistributive social policy fields now also to be considered as SGEI[51] (as with public utilities), which in principal fall under the regime of Article 106 para 2 TFEU. Insofar as the redistributive social policy fields do qualify as SGEI, in a second step the cases trigger the issue of whether the special or monopoly rights conferred in these sectors (i.e. the special structure of the member states welfare regimes outside the market system) can be regarded as justified restrictions in the sense of the EU market rules. This, by the way, has also been the core issue in the context of the liberalisation of public utilities.

On the other hand, the cases are based on the Union citizenship chapter (in connection with the general non-discrimination principle)[52] and the provision on the free movement of services in its passive conception. On this basis they in general deal with the question of whether and under which conditions the individuals of the EU have a right to cross-border access to welfare services within

---

49   E.g. social insurance carrier, hospitals, universities, non-for profit organisations providing social services, etc.
50   For on overview on these issues and cases, see Thomas Eilmansberger, Günter Herzig (2008), Study on Social Services of General Interest (SSGI), commissioned by the Federal Ministry of Social Affairs and Consumer Protection.
51   See e.g. in its last Communication on SGI: COM (2007) 725, at para 2.2.
52   Art 18–25 TFEU.

Europe.[53] This question, again, very much resembles the issues raised in context with the EU regulatory complex on the coordination of the member states' social security systems (originally under Article 51 EECT, now Article 48 TFEU): to what extent are migrant workers entitled to cross-border access to social benefits within the EU?

From the judgments issued so far by the ECJ within these cases, it is very difficult – if at all possible – to compose some sort of a broader EU framework for the redistributive social policy fields, which could unveil in a bit more structured way and on the basis of some more general principles and criteria how EU law relates to the member states' redistributive social policy fields, in particular to what extent its application might curtail the member states' sovereign rights in these fields. As the Commission has concluded (in particular as to the EU market rules):[54] whether the above-mentioned rules apply and if so, whether the member states' specific organisational and/or financing structures of their redistributive social policy fields can be regarded as proportional justifications in the meaning of the above-mentioned rules can only be decided on a case-by-case basis. That case-by-case approach, however, is not the problem as such. It is rather the fact that, from the ECJ's legal reasoning in these cases, it does not follow transparently enough how and why it makes a difference. For example, it is not fully comprehensible why services provided by public hospitals – even if completely financed by a social entity, i.e. in essence public funds – are to be regarded as economic services within the free movement rules,[55] whereas the services provided by public universities financed out of public funds are not. See e.g. fundamentally in C-263/86, *Humbel,* para 2; repeated in many other judgments. At the same time, the Court of First Instance expressly refuses to qualify public hospitals providing medical services funded from social security contributions and other state funding as undertakings according to the competition rules.[56] The ECJ so far did not rule otherwise on this issue, but implicitly confirmed the Court of First Instance's view on this point.[57] Likewise it is difficult to understand – at least from a legal perspective[58] – why the Court is so permissive when it comes

---

53 For an overview on these issues and case see Eleanor Spaventa (2008), Seeing the wood despite the trees? On the scope of Union Cirtizenship and its Constitutional Effects, Common Market Law Review 45(1), pp 13-45 at 13.

54 COM (2007)725, at para 2.1.

55 See e.g. Cases C-158/96 Kohll [1998] ECR I-1931 and C-120/95, Decker [1998] ECR I-1831; C- 157/99, Geraets-Smits & Peerbooms [2001] ECR I-5473; C-385/99, Müller-Fauré v Onderlinge Waarborgmaatschappij [2003] ECR I-4509 and C-372/04, Watts v Bedford Primary Care Trust [2006] ECR I-4325.

56 T-319/99 (Fenin v Commission), ECR II-357, ref. 39.

57 C-205/03 (Fenin v Commission), [2006] ECR I-6295, ref. 26.

58 That there might be political reasons is another issue, which is definitely an important one, but nevertheless not one on which the Court should rest its cases.

to cross-border access to higher education by students (on basis of the Union citizenship chapter) or to health care services by patients (on basis of the free movement rules), but is not, however, in the cases of cross-border access to other social benefits (except maybe from the unemployment benefits).[59]

In addition, the Commission has contributed quite substantially to misunderstandings with regard to the legal standing of the redistributive social policy fields within EU law, by drawing quite generalising and simplifying and so far not always accurate conclusions from the Court's case law. For example, from ECJ case law qualifying certain services as economic services pursuant to the free movement rules,[60] it does not necessarily follow that the provider of these services are to be qualified as undertakings under the competition or state aid rules,[61] as the Commission suggests by leading the discussion at the very general level of whether the services are to be considered as SGEI falling under the Article 86 para 2 TEC (now Article 106 para 2 TFEU) regime or not.

Notwithstanding these ambiguities and the case-by-case approach, one can still detect a general trend from the Court's and the Commission's activities in the field of redistributive social policies: to subject the member states' welfare systems increasingly under EU law, or in the Commission's diction (as to the EU market rules) to increasingly qualify them as SGEI. One can observe how the Commission since its first Communication on SGI in 1996, in which it categorised the redistributive social policy fields clearly as non-economic, has gradually moved on to conclude in its last Communication on SGI in 2007 that the redistributive social policy fields are in principle to be qualified as economic services.[62]

The fact that these areas are now also increasingly being subjected under EU law does not automatically impose changes upon the member states' welfare systems, as deviations from EU law by the member states' welfare systems can qualify as justified restrictions in the public interest and can be thus declared compatible with EU law. In fact, the Court in its cases allows for quite broad deviations from EU law under the title of 'justified restrictions in the public interest'. However, that the welfare systems are now to a great part subjected under EU law has substantially broadened the possibility of the private actors (both the

---

59   Siofra O'Leary (2009), Equal Treatment and EU Citizens: A New Chapter on Cross-border Educational Mobility and Access to Student financial Assistance, European Law Review 68, pp. 612-627.

60   As e.g. health care services provided by public hospitals and financed by social security systems.

61   See already Kamiel Mortelmans (2001), Towards Convergence in the Application of the Rules on Free Movement and on Competition? Common Market Law Review 38, pp. 613-649.

62   COM (2007) 725, para 2.1

market players and the beneficiaries of welfare services) to use litigation to promote their own interests at the EU level within the welfare systems and so to put considerable pressure onto a further dismantling of these systems in the future.[63]

7 Debate on a stronger Social Europe, in particular also with regard to the redistributive social policies

These activities of the Court and the Commission within the redistributive social policy fields have inflamed the debate on 'Social Europe' from anew at the beginning of this century. Compared to the 1980s, when the debate on 'Social Europe' was almost exclusively about the regulative social policy fields (labour and equality law), today its most controversial aspects refer to the redistributive social policy fields (the provision and organisation of health care, social security, social assistance, and public education).[64] At the European level these fields are also discussed as a category of the Services of General Interest (SGI).

The central argument put forward in this debate can be outlined as follows: The application of the EU market rules and the Union citizenship chapter – also denominated 'negative social integration' – might destabilise the member states' welfare systems by leading to an increased market opening of these sectors or social tourism within Europe. In any case, the application of these rules has curtailed the member states' sovereignty in these fields and therewith challenged their capacity to protect their social standards. As the process has its origin in single ECJ (or Commission) decisions, a European social dimension initiated by negative integration can only develop 'ad hoc and partial', 'as an unplanned collage',[65] and therefore is incapable of providing for a bigger vision of 'Social Europe' and a coherent approach to regulating and integrating the national welfare systems at the EU level. To counteract these developments, negative integration should be followed by 'positive integration', i.e. by the development of EU primary or secondary law rules, which could safeguard – in a general and coherent

---

63 As to the argument of the strategic utilisation of European legal procedures by private actors, see Renaud Dehousse (2000), Integration through Law Revisited: Some thoughts on the Juridification of the European Political Process, in: Francis Snyder (2000), The Europeanisation of Law. The Legal Effects of European Integration, Oxford: Hart Publishing, pp. 15-30 at 21.

64 There is, however, also very controversial ECJ case law referring to the regulative social policy fields, as e.g. the cases C-438/05, Viking [2007] ECR I-10779 and C-341/05, Laval [2007] ECR I-11767.

65 Gráinne de Burca (2005), Towards European Welfare? In: Gráinne de Búrca (ed.), EU Law and the Welfare State – In Search of Solidarity, pp. 1-9.

way – the social standards (that have evolved in a long tradition in the member states) also at the EU level.[66]

These claims have also been circumscribed by referring very generally to 'the development of a European Social Model',[67] therewith reviving a concept which had already been established at the beginning of the 1990s.

But in contrast to the 1990s when the development of the European Social Model (in the sense of a further EU integration within the regulative social policy fields) was primarily seen as a precondition for the EU economic integration process, today the term is increasingly intrumentalised just beyond economic integration, to argue for a further development of the European Union from a primarily economic to the true political Union. As Maduro[68] has put it:

> As the European project moves further towards the goal of political integration and beyond economic integration, questions about the nature and scope of the EU's social dimension, about the EU's 'social identity', become ever more pressing.

8   'Social Europe' under the Lisbon Treaty

Building on this argumentation, in the course of drafting the Constitutional Treaty 'Social Europe' has evolved into a true constitutional issue. In this sense, the Working Group on Social Europe of the Convention drafting the Constitutional Treaty held in its final report:[69]

> Social considerations constitute an essential part of European integration. The EU cannot be a credible force for good in the wider world if it is indifferent to questions of social jus-

---

66   For an overview on these arguments see e.g. Gráinne de Burca (2005), Towards European Welfare? In: Gráinne de Búrca (ed.), EU Law and the Welfare State – In Search of Solidarity, pp. 1-9 at 4 (with further references); Fritz W. Scharpf (2002), The European Social Model: Coping with the Challenges of Diversity, Journal of Common Market Studies 40 (4), pp. 645-670 at, 648; Miguel Poiares Maduro (2006), European Constitutionalism and Three Models of Social Europe, in: Martijn Hesselink (ed.), The Politics of a European Civil Code. The Hague: Kluwer Law International, pp. 125-141.
67   The term of the 'European Social Model' has been also used in a much broader sense, referring to the societal integration at the EU level, the European common good as such. In general it is missing clear contours. That's also why it has not been incorporated in the text of the treaty. The treaty instead refers to a 'Social Market Economy' (see Art 3 TEU). See the Report of the Working Group Social Europe, CONV 516/1/03, para 17.
68   Miguel Poiares Maduro (2000), Europe's Social Self: The Sickness Unto Death? In: Jo Shaw (ed.), Social Law and Policy in an Evolving European Union. Oxford: Hart Publishing, pp. 325-349 at 336.
69   Renaud Dehousse (2000), Integration through Law Revisited: Some thoughts on the Juridification of the European Political Process, in: Francis Snyder (2000), The Europeanisation of Law. The Legal Effects of European Integration, Oxford: Hart Publishing, pp. 15-30 at 12-14.

tice and poverty in European society or to how its citizens are treated at work or in retirement.

Given this strong rhetoric the amendments then achieved by the draft Constitutional Treaty on Social Europe were quite modest.[70] In fact, during the increasingly fraught ratification debates within the member states, the Constitutional Treaty was generally conceived to be insufficiently social in orientation. Consequently, the negative results of the French and Dutch referenda to the Constitutional Treaty were in part also explained by its 'social deficit'.[71]

Despite these concerns about the social deficit of the Constitutional Treaty, the Lisbon Treaty basically just carried over the set of rules that had been already contained in that failed treaty. In a nutshell this set of rules for a 'new Social Europe', which has finally come into force with the ratification of the Lisbon Treaty in December 2009, consists of:

A social clause that mainstreams social policy into all policy fields of the EU (Article 9 TFEU), several other provisions that affirm the importance of social values to the European integration process (Article 2 and 3 TEU), and a reference to the 'model of a social market economy' on which the EU's internal market shall be built (Article 3 TEU). These provisions establish social objectives as equivalent to economic objectives in the EU. Their central aim is to ensure a proper balance between social and economic values within the European integration process.[72] As mere principles they, however, do not provide any legal instruments and in particular not a legal base for positive integration at the EU level by which to achieve these aims.

The fundamental social rights of the EU Charter have now – with the entry into force of the Lisbon Treaty – also acquired binding legal force. They, however, do not establish a legal base on which a positive integration within the redistributive social policy fields could be established, either.[73] According to a quite widespread belief in EU law, they do not even provide individual rights, but are rather

70 For an overview on these amendments, Julio Baquero Cruz (2007), The Socioeconomic Model of the European Union: Stuck with the Status Quo, in: Giuliano Amato, Herve Bribosia, Bruno de Witte (eds.), Génèse et Destinée de la Constitution européenne – Genesis and Destiny of the European Constitution, Bruxelles: Bruylant, pp. 1105-1128 at 1117.

71 Jo Shaw (2005), Mainstreaming Equality and Diversity in European Union Law and Policy, Current Legal Problems 58, pp. 255-312;

72 See the Report of the Working Group on Social Europe, CONV 516/1/03, para 14.

73 According to Art 51(2) EU Charter, it does not 'establish any new power or task for the Union or modify powers and tasks as defined in the Treaties'. This point was hammered in again by the second sentence of the new Art 6 TEU stating that the 'provisions of the Charter shall not extend in any way the competences of the Union as defined in the Treaties.

to be conceived as mere principles.[74] So far, they just specify as to different aspects of a welfare regime (as e.g. health care, social security, and social protection) the above-mentioned horizontal social clauses and objectives of the Lisbon Treaty.

Finally, the new competence clause for SGEI (Article 14 TFEU) and Protocol No. 9 on the SGI[75] form an essential element of the new EU primary law framework for Social Europe. While the impact of the Protocol for the future Social Europe is generally described to be marginal, Article 14 TFEU, on the other hand, has the potential to develop into a EU legal base that could actually promote a true positive integration within the member states' redistributive social policy fields. This depends very much on how broad one draws the concept of the SGEI. As mentioned above, at least the Commission already adopts a very wide approach to this concept, subsuming under it beyond public utilities (the traditional SGEI) in principal also all areas of the redistributive social policies. At this point, however, it must be recalled that the Lisbon Treaty at the same time leaves the special competence clauses untouched, which reserve the areas of health care and public education to the member states or which require unanimity voting for the areas of social protection through the provision of social assistance or social security.

III   Conclusions

Getting back to the questions at the beginning of this chapter, and based on the outline given above on the various stages and phases in the developmental process towards an EU Social Constitution we can conclude the following:

1   The structure of the EU Social Constitution

For the regulative social policy fields (essentially labour and equality law) there exists a quite solid EU primary law base,[76] which was established first by the

---

74   On the right/principle discussion in relation to the social fundamental rights of the Charter, see Bruno de Witte (2005), The trajectory of Fundamental Social Rights in the European Union, in: Gràinne de Búrca, Bruno de Witte (eds.), Social Rights in Europe. Oxford: Oxford University Press, pp. 153-168 at 159.

75   The Protocol is the only norm among the above-mentioned, which was not already part of the Constitutional Treaty, but has been just added to the Lisbon Treaty during the IGC, which modified the Constitutional Treaty.

76   This is also why according to Art 2 para 4 lit 2 TEU 'social policy' is considered a shared competence within the EU. As such a shared competence, it virtually only refers to the

Maastricht Treaty and since then has been gradually evolved. Over the last 40 years the Union has made extensive use of this legal base by adopting a remarkable body of secondary EC legislation on issues of labour and equality law. EU integration by positive integration measures (i.e. primary and secondary law) has so far already reached a fairly high level within the regulative social policy fields.

The picture looks quite different within the redistributive social policy fields. Here the treaty on the one hand contains provisions that explicitly forbid any harmonisation within these fields (health care and education), or just allow for complementing measures (social assistance)[77] or, as to social security, just for EU coordination by unanimity voting.[78] On the other hand, by the use of the EU market rules (the internal market competence) and the Union citizenship chapter, the treaty allows at the same time – according to the ECJ's interpretation – for a harmonisation and/or coordination within these social policy fields.[79] The proposal for a directive on cross-border health care within Europe is an example for such an EU harmonisation of a redistributive social policy area on the basis of the EU's internal market competences.[80]

While social policy scientists and economists usually see a contradiction in the inclusion of both these sets of rules in the treaty,[81] lawyers, in contrast, ex-

---

regulative social policies. The limitation in Art 2 para 4 lit 2 TEU is formulated as follows: '*social policy, for the aspects defined in the treaty*'.

77   As to the 'combating of social exclusion' and 'social protection systems' (Art 153 lit j and k TFEU), the Treaty excludes any harmonisation or coordination measures and so far just allows for an EU integration by policy measures and not through legal instruments.

78   Art 48 TFEU. The unanimity requirement has been changed by the Lisbon Treaty to an ordinary legislative procedure. That has, however, again been combined with a veto right of each Member State. As of yet, social security coordination still requires unanimity voting.

79   Provided that from the application of these EU rules (the EU market rules and the Union citizenship chapter) by the ECJ to the member states' redistributive social policy fields, it automatically also follows that these EU rules can be used as a legal base to issue coordination or harmonisation measures by secondary law within these areas.

80   COM(2008) 414 final.

81   Conclusively Stephan Leibfried (2005), Social Policy. Left to the Judges and the Markets? In: Helen Wallace, William Wallace, Mark A. Pollack (eds.), Policy making in the European Union, 5th edition. Oxford: Oxford University Press, pp. 243-278 at 244: '*...it was assumed that initiatives to ensure the free movement of goods, persons, services and capital could be insulated from social policy issues, which should remain the province of member states. This dubious assumption runs directly contrary to the central tenets of political economy, which stress that economic action is embedded within dense networks of social and political institutions. There is significant evidence that the neat separation between "market issues" belonging to the supranational sphere and "social issues" belonging to the national spheres, is unsustainable...*' Similarly, Giandomenico Majone (2005), Dilemmas of European Integration: The Ambiguities & Pitfalls of Integration by

plain their compatibility with the so-called 'implied powers theory'. As long as the redistributive social policy fields are also relevant from other policy perspectives for which the Union has been conferred explicit competences (eg. the internal market), the Union has on the basis of these competences implied powers to regulate (harmonise and coordinate) also the redistributive social policy fields. Such a EU intervention does not interfere with the member states' reserved competences in these fields; respectively, the competences are only to that extent reserved to the member states insofar as they do not violate central EU principles and values (such as e.g. to establish an internal market based on open trade and fair competition).[82] Thereby, it is widely accepted that it is primarily the ECJ (and the Commission) which determine on a quite flexible basis to what extent the redistributive social policy fields are also relevant from policy perspectives for which the Union possesses competences, by deciding case by case whether they are to be subjected to the EU market rules or the Union citizenship chapter.

To this already quite irritating legal frame on the attribution of competences between the EU and the Member States within the redistributive social policy fields, the Lisbon Treaty has added a new legal base (Article 14 TFEU) according to which the Union might establish the principles and set the conditions which shall enable the SGEI to fulfil their mission, however, '*without prejudice to the competence of Member States, in compliance with the Treaties, to provide, to commission and to fund such services.*' Beyond still being unclear over whether this legal base will at all become relevant for the redistributive social policy fields (depends on whether they are to be classified as SGEI in the meaning of Article 14 TFEU), it is so far also quite difficult to discern what exactly the EU might regulate on this legal base with regard to the redistributive social policy fields and in particular how this new base for SGEI correlates with the EU's original rule for SGEI – now Article 106 TFEU. The wording of the provision is open to widely different interpretations.

Likewise it so far also seems quite unclear how the new social values, as included by the various programmatic provisions in the Treaty and the social fundamental rights of the Charter, could be embedded within the above-described so far developed EU primary law framework for the redistributive social policy fields, in particular when considering that these provisions shall not extend the competences of the Union as defined in the treaties.

Stealth. Oxford: Oxford University Press, pp. 181et seq., referring in this context to the 'Diminished Democracy Syndrom'.

82   On this doctrine in more detail, Armin von Bogdandy, Jürgen Bast (2002), The European Union's Vertical Order of Competences. The Current Law and Proposals for its Reform, Common Market Law Review 39(1), pp. 227-268.

2   The roles of the various EU actors within the developmental process towards the today's EU Social Constitution

The primary law framework for the redistributive social policy fields, as it currently stands, is in many respects the direct creation of the ECJ's case law and the Commission's practice. In particular the aspects that the EU market rules and the Union citizenship chapter do provide, including subjective rights and applicable to the redistributive social policy fields and so far allowing for a harmonisation or coordination within these fields, have been developed through the process of legal integration, i.e. through the application and therewith further development of the law by the ECJ and the Commission. In principle, these aspects have been then implicitly also accepted by the political actors (i.e. the member states 'as the masters of the treaties') through the various revisions of the treaties.

At the same time the member states, as the masters of the treaties, have refused ever since to adapt the special competence clauses for the welfare regimes to these by the ECJ's and the Commission's induced changes on the legal framework of the redistributive social policy fields. Political integration within the redistributive social policy fields so far still proceeds on the assumption that it is possible to exclude any EU harmonisation or coordination by legal instruments for health care, education, or the social protection systems,[83] even if the processes of legal integration clearly prove otherwise. This disparity between the legal and political integration processes within the redistributive social policy fields is in essence the cause for the many ambiguities within the legal framework for the redistributive social policy fields. It is again reflected in the wording of the new legal base for the SGEI (Article 14 TFEU), according to which the EU shall establish the principles and conditions for the provision of the SGEIs within the EU without, however, interfering with the member states' competences to provide (commission and finance) the SGEIs.

3   Potential future developments: 'A limited version of the Europe's social self'

First, through the inclusion of social policy values into the Treaty by programmatic provisions and by declaring the fundamental social rights as legally binding, it has been in principal safeguarded that any harmonisation or coordination of the redistributive social policy fields on the basis of EU policies other than so-

---

83   So at least the wording of these special competence clauses.

cial polices (e.g. the internal market policy) may not lead to a levelling down of social standards in Europe. Economic integration and in general further European integration has to find its limits where the common European social values might be jeopardised. The Commission and the EU legislator are obliged to evaluate their actions in this respect.[84]

Second, Article 14 TFEU could be used as a legal base to lay down by secondary law – with regard to the redistributive social policy fields that qualify as SGEI – those common social standards in Europe to which the social clause in Article 9 TFEU refers and which would have to be identified through an exercise in comparative law, i.e. by comparing and bringing together the different welfare systems of the member states.[85] Above all such a secondary law measure could specify what the proper balance between market and other EU values and the social policy values of the member states (as required by the social clause and the fundamental social rights) could be. As secondary law in general has to comply with EU primary law, in particular also in its interpretation by the ECJ, the content of such a measure in principle has to orientate on cases that have so far been issued by the ECJ and the Commission within the redistributive social policy fields. However, as the EU primary law framework has been changed significantly with regard to the aspect of balancing market and social values within the EU (through the inclusion of new social values and fundamental social rights in the Lisbon Treaty), deviations from the ECJ case law could be legitimate insofar as they find a base in these new provisions of the Treaty.

Such future developments in EU law with regard to the (redistributive) social policies would correlate with Maduro's second model of a Social Europe, according to which the role of the EU within the redistributive social policy fields is not to establish and exercise an independent redistributive function, but just to serve as a yardstick for the protection of the social systems at the national level.[86] The current EU Social Constitution so far allows – in the words of Maduro – just for 'a limited version of the Europe's social self'. It will be seen in the future whether the European project will get along with this limited version of Europe's social self or whether Maduro's third model – basically, the development of a European supranational welfare state, complementing if not replacing, the member states' welfare states, which today is clearly rejected by all the member

---

84 See in this context also the Commission's website on impact assessment: http://ec.europa.eu/governance/impact/index_en.htm

85 Miguel Poiares Maduro (2006), European Constitutionalism and Three Models of Social Europe, in: Martijn Hesselink (ed.), The Politics of a European Civil Code. The Hague: Kluwer Law International, pp. 125-141 at 133.

86 Ibid, p. 131.

states[87] – is indeed an inevitable developmental step towards a true political Union.

Bibliography:

Alter, K. (ed.) (2009), *The European Court's Political Power – Selected Essays*. Oxford: Oxford University Press..

Armstrong, K.A. (1998), Legal Integration: Theorizing the Legal Dimension of European Integration, *Journal of Common Market Studies* 36 (2), pp. 155-174.

Baquero Cruz, J. (2002), *Between Competition and Free Movement. The Economic Constitutional Law of the European Union*. Oxford: Hart Publishing.

Baquero Cruz, J. (2007), The Socioeconomic Model of the European Union: Stuck with the Status Quo, in: Giuliano Amato, Herve Bribosia, Bruno de Witte (eds.), *Génèse et Destinée de la Constitution européenne – Genesis and Destiny of the European Constitution*, Bruxelles: Bruylant, pp. 1105-1128.

Barr, N. (2004), *The Economics of the Welfare State*. Oxford: Oxford University Press.

Capelletti, M. et al (1986), *Integration through Law*, Book 1, Vol. 1, Chap. 2. Berlin/ New York: Walter de Gruyter.

Damjanovic, D.; De Witte, B. (2009), Welfare Integration through EU Law: The Overall Picture in the Light of the Lisbon Treaty, in: Ulla Neergard, Ruth Nielsen, Lynn Roseburry (eds.), *Integrating Welfare Functions into EU-Law. From Rome to Lisbon*. Copenhagen: DJØF, pp. 53-97.

De Búrca, G. (2005), Rethinking Law in Neofunctionalist Theory, *Journal of European Public Policy* 12(2), pp. 310-326.

De Burca, G. (2005), Towards European Welfare? In: Gráinne de Búrca (ed.), *EU Law and the Welfare State – In Search of Solidarity*, Oxford: Oxford University Press, pp. 1-9.

De Witte, B. (2005), The trajectory of Fundamental Social Rights in the European Union, in: Gràinne de Búrca, Bruno de Witte (eds.), *Social Rights in Europe*. Oxford: Oxford University Press, pp. 153-168 at 159.

Deakin, S.; Browne, J. (2003), Social Rights and Market Order: Adapting the Capability Approach, in: Tamara K. Hervey, Jeff Kenner (eds.), *Economic and Social Rights under the EU Charter. A Legal Perspective*. Oxford: Hart Publishing, pp. 27-43 at 28.

---

87 So far, in Europe the view predominates that a Single European Social Model that replaces and supersedes the national welfare systems is for various socio-political reasons neither a desirable nor a realistic option. '*The difficulty of conducting redistributive politics beyond the state*' (Giandomenico Majone (2005), Dilemmas of European Integration: The Ambiguities & Pitfalls of Integration by Stealth. Oxford: Oxford University Press, pp. 190f.) and the insufficient bonds of social solidarity amongst citizens of different states particularly in a much enlarged EU" (Michael Dougan, Eleanora Spaventa (2005), "Wish You Weren't Here..." New Models of Social Solidarity in the European Union, in: Michael Dougan, Eleanora Spaventa (eds.), Social Welfare and EU Law. Oxford: Hart Publishing, pp. 181-218 at 187) are just a few of the various reasons named in the debate.

Dehousse, R. (2000), Integration through Law Revisited: Some thoughts on the Juridification of the European Political Process, in: Francis Snyder (2000), *The Europeanisation of Law. The Legal Effects of European Integration*. Oxford: Hart Publishing, pp. 15-30.

Delhey, J. (2004), *European Social Integration. From Convergence of Countries to Transnational Relations between Peoples*, WZB Discussion Paper, Berlin, http://skylla.wzb. eupdf/2004/i04-201.pdf.

Dougan, M.; Spaventa, E. (2005), "Wish You Weren't Here..." New Models of Social Solidarity in the European Union, in: Michael Dougan, Eleanora Spaventa (eds.), *Social Welfare and EU Law*. Oxford: Hart Publishing, pp. 181-218

Edward, D.; Hoskins, M. (2005), Article 90: Deregulation and EC Law. Reflections arising from the XVI Fide Conference, *Common Market Law Review* 32 (1), pp. 157-186.

Eilmansberger, T.; Herzig, G. (2008), *Study on Social Services of General Interest* (SSGI), commissioned by the Federal Ministry of Social Affairs and Consumer Protection.

Falkner , G.(1998), *EU Social Policy in the 1990s. Towards a Corporatist Policy Community*. London: Routledge.

Griller, S. (2005), Die Europäische Union: Ein staatsrechtliches Monstrum? In: Ingolf Pernice, Ulrich Haltern, Gunnar Folke Schuppert (eds.), *Europawissenschaft*. Baden-Baden: Nomos

Hesselink, M. (ed.), *The Politics of a European Civil Code*. The Hague: Kluwer Law International.

Höpfner, M.; Schäfer, A. (2008), *Die Politische Ökonomie der europäischen Integration*. Frankfurt/ New York: Campus.

Kleinmann, M. (2002), *A European Welfare State? European Union Social Policy in Context*. Basingstoke: Palgrave Macmillan.

Leibfried, S. (2005), Social Policy. Left to the Judges and the Markets? In: Helen Wallace, William Wallace, Mark A. Pollack (eds.), *Policy making in the European Union*, 5th edition. Oxford: Oxford University Press, pp. 243-278

Majone, G. (2005), *Dilemmas of European Integration: The Ambiguities & Pitfalls of Integration by Stealth*. Oxford: Oxford University Press.

Marshall , T.H.(1975), *Social policy in the twentieth century*, 4th edition. Hutchinson University Library.

Mortelmans, K. (2001), Towards Convergence in the Application of the Rules on Free Movement and on Competition? *Common Market Law Review* 38, pp. 613-649.

O'Leary, S. (2009), Equal Treatment and EU Citizens: A New Chapter on Cross-border Educational Mobility and Access to Student financial Assistance, *European Law Review* 68, pp. 612-627.

Poiares Maduro, M. (2000), Europe's Social Self: The Sickness Unto Death? In: Jo Shaw (ed.), *Social Law and Policy in an Evolving European Union*. Oxford: Hart Publishing, pp. 325-349.

Poiares Maduro, M. (2006), European Constitutionalism and Three Models of Social Europe, in: Martijn Hesselink (ed.), *The Politics of a European Civil Code*. The Hague: Kluwer Law International, pp. 125-141.

Samuelson, P.A.; Nordhaus, W. (2005), *Economics*, McGraw Hill.

Scharpf, F.W. (2002), The European Social Model: Coping with the Challenges of Diversity, *Journal of Common Market Studies* 40, pp. 645-670.

Schmidt, S.K. (2008), Europäische Integration zwischen judikativer und legislativer Politik, in: Martin Höppner, Armin Schäfer (eds.), *Die Politische Ökonomie der Europäischen Integration*. Frankfurt/ New York: Campus Verlag, pp. 101-127.

Shaw, J. (2005), Mainstreaming Equality and Diversity in European Union Law and Policy, *Current Legal Problems* 58, pp. 255-312.

Shaw, J.; Hund, J.; Wallace, C. (2007), *Economic and Social Law and Policy of the European Union*. London: Palgrave Macmillan.

Spaventa , E.(2007), *Free Movement of Persons in the European Union. Barriers to Movement in their Constitutional Context*. Alphen aan der Rijn: Kluwer.

Spaventa, E. (2008), Seeing the wood despite the trees? On the scope of Union Cirtizenship and its Constitutional Effects, *Common Market Law Review* 45(1), pp. 13-45.

Van der Me, A.P.i (2003), *Free Movement of Persons within the European Community: Cross-border Access to Public Benefits*. Oxford: Hart Publishing.

Von Bogdandy, A.; Bast, J. (2002), The European Union's Vertical Order of Competences: The Current Law and Proposals for its Reform, *Common Market Law Review* 39(2), pp. 227-269.

Policy-Oriented Approaches to the European Common Good

Joint Action versus Free Ride: EU Financial Crisis Management Based on a Common Good?

Klaus Gretschmann[1]

> *We must all hang together, gentlemen...*
> *Else, we shall most assuredly hang separately.*
> Benjamin Franklin

> *The common weal of the peoples of Europe must be our maxim.*
> Helmut Schmidt

I   Introduction

'The situation is hopeless, people are helpless, markets are relentless and politicians are clueless'. This seems to characterise the general mood in Europe in 2012, as pundits and serious analysts hold alike.

Anti-Europeanism abounds, combined with mistrust in the political elites who are considered incapable of solving the multiple crises Europe has been facing ever since 2008.The alleged decline of Europe and notably the European Union (EU) is the subject of a whole legion of books,[2] articles, and newspaper headlines, which pinpoint this 'deplorable development' almost every single day. This is not an isolated phenomenon in individual member states of the EU, but rather a kind of generic characteristic all across the Union. Annoyance with Europe has become *à la mode* and is growing rapidly.

Over the past two years, EU heads of state and government have met 20 (!!) consecutive times at summits to deal with the fallout of financial crises without any convincing result in spite of the high hopes they had held to impress the markets. Numerous meetings of eurozone finance ministers, task forces, and pre-

---

1   Until July 2011, Professor Dr Klaus Gretschmann was Director-General at the General Secretariat of the Council of the EU responsible for competitiveness, internal market, industrial policy, tariffs, research, information society, energy, and transport. The following propositions are the sole responsibility of the author. They reflect his personal opinion and not the position of any EU institution.

2   For an excellent overview of the arguments see Paul Taylor (2008), The End of European Integration. Anti-Europeanism examined. London: Routledge.

paratory bodies (such as the well-known EFC[3]) have been called again and again in order to suggest and to shape the right emergency measures – most of them in vain! It has thus been proved that in European politics, more so than in national politics, the shortest distance between two points is never a straight line.

Scholars and students of European integration keep reminding us that crises and the determination of Europe's political elites to find common solutions have both been at the cradle of the European Communities and have often preceded the leapfrogging which has characterised the development of Europe over the past six decades.[4]

The choreography of EU development over time may be described as a swinging pendulum: alternating periods of europhoria and over-integration, and phases of stagnation and under-integration. The point of equilibrium has always been the 'locus' that marks the common good for both the member states and the Union as such.

In Section II we will search for this 'European common good'. We will try to determine what the common weal of Europe and the combined well being and shared values and interests of the member states might mean and imply, and answer the questions of whether such a European common good exists at all and if so, how it might be captured and defined.

In Section III we will investigate the multiple rationales of Europe and its approach towards ever closer integration, and we will question whether there is enough 'convergence of beliefs, values and interests' to build upon – notably in times of economic crises. On the one hand, Europe has indeed managed to create a common and free realm of mobility, communication, interaction, liberty, etc. without boundaries; on the other hand, it may have degenerated into what Habermas[5] recently criticised as a 'post-democratic threat of executive federalism', i.e. the heads of state and government decide whilst ignoring and blindsiding the will of the peoples and the citizens of Europe.

---

3   The Economic and Financial Committee (EFC) is a committee of the EU set up to promote policy coordination among the member states. It provides opinions to and works for the Council of the EU including assessments of the economic and financial situation, the coordination of economic and fiscal policies, contributions on financial market matters, exchange rate polices, and relations with third countries and international institutions.

4   Desmond Dinan (2004), Europe Recast: A History of European Union. London: Palgrave Macmillan; Tony Judt (2005), Postwar: A History of Europe after 1945. NYC: Penguin Press.

5   Jürgen Habermas (2011), Zur Verfassung Europas ('On Europe's Constitution'). Berlin: Suhrkamp Verlag.. Habermas criticises the European Council, which was given a central role in the Lisbon Treaty. He views the Council as a *governmental body that engages in politics without being authorized to do so.'*

The upshot of Section III will be further analysed in Section IV, which will discuss the possibilities and limits to economic policy coordination within the European Union.

Section V is devoted to the actions and reactions of major European players trying to fight the two financial crises since 2008. The tension between a common good approach and the prevalence of partial and national interests makes for interesting conclusions regarding where Europe and the EU presently stand and where they might be heading when the crisis is over.

Section VI will examine the feasibility of turning the eurozone into a fully-fledged fiscal union, concluding that there are both structural difficulties to make such a reform 'tick' and notional uncertainties about what a fiscal union might actually be and possibly entail.

This leads to some concluding remarks in Section VII and the crucial questions of what kind of Europe we want to strive for and which Europe mirrors the common good: a Europe of bureaucrats and the Brussels institutional machinery, a Europe of economic interests and enterprises in an unregulated free-market setting, a Europe of intellectuals and academics (widely neglected and side-lined so far), or a renewed and refreshed Europe beyond the alternative of 'deals versus ideals' and based on the will, preferences, and discourse of the normal citizen of Europe holding a national, regional, and European identity at the same time. Today the European *citoyen*, the sovereign of last resort, has become alienated and appears no longer aware of the spirit and purpose of the European Union, nor of its common good. The Brussels institutional apparatus has managed to create a distance between citizen and elites, which needs to be rapidly and drastically narrowed if Europe is to be revived.

II   In Search of the Common Good

The notion of 'common good'[6] encapsulates a deep-seated yet subjectivist politico-philosophical concept encompassing a juridical, sociological, political and, last but not least, economic dimension.[7]

---

6   The German Max Plank Society established an entire institute in Bonn for the 'Research on Collective Goods' and published a whole series of articles and papers under the heading *Common Goods: Law, Politics and Economics.*

7   Theories in the Social Sciences involve related concepts such as Social Goods, Collective Goods, Public Goods, and Club Goods, etc.

When talking about a common good from a medieval *Aquinian* perspective,[8] philosophers used to refer to the **bonum commune** as a natural quality – something which is a given and for which all humans strive. However, such a transcendental, abstract and *a priori* definition runs the danger of quickly turning totalitarian:[9] an idea, ideology or higher objective or purpose may be hijacked by a ruler or dictator and may be used to coerce his people and citizens into following what he defines as the common good. Whereas Rousseau[10] differentiated between the '*volonté de tous*' (the will of all individuals in a community) and the '*volonté génerale*', (the will of the community as a higher entity), the utilitarians in the Bentham tradition[11] defined the common good as the 'greatest happiness of the largest number principle'. Utilitarians claimed that the best course of action – and consequently the common good – is the one that maximises the overall 'happiness' of all. Similarly and in the same vein, classical philosophy considered the common good identical to the *res publica*![12] Modern theorists[13] believe that the common good may only be identified in a 'deliberative discourse', i.e. in an autonomous, non-hierarchical communicative situation undistorted by any kind of asymmetrical power relation in which all members of a community act as equals.[14] Other students of common good and a general (economic) interest at the European level[15] have pointed out that common good theory conceives of individual acting units – be they persons, citizens, families, clubs, communities, countries, peoples or states, and nations – as always having to take into account the interests and preferences of other such units, with whom they interact, live, or relate. In this vein, it goes without saying that the more homogeneous the various units, the easier it is to jointly define a common good and vice versa!

8   Thomas v. Aquin, Summa Theologiae I-II; Herfried Münkler, Harald Bluhm (2002) Gemeinwohl und Gemeinsinn. Historische Semantiken politischer Leitbegriffe. Berlin: Akademie Verlag.
9   Ernst Fraenkel (1941), The Dual State. New York: Octagon Books.
10   Jean Jacques Rousseau (1762), Du Contrat Social, Paris 1992, p. 40.
11   Philip Schofield (2006), Utility and Democracy. The Political Thought of Jeremy Bentham. Oxford: Oxford University Press.
12   *Res Publica,* meaning 'public affairs' or matters important to a community of individuals or groupings, dates back to classical philosophy and has accompanied political thinking ever since. Cf. Robert. E. Goodin, Philip Pettit. (eds.) (1995), A Companion to Contemporary Political Philosophy. Cambridge: Blackwell.
13   Dietmar von der Pfordten (2004), Normativer Individualismus, Zeitschrift für philosophische Forschung 58, pp. 321-346.
14   Jürgen Habermas (1986), The Theory of Communicative Action: Reason and the Rationalization of Society (original: Die Theorie des kommunikativen Handelns). Cambridge: Polity Press.
15   Gunnar Folke Schuppert, Friedrich Neidhardt (eds.) (2002), Gemeinwohl – auf der Suche nach Substanz, Berlin: WZB Jahrbuch. 'Les services d'intérêt économique général' have been part and parcel of the Roman Treaty of 1957: Art 86/2.

This points our reflections to the concept of spill-overs and externalities,[16] as developed and applied in public economics. The ubiquity of externalities was notably emphasised in the writings of Egon Matzner.[17] In addition, welfare economics in the Paretian and Kaldor-Hicksian tradition contributes to the thinking about the common good: according to the famous *Pareto criterium*, an initial allocation or distribution among individuals or units of action which may be changed and can make at least one individual better off without making any other one worse off is an improvement to strive for. An optimal allocation is reached when no further improvements are possible. This is a kind of steady state that defines an optimum in the sense of a common good. This theoretical approach was later complemented by Kaldor and Hicks, who argued that even if one individual (A) may suffer a loss by getting another individual (B) into a gainful position, such a reallocation may be efficient if and only if the gains of (B) will be sufficient to compensate for the pain (losses) of (A) and yielding an overall gain on top.[18]

Common goods can thus be defined as the action of individuals or units of action in any community with the aim of achieving cooperative, non-conflictual and pleasant 'togetherness', taking into account the (unintended) results of any individual action on the welfare of all other parties involved and concerned. This implies Subsidiarity,[19] Solidarity,[20] and Solidity,[21] and is the counter-model to private goods and individual interests.

Against this backdrop, our analysis will be based on a consequentialist notion of the common good that cannot be defined *a priori*, but is determined by its resulting outcome, i.e. *a posteriori*. This dovetails with the fact that Europe does not traditionally or historically have a *bonum commune*; rather we were – throughout the largest part of our history – a continent of fierce conflicts and wars. Therefore, no pre-defined *bonum commune* can serve as a precondition or

16 Concepts of externalities and spill-overs are best described in the seminal book of Richard Cornes and Todd Sandler (1996), The Theory of Externalities, Public Goods, and Club Goods. Cambridge: Cambridge University Press (2nd edition).
17 Egon Matzner (1982), Der Wohlfahrtsstaat von morgen, Entwurf eines zeitgemässen Musters staatlicher Interventionen. Wien: Österreichischer Bundesverlag.
18 Tibor Scitovsky (1941). A Note on Welfare Propositions in Economics. Review of Economic Studies 9 (1), pp. 77–88.
19 Klaus Gretschmann (1991), Le Principe de subsidiarité: Quelles responsabilités à quelle niveau de pouvoir dans une Europe intégré? Subsidiarité: défi du changement, Maastricht: EIPA, pp. 49-70.
20 Klaus Gretschmann (1986), Solidarity and Markets, in: Franz-Xaver Kaufmann, Giandomenico Majone, Vincent Ostrom (eds.), Guidance, Control and Evaluation in the Public Sector. Berlin/New York: Walter de Gruyter, pp. 387.
21 This pinpoints economising on scarce resources and the absence of a free-rider attitude on the good will and cooperative spirit of others. See further, the argument relating to the framework of a fiscal union below.

prerequisite, i.e. a sound basis for developing a coherent European political framework in its own right; rather it is Europe's history and tragedy that a common good will have to be the fateful *result of pooling sovereignty and hammering out previous joint action among member states of the Union.* Therefore, the European common good can only be identified knowing all the ultimate consequences of individual and common action at the EU level.

At this point, a related concept may come into play: public finance theory has developed the 'Theory of Public Goods', and ever since has differentiated between (pure) public goods and so-called 'club goods'. Whereas pure public goods imply unity in production and non-excludability in their use, i.e. consumption, club goods, in contrast, allow for partial excludability of non-club members. Both kinds of goods may constitute collective action problems[22] at the EU level: mutually beneficial outcomes (or public goods) can only be secured if member states have no incentives to 'free ride'[23] and if special interest groups are prevented from obtaining benefits to the detriment of the 'public interest'.

One final remark seems to be in order with regard to the European level: a good that is common between actor (A) and actor (B) may not necessarily be the same common good for actors (C) and (D). What may be considered in a local community as a common good, may turn into a particularistic interest at a higher – say, national – level. What may be considered a common good at the level of a nation or nation-state may easily change into a particular national interest not conducive to a common cause or concern at the European level.[24] Therefore, some scholars consider the European common good a result of mediation and compromise among competing and differing preferences, interests, and national priorities. Albeit partially true, this interpretation might end up in a smallest-common-denominator approach not apt to bring clarification to the matter.[25]

---

22 Elinor Ostrom (1990), Governing the Commons: The Evolution of Institutions for Collective Action. Cambridge: Cambridge University Press.

23 Mancur Olson (1965), The Logic of Collective Action: Public Goods and the Theory of Groups. Cambridge, Mass.: Harvard University Press; a critical view can be found in Robert Axelrod (2006), The Evolution of Cooperation (Revised ed.). New York: Perseus Books Group.

24 Therefore, European solidarity among citizens of the Union may be much less resilient and more abstract than national or local solidarity and communality among peers. In respect to the European Union, Alessandra Casella and Bruno S. Frey (1992), Federalism and Clubs: Towards an Economic Theory of Overlapping Political Jurisdictions, European Economic Review 36, pp. 639-46 advocate a structure of 'functional federalism' that allows for a system of overlapping political jurisdictions.

25 Paul Taylor (p.124) asserts that too much emphasis on 'the logic differentiation' and too little on 'the logic of synthesis' may attenuate the sense of common values and destiny in a community such as the EU.

III Europe's Multiple Rationale: Common Interests and Divergent Beliefs

Fundamentally, states seek to increase their power in international economic relations in order to create conditions that minimise the costs of pursuing their domestic economic priorities in an interdependent world economy. Their policy choices are conditioned by the constraints and opportunities they face in the international environment.

International interdependence provides both costs and opportunities for all actors involved. The main benefit of interdependence is the welfare gain that results from a more efficient allocation of resources. The foremost price of interdependence is a relative loss in national decision-making autonomy. Under the conditions of interdependence, the ability of a government to pursue its own domestic priorities is constrained by external forces over which it has little or no control. These costs of interdependence, however, are asymmetrical among the various participants. In other words, states possess different degrees of power to adjust to external pressures or to change the international environment under which they operate. The preferred option of states would be to push the costs of adjustment onto other actors in the system and to reduce domestic costs.

Governments can control domestic conditions only if they can influence the decisions taken in other countries. Thus, states want to avoid or constrain negative externalities of other governments' pursuits of domestic economic priorities. What is the rationale behind these developments? It is the growing interconnectedness of the global world that makes us feel the often unintended effects of the actions of others more directly and immediately. Such 'externalities' are changing the boundaries between domestic and international politics and are eroding the traditional modes of governance. This has profound implications: national decision makers must refocus on international cooperation; new institutional arrangements are needed to take up the new challenges; existing organisations must adapt their working methods; economic policy coordination both in the area of macroeconomics and at the level of micro-policies is badly needed.

Therefore, Moravcsik[26] argues convincingly that both the demand and the willingness to integrate and coordinate are determined by the extent to which it is necessary to manage international interdependence. It seems to be a kind of generic law in integration that, whenever a nation's ability to control its economy is constrained by either market forces, the most prominent of which is international capital mobility, or by spill-over from economic policy measures abroad, inte-

---

26 Andrew Moravcsik (1993), Preferences and Power in the European Community: A Liberal Intergovernmentalist Approach, Journal of Common Market Studies 31 (4), pp. 473-524.

gration provides a tool for regaining control and material sovereignty at a supra-national level, through the pooling of resources, cooperative governance, and in-stitutionalisation of rules for policymaking. Therefore, it will be necessary to re-concile conflicting national preferences, perceptions, interests, and 'beliefs'. This is particularly relevant since EU policymaking is only rarely built upon a shared, consistent, and coherent concept of policymaking for Europe as a whole.

Essentially, there are two major forces at work: *deals and ideals.* As we know from economic psychology, ideals tend to dominate in periods of economic well being, high growth rates, and stable political situations, in which certainty and security prevail, whereas interests and deals become the predominant force in situations of instability, economic slow-down, unemployment crises, etc. The advantage of ideals over deals is, as Thomas Shelling has put it, their self-binding function: in the pursuit of ideals, agents (be they governments or people) are inclined to act even beyond their narrow self-interest. When it comes to deals and interests playing the major role, there seems to be less leeway for selfless vi-sions: only if there is interest mediation and positive gains for those involved, will agents stick to treaties and contracts. If interests cannot be made compatible, agents will start to defect. It seems to be quite obvious that due to the many ele-ments of instability and uncertainty currently arising, which result from lower expected growth rates in the coming years, interests may dominate over ideals. This affects both citizens, voters, and taxpayers on the one hand, and institutional actors such as public authorities, administrations, and EU member states on the other hand.

When we search for the European common good in such a complex setting as described above, laden and interwoven with national interests, the question arises as to what brings nation-states to cooperate and integrate.

Non-conventional theory[27] holds that in the case of the EU the following ele-ments are constitutive:

The fact that in view of a growing number of *externalities* in an intercon-nected world, isolated national policies will no longer be able to work efficiently and effectively. Traditional deficit spending to stimulate the national economy of a country has become inefficient by leading to higher demand for imports; na-tional tax policy has failed in the face of the high international mobility of tax bases; national anti-pollution policy has been rendered useless in the face of emissions carried by wind across borders.

Economies of scale allow for economising resources in a larger Union – in an unrestricted single market, a wider range of goods can be produced at lower costs and sold at lower prices, compared to a smaller national market.

---

27 For a more traditionally theoretical approach, see: Antje Wiener (2009), European Inte-gration Theory. Oxford: Oxford University Press.

The **_pooling of resources and influence_** contributes to increasing the influence and power in wider settings. A small country like Luxembourg may not be able to promote its interest at the negotiation table of the World Trade Organization or elsewhere, but may possess greater bargaining weight by being an integral part of the EU as a negotiating party.

The well-known *'prisoner's dilemma'*[28] can be avoided between countries which cooperate and integrate closely.

Indeed, in an interdependent world and notably in an integrated area such as the EU, problems and solutions stretch across national borders, resulting in a growing need for collective action. Clean environment, health, knowledge, property rights, economic, and monetary policy are all examples of common and public goods. The main properties and distinguishing features of such international public goods are usually characterised by the fact that their benefits have strong qualities of *'publicness'* – i.e. they are marked by non-rivalry in consumption and non-excludability. This means, respectively, that when provided to one party, the public good is available to all, and consumption of the public good by one party does not reduce the beneficial effect to the others.

Regional public goods[29] are those whose benefits could in principle be consumed by the governments and peoples of all member states. Examples include mechanisms for ensuring financial stability, the creation of a common market, the promotion of research and scientific knowledge, and international regulations for aviation and telecommunications. European energy policy (security of energy supply to all members of the Union), a European patent (with equal legal rights and costs), European public service obligations (valid in all countries), free movement of labour, capital, goods and services with no discrimination, overcoming the financial and economic crisis, a European budget of its own right: these are all examples of European common goods in a wider sense.

If all member states of a Union can benefit from the provision of such common goods they should be easy to supply. However, literature argues convincingly

---

28   Anatol Rapoport, Albert M. Chammah (1965). Prisoner's Dilemma. Ann Arbor: University of Michigan Press.

29   "In the 1990s, it was noted that international public goods fall into the two categories of global and regional public goods, the latter differing from the former on account of the more limited geographical reach of the benefits conveyed. RPGs benefit spillover communities that can range from a couple of neighbouring countries to a continent or hemisphere. Their production typically requires cross border collective action that engages all (or most) of the members of the spillover group." See Marco Ferroni, Regional Public Goods: The Comparative Edge of Regional Development Banks, Paper prepared for the Conference on Financing for Development at the Institute for International Economics, February 19, 2002.

that the public nature of common goods means that this is not always the case, due to problems of:

1. *Sovereignty*: Governments are often unwilling to limit or constrain sovereign decision making, for example by accepting binding rules or international monitoring of their own compliance with agreements.
2. *Heterogeneous preferences*: Governments often have divergent interests and priorities as regards specific solutions, even where they share general long-term goals. Energy policy or CO_2 reduction policies may impact differently on individual EU member states. What might be a highly desirable public good for one country or group of countries may not be so for another.
3. *The 'free-rider' problem*: Once a common or collective good is produced and made available to one party, it is hard to exclude others from benefiting. Consequently, there is an incentive for every party to wait until somebody else provides and pays for that good.
4. *The 'weakest link' problem*. Some goods can only be produced when every government fully complies with a common approach, such as the reduction of CO_2 or banking regulation. Success can be eroded by a single act of non-compliance, sometimes due to a country that cannot – at a reasonable cost – carry the burden.

IV   Common Good and Policy Coordination

Nonetheless, despite the fact that the EU is often considered an 'unfinished union on the way to an unknown destination',[30] and in spite of being criticised as a 'soft power', it is moving ahead steadily: while undergoing major changes over the last 50 years from a 'trade-driven' (customs union) via a 'factor-driven' (single market) and a 'money-driven' (EMU) to an 'innovation-driven' undertaking – the EU has acquired both political and economic influence and reputation. Its model of regional integration incorporates unprecedented economic progress, new modes of international governance and new forms of collective leadership.

In a world of growing interconnectedness which makes us feel the often unintended effects of the actions of others more directly and immediately, such 'externalities' are changing the boundaries between domestic and international politics and are eroding traditional modes of governance. This has profound implications: national decision makers must refocus on international cooperation, new institutional arrangements are needed to face the new challenges, and existing

30   Joseph H.H. Weiler (1999), The Constitution of Europe. Cambridge, Mass.: Harvard University Press.

organisations must adapt their working methods and (economic) policy coordination both in the area of macroeconomics and at the level of micro-policies.

These observations lead us to what Le Cacheux[31] called

'the generic idea that the need for coordination arises in contexts characterized by interdependencies…(and the fact that) decentralized decision-making in the absence of coordination devices will lead to sub-optimal, non-cooperative, Nash equilibria'.

However, there seems to be an absence of substantial economic policy coordination in Europe. While Article 121 of the *Treaty on the Functioning of the European Union* requires member states to consider their economic policies as a matter of common interest, the reality is that policy coordination is still rather weak. Whereas *euroland* is characterised by a single currency and a single monetary authority, fiscal policy in Europe is still the domain of national governments. This raises questions of policy consistency and compatibility of decisions and instruments, as well as the timing and extent of policy changes.

There is no reason, Korkman[32] argues convincingly, to expect that the sum of the fiscal policies of 17 individual member states of the eurozone is always appropriate for the euro area. There seems to be general agreement that a genuine European economic policy in its own right is necessary, and that it should not be modelled on a single member state's approach. The problem, however, is that there is as yet no clear vision of where we are heading, nor is it evident which of the features from different national systems should be adopted.

Against this backdrop, there is a need to reconcile conflicting national preferences, perceptions, interests, and 'beliefs'. This is particularly relevant since the monetary union did not start out with a shared, consistent and coherent concept of economic policymaking for Europe as a whole; rather, it was built on the insulated introduction and management of a single currency. Its founders expected the necessary macroeconomic and fiscal institutions, instruments, and policy content to flow from monetary policy pressure.

Indeed, coordination is particularly difficult if policymakers do not agree on the 'true model' that is an accurate characterisation of how the economy functions. As discussed above, a common good requires the existence of both common perceptions and interpretations of what can be influenced as well as a sufficient degree of homogeneity among the relevant actors. Unfortunately, as ana-

31 Jacques Le Cacheux (2010), How to Herd Cats: Economic Policy Coordination in the Eurozone in Tough Times, Journal of European Integration 32 (1), pp. 41-58 at 43.

32 Sixten Korkman (2002), Fiscal Policy Coordination in EMU, in: Anne Brunilla et al. (eds.), The Stability and Growth Pact – the architecture of fiscal policy in EMU. Basingstoke: Palgrave Macmillan, p. 269.

lysed in the literature on policy coordination in the late 1980s[33] difficulties can be attributed to four main factors:

1. There are different national constraints on the policy instruments available *(limited domain);*
2. There is disagreement about the effects (both of their scale and nature) of specific policy changes on policy targets *(differences in beliefs);*
3. There are cross-country differences in the degree of (inter-)dependence *(differences in spill-over effects);*
4. There are different models of how national economies and the global economy work *(model uncertainties).*

Decision makers tend to have only limited knowledge about the functioning of their national economies. They know even less about the working of the European economy in its entirety. This means they are faced with the problem of having to decide between competing models, the properties and premises of which are only partially understood. This is already an intractable problem at the national level. It will be even harder to solve and even more complicated at the international level. Feldstein and Frenkel and Rockett[34] have proven conclusively that if policymakers do not agree on the true model, coordination may well entail welfare losses. In any international setting like the EU, the probability that there is model certainty and consensus is pretty low. The more uncertain and less consensual a policy model is, the less aggressively policymakers will use their policy instruments.

Siebert[35] pointed out that the conduct of a joint optimal economic policy would require near-perfect agreement on the model and the philosophy on which an economic policy is to be founded. In the same vein, he argues that a coherent and jointly acceptable paradigm of economic explanation and analysis is an indispensable prerequisite.

In principle, governments can coordinate either through *inter-governmental arrangements* or through *a transfer of sovereignty to a common institution.*[36] The

---

33   For an instructive overview, see Ralph C. Bryant (1995). International Coordination of National Stabilization Policies (Integrating National Economies: Promise & Pitfalls). Washington: Brookings Institution Press.

34   Martin S. Feldstein (1988), International Economic Cooperation. Chicago: University Press; Jacob A. Frenkel, Katherine E. Rockett (1988), International Macroeconomic Policy Co-ordination when Policymakers do not Agree on the True Model, American Economic Review 78 (3), pp. 318-340.

35   Horst Siebert (1997), Zu den Voraussetzungen der Europäischen Währungsunion, Kiel, Discussion Paper 289, Institut für Weltwirtschaft.

36   Jürgen von Hagen, Susanne Mundschenk (2001), The Functioning of Economic Policy Coordination, mimeo, Bonn: ZEI Working Paper.

more binding arrangement is, of course, the latter. The main problem is multidimensional and is confronted by the following dilemmas:

1. As long as there is no consensus on economic models and measures, self-binding arrangements are difficult to achieve;
2. As long as it is not clear which interests prevail in the common, supranational institution and whether it can be trusted to pursue the common goal, the transfer of sovereignty is risky; and
3. As long as spending and taxation are about the level and composition of *national* public goods and *at the same time* about European macroeconomic policy, a sacrifice of the former for the sake of the latter – in the face of varying national preferences – is very improbable.

Therefore, loose forms of coordination are to be preferred and a clear majority of eurozone member states seem to agree with former Commissioner Solbes[37] that economic policy coordination 'should not be seen to pursue a centralised economic governance with a uniform policy response to economic challenges, national policy should continue to have sufficient latitude to formulate and implement policies tailored to their needs.'

Economic policy coordination, as it is understood in the Brussels context, by no means dovetails with the conception of it in academic economics. In principle, economic coordination may have a narrow or a broad meaning.[38] The former implies a 'simple' surveillance and monitoring of the national policies of EU member states in order to veto those national policies that are expected to violate the European common good; i.e. that may produce – Paretian – welfare losses for the EU as a whole. Under this *regime-related coordination* come the Excessive Deficit Procedure and the Stability and Growth Pact, as well as – to a somewhat lesser extent – the Broad Economic Policy Guidelines. The coordination task is to identify and measure policies that might affect the EU's welfare position adversely and, in response, to push member states to refrain from adopting such policies. The broader notion of *strategic policy coordination* aims at developing cooperative policies in order to maximise welfare gains and positive externalities from policies adopted by one country that could affect economic variables in other countries. In this sense, the aim is not harmonisation of policy, but ensuring that it evolves in a coordinated manner maximising the common weal.

---

37 Pedro Solbes (2002), Economic Policy Co-ordination - the Way Forward, Brussels Economic Forum, 2 May 2002, mimeo, p.5.
38 Jürgen von Hagen, Susanne Mundschenk (2001), The Functioning of Economic Policy Coordination, mimeo, Bonn, ZEI Working Paper.

The above argument about model uncertainties and disparate beliefs demonstrates that in fact (economic and monetary) integration has not yet sufficiently overcome national interests and is still embedded in and constrained by disparate (economic) beliefs and ideas of what kind of Europe we should envisage. A fully-fledged and well-functioning Economic and Monetary Union would require the political will to steer (fiscal and monetary) politics and policies in line with a still to be defined common interest and a generally accepted common model. Considering the lack of these conditions and taking into account the challenges that the Union faces, the conceptual, theoretical, and political foundations on which the monetary union has been erected still appear rather shaky.

V   Common Good and Partial Interests: Europe fighting the crises of 2007-08 and 2010-11

At first glance, the movement towards *European Monetary Union* was built on an economic rationale: as a logical corollary of the *Single European Act* which was broadly about the removal of (non-tariff) barriers to intra-European trade. As an upshot, the single market in goods and services called for a commensurate liberalisation of cross-border movements of capital and labour. The creation of a single European currency and control of Union-wide monetary policy by a Union Central Bank was the capping stone of the whole venture. It was considered indispensable that one market operates on the basis of one currency. From this standpoint, an Economic and Monetary Union is principally a macroeconomic project, its target being essentially to shield the internal European market from the vagaries of fluctuating exchange rates and the perceived threats of *competitive devaluations*.

Some players in all of this, to be sure, have always entertained much more ambitious hopes. In their eyes, monetary union has always been the cornerstone of a far-reaching political strategy of integration yet to be consummated. The hope of the integrationists was to create a quasi-automatism in which the single market was to be followed by a monetary union, which might lead to a fiscal union and therefrom to a fully-fledged political union. Moreover, the idea to 'sell' was that the euro's economic mechanics might make everybody better off: if the poorer countries at the periphery shared a common currency with the strong core – like Germany and France – they could count on borrowing money at cheaper rates. The 'core' at the same time was able to export more of their products if the periphery was able to deficit-finance their imports at lower costs.[39] Some analysts called this a 'marriage of convenience'.

Against this backdrop, the original idea to 'sell' the euro to its critics and the general public as by and large compatible with a series of divergent national fiscal policies and on-going national economic sovereignty was attenuated over time. Economists had argued that the EU was no 'optimal currency area', and therefore so-called asymmetric shocks which in a monetary union could no longer be cushioned by exchange-rate adjustments had to be absorbed by means of wage and labour-market flexibility or through a system of transfers and fiscal federalism and a new 'unionised' fiscal policy. These arguments mirror the tension between those who advocate the 'unitary principle' and those who wish to maintain differentiation and diversity in European economic policymaking. Indeed, the risks for the EU as a whole and for any single member state depend on the policies and tools chosen by other member states.[40]

After ten years, during which time the euro worked perfectly and gained a strong reputation and position on the global financial markets due to its high internal stability (measured by inflation rates) and external stability (exchange rate vis-à-vis the US dollar), it was the financial and sovereign debt crises of 2008 and 2011 which laid bare its insufficient economic base and raised doubts about the economic 'principles' of EU integration.

Like the rest of the world, Europe has been going through major financial and economic crises and these are far from over. The crises have led to a search for solutions incorporating the European common good! This has involved a flurry of activity at various levels, including at member state and Union level. Yet the public perception of Europe's response has been rather mixed, with criticism focusing on the lack of decisive action and on the absence of a 'unitary response'.

At first glance, the EU response to the fall-out of crisis 1.0 – i.e. the so-called subprime crisis leading to a banking, financial market, and export crisis followed by a deep global recession – has been rather impressive: central banks cut interest rates to historically low levels, and provided huge amounts of liquidity to the financial system. Some of them embarked on unorthodox measures to provide credit to the economy. European governments channelled massive support to their banking systems through guarantees and recapitalisation. This was done in a well-coordinated fashion. The European Recovery Plan, which was proposed in November 2008, eventually received full endorsement from the European Council and included a significant and coordinated fiscal stimulus.

39 This argument has forcefully been put forward by Hans-Werner Sinn, President of the German Ifo-Institute in Munich.

40 If too many go for a restrictive fiscal policy, demand in the Union itself may decline and the result may be a negative economic dynamic for all.

This response has avoided a financial meltdown involving bank runs and a loss of confidence on the part of European citizens and has prevented an overall collapse of economic activity. Moreover, (1) the mere existence of the euro has prevented member states from choosing 'competitive devaluations' as a national way out of the crisis; (2) the internal market has held up remarkably well, despite all the loose talk about imminent protectionism, and (3) massive sums have been provided directly by the Union and indirectly through the IMF (under pressure from EU member states) to those countries confronted with sudden and drastic balance of payments problems.

The reaction to crisis 2.0 was however quite different:

It all started in October 2009. Trying to hide within the economic turbulence in the wake of crisis 1.0, the Greek government announced that its deficit figure for 2010 was 12.5 per cent, three times the amount officially acknowledged previously. Under market pressure, in February 2010 the Greek government launched a severe austerity package in order to control the fall-out on bond markets. Harsh debates in the European Council followed about the consequences of and solutions to the Greek situation, in particular how to prevent contagion, avoid bail-out discussions, and revise the Stability Mechanism. It soon became obvious that other member state such as Ireland, Portugal, and subsequently Italy and Spain were confronted with similar problems of sovereign debt and refinancing difficulties. In November 2011 the newly created European Financial Stability Facility lent money to Ireland with conditions attached.

It subsequently became evident that in the wake of crisis 1.0 the eurozone was caught in a downward spiral with European leaders left wanting in their approach to crisis management.[41] The sovereign debt crisis inside the eurozone soon laid bare the problems faced by European banks, which were holding government bonds of all types. Struggling banks and stumbling governments undermined the confidence of investors, which led to a kind of 'investment strike', deepening fears that governments might be unable to pay back their debts.

Objectively, the eurozone is still strong enough to cope with the crisis. It is less indebted than the United States and its deficit is manageable. It has the financial means to prevent the default of any of its member states. And if not hampered by rules, regulations, and ideologies, the European Central Bank (ECB) could buy out the weak bonds of crisis-stricken countries on the secondary market.

The real problem is that the governments of the eurozone are deeply at odds over what the crisis is really about, and riven by disagreement over what each country must contribute towards solving it. So long as the eurozone's members

41   For a chronological sketch of the developments and decisions since 2008 see Table 1.

cannot settle these arguments, or at least agree that their differences matter less than finding a solution, the collective action needed to defend the euro will remain impossible.'[42]

In theoretical terms a coordinated approach by no means implies a harmonisation in which everyone does the same thing, but rather a well-orchestrated coordination, nationally diversified, designed to guarantee a welfare maximum for the whole of Europe. EU member states can *choose from a broad portfolio of measures ('toolkit') the combination that seems to them to be most advantageous*: reducing public spending, increasing the tax burden and revenues, cutting subsidies and the support of specific branches of business, or reducing wages and pensions, often of low-income households. The measures taken to combat the crisis in the short term should be carefully considered as regards their coherence with the mid- to long-term endeavours to accomplish national goals and the Lisbon structural reforms. This means, primarily, intensified investment in infrastructure and innovation, greater support for SMEs and stimulation of employment, innovation, research and development, as well as education and training in order to increase competitiveness. In parallel, the European Council has repeatedly stressed that a strengthened *stability and growth pact continues to be the cornerstone of the fiscal framework of the EU*. However, criticism has been voiced vis-à-vis the 'toolkit approach' since, in addition to a gratifying commitment to flexibility, the approach is characterised by a lack of both conceptual stringency and of a common interpretation of the economic situation and its consequences for the diversity of economic interests in the Union.

In the wake of crisis 1.0 the analysis of the benefits of coordinating fiscal policies (or the lack thereof) was focused on joint stimulus programmes and was based on the notion of spill-overs. If a fiscal stimulus programme in one country also stimulates economic activity in other countries and if that country does not coordinate its actions with the other countries, we are faced with a free ride. The reason is that the other countries benefit from that country's stimulus and thus may decide to reduce their own stimulus effort. This way they can profit from the externally generated expansion without having to run costly budget deficits. This free-riding behaviour creates a problem for the first country – the benefits of its stimulus programme spill over (partially) to the other countries, while it alone bears the costs of the budget deficits. The country will therefore have an incentive to reduce its own stimulus programme. If all countries reason in the same way, they will not enact sufficiently ambitious stimulus plans. These very

---

42   Economist 12 November 2011: Special report: Europe and its currency. Edward Carr, Staring into the abyss.

general principles also apply when countries disengage by withdrawing from their stimulus programmes because their leaders feel constrained to do so.

In the debate about crisis 2.0 and the management thereof, the reverse logic is valid: when one country starts a policy of fiscal contraction and debt reduction, this reduces domestic economic activity and also negatively affects economic activity in the other countries. In this case, part of the cost of fiscal restriction spills over to other countries, while the benefit of the restrictive policy (which is the reduction of the budget deficit) is enjoyed solely by the first country. As a result, the other countries find themselves in a worse situation – economic activity declines and this in turn tends to increase their budget deficits. They are likely to respond by following restrictive budgetary policies thereby reducing economic activity both domestically and in the other countries. This process triggers a further deflationary dynamic that hurts everybody and complicates the task of reducing the budget deficits elsewhere.

Unfortunately, there is not much agreement either within the relevant decision-making bodies, such as the Competitiveness or Economic and Financial Affairs Councils or in academic circles, about how much and what kind of economic coordination is required. Ministers meeting in the Council of the EU collectively exercise many governmental functions, including legislation, but always with the intention, at the same time, of furthering what they consider to be their individual national interests. Jabko[43] (2011) has coined the notion of 'divided sovereignty' to capture this ambivalence.

Governance of the EU is indeed conceived of as an *aggregation* **of national interests rather than a** *disaggregation* **of a European common good.** EU economic policy is not driven by an operative conception of its own common interest. **So far, there is no clear-cut conception of** *the common good of a European economy,* because there is no consciousness of a European communality and no joint model of European economics and how such an economy should and could work.

VI   On the Way to a Fiscal Union?

The discussion about how best to fight the sovereign debt crisis has rolled out into two tracks: a short-term dimension to calm and soothe the financial markets and so put their unease to rest, and a longer-term reform of the economic governance structure of the eurozone and ultimately the EU as such.

43   Nicolas Jabko (2011), Which Economic Governance for the European Union? Facing up to the Problem of Divided Sovereignty; SIEPS Paper.

Whereas the discussion of tools such as Eurobonds, the ECB 'bazooka', or other instruments belonging to the first category represents one pillar of the political debate, the second pillar deals with the creation of a fiscal union and essentially, a European Ministry of Finance[44] that will steer the economic policy of the Union towards its best common interest.

What is a fiscal union?[45] According to the textbooks of public economics, a fiscal union comprises the joint determination of public activities in a market economy, i.e. public spending and public expenditures, as well as revenues, primarily taxes and loan financing. This may include strict rules to limit sovereign debt.[46]

However, measures to streamline, coordinate, or harmonise such elements carry the risk of producing externalities and unwanted policy results.

In this respect several summits, including the one in December 2011, tried hard to find agreement on the ways and means to close the institutional gaps in the Union. Quite simply, they failed. As Simon Tilford put it so aptly: 'What has been agreed falls far short of a «fiscal union". There will be no joint debt issuance, no shared budget, and no mechanism to transfer monies between the participating countries. Essentially, the agreement hard-wires pro-cyclical fiscal austerity into the institutional framework of the Eurozone, with no *quid quo pro* in terms of a commitment to move gradually to debt mutualisation. It is little more than a revamped version of the EU's existing Stability and Growth Pact.[47]

The reproach is that the heads of state and government under German-French leadership have exclusively concentrated their efforts on austerity measures. Such a strategy cannot solve the crisis but may actually pose part of the problem. As *Standard and Poor's*, the world's largest rating-agency, have voiced in their sharp criticism in the week running up to the December 2011 summit, markets may become even more unsettled when taking into account the deflationary and contractive effects from austere public savings in an already-threatening recession.

While, as Annunziata puts it, 'Requiring countries to amend their constitution sets the bar high – but it is the kind of step that would demonstrate an irrevocable commitment to fiscal discipline, and the dividends in terms of credibility would

44   Jean-Claude Trichet (2011), Building Europe – building institutions, speech on occasion of receiving the Karlspreis, in: Olaf Müller, BerndVincken (eds.), Challenges in Times of Crises, Aachen, pp 41-75.

45   Benedicta Marzinotto, André Sapir, Guntram B. Wolff, (2011) What kind of fiscal union? Bruegel Policy Brief No 6/2011.

46   Donatella Gatti, Christa van Wijnbergen (2002), Coordinating Fiscal Authorities, Oxford Economic Papers 54 (1), pp. 56-71.

47   Tilford Simon, EU Summit: Enough to save the euro? Friday, December 09, 2011 CER Paper.

be enormous',[48] it remains to be seen whether and by how much market expectations will be impacted by this kind of approach, which may well change the risk structure, the expectations, and calculations of market participants. However, what remains dubious is the hope it might help in returning government bonds back to the realm of confidence and zero risk weight.

Admittedly, 'there is no easy way to prevent the decisions of national governments from becoming an unsatisfactory aggregate for the European Union as a whole. This could arise in various circumstances: too many governments pursuing fiscal policies that are restrictive and thus exert a collective squeeze on demand or, vice-versa that are lax, fuelling inflationary pressures; over-reliance on net exports as the principal source of growth; or a reluctance to implement politically difficult supply-side reforms.'[49]

VII   By Way of Conclusion

The dominance of both financial and asset markets over goods markets and labour markets during the past two decades has created **a house of cards of 'over-leveraged', i.e. super-credit-based national economies**. The saying, '*This house of cards has gone down – we'll bring it back*', seems to be the order of the day in many quarters. But rebuilding this house of cards will simply not do. New business models for banks and companies and new regulatory considerations in business and society appear absolutely indispensable. *The undisputed growth model of an overleveraged, credit-based and borrowing economy will have to be revised substantially and replaced by a sound alternative.* Over the past 20 years the financial sector has boomed with hitherto unknown intensity and has become too powerful. The dominance of the financial markets spawned the *Masters of the Universe* (previously mere investment bankers) and lured policymakers into excessive public loan financing.[50] The wealth that the financial sector created and concentrated in the banking system allowed bankers to influence the political system to a degree that had never before been achieved.

---

48   Marco Annunziata (2010), Moral Hazard in the Eurozone: A Proposed Solution'. Uni-Credit, Economic Special.
49   Iain Begg (2011), Prevent or Cure, in: Iain Begg et. al. (2011), European Economic Governance. Gütersloh: Bertelsmann Stiftung, p. 24
50   Between 1973 and 1985 the share of the financial sector never amounted to more than 16 per cent of US corporate profits. In 1986 it rose to 19 per cent and in the 1990s it oscillated between 21 and 30 per cent. Since 2000, this share has been about 35 per cent. This figure carries enormous weight considering that the total contribution of the financial sector to US GDP is only about 7 per cent.

Therefore, mastering the crisis means recasting the Common Good and 'reconstructing responsibility', which means transparency, control, and setting incentives correctly. Runaway speculative financial capitalism must be reshaped to become a reliable and servient means of support for business and the real economy. The traditional, old European virtues of the respectable businessman, such as reliability, honesty, dependability, long-term business relations, trust, considerateness, and continuity have been lost. This is what we will have to bring back!

The era of excessive liberalism, deregulation and privatisation – which was accompanied by the destruction of social and collective values and a development towards ignoring common goods – obviously contained the seed of its own decay. The philosophy of minimal state intervention has turned out to be a mere illusion. Massive growth and artificial profitability of the financial sector, financial innovations, economic imbalances, etc. have led to speculative bubbles on the housing, asset, and securities markets, to insolvency of households and companies, to undercapitalised banks, and to fragile financial markets. Eventually the saviours – i.e. the public and political agents – fell into the abyss, since the loan-financed rescue packages turned out to destroy the credibility of the bond markets. In a globalised world marked by ubiquitous *spill-overs*, Europe could not remain completely unscathed by these developments. The role of the state will have to be redefined and revised in the process. To master the crisis we *do* need a convergence of *economic beliefs around fresh ideas of a European common good.*

The crises have demonstrated the importance of a common coordinated crisis-management framework; joint action rather than free rides. What is required is:

1. *Crisis prevention* to avoid future repetition. This should be mapped onto a collective judgment as to what the principal causes of the crisis were and how changes in macroeconomic, regulatory, and supervisory policy frameworks could help prevent their recurrence. Policies to boost potential growth and competitiveness would also bolster the resilience to future crises.
2. *Crisis control and mitigation* to minimise the damage by preventing systemic defaults or by containing the output loss and easing the social hardship stemming from recession. Its main objective is thus to stabilise the financial system and economic activity in the short run. To strike the right balance between national preoccupations and spill-over effects affecting other member states, it must be coordinated across the EU.
3. *Crisis resolution* to bring crises to a definitive end, at the lowest possible cost for the taxpayer, while containing systemic risk and securing consumer protection. This requires reversing the temporary support measures and ac-

220

tion to restore economies to sustainable growth and fiscal paths. This includes policies to restore banks' balance sheets, restructure the banking sector, and bring about an orderly policy 'exit', especially from expansionary
macroeconomic policies.

In generic terms, we will have to strike new balances between risks and security,
rewards and sanctions, consolidation and dynamics, wealth and distribution, the
state and markets, finance and production, global and local, hope and resigna-
tion, equity and efficiency, macro and micro, rhetoric and practice, competition
and competitiveness, trust and control, regulation and de-regulation, and europhoria and euro-scepticism, to name just a few.

Against this backdrop, Europe today needs a new economic strategy, a new
vision for the future.[51] Its representatives must explain how they intend to foster
creativity, to promote science and technology, and enhance human capital, and
how they will reinvigorate entrepreneurial spirit in order to transform and mod-
ernise the European economy to create more jobs, growth and welfare. Unless
Europe's leaders can come up with convincing and compelling answers, the EU
is bound to lose credibility, confidence, and trust. However, it goes without saying that the vision of a renewed European economy based on an agreed common
economic policy for the Union in its entirety is a tall order. It is in this very
realm that Europe's common good will emerge and take shape. What is required
are the three I's: *intellectual* rigor, *innovative,* out-of-the-box thinking, and *in-
spiring* visions for the future. These I's will be indispensable in the process of
(re-)constructing the European common good.

ANNEX: The Ten Commandments for the Eurozone

1. **Thou shalt not live beyond your means** – no member state may exceed its
   deficit-to-GDP ratio of 3 per cent.
2. Thou shalt not prevent punishment – *automatic sanctions must be accepted.*
3. Thou shalt consider the interest of future generations – *introduce a national
   'debt brake'.*
4. **Thou shalt honour the European Court of Justice** – which is supposed to
   ensure good fiscal governance and prosecute any violation of the treaty.

---

51 The German Daily Handelsblatt put together (in December 2011) – by way of irony – the
    10 Commandments for the Eurozone which the author has attached in this Annex. He is
    sure, however, that these Commandments do not represent what may be considered the
    European Common Good!

5. **Thou shalt not unsettle financial investors** – refrain from inflicting losses on private sector creditors (no involvement of the private banking sector).
6. **Thou shalt procure economic growth** – by means of the Euro Plus Pact and the creation of a European economic government.
7. **Thou shalt respect the independence of the European Central Bank** – don't give unwanted advice or demand bond market interventions or liquidity provision.
8. Thou shalt not seek your neighbour's money – *no Eurobonds*.
9. **Thou shalt listen to what the large national economies demand** – the leadership role (directorate) of Germany and France has to be acknowledged.
10. **Thou shalt serve the new 'core Europe'** – the eurozone is the exclusive new frame of reference.

Table 1: Chronological Order of the Crisis

2007	United States/World financial crisis: the collapse of the US housing bubble had dramatic consequences on financial institutions on a global scale. Economies worldwide slowed during this period as credit supply tightened and international trade declined.
2008 September	Lehman brothers filed for Chapter 11 bankruptcy protection on 15 September 2008. This bankruptcy is considered to be the trigger point of the global financial and economic crisis. It sparked 'contagion' and a massive liquidity shortfall in the US and EU banking systems.
2008 -2009	The EU was hit hard by the fall-out of the banking crisis, and as a consequence almost all member states suffer from severe economic recession.
2008 November	On 26 November 2008 the European Commission proposed a European Stimulus Plan amounting to €200 billion to cope with the effects of the global financial crisis on the economies of the member states.

2009 February	Publication of the De Larosière report. A high level working group chaired by former managing director of the International Monetary Fund and former governor of the Bank of France, Jacques De Larosière, produced its findings on how to reform financial supervision in Europe.
2009 September	The European Commission suggested measures for a new European financial supervisory architecture.
2009 October	Trying to hide within the economic turbulence in the wake of the crisis, the Greek government announced that its deficit figure for 2010 was 12.5 per cent, three times the amount officially acknowledged previously.
February 2010	Under market pressure, the Greek government launched a severe austerity package in order to control the fall-out on bond markets.
11 February 2010	Harsh debates occurred in the European Council about the consequences of the Greek situation: prevent contagion, avoid bail-out discussion, and revise the Stability Mechanism. Heads of state and government declared their willingness to support Greece if it so desired.
25/26 March 2010	European Council Conclusions called for the establishment of a Van Rompuy Task Force to draw up measures to improve economic governance in the eurozone. The Task Force held its first meeting on 21 May 2010.
2010 May	Peak of Greek sovereign debt crisis, and the Council decision to 'save' Greece by adopting the European Financial Stability Facility (EFSF) and the European Financial Stability Mechanism (EFSM).
29 September 2010	The European Commission submitted six legislative proposals – the so-called 'Six-Pack' – to strengthen economic governance: broader macroeconomic surveillance and greater fiscal discipline.
18/19 October 2010	At the Deauville Summit a Franco-German deal was hammered out. Germany accepted less automated sanctions in exchange for a French concession to support the eventual changing of the EU treaties to create a new, permanent mechanism to manage future (Greek-style) bail-outs.

21 October 2010	The final report of the Van Rompuy Task Force was submitted to the European Council involving: (1) broader macroeconomic surveillance, (2) greater fiscal discipline in the form of a stronger and more efficient Stability and Growth Pact, (3) deeper and broader policy coordination, e.g. the European Semester, (4) a more robust framework for (financial) crisis management, i.e. the temporary European Financial Stability Facility (EFSF) and the European Financial Stability Mechanism (EFSM) to be turned into the permanent European Stability Mechanism (ESM), and (5) stronger institutions such as the European System of Financial Supervision (ESFS).
28 October 2010	Heads of state and government agreed upon the setting up of a permanent crisis mechanism (ESM), supposed to replace the EFSF. Merkel declared: We have taken the necessary decision and can, from this moment on, guarantee the stability of the euro in perpetuity!
21 November 2010	Irish crisis due to unlimited bank guarantees through public money forced Ireland under the rescue umbrella. The European Financial Stability Facility lent money to Ireland with conditions attached. Van Rompuy issued caution regarding exaggeration of the fiscal fragility of Portugal.
1 January 2011	The European System of Financial Supervision (ESFS) was set up, comprising: the European Systemic Risk Board (ESRB), and the three European Supervisory Authorities (ESAs), namely the European Banking Authority (EBA), the European Insurance and Occupational Pensions Authority (EIOPA), the European Securities and Markets Authority (ESMA) and the Joint Committee of the European Supervisory Authorities (ESAs).
12 January 2011	The European Commission presented its first Annual Growth Survey, marking the start of the first European Semester, a procedure by which the Commission can monitor and control the budget planning of individual member states.
4 February 2011	European Council Summit adopts the Franco-German Competitiveness Pact – later called the Euro Plus Pact – signed-up by 17 eurozone members + 6 EU member states.

11 March 2011	Extraordinary eurozone summit to identify priorities for structural reforms and fiscal consolidation.
24/25 March 2011	Final decision on the limited treaty change and the setting up of the European Stability Mechanism by the heads of state and government
8 April 2011	Further to a call for help from Portugal, the EU establishes a €80 billion rescue package.
20 June 2011	Finance ministers agree on an enlargement of the EFSF: in order to enable the facility to hand out loans up to €440 billion, guarantees have to be increased to €750 billion. Germany considers this move indispensable: 'If the euro fails, Europe fails!'
21 July 2011	Heads of state and government decided to increase the financial support to Greece by up to €109 billion. The private sector creditors joined in with a 'voluntary' contribution of €37 billion.
26 October 2011	After hefty discussions among both the heads of state and government of the eurozone and the EU, Greece received a debt relief of 50 per cent. The private investors realised losses of 50 per cent vis-à-vis the nominal value of Greek bonds. European banks were forced to increase their core capital share to 9 per cent and the EFSF was supposed to be 'leveraged' up to €1000 billion. France claimed: There was a risk of implosion; this is our credible and compelling answer!
8/9 December 2011	Heads of state and government endorsed a series of rules tightening budget surveillance and setting limits to public spending: the 'fiscal compact'. The key element is a 'golden rule' enforcing balanced budgets defined as deficits not exceeding 0.5 per cent of GDP to be inscribed in domestic constitutions. The European Court of Justice has been tasked with monitoring the transposition into national law. Countries breaching deficit rules would be subject to 'automatic consequences' unless a qualified majority of states decided otherwise. Members of the eurozone are obliged to submit their budgets to the EU Commission before they are discussed in national parliaments. The whole package is supposed to be the launching pad of a fiscal union and a means to regain the confidence of financial markets and investors.

225

Bibliography

Annunziata, M. (2010), *Moral Hazard in the Eurozone: A Proposed Solution*. UniCredit, Economic Special.

Axelrod, R. (2006), *The Evolution of Cooperation* (Revised ed.). New York: Perseus Books Group.

Begg, I. (2011), Prevent or Cure, in: Iain Begg et. al. (2011), *European Economic Governance*. Gütersloh: Bertelsmann Stiftung.

Bryant, R.C. (1995), *International Coordination of National Stabilization Policies* (Integrating National Economies: Promise & Pitfalls). Washington: Brookings Institution Press.

Casella, A. and Frey, B.S. (1992), Federalism and Clubs: Towards an Economic Theory of Overlapping Political Jurisdictions, *European Economic Review* 36, pp. 639-646.

Cornes, R.;Sandler, T. (1996), *The Theory of Externalities, Public Goods, and Club Goods*. Cambridge: Cambridge University Press (2nd edition).

Dinan, D. (2004), *Europe Recast: A History of European Union*. London: Palgrave Macmillan.

Feldstein, M.S. (1988*), International Economic Cooperation*. Chicago: University Press.

Ferroni, M. (2002), *Regional Public Goods: The Comparative Edge of Regional Development Banks,* Paper prepared for the Conference on Financing for Development at the Institute for International Economics, February 19, 2002.

Fraenke, E.l (1941), *The Dual State*. New York: Octagon Books.

Frenkel, J.A. and Rockett, K.E. (1988), International Macroeconomic Policy Co-ordination when Policymakers do not Agree on the True Model, *American Economic Review* 78 (3), pp. 318-340.

Gatti, D.; Van Wijnbergen, C. (2002), Coordinating Fiscal Authorities, *Oxford Economic Papers* 54 (1), pp. 56-71.

Goodin, R.E. and Pettit, P. (eds.) (1995), *A Companion to Contemporary Political Philosophy*. Cambridge: Blackwell.

Gretschmann, K. (1986), Solidarity and Markets, in: Franz-Xaver Kaufmann, Giandomenico Majone, Vincent Ostrom (eds.), *Guidance, Control and Evaluation in the Public Sector*. Berlin/New York: Walter de Gruyter.

Gretschmann, K. (1991), Le Principe de subsidiarité: Quelles responsabilités à quel niveau de pouvoir dans une Europe intégrée? Subsidiarité: défi du changement, Maastricht: EIPA, pp 49-70.

Habermas, J. (2011), *Zur Verfassung Europas* ('On Europe's Constitution'). Berlin: Suhrkamp Verlag.

Habermas, J. (1986), *The Theory of Communicative Action: Reason and the Rationalization of Society* (original: Die Theorie des kommunikativen Handelns). Cambridge: Polity Press.

Jabko, N. (2011), *Which Economic Governance for the European Union? Facing up to the Problem of Divided Sovereignty*; SIEPS Paper.

Judt, T. (2005), *Postwar: A History of Europe after 1945*. NYC: Penguin Press.

Korkman, S. (2002), Fiscal Policy Coordination in EMU, in: Anne Brunilla et al. (eds.), *The Stability and Growth Pact – the architecture of fiscal policy in EMU*. Basingstoke: Palgrave Macmillan, p. 269.

Le Cacheux, J. (2010), How to Herd Cats: Economic Policy Coordination in the Eurozone in Tough Times, *Journal of European Integration* 32 (1), pp. 41-58.

Marzinotto, B.;Sapir, A.; Wolff, G.B.(2011) *What kind of fiscal union?* Bruegel Policy Brief No 6/2011.

Matzner, E. (1982), *Der Wohlfahrtsstaat von morgen, Entwurf eines zeitgemässen Musters staatlicher Interventionen.* Wien: Österreichischer Bundesverlag.

Moravcsik, A. (1993), Preferences and Power in the European Community: A Liberal Intergovernmentalist Approach, *Journal of Common Market Studies* 31 (4), pp. 473-524.

Münkler, H. and Bluhm, H. (2002) *Gemeinwohl und Gemeinsinn. Historische Semantiken politischer Leitbegriffe.* Berlin: Akademie Verlag.

Olson, M. (1965), *The Logic of Collective Action: Public Goods and the Theory of Groups.* Cambridge, Mass.: Harvard University Press.

Ostrom, E. (1990), *Governing the Commons: The Evolution of Institutions for Collective Action.* Cambridge: Cambridge University Press.

Rapoport, A. and Chammah, A. (1965). *Prisoner's Dilemma.* Ann Arbor: University of Michigan Press.

Rousseau, J.J. (1762), *Du Contrat Social*, Paris 1992.

Schofield, P. (2006), *Utility and Democracy. The Political Thought of Jeremy Bentham.* Oxford: Oxford University Press.

Schuppert, G.F. and Neidhardt, F. (eds.) (2002), Gemeinwohl – auf der Suche nach Substanz, *WZB Jahrbuch*, Berlin.

Scitovsky, T. (1941). A Note on Welfare Propositions in Economics. *Review of Economic Studies* 9 (1), pp. 77–88.

Siebert, H. (1997), *Zu den Voraussetzungen der Europäischen Währungsunion*, Kiel, Discussion Paper 289, Institut für Weltwirtschaft.

Simon, T. (2011*), EU Summit: Enough to save the euro?* Friday, December 09, 2011 CER Paper.

Solbes, P. (2002), Economic Policy Co-ordination - the Way Forward, Brussels Economic Forum, 2 May 2002, *mimeo*, p.5.

Taylor, P. (2008), *The End of European Integration. Anti-Europeanism examined.* London: Routledge.

Trichet, J.-C. (2011), Building Europe – building institutions, speech on occasion of receiving the Karlspreis, in: Olaf Müller, Bernd Vincken (eds.), *Challenges in Times of Crises*, Aachen, pp 41-75.

Von Aquin, T. *Summa Theologiae* I-II.

Von der Pfordten, D. (2004), Normativer Individualismus, *Zeitschrift für philosophische Forschung* 58, pp. 321-346.

Von Hagen, J. and Mundschenk, S. (2001), The Functioning of Economic Policy Coordination, *mimeo*, Bonn: ZEI Working Paper.

Weiler, J.H.H. (1999), *The Constitution of Europe.* Cambridge, Mass.: Harvard University Press.

Wiener, A. (2009), *European Integration Theory.* Oxford: Oxford University Press.

Energy and climate policy and the common good

Volkmar Lauber

I   Introduction

Defining the common good is not just a matter of substantive goals; it is also a matter of which principles, rules, and instruments are considered appropriate for guiding government action. Particularly in liberal-democratic states, strong differences emerged in the 1970s regarding this issue. A dominantly Keynesian understanding of public policy was replaced by a return to neoclassical economics as the foundation of policymaking. The attendant waves of privatisation, liberalisation, deregulation, slimming of the state, etc. often had a fundamentalist touch to it. While this philosophy has been placed into doubt in the course of the financial crisis of 2008, there is now a policy legacy in many areas that reflects the market fundamentalist approach which emerged in the 1970s and which shaped whole areas of public policy. This is widely known with regard to the banking sector. Energy and climate policy is another case in point.

The chief argument of this chapter is that market fundamentalist approaches have directed – and are still directing – energy and climate policy towards 'market' frameworks which supposedly steer developments in a general direction but then rely on market competition to select the means to achieve those ends.[1] It also argues that, contrary to widespread assumption, these frameworks are rather inefficient in terms of basic results. Nor are they replacing complex regulations by simple and elegant tools of governance; the opposite is closer to reality. Due to their complexity they also seem to be particularly intransparent and inaccessible to democratic control. However, they are attractive to the incumbents of the sectors that are the target of these policy frameworks as well as to a large group of specialists of all kinds involved in formulating policy or in contributing, such as auditors, consultants, lawyers, traders and the like who are necessary to assist with implementation.

It is commonplace today to argue that we need an 'energy revolution' to overcome 'carbon lock-in'[2] if we want to avoid dire scenarios of climate change or of

---

1   Catherine Mitchell (2008), The Political Economy of Sustainable Energy. Basingstoke: Palgrave Macmillan, p. 1.

2   Gregory C. Unruh (2000), Understanding Carbon Lock-in, Energy Policy 30 (4), pp. 317-325.

energy scarcity, resulting from the fact that fossil fuels are probably about to enter a phase of decline (as in the case of 'conventional' oil) or will reach this point within a few decades (the likely case of gas and coal). Improving efficiency and shifting towards renewable energy are widely seen as the most promising avenues. The question is whether, given the urgency of the climate problem and that of peak oil, the transition can still be made in time. What is the impact of market frameworks on this issue?

The problem of carbon lock-in is not just one of finding new sources of energy. It is also a political problem – one of overcoming resistance from the incumbents, i.e. the fossil fuel-based corporations. To be sure, this includes a much wider network of actors, as well as legal and cultural institutions. All these elements combine to make the transition – and especially a rapid transition to other sources of energy, i.e. one that would largely take place before the middle of the twenty-first century (remember the EU goal of an 80 to 95 per cent decarbonisation by 2050) – appear as a particularly difficult enterprise. It is my hypothesis that 'market' approaches to energy and climate policy compound the political problem of the energy transition since they are in fact designed to favour incumbents and to impede the development of renewable energy.

This hypothesis shall be explored by reviewing four areas of 'market' policy affecting the field of electricity generation for the kinds of problems mentioned above: First, US acid rain policy since 1990; second, the policy transfer from this US approach to the Kyoto Protocol; third, the EU Emission Trading Scheme with regard to windfall profits and carbon capture and storage (CCS); and fourth, the fate of support schemes for renewable energy, an area in which several types of schemes have been implemented, some supposedly market oriented, others supposedly closer to the command-and-control approach.

II   The analogy with the banking sector

Perhaps it will help to compare the behaviour of energy incumbents with that of banks in the twentieth century. As a result of the crisis that led to the Great Depression, it became clear in the United States that banks had played a decisive role in creating the economic havoc that characterised this period. Existing banking regulations were insufficient to produce responsible behaviour. As a result, banks were strictly regulated under the New Deal by a legal and administrative framework. But the sector remained in private hands and the government did not intervene in its day-to-day affairs. As a result, banking became less adventurous; bankers became the very paradigm of solidity and reliability. But beginning in the 1970s, the sector was deregulated, a process which picked up speed under the influence of market fundamentalists – under Reagan and Thatcher[3] – and reached its apex during the second Bush administration, leading to the casino capitalism and the disasters of 2008 (presumably we have not seen their end yet) that Strange described and anticipated so well. Contrary to market fundamentalist expectations, bankers in pursuit of their self-interest did not achieve the public interest; the market did not 'know best'. In 2010, the near-consensus among government policymakers is that it is necessary to return once more to a more regulated market for banks and similar institutions in order to prevent them from repeating a financial crisis of a dimension that few thought was even possible, much less likely. It remains to be seen to which extent reversing the process of liberalisation is politically feasible, as it created new constituencies as it progressed, which contributes to its political clout.

The history of energy and environmental policy shows a similar influence of changing public philosophy in the name of the common good when it comes to regulatory frameworks and particularly the design of instruments.[4] When modern environmental policy first emerged in the second half of the twentieth century, it 'naturally' took the form of regulation, although in the United States a school of environmental economists grew up which, applying neoclassical economics, designed market instruments which they held to be superior to regulation; In their view, these instruments could be designed in such a way as to make sure that the market would solve problems elegantly and without legalistic complications, without the intervention of a wasteful and expensive bureaucracy which unduly burdened citizens and industry alike. For a long time however, the environmental economists only occupied niches in academic programs. Their hour came decades later, after the rise of market fundamentalism under Reagan. In the early 1990s US acid rain policy first introduced trading – of SO2 certificates – on a grand scale; this was touted as the 'market approach' that would solve problems with less bureaucracy and at a lower cost. The general opinion of the US economists who came to dominate the environmental policy community was to view this as a major breakthrough. In Kyoto, the US made their participation in an international GHG treaty dependent on emission trading. After initial reluctance, the European Union accepted this and introduced its own emission-trading scheme. From there, the idea travelled to the design of frameworks for the support of renewable energy that were on the agenda at that time. In all of these areas, certificate trading – the creation of a market – was viewed with the same high expectations regarding goal achievement. It was supposed to yield low-cost

3   Susan Strange (1986), Casino Capitalism. Oxford: Blackwell.
4   Jan-Peter Voss (2007), Designs on Governance. Development of Policy Instruments and Dynamics in Governance. Enschede: Iskamp.

yet effective SO2 or GHG reduction *viz.* low-cost yet effective support for renewable energy. The results achieved so far contradict those expectations; they show that – not surprisingly – those schemes systematically favour incumbents while they are slow on goal achievement.

On the following pages several major steps in the development of 'market approaches' to climate and energy will be reviewed.

III   The US Clean Air Act Amendments of 1990

EU ETS was largely inspired by the US Clean Air Act Amendments of 1990 and subsequent legislation on trading, taking over not only the mechanism of emissions trading but the whole structure of an instrument that reflected a very peculiar political constellation. In the late 1980s, regulation – and especially environmental regulation – was the whipping boy of the Reagan Republicans and blamed for the recession. Congressional clean air legislation requiring particular technologies such as scrubbers (as were common in Europe by that time) was successfully opposed by the operators of fossil fuel power plants and blocked by the president; all new acid rain legislation practically came to a halt.[5] With President G.H.W. Bush, who had declared himself an environmentalist during his campaign to accommodate a new rise in environmentalism but also remained a stout supporter of business, a policy window opened for new initiatives, in particular for the free market environmentalist Project 88[6] which developed a cap-and-trade system for sulphur dioxide emissions.

The adoption of this scheme represented a breakthrough for acid rain legislation, but at a cost that was a concession to political realism. This required that SO2 certificates must not be costly for emitters. In order to secure consent by the industry, grandfathering – allocating emission rights according to earlier emissions – was introduced. Trading of certificates created an incentive to use the cheapest opportunities for SO2 reduction first; these would be the most lucrative, while at the same time their realisation would hold down certificate prices. Grandfathering also created property rights and in fact windfall profits for emitters. Technological innovation – renewable energy in particular – was put on the back burner as volatile certificate prices created insufficient incentives. The reduction goal for sulphur dioxide of 50 per cent between 1980 and 2010 – the diminishing cap – was exceedingly modest (see below); it was more important, as

5   Don Munton (1998), Dispelling the myths of the acid rain story, Environment 40 (6), pp. 27-33.
6   Brian Tokar (1996), Trading away the earth. Pollution credits and the perils of "free market environmentalism". Dollars and Sense, March/ April, pp. 24-29.

Bush put it, to generate 'the most environmental protection for every dollar spent', allowing him to bolster his environmentalist image and yet to accommodate 'the business interests that supported his administration and the Republican Party'.[7] Cap-and-trade for SO2 was probably realistic at the time, aiming for what was politically possible. Strangely enough, it inspired policymakers in very different political constellations.

Neither the goals nor the results of this legislation are particularly impressive in terms of environmental improvement. The United States may well reduce sulphur emissions by 50 per cent from 1980 to 2010 as planned in the legislation. But then the EU has already reduced them by nearly 80 per cent from 1980 to 2004.[8]

IV   Greenhouse gas (GHG) emission trading: From the United States to Kyoto

In 1993, President Clinton submitted a kind of ecological tax reform to Congress – the so-called BTU tax, which was meant to be a key measure of his first term in office. While the House of Representatives adopted the bill, the Senate rejected it when several Democratic senators from fossil fuel producing states 'deserted', led by the senator from Oklahoma, one of the leading oil states. The BTU tax bill became a favourite target for Republican attacks. Subsequently, the Republicans gained a majority in both houses of Congress and showed a particular determination to oppose new taxes, international treaty commitments, and climate change measures. The adoption of the Byrd-Hagel resolution with 95:0 votes[9] a few months before the Kyoto conference made clear that the Senate would reject any measure that 'would result in serious harm to the economy of the United States', taking up the earlier Republican argument against the BTU tax. This did not leave much leeway to the Clinton administration's climate policy. Under these circumstances it fell back on emission trading as a solution that might prove acceptable to the fossil fuel industry and its political representatives (many of which at this time still denied that there was a climate problem). There

7   Jeffrey M. Hirsch (1999), Emission Allowance Trading Under the Clean Air Act: A Mode for Future Environmental Regulations, NYU Law Journal 7, pp. 352-397.

8   EMEP (2006) Inventory Review: Emission Data reported to the LTRAP Convention and NEC Directive. http://www.emep.int/publ/reports/2006/emep_technical_1_2006.pdf (accessed 28 April 2010) and EMEP (2009), Inventory Review 2009, http://www.emep.int/publreports/2009/emep_technical_1_2009.pdf, (accessed 28 April 2010).

9   Byrd-Hagel Resolution (1997), http://www.nationalcenter.org/KyotoSenate.html (accessed 4 May 2010).

were widespread expectations in Kyoto that emission trading would not hurt this industry.[10]

Thus in Kyoto, the US delegation – with strong support from the international business community[11] – made emissions trading a condition for US participation in a global climate policy scheme. At the same time the delegation and its experts praised the superior performance of the US sulphur reduction cap-and-trade scheme, a claim that has since been repeated quite frequently.[12] As described above, at least in hindsight the US experience with sulphur emissions trading is not the success story it is often made out to be, due to much slower reductions than in Europe. The 'real' success of sulphur trading was probably political – the fact that it was made palatable to business (though at a cost).

In the EU, there was considerable scepticism concerning emissions trading arrangements prior to Kyoto.[13] The Commission had long argued in favour of other instruments (such as an energy tax). But its efforts to introduce a European energy/carbon tax in 1992 and 1995 had foundered on the unanimity requirement in the Council. National efforts on emission reductions had been disappointing and were likely to become incompatible. By contrast, emission trading presented certain advantages from the Commission perspective. Since the Single European Act in 1987 the Commission had expanded its powers through its – neoliberal – internal market activities of deregulation and liberalisation.[14] Unlike energy taxation, emissions trading could be adopted by a simple majority.[15]

In the late 1990s and early 2000s, first experiments started with emission trading in Europe, first at the firm level (BP and soon thereafter Shell), then at the

10   Michael Grubb, Christiaan Vrolijk, Duncan Brack (eds.) (1999), The Kyoto Protocol. A Guide and Assessment. London: Royal Institute of International Affairs; Peter Newell (2000), Climate for Change: Non-State Actors and the Global Politics of Greenhouse. Cambridge: Cambridge University Press; Christiaan Vrolijk (ed.) (2002), Climate Change and Power. Economic Instruments for European Electricity. London. Earthscan.
11   Jan-Peter Voss (2007), Designs on Governance. Development of Policy Instruments and Dynamics in Governance. Enschede. Iskamp.
12   Chad Damro, Pilar Luaces-Mendez (2003), Emissions Trading at Kyoto: From EU Resistance to Union Innovation, Environmental Politics 12 (2), pp. 71-94; George Pring (2006), A decade of emissions trading in the USA: Experiences and observations for the EU, in Marjan Peeters, Kurt Deketelaere (eds.), EU Climate Change Policy. Cheltenham: Edward Elgar, pp. 188-204.
13   Sebastian Oberthür, Hermann E. Ott (1999), The Kyoto Protocol: International Climate Policy for the 21st century. Berlin: Springer.
14   Michelle Cini, Lee McGowan (1998), Competition Policy in the European Union, Basingstoke: Palgrave Macmillan; Alan W. Cafruny, Magnus Ryner (2003), A ruined fortress? Neoliberal hegemony and transformation in Europe. New York: Rowman Littlefield.
15   Jan-Peter Voss (2007), Designs on Governance. Development of Policy Instruments and Dynamics in Governance. Enschede: Iskamp, p. 112.

national level in Denmark and the UK. The OECD also 'picked up tradable permits and emissions trading as a pet proposal...'[16]. As Voss put it:

> The cumulation of these developments on various governance levels created a global hype around emissions trading as the instrument of future environmental policy. It nurtured the expectation that emissions trading would come anyway and reversed scepticism and criticism in European policy circles into widespread attempts to become part of the emerging movement.[17]

Once the United States had withdrawn from the Kyoto Protocol in 2001, the EU took over leadership in climate policy (Wettestad 2005).[18] According to Voss:

> [A] substantial effort...had to be invested to reframe emissions trading: from a strategic device to water down binding emission reduction commitments in the hands of the USA, to an effective and efficient instrument for the European Union.[19]

It remains to be seen just how fundamental this change was in reality. The business community in any case became increasingly eager in its support for emissions trading when it realised the potential for windfall profits that it contained.

Eventually, EU ETS was introduced via two directives in 2003 and 2004. It covers nearly half of the total carbon emissions in the EU, including power generation and most large-scale energy-intensive industry. Emitters are given allowances and these allowances add up to a cap that is gradually reduced to below 'business as usual'. As in the United States, emission trading was supposed to secure efficiency, since the cheapest ways to avoid GHG emissions would be the most lucrative and therefore be mobilised first. For this reason EU ETS was (and is) widely considered as the most cost-efficient way to reduce emissions. For the same reason it does little to develop new technologies as an initially low price of certificates is not a sufficient incentive to develop such technologies (more on this later). In the early days of EU ETS it was often argued that 'once the EU ETS becomes operational, the effectiveness of all other policies to reduce CO2 emissions of the participating sectors becomes zero'.[20] Other policy instruments should be abandoned unless there was evidence of market failure or over-riding priorities involving national energy security. Even in these cases it was argued that coexisting instruments 'may raise overall abatement costs while contributing

16   Ibid, p. 110.
17   Ibid, p. 109.
18   Jørgen Wettestad (2005), The Making of the 2003 EU Emissions Trading Direvtive: An Ultra-Quick Process due to Entrepreneurial Proficiency? Global Environmental Politics 5 (2), pp. 1-22.
19   Jan-Peter Voss (2007), Designs on Governance. Development of Policy Instruments and Dynamics in Governance. Enschede: Iskamp, p. 112.
20   Jos Sijm, Angela van Dril (2003), The Interaction between the EU Emissions Trading Scheme and Energy Policy Instruments in the Netherlands. Implications of the EU Directive for Dutch Climate Policies: ECN-C—03-060, ECM: ZG Petten, The Netherlands.

nothing further to emission reductions'.[21] Economists such as Hans-Werner Sinn[22] are still arguing along these lines when they take position against measures such as the German feed-in tariff (one of the most successful so far) to support renewable energy development, ignoring the fact that developing such technologies is a matter of decades and should probably not wait until the time when carbon certificates have sufficiently risen in price.

V   The secret charm of the 'market' approach: Billions of windfall profits from ETS for the incumbents of the power sector

One of the basic elements underlying the deal between the US government and US coal power plant operators consisted in the introduction of a trading scheme for SO2 certificates for those operators – certificates which those operators had obtained free of charge from the government, based on the grandfathering principle (i.e. that those who had emitted in the past would receive certificates to cover their emissions; at the same time a cap would be introduced on total emissions that would be reduced over time). The value of those certificates was a windfall profit to the companies – the lubricant that made the deal politically possible. Better yet from the perspective of the incumbents, there was not much transparency to the deal since the value of the windfalls depends on the market value of the certificates, which was supposed to vary over time. This makes it impossible to put a figure on windfall profits and helps to largely keep them out of controversy.

When the EU adapted the US trading scheme for SO2 to those of CO2 under the Emissions Trading Directive, it also took over this feature of grandfathering permits viz. certificates. One analysis of industry lobbying and its impact on Commission legislative proposals on carbon trading observes that one of the chief successes of industry was to secure free initial allocations on the basis of grandfathering (historical emissions) from a number of possibilities – including auctioning – listed in the Commission Green Paper. Member states could auction up to 5 per cent of the permits in the first trading period (2005 to 2008) and 10 per cent in the second (2009-2012), but even this restrictive provision was little

---

21   Steven Sorrell, Jos Sijm (2003), Carbon Trading, in the Policy Mix, Oxford Review of Economic Policy 19 (3), p. 420.
22   Hans-Werner Sinn (2008), Das Grüne Paradoxon. Plädoyer für eine illusionsfreie Klimapolitik. Berlin: Econ.

used. Grandfathering acts as a barrier to new entrants and reflects 'strong industrial rent-seeking'.[23]

In Germany as in most member states, allocation was completely free of charge. The Association of German Electric Utilities (VDEW) in a communication to the European Parliament in 2002 argued that this would avoid burdening energy-intensive industries and other consumers with additional costs (Bundesregierung 2006). The German government endorsed VDEW's position. VDEW, however, changed its mind about sparing consumers once trading started in 2005 and added the 'opportunity cost' of carbon certificates to the electricity price. The German Council of Environmental Experts (SRU 2006) – and later on the International Energy Agency (IEA 2007) – argued that this price increase was justified as a market signal of scarcity but did not address the question of why the resulting income – or rent – should be 'privatised' by the utilities. By contrast, some critics even argue that free allocation represents illegal state aid under the EU Treaty.[24] The European Parliament for its part consistently argued in favour of auctioning.

Similar windfall profits occurred in most EU member states. Most of them reacted by reducing allocations to the power sector by a modest amount, reducing windfall profits by the same percentage. Only few – e.g. Sweden – considered a windfall profit tax.[25] When the German government for its part announced its intention to auction 10 per cent of permits for electricity companies in the period 2008-2012, the latter responded that this would inevitably increase prices another time.[26]

To sum up: The fossil fuel-burning power sector received certificates free of charge in most cases, but could pass their 'cost' (i.e. opportunity cost) on to its customers at market value, at a rate estimated roughly at 80 per cent.[27] This led to tremendous windfall profits for power generators, particularly from coal plants, based on the estimate of nearly €6 billion of windfall profits for German utilities just in 2005 and Capgemini's estimate of €5 billion just for E.ON and

23   Peter Markussen, Gert T. Svendsen (2005), Industry lobbying and the political economy of GHG trade in the European Union, Energy Policy 33 (2), pp. 245-255.
24   Angus Johnston (2006), Free allocation of allowances under the EU Emissions Trading System – legal issues, Climate Policy 6, pp. 136f.
25   Bundesregierung (2006), Antwort der Bundesregierung auf die kleine Anfrage der Abgeordneten Eva Bulling-Schröter et.al. Nationaler Allokationsplan 2008-2012; Anfrage Teil I – Extraprofite und Strompreise, Bundestags-Drucksache 16/1459, 12.7.2006.
26   Frankfurter Allgemeine Zeitung (2007), 5 June 2007, CO2-Versteigerungen – Industrie und Versorger warnen vor höheren Strompreisen.
27   J. Sijm, K. Neuhoff, Y. Chen. (2006), CO2 cost pass through and windfall profits in the power sector, Climate Policy 6, pp. 49-72; Point Carbon (2008), EU ETS Phase II – The potential and scale of windfall profits in the power sector.

RWE in 2007.[28] Considering that this system of 90-95 per cent grandfathering will last for eight years before it expires (2005-2012), it seems safe to assume that the European fossil fuel power sector was set to extract windfall profits in the range of €50-€100 billion; the recent decline of carbon prices reduced this result. Even so, the accumulated amounts must have strengthened power incumbents – the chief beneficiaries of these funds – considerably. Ironically, this additional cash flow seems to play an important role in the actual and planned expansion of coal-fired plants in the European Union (see below). It also helps the incumbents to better ward off challengers such as those coming from the renewable energy sector.

VI   ETS favours more new coal-fired power plants – with or without CCS

One of the expectations regarding the introduction of ETS was that it would change the structure of power production. A price on carbon, it was argued, would make less attractive those forms of power generation that are producing more carbon dioxide per kilowatt hour (kWh); in practice, this means coal-fired plants. And in fact, a new generation of gas thermal plants emerged in Europe in the 1990s, displacing coal, as natural gas – consisting of CH4 – emits only half as much carbon dioxide as coal.

This situation changed towards the end of the new century's first decade. Coal, not gas, now seems to be the fossil fuel of choice for the next generation of centralised utility power plants. This is not just an accident but the direct result of the incentive system produced by ETS. The utility proponents of ETS were in favour of coal from the beginning, as this allowed the extension of the present structure – and assets – of the electricity industry, with its emphasis on centralised, fossil-fuel-based generation. But coal power, they have been arguing for some time now, will become 'clean coal' and eventually low carbon-emission coal power thanks to the development of carbon capture and storage (CCS). In the meantime, 'capture-ready' plants could be built. To them, CCS is neither a transition technology nor a supplement to renewable energy; it is rather the alternative to it.[29]

28   Ben Schlemmermeier, Hans-Peter Schwintowski (2006), Das deutsche Handelssystem für Emissionszertifikate: Rechtswidrig? Zeitschrift für neues Energierecht 10 (3), pp. 195-199; Capgemini cited in: Michael Pahle (2010), Germany's dash for coal: Exploring drivers and factors, Energy Policy 38 (7), pp. 3431-3442.
29   G. Goerne, F. Lundberg (2008), Last gasp of the coal industry. Air Pollution and Climate Secretariat, Göteborg, http://www.airclim.org/reports/documents/APC21.pdf (accessed 28 April 2010).

In 2010 there is still much speculation about whether CCS will ever become a viable technology for the power sector – both in technical and in economic terms. It has huge requirements for underground space – each kWh of CCS, coal-based power produces nearly one kg of carbon dioxide (Bossel 2009, 21), and it is not certain whether carbon dioxide will not leak out in future millennia (because essentially it has to stay in the ground forever if it is not to endanger human settlements). Carbon removal and its transport through pipelines to underground storage require considerable additional energy, so that the amount of coal needed for one kWh will increase by one third.[30] CCS-equipped coal plants will still avoid only about two-thirds of the emissions they cause.[31] Nor is it not certain that installing CCS on a grand scale will bring down costs in the same way as what usually happens with mass production.[32] Even if it works, the technology will not be available before 2020, and possibly only decades later.[33] Even if it is available, its use will depend on the price of ETS carbon certificates. If certificate prices do not rise as expected by the European Commission, it may well remain cheaper to emit carbon and to buy the attendant certificates than to install CCS equipment (or to shift to gas). It is by no means certain that ETS carbon prices will be high enough in the next few decades to motivate the installation of CCS. Fluctuating prices for carbon certificates – so essential to market fundamentalists – compound the problem. But if CCS is not installed on a large scale, then what happens to the reduction of GHG in countries using – or about to expand – the use of coal?

These are not just fantasies. At the start of 2010 the four big utilities in Germany dominating electricity generation showed new financial strength following a decade of concentration via mergers and acquisitions (due to EU-style liberalisation) and a half–decade of considerable windfall profits resulting from the introduction of ETS. They did not have any plans for the addition of significant gas plants (only 15-20 per cent of new generation). Ten years ago gas-fired plants – usually CCGT – seemed the only ones acceptable due to both their lower capital requirements (quicker amortisation is essential in a liberalised market) and their lower carbon emissions (about half those of coal per kWh; this was expected to represent an advantage under carbon trading). Often they also received environmentally motivated tax privileges. New types of investors entering the market

30   S. C. Page, A.G. Williamson, I.G. Mason (2009), Carbon capture and storage: Fundamental thermodynamics and current technology. Energy Policy, 37(9), pp. 3314-3324.

31   Hans-Jochen Luhmann (2009), Carbon Dioxide capture and Storage (CCS) at Coal-Fired Power Plants does not Contribute to Stopping Climate Change, GAIA 18(4), pp. 294-299.

32   Varun Rai, David G. Victor, Mark C. Thurber (2010), Carbon Capture and Storage at scale: Lessons from the growth of analogous energy technologies. Energy Policy, 38(8), pp. 4089-4098.

33   European Environment & Packaging Law (2007), 15 June, p. 11.

preferred these plants. But in 2010, the large integrated utilities were back in the central position they had before liberalisation – and they plan almost only coal-fired plants. 'Coal represents around 80% of all new capacity, whereas natural gas falls back to 20%'.[34]

Pahle concludes that, given current market assumptions about the future prices of gas, coal, capital, and carbon emissions, it simply makes more sense for the big utilities to favour coal plants; this is a rational market calculation supported by ETS rules and price expectations and probably prevails outside of Germany as well. The price of coal is expected to increase less than that of gas; the price of carbon under the ETS is widely estimated to rise no higher than €30-€50 by 2020[35]. The cost of installing CCS for its part is viewed as reaching $35-$60 around 2030, and $30-$45 if CCS reaches maturity by then. So depending on market prices of these various inputs, CCS may become interesting to install between 2020 and 2030 – or it may not. If not, our electricity generation infrastructure may well include coal plants without CCS that continue to operate for decades. There is clearly no great sense of urgency about the climate in this scheme. The mere promise of CCS seems to allow extending – or reinstating – the use of coal for several decades, helping to keep the incumbents of the electricity generating sector in their dominant position.

At least one of the problems of CCS described above could be resolved differently. Governments – nationally or at the EU level – could require that CCS be installed in an obligatory fashion, without regard to carbon certificate prices; and this could be done immediately at least for a proportion of the emissions. Such plans were debated in some member states' governments – in the UK (Miliband 2009) and in others[36] – and in the European Parliament. The position of the European Commission on this issue, however, has been consistently negative. Thus it argued in early 2010 that an amendment to the IPPC Directive made in 2003 (when the ETS Directive was introduced) bars member states from setting national performance emission standards, caps, or other emission limits. When the European Parliament discussed the proposal of the Industrial Emissions Directive (IED) which could have contained an emission performance standard (EPS) – i.e. a benchmark value – for CO2, Marianne Wenning, head of the European Commission's IED unit, rejected such a scheme with the argument that, with an unchanged cap of the ETS, a performance standard for power generation would

34 Michael Pahle (2010), Germany's dash for coal: Exploring drivers and factors, Energy Policy 38 (7), pp. 3431-3442.

35 Point Carbon (2009) Carbon 2008. For the sake of perspective, the price of certificates declined below €8 in 2012.

36 James Thornton (2010), A carbon riddle that is in need of political answers, European Voice 16(7), p. 9.

reduce the power sector's demand for emission allowances, reduce the price of allowances, and therefore increase emissions in other sectors. It appears that she did not even consider the possibility of redefining the ETS cap, stating that 'an EPS would affect the carbon market which we had so carefully crafted and worked so hard to build'[37] and that ETS was the most effective way of reducing CO2 emissions from industrial plant. Opposition to a carbon performance standard for power plants also came from the utility companies who stated that it would make CCS compulsory and thus make electricity more expensive but not accelerate CCS R&D – yet cost €6 billion for premature development and result in the closure of coal-fired power plants. Indeed, Eurelectric favours a carbon-neutral power supply by...2050[38]. The message seems clear. It seems as though the Commission were protecting the deal it made with carbon emitters at the time ETS was introduced. The emitters' consent to carbon trading was exchanged against initial windfall profits and protection against 'command-and-control regulation' that would directly interfere with management (such as obligatory, physical controls on carbon emissions).

VII   EU ETS as a playground for creative carbon finance

Emissions trading started out with a claim to provide a simple instrument, one that would free business from meddling by government. Real life emissions trading is no such thing. Instead, it has developed much like banking, leading to a multitude of special instruments which emerged in the process of implementation and which made it 'an impervious complex of new rules and administrative structures that spans the public and the private sector' which 'decreases transparency and creates practical difficulties of exercising democratic control over policy development'.[39] Its complexity is such that the European Parliament resigned itself to a passive role in its design. That work is conducted by a specialised expert community, especially from the carbon finance industry. This community of 'specialised researchers, evaluators, consultants, verifiers, lawyers, financial service providers etc.' contribute to the cost of the emission trading policy, but this substantial cost – in particular carbon trading – is itself presented as a benefit and a new opportunity created by the new industry, not as a cost. Voss concludes that

37   European Environment & Packaging Law Weekly, No 194, 3 Feb. 2010, p. 6.
38   Ibid.
39   Jan-Peter Voss (2007), Designs on Governance. Development of Policy Instruments and Dynamics in Governance. Enschede: Iskamp.

'What gives emission trading as a design on governance its strength is at the same time the reason for it escaping control'. [40]

Now trading is certainly good for the banking sector, but its benefit to society at large is supposedly based on the fact that it motivates emitters to accept the cap, which is essential for trading. Banks may plan a useful role in this context – or they may just have discovered a new terrain for its activities without much benefit to society at large, as we know from other creative products invented by the banking sector during the last decade. In fact, it is not just banks that benefit; in 2009 organised crime also took its cut. Emission trading was used as a vehicle for large-scale tax fraud and – according to Europol – caused a loss of about €5 billion to EU member states before this was even publicised, much less stopped. Its institutions were also used for money laundering at an unknown scale as it lacks the strict regulations that supposedly prevent such activities in banking.[41]

This brief review has shown some interesting features of carbon trading. It is so little transparent that it may indeed be impossible to judge its cost-efficiency in terms of emission reduction per euro spent. It is not even possible to determine the precise cost of grandfathered emission certificates to electricity consumers since the ability to pass on opportunity costs depends on competition in the sector (which in most sectors is higher than in that of electricity). It is also difficult to know the impact of ETS on actual emissions. We know that the most important carbon reductions in the EU took place in the 1990s: in the UK during the dash for gas (which replaced coal-fired power plants on a grand scale) and in Germany due to East German deindustrialisation. The increasing cost of energy after 2005 and the financial crisis after 2007 also contributed their share. But it seems that we must not be impatient. EU ETS is supposed to show its real virtue in the future, with the advent of higher certificate prices.

VIII Support schemes for renewable power

Renewable power is important for the energy transition. For the time being, most of it is in need of policy support of some kind. As there are a variety of support schemes in this area, this allows for comparative study and assessment. As in the other fields of energy and climate policy, many actors have consistently favoured 'market approaches' to energy policy (in fact arguing for very peculiar markets) and on this basis opposed feed-in tariffs – the chief competing scheme – which they likened to 'command and control' legislation. They argued that market approaches will reduce prices of renewable electricity more quickly, stimulate its

---

40   Ibid. pp. 119-120.
41   European Environment & Packaging Law 2009, No. 188, p. 20.

deployment, spur innovation and prevent the rise of protectionist regulation in the renewable electricity sector. In retrospect, experience has refuted most of those claims.

In 1999, the EU Commission was clearly under the impact of the 'discovery' of emissions trading in the Kyoto negotiations. DG Energy argued the case of tradable certificates for renewable energy when it wanted a quota and certificate system as part of a directive on electricity from renewable energy sources. It claimed that this was the most efficient and effective approach. At the same time DG Competition supported the complaints by German energy incumbents against the country's electricity feed-in law of 1990 (which they had wanted to prevent from the very beginning) and argued that it amounted to state aid and was incompatible with the liberalised internal market for energy. DG Competition even joined a legal challenge to this law by German electricity incumbents before the European Court. Eventually, in its final proposal for what became renewable energy directive 2001/77/EC, the Commission took a more neutral position regarding the different support schemes; DG Competition also lost its case in the Court. The Commission made a new effort to introduce renewable energy quotas and certificate trading in 2007-08 but failed again.[42] Similar arguments against the German feed-in tariff came from the IEA until 2007.

A quota-cum-certificates system requires an authority to set a (normally increasing) quota for renewable electricity and leaves its price to the market. A feed-in system such as the German one, which became a model for many other countries, sets an obligation for utilities (or distributors, or grid companies) to purchase all renewable electricity from any generator at a specific tariff which varies with technologies, reflecting 'reasonable costs' and the need for a fair return; photovoltaic power is thus paid considerably more per kWh than e.g. on-shore wind power. This led to a large number of new market entrants; in Germany, their number surpasses one million. For both feed-in tariffs and certificate systems the extra cost is borne by electricity consumers. The advocates of quota-certificate systems claim that their arrangement will induce direct price competition and, as a result, reduce prices for renewable electricity more rapidly. Competition will also favour innovation, and lower prices will in turn favour more rapid deployment. They also argue that governments will find it difficult to lower feed-in tariffs as costs come down as firms can defend their extra profits with

42   Volkmar Lauber, Elisa Schenner (2011) The Struggle over Support Schemes for Renewable Electricity in the European Union: A Discursive-Institutionalist Analysis. Environmental Politics, 20(4), pp. 508-527.

populist arguments. As a result, feed-in tariffs will in the long run supposedly become an obstacle to cheap renewable energy and to its deployment.[43]

When presenting its arguments in 1999, the Commission invoked 'economic theory', meaning presumably neoclassical theory. Fortunately, the support schemes for renewable electricity are more transparent than emission trading, and fortunately there are very thorough quantitative studies comparing the different renewable electricity support schemes. In 2008, the EU submitted such a study together with its new directive proposal.[44] The conclusion of this study could not be clearer: feed-in tariffs offer substantially lower rewards to generators (except in Sweden), yet they are much more successful at encouraging deployment. They are also far more successful at encouraging the setting up of an investment goods industry for renewable energy and thus industrial innovation in this field.[45] All of this is the very opposite of what the Commission predicted in 1999 and what quota-certificate advocates were saying all along. At the same time, the 1990s showed a remarkable side effect of quota/certificate systems. They only mobilised the cheapest sources, in the same way as the Kyoto Protocol or ETS, and did not support technologies which may hold great promise but which will take support over an extended time period to become cheap – such as photovoltaics. More importantly, they discouraged new market entrants even for low-cost technologies because these cannot absorb the potential volatility of renewable energy certificate prices and thus are exposed to the constant threat of collapse in case the quota is over-fulfilled. Incumbents are better able to absorb such risks – and derive high windfall profits.[46] In the area of wind power, quota-cum-certificate scheme countries (except Sweden) combine the highest profit rates – at values which are a multiple of feed-in countries such as Germany, France or even Spain – with the lowest deployment.[47] So much for 'economic theory' in real life.

It is true that in recent years many national feed-in tariffs for photovoltaics have become a victim of their own success when they were not adjusted in time to reflect the rapid decline in PV prices they had brought about; this caused an over-

43   Volkmar Lauber, David Toke (2005), Einspeisetarife sind billiger und effizienter als Quoten-/ Zertifikationssystem, Zeitschrift für neues Energierecht 9(2), pp. 132-139.
44   Commission of the European Communities (2008), Commission Staff Working Document – The support of electricity from renewable energy sources, SEC(2008)57.
45   Staffan Jacobsson et. al. (2009), EU renewable energy support policy: Faith or facts? Energy Policy, 37(6), pp. 2143-2146.
46   Aviel Verbruggen, Volkmar Lauber (2009), Basic concepts for designing renewable electricity support aiming at a full-scale transition by 2050, Energy Policy 37(12), pp. 5732-5743.
47   Commission of the European Communities (2008), Commission Staff Working Document – The support of electricity from renewable energy sources, SEC(2008)57, p. 34.

reaction in several member states. They are also meeting with renewed resistance as they are beginning to cut more deeply into the profits of fossil incumbents. At the same time, they are a highly promising and effective instrument to advance the transition to an all-renewable electricity supply within a few decades.

IX   Conclusion

The chief thesis of this chapter is that the approaches which were fashionably termed 'market approaches' (because they were relying on a trading mechanism and supposedly on competition) do not live up to expectations. This may be a surprise to their authors, many of whom seem to have truly believed in the superiority of those instruments. For some incumbents it may be less surprising.

Mitchell writes that market approaches such as the ones discussed here (she is writing about sustainable energy in the UK) have as their common feature 'to promote narrow, short-term economic considerations which are unlikely to deliver the technical industrial, institutional and human innovations required. Government must intervene more effectively...'.[48]

What the 'market' frameworks described here did deliver shall now be summed up. There is a lack of ambitious goals that characterises trading schemes generally, possibly due to the political weight they accorded to incumbents in the process of introduction. There is a lack of transparency and accountability, possibly a structural problem to produce those qualities. A flow of money is organised supposedly to solve the problems of climate and energy and this seems in fact to be the feature that works best. But the problem is that this money, often in the form of windfall profits, ends up with incumbents – an unlikely source of change. Deployment of renewable electricity under these schemes is slower and more costly. The feed-in tariff scheme, often contrasted in the past with 'market approaches', shows that there is a regulatory alternative which serves the goals proclaimed by certificate systems quite well: lower prices, rapid deployment and innovation, competition (mainly between equipment producers) and few windfall profits.

Since the time of the Single European Act, the market approach in Europe had one chief supporter, i.e. the UK, also the first EU member state to liberalise its electricity sector. In March 2010 UK energy regulator Ofgem and government admitted 'that the current free-market approach will not achieve the country's green goals – nor provide the certainty that investors in new generation need in

48   Catherine Mitchell (2008), The Political Economy of Sustainable Energy. Basingstoke: Palgrave Macmillan, p. 1.

today's difficult financial climate'.[49]. A Deutsche Bank analysis came to a similar conclusion, stressing that many countries do not offer enough transparency, longevity, and certainty in their policies, such as those countries that 'rely on a more volatile market incentive approach'[50]; it too compares this with the more advantageous solution of the German feed-in tariff.

The challenge is to develop a regulatory instrument that incorporates the advantages of the feed-in tariff scheme (incentives for many new entrants enabling them to compete with incumbents) to other sectors central to climate change. This is no small challenge – not just due to the influence of incumbents and 'market' advocates, but also due to the need for regulatory imagination combined with political clout.

Bibliography

Cafruny, A.W.; Ryner, M. (2003), *A ruined fortress? Neoliberal hegemony and transformation in Europe.* New York: Rowman Littlefield.

Cini, M.; McGowan, L. (1998), *Competition Policy in the European Union.* Basingstoke: Palgrave Macmillan.

Damro,C.; Luaces-Mendez, P.(2003), Emissions Trading at Kyoto: From EU Resistance to Union Innovation, *Environmental Politics* 12 (2), pp. 71-94.

Grubb, M; Vrolijk, Ch.; Brack, D. (eds.) (1999), *The Kyoto Protocol. A Guide and Assessment.* London: Royal Institute of International Affairs.

Hirsch, J.M. (1999), Emission Allowance Trading Under the Clean Air Act: A Mode for Future Environmental Regulations, *NYU Law Journal* 7, pp. 352-397.

Jacobsson, S. et. al. (2009), EU renewable energy support policy: Faith or facts? *Energy Policy* 37(6), pp. 2143-2146.

Johnston, A. (2006), Free allocation of allowances under the EU Emissions Trading System – legal issues, *Climate Policy* 6, pp. 136f.

Lauber, V.; Schenner, E. (2011) The Struggle over Support Schemes for Renewable Electricity in the European Union: A Discursive-Institutionalist Analysis. *Environmental Politics*, 20(4), pp. 508-527.

Lauber, V.; Toke, D. (2005), Einspeisetarife sind billiger und effizienter als Quoten-/Zertifikationssystem, *Zeitschrift für neues Energierecht* 9(2), pp. 132-139.

Luhmann, H.J. (2009), Carbon Dioxide capture and Storage (CCS) at Coal-Fired Power Plants does not Contribute to Stopping Climate Change, *GAIA* 18(4), pp. 294-299.

Markussen,P.; Svendsen, G.T. (2005), Industry lobbying and the political economy of GHG trade in the European Union, *Energy Policy* 33 (2), pp. 245-255.

49   Windpower Monthly (2010), 26 (3), p. 34.
50   Deutsche Bank Climate Change Advisors (2009), Global Climate Change Policy Tracker: An Investor's Assessment.

Mitchell , C.(2008), *The Political Economy of Sustainable Energy.* Basingstoke: Palgrave Macmillan.

Munton, D. (1998), Dispelling the myths of the acid rain story, *Environment* 40 (6), pp. 27-33.

Newell, P. (2000), Climate for Change: Non-State Actors and the Global Politics of Greenhouse. Cambridge: Cambridge University Press.

Oberthür, S.; Ott, H.E. (1999), The Kyoto Protocol: International Climate Policy for the 21st century. Berlin: Springer.

Page, S.C.; Williamson,A.G.; Mason, I.G. (2009), Carbon capture and storage: Fundamental thermodynamics and current technology. *Energy Policy* 37(9), pp. 3314-3324.

Pahle, M. (2010), Germany's dash for coal: Exploring drivers and factors, *Energy Policy* 38 (7), pp. 3431-3442.

Pring, G. (2006), A decade of emissions trading in the USA: Experiences and observations for the EU, in: Marjan Peeters, Kurt Deketelaere (eds.), *EU Climate Change Policy.* Cheltenham: Edward Elgar, pp. 188-204.

Rai, V.; Victor, D.V.; Thurber, M.C. (2010), Carbon Capture and Storage at scale: Lessons from the growth of analogous energy technologies. *Energy Policy* 38(8), pp. 4089-4098.

Schlemmermeier, B.; Schintowski, H.P. (2006), Das deutsche Handelssystem für Emissionszertifikate: Rechtswidrig? *Zeitschrift für neues Energierecht* 10 (3), pp. 195-199;

Sijm, J.; Neuhoff, K.; Chen, Y. (2006), CO cost pass through and windfall profits in the power sector, *Climate Policy* 6, pp. 49-72.

Sijm, J.; Van Dril, A. (2003), *The Interaction between the EU Emissions Trading Scheme and Energy Policy Instruments in the Netherlands.* Implications of the EU Directive for Dutch Climate Policies: ECN-C—03-060, ECM: ZG Petten, The Netherlands.

Sinn, H.W. (2008), *Das Grüne Paradoxon. Plädoyer für eine illusionsfreie Klimapolitik.* Berlin: Econ.

Sorrell, S.; Sijm, J. (2003), Carbon Trading, in the Policy Mix, *Oxford Review of Economic Policy* 19 (3), pp. 420-437.

Strange, S. (1986), *Casino Capitalism.* Oxford: Blackwell.

Thornton, J. (2010), A carbon riddle that is in need of political answers, *European Voice* 16(7), p. 9.

Tokar, B. (1996), Trading away the earth. Pollution credits and the perils of "free market environmentalism". Dollars and Sense, March/ April, pp. 24-29.

Unruh, G.C. (2000), Understanding Carbon Lock-in, *Energy Policy* 30 (4), pp. 317-325.

Verbruggen, A.; Lauber, V. (2009), Basic concepts for designing renewable electricity support aiming at a full-scale transition by 2050, *Energy Policy* 37(12), pp. 5732-5743.

Voss, J.P. (2007), *Designs on Governance. Development of Policy Instruments and Dynamics in Governance.* Enschede: Iskamp.

Vrolijk, Ch. (ed.) (2002), *Climate Change and Power. Economic Instruments for European Electriciy.* London. Earthscan.

Wettestad, J. (2005), The Making of the 2003 EU Emissions Trading Direvtive: An Ultra-Quick Process due to Entrepreneurial Proficiency? *Global Environmental Politics* 5 (2), pp. 1-22.

Social Citizenship. Past and Future of a European Common Good

Sonja Puntscher Riekmann[1]

> *Conscious of its spiritual and moral heritage, the Union is founded on the indivisible,*
> *universal values of human dignity, freedom, equality and solidarity; it is based on the*
> *principles of democracy and the rule of law. It places the individual*
> *at the heart of its activities, by establishing the citizenship of the Union and*
> *by creating an area of freedom, security and justice.*

Charter of Fundamental Rights of the European Union, Preamble

I   Introduction

Will Europe's social model survive the financial and fiscal crisis?[2] In view of the new European fiscal compact[3] that will considerably reduce member states' room for manoeuvre in terms of public spending and thus of sustaining current and conceiving future national welfare policies, the question is compelling. The compact together with other measures is to save the troubled euro identified by President Van Rompuy as the European 'common good'.[4] While it is hard to consider the single currency as being a common good in itself, in the last two years rescuing the member states that by their sovereign debt endanger the euro has become the most important issue to Europeans. Despite contestation on legal and political grounds, bail-out procedures were put in place on strict conditions

---

1   My acknowledgement goes to Philippe Schmitter, Carlos Closa, Alexander Somek, and Michael Blauberger for critical comments on earlier versions of this chapter. The usual disclaimer applies.
2   Europe's social model is meant here to define the very European concept of the national welfare state not a supranational version of it. If only by way of anecdote, it was interesting to observe that the question about whether the European welfare states will survive the current financial crisis was raised by one Russian and one Chinese economist, Olga Butorina (Moscow) and Dai Bingran (Shanghai), at the Global Jean Monnet Conference 'European Economic Governance in an International Context' held in Brussels on 24-25 November 2011 (http://ec.europa.eu/education/jean-monnet/doc3156_en.htm).
3   European Council, Statement by the Euro Area Heads of State or Government, Brussels, 9 December 2011.
4   Van Rompuy at the press conference on 9 December 2011. See also Klaus Gretschmann in this volume.

for beneficiaries to reduce debts and deficits. Such conditions are curbing national welfare states and thus redefining the whole concept of social citizenship that for long has been part and parcel of the common good in Europe. In this chapter I will, however, not speculate about the survival of the euro. I will instead tackle the question of the future of the European welfare state and the chances of its revival at the supranational level.

For almost two centuries, the common good was defined in Europe as the pursuit of democracy and social citizenship. Indeed, T.H. Marshall's famous essay on *Citizenship and Social Class* of 1950 summarised past struggles and projected future perspectives. In Marshall's terms the concept of social citizenship encases two intertwined aspects: citizenship as a political-democratic norm, and social rights as their commensurate underpinning. In post-war Europe democratic citizenship and social rights as two sides of the same coin became palatable even to economic liberals who accommodated to a vision of reconstructing the shattered economies in terms of a social market economy.[5] Although from a liberal capitalist perspective the concept remained contested due to fears about encroachments of the social aspect upon market economy, it turned into a political and legal principle driving political discourse and practice well into to 1980s: 'Empirically, the post war democratic welfare state was committed to reconciling free markets with a stable social order, by a variety of economic, political, and social intervention. *Public interest* came to be identified with a combination of social integration – to be achieved by way of protection and stabilization of social relations against unpredictably fluctuating of prices – and system integration providing for stable cooperation between capital and labor....'[6]

Social citizenship, its continuous pursuit, the quantitative and qualitative growth of the relevant legal provisions, and of the social budgets concomitant with it, mark the *differentia specifica* characterising Europe vis-à-vis other world regions. Whereas democracy, if in different forms and degrees, has been adopted by many states throughout the world, fully-fledged welfare models mainly remain a European characteristic. Even if in one way or another social justice is a

5   See Tony Judt (2005), Post-War. A History of Europe since 1945. London: William Heinemann, pp. 324-389; for a broader historical overview see Abram de Swaan (1988), In Care of the State. Health Care, Education and Welfare in Europe and the USA in the Modern Era. Cambridge: Polity Press. De Swaan describes the welfare state as the outcome of a 'collectivizing process' as concomitant with the formation of the state and the rise of capitalism (pp. 218 et seq.), but he concludes that '[e]ven though the dynamics of interdependency between rich and poor and the dilemmas of collective action among the established repeat themselves on a world scale, there is no historical necessity for the collectivizing process to proceed at a global level.' (p. 257) However, he does not tackle such necessity in the EU framework.

6   See Wolfgang Streeck (2009), Re-Forming Capitalism. Institutional Change in the German Political Economy. Oxford: Oxford University Press, p. 7 (emphasis in the original).

notion common to all societies, nowhere has social citizenship reached such political importance and institutionalisation as in modern Europe.[7] In her famous book, *On Revolution*, Hannah Arendt dedicated a whole chapter to the *Social Question* as being *the* issue of European revolutions, whereas the American Revolution had shunned it in the very general idea of the individual 'pursuit of happiness'.[8] In Europe, on the contrary, concepts of a socialist society, of the welfare state, and of social market economy stem from a vision of the world based on social justice, solidarity, and security. To become effective political freedom, so it seemed, had to realise these values and, thus, citizenship had to be also social citizenship.

Even if meanings are ambiguous and positions diverge, discourses on a European Social Model in supranational terms are developed in this vein.[9] European integration, however, has largely been conducted in the all-pervading spirit of the single market and its freedoms, thus creating the asymmetry between European market-making and national social policy-making. This was to a degree compensated by the European Court of Justice that substantiated the social implications of the treaties in particular for mobile workers and women, but its rulings quite logically are based on a concept of individualism,[10] to the detriment of collective self-determination.[11] Nevertheless, political awareness of the negative consequences of such asymmetry has also grown. How else are we to explain the inclusion of the chapter on employment into the Treaty of Amsterdam, or of solidarity into the European Charter of Fundamental Rights, or the introduction of a general social clause into the Treaty of Lisbon? How are we to explain the social

7   I share Maurizio Ferrera's qualification of Europe as unique in this respect: 'It is not exaggerated to say that what makes our continent uniquely distinctive and recognizable nowadays at the global level are, precisely, its "social model" centred on the EU's novel system of multi-level governance and shared sovereignty, especially in the economic and monetary field.' Maurizio Ferrera (2009), The JCMS Annual Lecture: National Welfare States and European Integration: In Search of a 'Virtuous Nesting', Journal of Common Market Studies 47(2), pp. 220.

8   Hannah Arendt (1963), On Revolution. New York: The Viking Press. Ch.II.

9   Maria Jepsen, Serrano Pascual (2006), The Concept of the ESM and supranational legitimacy-building, in: Maria Jepsen, Serrano Pascual (eds.), Unwrapping the European Social Model, Bristol: Polity Press, pp.25-45; Robert Rebhahn (2009), Europäisches Sozialmodell – oder nationale Sozialmodelle für Arbeitsbeziehungen und Welfare?, Thomas Eilmansberger, Günter Herzig (eds.) Soziales Europa. Wien: Nomos-Facultas WUV, pp. 15-56.

10   Alexander Somek (2009), Individualism. An Essay on the Authority of the European Union. Oxford: Oxford University Press.

11   Fritz W. Scharpf (2010), The Double Asymmetry of European Integration – Or Why the EU Cannot Be a Social Market Economy, in: Fritz W. Scharpf (ed.), Community and Autonomy. Institutions, Policies and Legitimacy in Multilevel Europe. Frankfurt/ New York: Campus Verlag, pp. 353-391; p. 364.

promises of the Europe 2020 strategy or the recurrent appeals to solidarity and social cohesion in treaty articles and EU programmes? Are they merely 'cheap talk'?[12] The Preamble of the Constitutional Treaty did not only and repeatedly mention justice and equality, but also claimed that the Union had become a 'special area of human hope', whereas Article I-3 (3) stated the commitment to:

> ...[W]ork for the sustainable development of Europe based on balanced economic growth and price stability, a highly competitive social market economy, aiming at full employment and social progress. ... It shall combat social exclusion and discrimination, and shall promote social justice and protection, equality between women and men, solidarity between generations and protection of the rights of the child. It shall promote economic, social and territorial cohesion, and solidarity among Member States.[13]

The Charter of Fundamental Rights enshrined in the Constitutional Treaty spelled out a number of social principles and rights.[14] The Treaty of Lisbon took up many of these commitments and provisions, whereas in the aftermath of the 2009 elections the European Parliament setting out its new agenda mainly refers to social issues to be tackled in the near future.[15] Reading these documents and the concomitant literature on the European Social Model, any observer could reach the conclusion that the Union is driven by the same welfare logic as the member states were in the past. Yet, reality does hardly live up to the standards set by the documents, and problems loom large: when asked, citizens have time and again rejected a treaty in spite of its abundance of classical social rhetoric, and EU-scepticism is on the rise almost everywhere.[16]

It is my thesis that there is a deep cleft between the rhetoric and the competencies given to the supranational organs to meet expectations raised by treaty promises. The cleft, however, stems from mainly two phenomena: *first*, from the apparently indissoluble bond between the nation-state and the welfare state, and *second*, from the rather peculiar division of labour between national welfarism

---

12   Ibid. p.353.
13   Treaty establishing a Constitution for Europe, Official Journal of the European Union C 310/11, 2004.
14   Von Bogdandy argues that these rights as well as ECJ interpretations of Union Citizenship justify the inclusion of 'solidarity' in his list of four constitutional principles besides 'equal liberty', 'rule of law', and 'democracy'. See Armin von Bogdandy (2006), Constitutional Principles, in Armin von Bogdandy, Jürgen Bast (eds.), Principles of European Constitutional Law. Oxford and Portland, Oregon: Hart Publishing, pp. 3-52, pp. 32et seq.
15   http://www.europarl.europa.eu/news/public/story_page/008-56961-166-06-25-901-20; 12 June 2009.
16   Christian Joerges and others have pointed to the interdependence of the democratic and the social deficit of the Union, concluding that '[a] social deficit is likely to provoke a crisis in the social acceptance of Europe and is challenging the potential of Europe's constitutionalism'. See Christian Joerges (2005), Introduction to the Special Issue: Confronting Memories: European "Bitter Experiences" and the Constitutionalization Process: Constructing Europe in the Shadow of its Past, German Law Journal 6, pp. 245-254.

and European economic liberalism. The first phenomenon constitutes the relations between governments and their electorate through re-distributive policies, whereas the second is responsible for enhancing the competitiveness of the European economy, thereby continuously 'de-stabilising' national welfare achievements. Thus, European policies became the culprit in the eyes of citizens who scapegoat the Union for ushering in liberalism enhanced by global dynamics. Citizens, however, hardly perceive that this has been the agreement of the Founding Fathers and their successors.[17] The fall of the iron curtain and EU enlargement exacerbated the economic liberal position, as many new member states' governments dismissed the welfare discourse reminding them of the communist past.[18] Moreover, in the process of catching up with old EU members, the new economies tried to compete on the single market by cheaper products and services and by lower wages.

I aim, *first*, to describe briefly the European legacy of social discourse common to all member states. Whereas concrete social policies and legal arrangements might differ from member state to member state (or rather between groups of member states), they all concur in the ultimate goal of reducing inequalities and protecting citizens in case of misfortune. In Europe, poverty, illness, unemployment, and ageing are not seen as merely individual fates, but as events to be corrected or at least alleviated by collective solidarity and responsibility. Such thinking was the result of the eighteenth-century Enlightenment, but even more so of the conflicts emerging from growing social cleavages of the nineteenth century and assuaged by Bismarckian policy response. Moreover, education geared towards the formation of skilled workers and thus towards the creation of more equal opportunities was considered to be a public responsibility of paramount importance. The policies resulting thereof were, however, national policies that gradually came to dominate liberalism. The era of liberal capitalism endorsed by global 'imperialism' entered a phase of grave crisis with World War I, communist revolutions, fascism and National Socialism.

I argue, *second*, that after World War II economic liberalism returned and was reinstated not only at the national but also and far more consistently at the Euro-

---

17 Even if some consequences resulting from the treaties may have been more unintended than intended and even if a number of important developments stem from ECJ interpretation of the treaties, it is the member states' responsibilities to negotiate, write, and ratify the treaties. Thus, I am not so convinced by Scharpf's reference to Carl Friedrich's 'law of anticipated reaction' to ECJ judgements as applying to EU member states (see Scharpf p. 379). At least one may also ask whether politicians are delegating difficult decisions to courts.

18 The position of the new member states is at least ambiguous considering the fall and the return of socialist or communist parties in the last two decades, but also reading the social commitments enshrined in the national constitutions to which I will return later in this paper.

pean level. With the project of the single market launched in the second half of 1980s and after the Thatcher revolution, European integration was first and foremost 'negative integration' due to its liberalising effects. It thus provoked resistance from national electorates who saw their social achievements jeopardised by the Union. However, this development is intimately linked to a dilemma created by national political actors captured in their 'Faustian bargain'[19] in that they try to preserve their national prerogatives regarding re-distributive social policies, whereas they delegate the implementation of liberal economic policies to the European level. Moreover, the tensions between national welfare states and European acts impinging upon them are not exclusively in the hands of the member states, as can be demonstrated by Commission activities and in particular by ECJ judgements.

Hence, *third*, I argue normatively that European citizenship is to remain a term void of significance if not complemented by social citizenship. European political actors seem to acknowledge this by considerably strengthening normative commitments to the Social Question. However, while there has always been a lack of consensus among actors as to how much substantive European social policy there should be, the financial and economic crisis is obviously changing the parameters of integration. The considerable asymmetries between member states in terms of productivity and thus of competitiveness that were neglected in the first decade of the euro have come to the surface in what is now a sovereign debt crisis. The response to the need for European solidarity is the creation of the EFSF/ESM on the condition of respect for the compact of strict fiscal rules. Whether such a compact will operate as a catalyst for greater convergence of the different economies remains doubtful. However, and equally important, is the question of whether its austerity implications will further erode social acceptance of the Union. By way of conclusion, I will, *fourth*, reflect upon the question of how the European pursuit of social justice is to become compatible with European and global market economy. Such reflection draws on existing European legal provisions and builds on the idea of nesting national welfare regimes in a supranational regime, i.e. in a European Social Model. The latter approach, however, does imply a re-launch of the debate about the direction of integration and hence of the Union's *finalité*.

---

19 I use the term coined by Guy Peters and Jon Pierre to describe the trade-offs between democratic values and political effectiveness and efficiency in different context, but where it seems just as appropriate. See Guy Peters, Jon Pierre (2004), Multi-Level Governance and Democracy: A Faustian Bargain, in: Ian Bache, Matthew Flinders (eds.), Multi-Level Governance. Oxford: Oxford University Press, pp. 79-92.

II   The Welfare State as Instrument of National Unity

Liberalism and socialism are both European inventions. The controversy between the two strands of thinking has marked more than two centuries of theoretical work and political struggle in Europe.[20] I use 'socialism' here as a meta-term without referring to concrete political orders. It simply describes the idea that social justice is a value to be pursued by a society whose traditional order had been upset by capitalism as the rising and ultimately dominant form of economy. As regards political actors, the term refers to Social Democratic as much as to Christian Socialist parties.

Liberalism and socialism share one important value, i.e. the freedom of the human being, albeit they pursue it by different means. Thus, liberalism was interested in the civil and political part of citizenship, whereas socialism focused on the social part, as it thought the first two parts remained incomplete without the third part. Indeed, civil and political rights without a social underpinning would hardly lead to the freedom of the individual to make appropriate choices. In particular, without education and minimum income, the exertion of political rights would be difficult at least. As Marshall put it, the right to freedom of speech is useless if you have nothing to say or if you lack the power to make yourself heard. And the latter for a long time was tied to property and wealth. 'Civil rights…confer the legal capacity to strive for things one would like to possess but do not guarantee the possession of any of them'.[21] It is the contradiction between rights and the possibility to fully enjoy them that has driven the nineteenth-century revolutions and reforms.

> 'Citizenship is a status bestowed on those who are full members of a community. All who possess the status are equal with respect to rights and duties with which the status is endowed. There is no universal principle that determines what those rights and duties shall be, but societies in which citizenship is a developing institution create an image of an ideal citizenship against which achievement can be measured and towards which aspiration can be directed.'[22]

Hence, if being a full member of a community forms the core of an ideal citizenship, opening ways for potentially all individuals to participate becomes an important goal of such society. In Europe, this goal was pursued by nation-builders geared towards constructing the loyalty of the subjects. It goes without saying that inter-national economic competition and even more so wars made the construction of nationhood and loyalty of subjects and thus of citizenship an urgent

---

20   Such a struggle has been exported to other world regions developing into different directions depending on specific socio-economic contexts.

21   Thomas H. Marshall (1950), Citizenship and Social Class and other essays. Cambridge: Cambridge University Press, pp. 34-35.

22   Ibid. p. 29.

task of the states. However, also capitalism was interested, at least in the civil emancipation of workers who would be freed from traditional bonds by gaining civil rights that 'gave to each man, as part of his individual status, the power to engage as an independent unit in the economic struggle and made it possible to deny him social protection on the ground that he was equipped with the means to protect himself.'[23] But then, capitalism was also interested in better-educated workers and welcomed the institutionalisation of general schooling that in the eyes of policymakers had become a tool to form the future adult.[24] However, the creation of civil and political rights, if it did not abolish inequalities, did gradually undermine the old class system. In particular, political rights helped to create workers' representation organs and hence a powerful tool to fight for ever-growing social rights. Civil and political rights also 'provided the foundation of equality on which the structure of inequality could be built.'[25] That is, while education or housing policies were conceived to deliver services to an ever-growing number of citizens, they were of course not detached from other goals such as occupation or town planning. And in this respect they would create new stratification of a given society, e.g. by sifting children through the educational system for the purpose of specific labour market demands, or by segregating groups according to specific housing needs.

Thus, the developments of the nineteenth century laid the foundations for the modern welfare state that became an integrative part of the very idea of nationhood. In the fight for civil and political rights, modern political parties were formed who then became representatives of socio-economic forces striving for social rights. This development did not occur in the same way in all European countries, nor did it lead exactly to the same outcomes. As Philip Manow has shown, different structures of social cleavages gave birth to diverse party coalitions and electoral rules which account for the differences in the European welfare state regimes as proposed by Esping-Andersen.[26] Yet, whatever differences in terms of capitalist market orders, redistributive generosity, or legally binding social rights,[27] we also witness Europeans converging on some concept of social

23   Ibid. pp. 33-34.
24   Ibid. p.25.
25   Ibid., pp. 30-34.
26   Philip Manow (2009), Electoral rules, class coalitions and welfare state regimes, or how to explain Esping-Andersen with Stein Rokkan, Socio-Economic Review 7, pp. 101-121.; Gosta Esping-Andersen (1990), The Three Worlds of Welfare Capitalism. Cambridge: Polity Press.
27   As for the reasons of such differences see also Torben Iversen, David Soskice (2006), Electoral Institutions and the Politics of Coalitions: Why Some Democracies Redistribute More Than Others, American Political Science Review 100, pp. 165-181; and Peter A. Hall, Kathleen Thelen (2009), Institutional change in varieties of capitalism, Socio-Economic Review 7, pp. 7-34.

justice and solidarity as important preconditions of the citizens' loyalty to the nation-state. It is in this context that collective bargaining and 'trade unionism has…created a secondary system of industrial citizenship parallel with and secondary to the system of political citizenship'.[28] Socio-economic changes at the beginning of the twentieth century led to the diminution of inequality strengthening the demand for its abolition. Thus the focus was no longer on how to alleviate destitution but on how to modify the whole pattern of social inequality: 'It has begun to remodel the whole building, and it might even end by converting a sky-scraper into a bungalow'.[29] It is perhaps no exaggeration to hold that in the twentieth century if to different degrees the welfare state became the 'civilising moment' of the European nation-state. 'Citizenship requires a bond of a different kind (as kinship or the fiction of common descent, SPR), a direct sense of community membership based on the loyalty to a civilisation which is common possession'.[30]

However, such sense of community membership did also entail a drive to closure. As Maurizio Ferrera put it: 'The welfare state essentially rests on a logic of «closure"; it presupposes the existence of a clearly demarcated and cohesive community, whose members feel that they belong to the same 'whole' and that they are linked by reciprocity ties vis-à-vis common risks and similar needs. Since the nineteenth century (or even earlier in some cases) the nation-state has provided the closure conditions for the development of an ethos of social solidarity and redistributive arrangements within its geographical territory'.[31] Such logic is not only colliding with the 'logic of opening' guiding European integration which will be my topic later, but it has also been one driving force in the establishment of the authoritarian and totalitarian regimes in the inter-war period. As regards the latter, the logic of closure in a dialectical leap became a force of de-civilisation in the Shoah and the subjugation of foreign peoples for the sake of national welfare.[32] And so has the extirpation of specific classes in the process of collectivisation and 'de-koulakisation' in the Soviet Union.[33]

28   T.H. Marshall (1950), Citizenship and Social Class and other essays. Cambridge: Cambridge University Press, p. 44.
29   Ibid., p. 47.
30   Ibid., pp. 40-41.
31   Maurizio Ferrera (2009), The JCMS Annual Lecture: National Welfare States and European Integration: In Search of a ‚Virtuous Nesting', Journal of Common Market Studies 47 (2), pp. 220.
32   See e.g. Götz Aly (2005), Hitlers Volksstaat: Raub, Rassenkrieg und nationaler Sozialismus. Frankfurt am Main: Fischer.
33   See e.g. Stéphane Courtois et al. (1997), Le livre noir du communisme. Crime, terreur, repression. Paris: Robert Laffont, pp. 164-177; Mark Mazower (1998), Dark Continent: Europe's Twentieth Century. London: Penguin Books, chapters 3 and 4.

After the dark era had come to an end, a growing number of welfare states lying west of the iron curtain were to be rescued by European integration.[34] A novel process of European civilisation was launched through institutionalised supranational cooperation in selected but ever-growing policy fields. In regard to social policy, however, the construction of the novel polity spawned a European dilemma: while continuous expansion of social security entitlements for national constituencies became the hallmark of the *Trente Glorieuses*, the socio-economic national orders stemming thereof are simultaneously 'de-constructed' by the integration process.[35]

III   Common Market Policy as Instrument of European Integration

T.H. Marshall wrote his essay on *Citizenship and Social Class* in the attempt to find an answer to the question about the limits of social citizenship in a market economy. His was the quest for the 'possibility of combining in one system the two principles of social justice and market price'.[36] For three post-war decades it seemed that there were no limits to that combination. But then such limits came to the fore in the late 1970s when the EEC members entered a phase of stagnation or Eurosclerosis, a term coined not only to define integration stalemates, but also the decline of growth and the rise of unemployment. In the mid-1980 the EEC governments together with the Delors Commission started to re-launch the integration process, first by creating the Single European Act, second by the Project 1992 geared towards the completion of the single market, and third by the Treaty of Maastricht enshrining the Economic and Monetary Union (EMU).[37] The demise of the Soviet Empire and the fall of the iron curtain in 1989 certainly spurred developments that had been in the pipeline since quite some time, whereas the now directly elected European Parliament demonstrated a new determination to participate in the integration process by opening the debate on the constitutionalisation of the would-be polity.

The new drive towards the 'ever closer union' did not, however, go hand in hand with entirely new instruments, but rather by taking the four freedoms more seriously. Thus the European Economic Community, now crowned by the European Union, enhanced what Ferrera has called the 'logic of openness' in an un-

---

34   Allen St. Milward (2000), The European Rescue of the Nation State, 2nd edition. London: Routledge.
35   Stefano Bartolini (2005), Restructuring Europe. Oxford: Oxford University Press.
36   Thomas H.Marshall (1950), Citizenship and Social Class and other essays. Cambridge: Cambridge University Press, p. 48.
37   The Treaty of Maastricht enshrined two other new pillars concerning Foreign and Security Policy and Justice and Home Affairs that however will not be tackled here.

precedented way and 'aimed at fostering free movement (in the widest sense) and non-discrimination by weakening or tearing apart those spatial demarcations and closure practices that nation-states have historically built around (and often within) themselves.'[38] A number of initiatives evolving in the course of the implementation of European Economic and Monetary Union, such as the Stability and Growth Pact, the Lisbon and the Employment Strategy buttressed by the Open Method of Coordination, if with varying effects started to impinge upon national socio-economic orders. Particularly from a Neo-Keynesian perspective, the EMU agreement was qualified 'as a substantial, even if incomplete, victory of neo-liberalism and a Trojan horse for an economic-policy revolution in Europe based on supply-side economics and an agenda of deregulation and privatization. It empowered both finance ministries and central banks to push through what they judged to be overdue reforms in EC member states, extending beyond the specific terms of the Treaty to include reform of social policies as well as of labour markets.'[39]

While fostering the logic of openness, milestone rulings of the ECJ also provoked questions about the legitimacy of judge-made law.[40] The pro-integrationist judiciary enforcing the four freedoms as well as competition law leading up to cases such as *Rüffert*, *Viking* or *Laval* came to 'involve a distributive conflict between high-wage and low-wage member states whose fair resolution would have raised difficult normative issues', which the ECJ seems to ignore: 'Its self-referential legal framework prevents any consideration of the normative tension between solidarity achieved, with great effort, at the national level and a moral commitment to the 'inclusion of the other' in an European context.'[41] This may be exaggerated, as in other cases such as *Poucet* and *Pistre* the ECJ did indeed demonstrate judicial self-restraint. Moreover, recent studies on national responses to supposedly disruptive ECJ rulings show that there still is 'considerable room for manoeuvre', and thus contradict 'the gloomy forecasts of early legal

---

38   Maurizio Ferrera (2009), The JCMS Annual Lecture: National Welfare States and European Integration: In Search of a ‚Virtuous Nesting', Journal of Common Market Studies 47 (2), p. 220.

39   Kenneth Dyson, Kevin Featherstone (1999), The Road to Maastricht. Negotiating Economic and Monetary Union. Oxford: Oxford University Press, p. 791.

40   See Fritz Scharpf (2009), Legitimacy in the multilevel European Polity, European Political Social Science Review, 1 (2), pp. 173-204: 'By enforcing its (the ECJ's, SPR) "liberal" programme of liberalization and deregulation, the ECJ may presently be undermining the "republican" bases of member-state legitimacy. Where that is the case, open non-compliance is a present danger, and political controls of judicial legislation may be called for.' (p. 173), and 'The Court can only destroy existing national solutions, but it cannot itself create "Social Europe"'. (p. 198).

41   Fritz Scharpf (2009), Legitimacy in the multilevel European Polity, European Political Social Science Review 1 (2), pp. 173-204 at 199.

commentaries on judgements'.[42] However, legal scholars argue that, even if the Court for instance refrained from qualifying public social insurance services as economic undertakings, the justification is far from stringent. In particular, a clear dogmatic line of argumentation is difficult to discern, and so is future jurisdiction. Indeed, in other cases the ECJ has defined health services as subjected to commodification and hence to the freedom of services.[43] The Commission adds to the blurring of demarcation lines between what is and what is not subjected to pertinent rules as defined by Articles 43 seq. or Articles 81 seq. EC when it states that, in practice, single market provisions apply to the overwhelming majority of services which are to be considered as economic activities.[44] Even if the ECJ seems to be more interested in promoting the coordination of national welfare systems rather than transforming them into purely marketised areas, Damjanovic argues that this might in the end be the result. Owing to a broad interpretation of market rules (that in principle apply also to welfare systems) in combination with anti-discrimination and Union citizenship rules, the ECJ could indeed 'create' a competence to decide on issues that the legislator shuns to decide. The court could thereby open a new port of entry also for actors advocating more pronounced market orientation also in the social services.[45] Even if this sounds speculative, it would hardly be the first time for the Commission and the ECJ to gradually and stealthily make important inroads into national legal and socio-economic orders.[46] However, while both supranational organs are acting in a logic of 'opening up', the member states do so not in undue arbitrariness, but in the spirit of the treaties and driven by interests of citizens as socio-economic actors

42 Michael Blauberger (2012), With Luxembourg in mind…The re-making of national policies in the face of ECJ jurisprudence, Journal of European Public Policy 19(1), pp. 108-125 at 121. See also the GA's argument in the case Cruz Villalón C-515/08, 53: 'To the extent that the new primary law framework provides for a mandatory high level of social protection, it authorises the Member States, for the purpose of safeguarding a certain level of social protection, to restrict a freedom, and to do so without European Union law's regarding it as something exceptional and, therefore, as warranting a strict interpretation. That view, which is founded on the new provisions of the Treaties cited above, is expressed in practical terms by applying the principle of proportionality.'

43 Dragana Damjanovic, Die Marktregeln der EG, p. 211; John Temple Lang, Privatisation of Social Welfare: European Union Competition Law Rules, in Eleanor Spaventa and Michael Dougan (2005), Social Welfare and EU Law, Oxford and Portland. Oxford: Hart Publishing 2005, pp. 45-77; Malcolm Ross (2007), Promoting Solidarity: From Public Services to a European Model of Competition? Journal of Common Market Law Review 2007, 44(4), p. 1067 et seq.

44 European Commission, Communication on services of general interest, COM (2007) 724 final, 6 (2.1).

45 Dragana Damjanovic (2009), Die Marktregeln der EG, in: Thomas Eilmansberger, Günter Herzig (eds.), Soziales Europa, Vienna: Nomos and facultas.wuv 2009, p. 216-7.

46 Sonja Puntscher Riekmann (1998), Die kommissarische Neuordnung Europas. Das Dispositiv der Integration, Wien/ New York: Springer.

and plaintiffs seeking respect for their rights.[47] Whether member states as 'arbiters of treaties' ignore the consequences of their creation of primary or secondary law or whether they stealthily pursue them is often difficult to say, in particular when governments play both cards: the card of openness in Brussels and the card of closure in the domestic sphere.

Since the early 1990s the problems arising from the clash of the two logics of openness and closure became tangible in the ratification processes of the Treaty of Maastricht (rejected by the Danish and accepted by the *petit oui* of the French) and the treaties of states forming the European Economic Area (rejected by the Swiss), by the referenda on accession in the Northern enlargement (rejected for the second time by Norwegians). But also the following treaty revisions (Amsterdam, Nice, Rome, and Lisbon) undertaken to prepare the Union for the great enlargement towards Central and Eastern European countries were contested, the rejection of the Constitutional Treaty by large majorities in the two founding members France and the Netherlands being the most impressive case in point. The permissive consensus of citizens regarding European integration definitely seemed to belong to the past.

European integration is, however, not only following the logic of openness, but at the same time the logic of a new closure through the building of a supranational polity. Thus the logic of openness through European integration is propelled by a set of supranational and inter-governmental institutions unleashing a remarkable shift of power to the supranational level of governance. Indeed, the transformation of the old national polities into a new one whose *finalité* is unclear and contested exacerbates the clash of logics identified by Ferrera. To reconcile the two logics, Ferrera proposes a model of three overlapping spaces in which the nation-based welfare state is central and at the same time embedded in the EU economic space on the one hand, and in the EU social space on the other. Such 'virtuous nesting'[48] of the national welfare state within the wider institution of the EU would allow for 'internal convenience' and 'external adjustment'. Conceived as 'strategy of reconciliation' between the two logics, it should take the social provisions already inherent in EU primary and secondary law as a starting point for delineating the European social space. However, the fiscal compact developed to tackle the financial crisis makes such demarcations ever more difficult.

---

47 Fritz W. Scharpf (2009), The Double Asymmetry of European Integration Or Why the EU cannot be a Social Market Economy, MPIfG Working Paper. Scharpf stresses the role of 'private enforcers' of liberalisation that favours the individual while it prevents the emergence of supranational forms of collective self-determination.

48 Maurizio Ferrera (2009), The JCMS Annual Lecture: National Welfare States and European Integration: In Search of a ‚Virtuous Nesting', Journal of Common Market Studies, 47 (2), p. 223.

IV   From Economic and Monetary Union to Social Union?

From the outset and until the 1980s, the creation and maintenance of public services as well as the reallocation of resources in terms of social security were seen as outside the Community competencies. Only where required for the functioning of the common market, as e.g. induced by the transnational mobility of workers, were Community activities foreseen. In the 1990s, however, the Union chose a more expansive approach. In particular we witness that the coordination of national security systems as a precondition for the functioning of the common market, buttressed by the European Court of Justice already in the preceding decades, now was extended to all persons that could be somehow defined as economically active and, potentially, to all welfare provisions.[49] With regard to health issues the Court did not invoke the rationale of the single market but rather the rationale of the freedom of services, thereby qualifying health benefits in terms of 'services provided against remuneration' and hence accessible for all Union citizens. Thus, the 'social turn' in the ECJ jurisdiction is constructed by an intriguing combination of market and social citizenship related arguments, whereas owing to the precariousness of transnational solidarity in the would-be polity the ECJ seemed to be well aware of their limits, and thus repeatedly invoked the principle of proportionality.[50]

Two caveats are important as regards such 'social turn': First, the dominant trend of negative integration in the name of single market building is likely to continue.[51] Second, speaking of European social policy is inappropriate as long

---

49   See Stefano Giubboni (2007), Free Movement of Persons and European Solidarity, European Law Journal 13 (3), pp. 360ff; in Eleanor Spaventa (2007), Free Movement of Persons in the European Union. Barriers to Movement in their Constitutional Context. Alphen Aan den Rijn: Kluwer Law International; for the effects of ECJ rulings on the mobility of patients see Vassilis Hatzopoulos (2002), Killing National health and Insurance Systems but Healing Patients? The European Market for Health Care services after the Judgements of the ECJ in Vanbraekel and Peerbooms, Common Market Law Review 39, pp. 683ff; on the 'social turn' in the ECJ jurisdiction in general see Dragana Damjanovic (2009), Die Marktregeln der EG, in: Thomas Eilmansberger, Günter Herzig (eds.), Soziales Europa. Vienna: Nomos and facultas.wuv 2009, p. 205.

50   See Michael Dougan, Eleanor Spaventa (2005), 'Wish You Weren't Here…' New Models of Social Solidarity in the European Union, in: Michael Dougan, Eleanor Spaventa (eds), Social Welfare and EU Law. Oxford: Hart Publishing, p 191. Eleanor Spaventa (2008), Seeing the wood despite the trees? On the scope of Union citizenship and its constitutional effects, Common Market Law Review 45(1), pp. 13 et seq.

51   Julio Baquero Cruz (2005), Beyond Competition: Services of General Interest and European Community Law, in: Gráinne de Búrca (ed.), EU Law and the Welfare State. In Search of Solidarity. Oxford: Oxford University Press, pp. 169-212.

as the regulatory approach will prevail.[52] While social regulation occurs in a number of fields (largely based on the Articles 137, 138, 139, 141 or 153 EC), redistribution is minimal: as a matter of fact, the Union does not command a 'social budget'. While the European Social Fund created on the basis of Articles 146-148 EC is part of regional cohesion policy, it does not allocate resources directly to individuals. Moreover, the concept of the market slowly penetrating the realm of welfare provisions[53] has unleashed a re-shaping of national redistribution policies.

Despite these caveats, however, we witness a change in political discourse: even if is difficult to assess whether there is a subterraneous causal link between the Court's jurisdiction, the citizens' expectations, and the constitutionalisation process of the last decade, the rise of 'Social Europe' is striking. In particular, the Convention drafting the Charter of Fundamental Rights in 2000 dedicated one title explicitly to 'Solidarity', while it spread a number of relating rights and principles all over the text. The Charter was preceded by the Simitis Report (1999) prepared for the Commission that recommended to follow international legal standards and to divide fundamental rights into civil-political and economic-social rights. Despite the deep conflicts between supporters and detractors of fundamental social rights, the Convention in less than one year of negotiations created a Charter enshrining principles and rights going beyond international laws and in many cases also national constitutions. In regard to the latter, it is important to stress that there is a significant variance among member states' constitutional settings: Only the UK and Austria are silent about social constitutional rights, whereas Germany, Ireland and Sweden recognise pertinent principles and general state objectives in their constitutions. A third group formed by Denmark, Finland, Greece, Luxembourg, the Netherlands, and Spain has constitutions combining such general objectives with some social rights, whereas a fourth group comprising Belgium, France, Italy, and Portugal pursues an approach of constitutionally guaranteed rights. Strikingly, it is the fourth group that grew after enlargement: Bulgaria, Estonia, Latvia, Lithuania, Poland, Rumania, Slovenia, Slovakia, Hungary, and the Czech Republic introduced (or kept) constitutionally guaranteed social rights.[54] There is, apparently, a paradoxical relation-

---

52 Giandomenico Majone (1993), The European Community between Social Policy and Social Regulation, Journal of Common Market Studies, 31 (2).
53 Stefan Leibfried (2005), Social Policy. Left to the Judges and Markets? In: Helen Wallace, William Wallace and Mark Pollak (eds.), Policy Making in the European Union, 5th edition. London: Routledge, pp. 243-278.
54 The trend towards constitutionalisation of social rights can also be observed in the members of the Council of Europe, where the fourth group now encompasses 29 states. For an overview see Ewald Wiederin (2009), Soziale Grundrechte in der Europäischen Grundrechtecharta, in: Thomas Eilmansberger, Günter Herzig (eds.), Soziales Europa, Wien:

ship between high social protection through normal legislation and constitutional rights. Or as the legal scholar Wiederin writes, constitutional rights may have a compensatory function in view of the difficulties to find appropriate compromises in the legislative process.[55] Is this also the case in the European Union? Although the Treaty of Lisbon after a difficult process of ratification finally entered into force on December 1, 2009, it will take some time to assess the political and legal implications of the new primary law, while optimists and pessimists will most certainly continue their hermeneutic battle.

May that be as it is, a brief glance at the Charter of Fundamental Rights[56] shows that the Convention succeeded in negotiating a text that may be considered as the *summa* of a long-standing European discourse. The Charter's Preamble states that the Union is based on a number of values, namely 'human dignity, freedom, equality and solidarity' to be pursued by democratic means and the rule of law. In the same paragraph the Charter continues that at the heart of European political activities lies the individual enjoying citizenship within an area of freedom, security, and justice. The latter, though, refer to social rights only indirectly in that the three terms actually circumscribe matters of justice and home affairs. Yet, in the second paragraph the Charter reiterates older values such as the respect for the diversity of the cultures and traditions of the peoples, as well as the identity of member states (later underpinned by the principle of subsidiarity) and, of course, the famous four freedoms. Interestingly, the Charter also states the respect for the member states' 'organisation of their public authorities at national, regional and local levels.' This is important also for provisions of social services and more general services of public interest.

The Preamble also makes references to the constitutional traditions of the member states (which are however diverse, as aforementioned) and international obligations such as the European Convention for the Protection of Human Rights and Fundamental Freedoms, the Social Charters adopted by the Council of Europe and the Union, and their respective case law. In particular the Treaty of Lisbon opens the way for the Union to become a member of the European Convention for the Protection of Human Rights and Fundamental Freedoms. Remarkably, the interdependence with regard to international law was also stressed by the intervention of the UN Committee on Economic, Social and Cultural Rights,

Nomos-Facultas.WUV, pp. 116-119, and Julia Iliopoulos-Strangas (ed.) (2000), La protection des droits sociaux fondamentaux dans les états membres de l'Union Européenne: étude de droit comparé. Athènes: Sakkoulas and Bruxelles: Bruylant.

55   Ewald Wiederin (2009), Soziale Grundrechte in der Europäischen Grundrechtecharta, in: Thomas Eilmansberger, Günter Herzig (eds.), Soziales Europa. Wien: Nomos-Facultas.WUV, pp. 116-119 at 117.

56   All quotations are from Charter of Fundamental Rights of the European Union, Official Journal of the European Union, C 303/1, 14.12.2007.

who in a letter to the Presidium of the Convention uttered concern about the controversy on the inclusion of social rights. The Committee wrote that the international community would indeed perceive the omission of such rights from a European Charter as backlash and that this could eventually create tensions with international obligations.[57]

However, in the end social rights were enshrined in the Charter in a number of articles ranging from the prohibition of slavery, forced labour, and human trafficking (Article 2), to freedom rights including the right to education (Article 14), choice of occupation, and the right to engage in work (Article 15), to equality and non-discrimination (Article 21-23), to the rights of the child (Article 24), of the elderly (Article 25), and of disabled persons (Article 26). Some of these rights have a long-standing tradition also in EU primary law, the non-discrimination between women and men being the most important case in point as shown by an extensive ECJ case law. The case law could refer not only to provisions of the primary law but also of secondary law. [58]

Title IV on Solidarity constitutes the centrepiece of social rights in that it recalls the notion of 'industrial citizenship' coined by Marshall. Indeed, Articles 27 to 38 define workers' rights at the workplace. They deserve special analysis also because to a large degree they are not formulated as objectives but constitute enforceable rights. However, none is entirely new as all rights have a basis in the European Social Charter and the Community Charter on the rights of workers and have, if to a different extent, been buttressed by the Union *acquis*: this holds true for the 'Workers' right to information and consultation within the undertaking' (Article 27), the 'Right of collective bargaining and action' (including strike action, Article 28), the 'Right of access to placement services' (Article 29), the 'Protection in the event of dismissal' (Article 30),[59] the 'Fair and just working conditions' (Article 31), the 'Prohibition of child labour and protection of young people at work' (Article 32), 'Family and professional life' (Article 33), 'Social

57 Ewald Wiederin (2009), Soziale Grundrechte in der Europäischen Grundrechtecharta, in: Thomas Eilmansberger, Günter Herzig (eds.), Soziales Europa. Wien: Nomosfacultas.wuv, p. 121.

58 See Article 157 (1) in the version of the Treaty of the Functioning of the European Union and Article 2(4) of the Council Directive 76/207/EEC on the implementation of the principle of equal treatment for men and women as regards access to employment, vocational training and promotion, and working conditions. For a general overview see among many others Lilja Mósesdóttir (2006), The European Social Model and Gender Equality, in: Maria Jepsen, Serrano Pascual (eds.), Unwrapping the European Social Model. Bristol: Polity Press, pp. 145-166.

59 In this regard two important directives are noteworthy: Directive 2001/23/EC on the safeguarding of employees' rights in the event of transfer or undertakings, and the Directive 80/987/EEC on the protection of employees in the event of the insolvency of their employers, as amended by the Directive 2002/74/EC.

security and social assistance' (Article 34), 'Health care' (Article 35), 'Access to services of general economic interest' (Article 36),[60] 'Environmental protection' (Article 37), and 'Consumer protection' (Article 38). It is perhaps no exaggeration to state that these rights form the core of the European Social Model. Yet, enthusiasm is to be quelled as long as we do not know whom they bind and how deep their implications are. *First*, Article 51 describing the field of application states that 'the provisions of the Charter are addressed to the institutions, bodies, offices and agencies of the Union with due regard for the principle of subsidiarity and to the Member States only when they are implementing Union law.' Paragraph 2 clarifies beyond doubt that 'The Charter does not extend the field of application of Union law beyond the powers of the Union or establish any new power or task for the Union, or modify powers and tasks as defined in the Treaties'. *Second*, Article 52 subjects all rights and freedoms as enshrined in the Charter to the principle of proportionality (1) and stipulates rules of interpretation to be carried out in harmony with national traditions (4). Owing to the variety of such traditions, the latter might prove difficult. However, the difficulties may be not only of legal, but even more so of political importance: they may arise from expectations citizens associate with the Charter's normative thrust, which is not or not fully met by the powers given to the Union.

In this respect, the Charter is to be read synoptically with the Treaty of Lisbon. While it is true that the Treaty does hardly create any new competencies particularly in the field treated here, the introduction of a horizontal 'social clause' needs explanation. The clause reads: 'In defining and implementing its policies and activities, the Union shall take into account requirements linked to the promotion of a high level of employment, the guarantee of adequate social protection, the fight against social exclusion, and a high level of education, training and protection of human health'.[61] Are these instances of a new integration vision or of mere lip service to social responsibility producing nothing more than 'constitutional minimalism'?[62] It is at least the normative recognition of what constitutes the very basis of the cohesion of societies within member states as much as a sign of awareness that European policymaking may jeopardise the

---

60 Interestingly, there is a cautionary addendum in the explanation to this article that is said to be 'fully in line with Article 14 of the Treaty on the Functioning of the European Union and does not create any new right. It merely sets out the principle of respect by the Union for the access to services of general economic interest as provided for by national provisions, when those provisions are compatible with Union law.' (Explanations relating to the Charter of Fundamental Rights, Official Journal of the European Union, C 303/17, 14.12. 2007).

61 Article 9, Consolidated Version of the Treaty on the Functioning of the European Union, *Official Journal of the European Union*, C115/47, 9.5.2008.

62 Hans-Wolfgang Platzer (2009), Konstitutioneller Minimalismus: die EU-Sozialpolitik in den Vertragsreformen von Nizza bis Lissabon, integration 1, pp. 33-49.

achievements of national social orders. Hence, in an optimistic reading the clause can be appreciated as the legal basis for Ferrera's model of 'virtuous nesting'. In the concluding chapter I shall discuss whether such optimism is at all realistic.

V Envisioning a European Area of Social Security, Justice and Solidarity[63] in Times of Crisis?

While all constitutional achievements described above appear to reinforce the European *differentia specifica*, they are overhauled by the momentum of the financial and the ensuing fiscal crisis. At the time of writing, the Union lingers on the brink of an abyss. Exacerbating from day to day the financial crisis has put some states in danger of default and others in a position of loosing the triple-A status attributed by international rating agencies. Time and again European leaders have come up with plans to resolve the sovereign debt debacle by combining transfers and guarantees with austerity measures. Whereas in the 'state of emergency' the no-bail-out-taboo was breached and national parliaments were 'forced'[64] to endorse guarantees of hundreds of billions of euros, beneficiaries in turn are forced to implement provisions that will cut back on pensions, unemployment, and health benefits.[65] The sovereignty of national parliaments to autonomously decide upon their budgets – defined as the 'crown jewels' of parliaments by the German Constitutional Court[66] – is curtailed by the so-called European Semester that requires governments to present their budget proposals to the European Commission and to their peers for approval first. The Memoranda of Understanding for Greece and Ireland on Specific Economic Policy Conditions

---

63 I use this title as proposed by Johannes Voggenhuber (2002), The Unity of Europe. Outline for a European Constitution, Brussels 2002. The Green MEP and member of both Conventions submitted this proposal for a European Constitution to the Convention in 2002.

64 This appears to have particulary been the case in Germany, where Minister of Finance Wolfgang Schäuble presented the bail-out to national MPs as a strategy „'without alternative". (Deutscher Bundestag, 17. Wahlperiode, 41. Sitzung, 7 May 2010, pp. 4001-4002).

65 See the Italian budget law presented by the new government led by Mario Monti to the parliament. On 14 December 2011 the Camera dei deputati, Italy's first chamber, started a highly controversial discussion on the 'Conversione in legge del decreto-legge 6 dicembre 2011, n. 201, recante disposizioni urgenti per la crescita, l'equità e il consolidamento dei conti pubblici' (C. 4829-A) but approved it already one week later (22 December 2011).

66 Such was the formula chosen by the German Constitutional Court's Judge Di Fabio during negotiations on the rescue operation of Greece and the EFSF. 'The right to decide on the budget is the crown jewel of the parliament, but if the sovereign starts to bond its crown jewels, its freedom might be limited' (quoted in Der Spiegel 36/2011, p. 21, my translation).

will cut deeply not only into national welfare provisions, but also into parliaments' rights to define them.

The fiscal rule guiding such scrutiny stipulates that 'general government budgets shall be balanced or in surplus; this principle shall be deemed respected if, as a rule, the annual structural deficit does not exceed 0,5% of nominal GDP.' What is more, 'member states in Excessive Deficit Procedure shall submit to the Commission and the Council for endorsement, an economic partnership programme detailing the necessary structural reforms to ensure effectively durable correction of excessive deficits.' While as of today it is impossible to gauge the consequences of this agreement (accepted by all euro members, but not by the UK, whereas nine other states wish to consult their parliaments before consenting) in terms of compliance, its thrust appears quite clear: centralisation and sound finances.[67] The Fiscal Stability Union will rest upon 'enhanced governance to foster fiscal discipline and deeper integration in the internal market as well as stronger growth, enhanced competitiveness and social cohesion.'[68] However, while the compact is explicit on fiscal discipline, it is rather silent in regard to measures enhancing growth and even more so in regard to cohesion policy.[69]

Solidarity comes at a price. This holds true for both sides: for net payers and for net receivers. The bail-out of troubled member states requires the first to agree to an increase of national debts despite relatively sound domestic fiscal policy, whereas the latter must accept the austerity conditions imposed by the creditors. Certainly, it does foster public dissensus by those who have to shoulder the hea-

---

67 On the problematic economic and social implications of the 'Rescue-cum-Retrenchment Program' see Fritz W. Scharpf (2011), Monetary Union, Fiscal Crisis and the Preemption of Democracy, in: Joachim Jens Hesse (ed.), Zeitschrift für Staats- und Europawissenschaften 9 (2), 163 198. (http://www.zse.nomos.de/fileadmin/zse/doc/Aufsatz_-ZSE_11_02.pdf)

68 European Council, Statement by the Euro Area Heads of State or Government, Brussels, 9 December 2011. Moreover, 'such rule will be introduced in member states's national legal systems at constitutional or equivalent level. The rule will contain an automatic correction mechanism that shall be triggered in the event of deviation.'

69 The Excessive Deficit Procedure (EDP) as much as the Excessive Imbalance Procedure (EIP) do not foresee active European policies in this regard, whereas the EIP scoreboard that finally also focuses on important aspects of national economic performance including public and private indebtedness does not take into account the fact that national governments may have little influence on such criteria (see Scharpf, Monetary Union, Fiscal Crisis, and the Pre-emption of Democracy, Fritz W. Scharpf (2011), Monetary Union, Fiscal Crisis and the Pre-emption of Democracy, in: Joachim Jens Hesse (ed.), Zeitschrift für Staats- und Europawissenschaften 9 (2), 163 198. (http://www.zse.nomos.de/-fileadmin/zse/doc/Aufsatz_ZSE_11_02.pdf) at 188-189).

viest burdens.[70] Here we may ask: Are advocates of a European fiscal and trans-fer union all too facile as they shun the question about the size and diversity of a community capable of solidarity? Perhaps they are, but then ideas about the size of a political community change over time, and they do so in response to real problems and needs.[71] Europe's single market and single currency have created such a degree of interdependence between national economies that disentangling them may entail huge costs, while the prospects for states on the brink of insol-vency to recover outside the eurozone remain doubtful as well.[72] Europeans might therefore have no choice but to tackle their problems and needs within the given community. The economic problems quite obviously need responses that start from an appropriate analysis of the fallacies of past monetarism. While con-vergence on the Maastricht criteria did not eliminate the structural and institu-tional divergences between euro members neither before nor after access to the single currency, the 'ECB monetary impulses reflected average conditions in the eurozone and hence could not be targeted at the conditions of specific national economies'.[73] It is indeed astounding that 'the escalating economic imbalances and vulnerabilities were also of no concern to the EMU policy makers, neither for the Commission enforcing the Stability Pact nor for the ECB carrying out its mandate to ensure price stability.'[74]

70   As to the rising dissensus among European citizens about European integration see Lies-bet Hooghe and Gary Marks (2008), A Postfuncionalist Theory of European Integration: From Permissive Consensus to Constraining Dissensus, 39 British Journal of Political Science, pp. 1-23. However, this article was written before the current crisis. One is to expect such dissensus to exacerbate as a consequence of it, the recurrent strikes of work-ers, employees, and civil servants in Greece, Spain, and Italy serving as important in-stances.

71   In this respect a reading of the Anti-Federalist Papers can teach modern scholars an inter-esting lesson. See Agrippa IV, 3, December 1787, where a member of the Massachusetts Convention held that 'the idea of an uncompounded republic...containing six millions white inhabitants all reduced to the same standard of morals, of habits, of laws, is itself an absurdity and contrary to the whole experience of mankind.' Quoted in Cécile Leconte (2008), Opposing Integration on Matters of Social and Normative Preferences: A New Dimension of Political Contestation in the EU, Journal of Common Market Studies 46 (5), pp. 1071-1091 at 1088.

72   See Fritz W. Scharpf (2011), Monetary Union, Fiscal Crisis, and the Pre-emption of De-mocracy, p. 183. Besides the compelling story told by Scharpf about the impact of 'mo-netarism in a non-optimal currency area' (ibid. p. 172 et seq.), it is somewhat ironic that the 50 per cent increase in German military export is mainly due to Greek and Portuguese imports (see Frankfurter Allgemeine Zeitung, 8 December 2011).

73   Fritz W. Scharpf (2011), Monetary Union, Fiscal Crisis, and the Pre-emption of Democ-racy, p. 173. In the following, Scharpf describes how this one-size-fits-all approach af-fected national policy-making by victimising not only Greece, Ireland, Spain, and Por-tugal, but also Germany (pp. 175-181).

74   Ibid., p. 181.

Yet, the crucial question today goes beyond pure economics: are European citizens and their leaders willing to and capable of deepening the Union towards a fiscal and transfer union that will safeguard the common good of social citizenship? The price of such an undertaking is high as it implies a considerable degree of solidarity between member states of quite diverse economic performance and welfare traditions: it entails the willingness to transfer resources from the most advanced member states to the laggards as much as the compliance of the latter with the rules imposed by the former. Moreover, decisions on relevant provisions on both sides have to be taken according to democratic rules. The crisis does indeed put into question both elements of the European common good: social citizenship and democracy. As long as agreements on rescue funds are largely intergovernmental, the challenge is paramount for national parliaments. This may be a unique opportunity for national MPs to debate the Social Question in a 'logic of openness' and thus in a European dimension. While this could finally create a parliamentarian ownership of Europe, it would hardly be astounding if the 'logic of closure' were to prevail. Until now national parliaments rarely had to justify European policymaking even if they enjoyed considerable rights to control their executives.[75] Moreover, considering the rise of Eurosceptic parties in most parts of the Union,[76] advocating European solutions will become more difficult than scapegoating Brussels.

Is the Union then doomed to fall apart? I hold that the current 'state of emergency' could be conducive to further deepening and thus to Ferrera's vision of 'virtuous nesting' of the different levels of competencies. It was my aim to demonstrate that primary as well as secondary law have opened doors in this respect. Important problems, though, loom large: First, integration through law has its limits. While I entirely agree with Fritz Scharpf on this point, I disagree as to his recommendation to withdraw allegiance to the ECJ.[77] What is needed is political determination to bring the Social Question onto the European agenda and the democratic debate about a European Social Model. History does not repeat itself in the same form, but it may well be that Europeans today find themselves in conditions to heed the famous dictum attributed to Benjamin Franklin: 'We

75 This holds particularly true for Austrian parliamentarians who by constitutional law are granted to bind the government on European stances: see Johannes Pollak and Peter Slominski (2009), Zwischen De- und Reparlamentarisierung – Der österreichische Nationalrat und seine Mitwirkungsrechte in EU-Angelegenheiten, in: Österreichische Zeitschrift für Politikwissenschaft 38(2), pp. 193-212.

76 See Aleks Szczerbiak and Paul A.Taggart (2008), Opposing Europe? Oxford: Oxford University Press.

77 Fritz W. Scharpf on a variety of cases (http://www.mpifg.de/service/pressestelle/Pressespiegel/2008%5C08-07-24_Scharpf_Mitbestimmung.pdf). See also Roman Herzog on the Mangold Case where he argues that the Court is in need of brakes (http://4topas.wordpress.com/2008/09/14/roman-herzog-stoppt-den-europaischen-gerichtshof/)

must, indeed, all hang together, or assuredly we shall hang separately'. Even if the hangmen are no longer military forces, but global financial markets, pondering on how much and in which areas hanging together is necessary in order to safeguard the Europe's *differentia specifica* is urgent.

If the outcome of such pondering were to at least partially re-locate authority in social affairs at the European level, such authority must be justified. To put it in Somek's words: 'A justification of authority presupposes, hence, a *conception of citizenship*; by which I mean a normative perspective with regard to where the limits to plurality may legitimately be drawn and the types of processes that are necessary in order to for citizens to be able to live together despite disagreements.'[78] Taking the pursuit of social citizenship as the common starting point, authorising the Union to spell out relevant legislation implies a perspective not only on the European Social Model but also on European democracy. To achieve such perspective under the bombarding of global financial markets is a task of a kind. It does not need to be a mission impossible. First, European policymakers should take their treaty commitments seriously, second, austerity plans should be complemented by growth strategies tailored to regional differences,[79] but, third and most importantly, policymakers need to enter the democratic arenas at the national and at the European level to justify their decisions. All three points smack of idealism. However, it would simply be grotesque if the biggest world economy in terms of population and GDP and with the second most important international currency after the dollar[80] were incapable of tackling its internal imbalances.

Bibliography

Aly, G. (2005), *Hitlers Volksstaat: Raub, Rassenkrieg und nationaler Sozialismus*. Frankfurt am Main: Fischer.

Arendt, H. (1963), *On Revolution*. New York: The Viking Press.

---

78 Alexander Somek (2008), Individualism: An Essay on the Authority of the European Union. Oxford: Oxford University Press, p. 26.
79 The need for the ECB to differentiate approaches towards national economies is briefly discussed by Scharpf, recalling the work of the Swedish economist Eric Lindahl (Scharpf, Monetary Union, Fiscal Crisis, and the Pre-emption of Democracy, p. 178, Fn 29). It seems, however, that the pursuit of such differentiation in regard to monetary and more generally to economic policy would presuppose an ideological shift in the mind-set of European policymakers.
80 See David Marsh (2011), Faltering Ambitions and Unrequited Hopes: The Battle for the Euro Intensifies, Journal of Common Market Studies 49, Annual Review, pp. 45-55, p. 45-46; The Economist, July 10-16, 2010, p. 11-12.

Baquero Cruz, J. (2005), Beyond Competition: Services of General Interest and European Community Law, in: Gráinne de Búrca (ed.), *EU Law and the Welfare State. In Search of Solidarity*. Oxford: Oxford University Press, pp. 169-212.

Bartolin, S.i (2005), *Restructuring Europe*. Oxford: Oxford University Press.

Blauberger, M. (2012), With Luxembourg in mind...The re-making of national policies in the face of ECJ jurisprudence, *Journal of European Public Policy* 19(1), pp. 108-125.

Courtois, S. et al. (1997), *Le livre noir du communisme. Crime, terreur, repression*. Paris: Robert Laffont.

Damjanovic, D. (2009), Die Marktregeln der EG, in: Thomas Eilmansberger, Günter Herzig (eds.), *Soziales Europa,* Vienna: Nomos and facultas.wuv.

De Swaan, A. (1988), *In Care of the State. Health Care, Education and Welfare in Europe and the USA in the Modern Era*. Cambridge: Polity Press.

Dougan, M.; Spaventa, E. (2005), 'Wish You Weren't Here...' New Models of Social Solidarity in the European Union, in: Michael Dougan, Eleanor Spaventa (eds), *Social Welfare and EU Law*. Oxford: Hart Publishing.

Dyson, K.; Featherstone, K. (1999), *The Road to Maastricht. Negotiating Economic and Monetary Union*. Oxford: Oxford University Press.

Esping-Andersen, G. (1990), *The Three Worlds of Welfare Capitalism*. Cambridge: Polity Press.

Ferrera, M. (2009), The JCMS Annual Lecture: National Welfare States and European Integration: In Search of a 'Virtuous Nesting', *Journal of Common Market Studies* 47(2), pp. 219-233.

Giubboni, S. (2007), Free Movement of Persons and European Solidarity, *European Law Journal* 13 (3), pp. 360-379.

Hall, P.A.; Thelen, K. (2009), Institutional change in varieties of capitalism, *Socio-Economic Review* 7, pp. 7-34.

Hatzopoulos, V. (2002), Killing National Health and Insurance Systems but Healing Patients? The European Market for Health Care services after the Judgements of the ECJ in Vanbraekel and Peerbooms, *Common Market Law Review* 39, pp. 683-729.

Hooghe, L.; Marks, G. (2008), A Postfuncionalist Theory of European Integration: From Permissive Consensus to Constraining Dissensus, *British Journal of Political Science* 39 (1), pp. 1-23

Iliopoulos-Strangas, J. (ed.) (2000), *La protection des droits sociaux fondamentaux dans les états membres de l'Union Européenne: étude de droit comparé*. Athènes: Sakkoulas and Bruxelles: Bruylant.

Iversen, T.; Soskice, D. (2006), Electoral Institutions and the Politics of Coalitions: Why Some Democracies Redistribute More Than Others, *American Political Science Review* 100, pp. 165-181;

Jepsen, M.; Pascual, S. (2006), The Concept of the ESM and supranational legitimacy-building, in: Maria Jepsen, Serrano Pascual (eds.), Unwrapping the European Social Model, Bristol: Polity Press, pp.25-45.

Joerges, C. (2005), Introduction to the Special Issue: Confronting Memories: European "Bitter Experiences" and the Constitutionalization Process: Constructing Europe in the Shadow of its Past, *German Law Journal* 6, pp. 245-254.

Judt, J. (2005*), Post-War. A History of Europe since 1945*. London: William Heinemann.

Lang, T. (2005), Privatisation of Social Welfare: European Union Competition Law Rules, in: Eleanor Spaventa and Michael Dougan (eds.), *Social Welfare and EU Law*. Oxford: Hart Publishing, pp. 45-77.

Leconte, C. (2008), Opposing Integration on Matters of Social and Normative Preferences: A New Dimension of Political Contestation in the EU, *Journal of Common Market Studies* 46 (5), pp. 1071-1091.

Leibfried, S. (2005), Social Policy. Left to the Judges and Markets? in: Helen Wallace, William Wallace and Mark Pollak (eds.), *Policy Making in the European Union*, 5th edition. London: Routledge, pp. 243-278.

Majone, G. (1993), The European Community between Social Policy and Social Regulation, *Journal of Common Market Studies*, 31 (2), pp. 153-170.

Manow, P. (2009), Electoral rules, class coalitions and welfare state regimes, or how to explain Esping-Andersen with Stein Rokkan, *Socio-Economic Review* 7, pp.101-121.

Marsh, D. (2011), Faltering Ambitions and Unrequited Hopes: The Battle for the Euro Intensifies, *Journal of Common Market Studies* 49, Annual Review, pp. 45-55.

Marshall, T.H. (1950), *Citizenship and Social Class and other essays*. Cambridge: Cambridge University Press.

Mazower, M. (1998), *Dark Continent: Europe's Twentieth Century*. London: Penguin Books.

Mósesdóttir, L. (2006), The European Social Model and Gender Equality, in: Maria Jepsen, Serrano Pascual (eds.), *Unwrapping the European Social Model*. Bristol: Polity Press, pp. 145-166.

Peters, G.; Pierre, J. (2004), Multi-Level Governance and Democracy: A Faustian Bargain, in: Ian Bache, Matthew Flinders (eds.), *Multi-Level Governance*. Oxford: Oxford University Press, pp. 79-92.

Platzer, H.W. (2009), Konstitutioneller Minimalismus: die EU-Sozialpolitik in den Vertragsreformen von Nizza bis Lissabon, *integration* 1, pp. 33-49.

Pollak, J.; Slominski, P. (2009), Zwischen De- und Reparlamentarisierung – Der österreichische Nationalrat und seine Mitwirkungsrechte in EU-Angelegenheiten, *Österreichische Zeitschrift für Politikwissenschaft* 38(2), pp. 193-212.

Puntscher Riekmann, S. (1998), *Die kommissarische Neuordnung Europas. Das Dispositiv der Integration*. Wien/ New York: Springer.

Rebhahn, R. (2009), Europäisches Sozialmodell – oder nationale Sozialmodelle für Arbeitsbeziehungen und Welfare? In: Thomas Eilmansberger, Günter Herzig (eds.) *Soziales Europa*. Wien: Nomos-Facultas WUV, pp. 15-56.

Ross, M. (2007), Promoting Solidarity: From Public Services to a European Model of Competition? *Journal of Common Market Law Review* 44(4), pp. 1057-1080.

Scharpf, F. (2009), Legitimacy in the multilevel European Polity, *European Political Social Science Review*, 1 (2), pp. 173-204.

Scharpf, F.W. (2009), *The Double Asymmetry of European Integration Or Why the EU cannot be a Social Market Economy*, MPIfG Working Paper.

Scharpf, F.W. (2010), The Double Asymmetry of European Integration – Or Why the EU Cannot Be a Social Market Economy, in: Fritz W. Scharpf (ed.), *Community and Autonomy. Institutions, Policies and Legitimacy in Multilevel Europe*. Frankfurt/ New York: Campus Verlag, pp. 353-391.

Scharpf, F.W. (2011), Monetary Union, Fiscal Crisis and the Pre-emption of Democracy, in Joachim Jens Hesse (ed.), *Zeitschrift für Staats- und Europawissenschaften* 9 (2), pp. 163-198.

Somek, A. (2009), *Individualism. An Essay on the Authority of the European Union*. Oxford: Oxford University Press.

Spaventa, E. (2007), *Free Movement of Persons in the European Union. Barriers to Movement in their Constitutional Context.* Alphen Aan den Rijn: Kluwer Law International.

Spaventa, E. (2008), Seeing the wood despite the trees? On the scope of Union citizenship and its constitutional effects, *Common Market Law Review* 45(1), pp. 13-45.

St. Milward, A. (2000), *The European Rescue of the Nation State*, 2nd edition. London: Routledge.

Streeck, W. (2009), *Re-Forming Capitalism. Institutional Change in the German Political Economy.* Oxford: Oxford University Press.

Szczerbiak , A.; Taggart, P.A. (2008), *Opposing Europe?* Oxford: Oxford University Press.

Voggenhuber, J. (2002), *The Unity of Europe. Outline for a European Constitution*, Brussels.

Von Bogdandy, A. (2006), Constitutional Principles, in: Armin von Bogdandy, Jürgen Bast (eds.), *Principles of European Constitutional Law*. Oxford/ Portland, Oregon: Hart Publishing, pp. 3-52.

Wiederin, E. (2009), Soziale Grundrechte in der Europäischen Grundrechtecharta, in: Thomas Eilmansberger, Günter Herzig (eds.), *Soziales Europa*, Wien: Nomos-Facultas WUV, pp. 116-119.

Dragana Damjanovic is a post doc researcher financed by the Elise-Richter programme of the FWF. She is affiliated both with Vienna University of Economics and the Salzburg Centre of European Union Studies. Her publications cover a number of pieces on the EU legal framework within the Member States' both public utilities and welfare regimes. The project 'Social market rules for Europe' is her "habilitation" project.

Thomas Eilmansberger is Professor for European Law at the Department for Labour, Economic and European Law at the University of Salzburg. Before returning to the Law Faculty in Salzburg in 2000, he was a Fulbright Scholar visiting professor at Southwestern University School of Law. He also served as resident counsel for the international law firm Bruckhaus Westrick Heller Löber (now Freshfields Bruckhaus Deringer) in Brussels. He was a Member of the Austrian Federal Procurement Review Commission, as well as a member of the group of experts advising the German government on the reform of the GWB (German competition law). He has been representing the European Commission in proceedings before the Court of Justice on a regular basis. Recently, Thomas Eilmansberger has been acting as special advisor to Commissioner Reding regarding the review of the regulatory framework for electronic communications. He is the author of several books and numerous articles on European economic law.

Klaus Gretschmann was Director-General, EU Council of Ministers in Brussels (2001-2011), responsible for Competitiveness, Internal Market, Industrial Policy, Research and Innovation, Energy and Transport. After an academic career as a tenured professor of public and international economics at various universities inside and outside Europe between 1980 and 1998 he held the position of the Director-General for Economics and Finance in the German Chancellery and as the personal representative of the German Prime Minister for the preparation of G8 summits. He is the author of numerous publications on European integration, EU economic policies, public finance, etc. Today he is an independent advisor to EU governments and business leaders and is bearer of the Commander's Cross of the French Legion of Honor and the Federal Cross of Merit of Germany.

Peter Koller is Professor of Law at the University of Graz where he teaches jurisprudence, social philosophy, legal theory and sociology of law. His main research interests are in the areas of political philosophy and legal theory. His publications on these areas include: Current Issues in Political Philosophy: Justice in Society and World Order (ed.), Vienna 1997; Gerechtigkeit im politischen Diskurs der Gegenwart (ed.), Wien 2001; Die globale Frage. Empirische Befunde und ethische Herausforderungen (ed.), Wien 2005; International Law and Global

Justice, in: Lukas Meyer (ed.), Legitimacy, Justice and Public International Law, Cambridge 2009, 186-206; On the Legitimacy of Political Communities, in: M. Baurmann and B. Lahno (eds), Perspectives in Moral Science, Frankfurt/Main 2009, 309-326; On the Interrelations Between Domestic and Global (In)Justice, Critical Review of International Social and Political Philosophy 13, 2010, 137-158.

Volkmar Lauber is trained both in law (Vienna, Harvard) and political science (Chapel Hill, NC). He is professor of political science at the University of Salzburg, Austria and did most of his research on economic and environmental policy. During the past decade his research focused on renewable energy policy and the political struggles underlying it, particularly at the EU level as well as in Germany and Britain.

Agustín José Menéndez is Lecturer of Natural Law and Jurisprudence at the University of León (Spain) and European fellow of ARENA at the University of Oslo. He is the author of Justifying Taxes (2000), Una difesa (moderata) della sentenza Lisbona della Corte costituzionale tedesca (2012) and of De la crisis económica a la crisis constitucional (2012), and co-author (with John Fossum) of Constitution's Gift (Rowman, 2011, Firenze University Press, 2012).

Patrick Riordan SJ received his doctorate in Philosophy from the University of Innsbruck in 1985, and taught in Dublin for fifteen years before moving to Heythrop College, University of London, where he now teaches political philosophy. Patrick Riordan has contributed to debates in the Philippines, where he has been visiting professor both in Manila and Naga. Publications arising from this involvement have addressed the issues of capital punishment, law and morality, constitutional change, and people power. His current research interests include the Common Good, Religion in Public Life, and the Philosophy of Justice.

Rainer Palmstorfer has studied law, history and English at Salzburg University. From 2007 to 2010 he worked as a pre-doc research assistant at the Institute of European Union law, writing his doctoral thesis in the field of EU competition law. Since December 2010 he has been working at the Department of Public Law as a post-doc research fellow. In this position he has done research in the fields of human rights law (religion and education) and European Monetary Union law. At present he is writing his habilitation thesis on 'EU rights and their protection'.

Johannes Pollak is Professor of Political Science at Webster University Vienna and Head of the Political Science Department of the Institute for Advanced

Science in Vienna. Among his publications are *Repräsentation ohne Demokratie?* (Springer 2007) and he is the editor of the series *Europa Kompakt* (UTB).

Sonja Puntscher Riekmann is Jean Monnet Professor, Professor of Political Theory and European Integration at the University of Salzburg and Head of the Salzburg Centre of European Union Studies/Jean Monnet Centre of Excellence. She is Member of the Austrian Academy of Sciences where she was head of the Institute of European Integration research until 2008. She held the position of Vice-Rector for International Relations at Salzburg University until 2011. She published widely on EU issues with a special focus on institutional questions, on European constitutionalism and democracy, on the transformation of Austria's political system in the EU system of governance as well as on theory of power and democracy.

Gerhard Seel is Professor emeritus of Philosophy at the University of Bern. His publications include Sartres Dialektik (Bonn, 1971), Die Aristotelische Modaltheorie (Berlin and New York, 1982), Ammonius and the Sea Battle (with J.-P. Schneider and D. Schulthess, Berlin, 2001), End of Art – Endings in Art (Basel 2006) and Minderheiten, Migranten und die Staatengemeinschaft.Wer hat welche Rechte? (Bern 2006). He is Secretary General of the International Academy of Philosophy of Art, Co-editor (with Lloyd Gerson and Carlo Natali) of International Aristotle Studies and member of the Steering Committee of FISP.

Alexander Somek holds the Charles E. Floete Chair in Law at the University of Iowa. His research focuses on European Union law, constitutional law and legal philosophy. His more recent publications include Engineering Equality: An Essay on European Anti-discrimination Law (Oxford: Oxford University Press, 2011), Individualism: An Essay on the Authority of the European Union (Oxford: Oxford University Press, 2008) and Rechtliches Wissen (Frankfurt/Main: Suhrkamp, 2006). His current research focuses on the transformation of constitutionalism in a transnational context.